RUSSIAN
CIVILIZATION

By
David A. Law

CONTENTS

MAPS, CHARTS AND ILLUSTRATIONS

PREFACE

The need for a better understanding of the Russian people and their way of life has inspired the author to write this book. Many books have already been written concerning the Soviet Union. However, most of them are too specialized to give an overview of life in the Soviet Union. Other books are only introductory writings or encyclopedic reference books. There is also the problem of bias on the part of those who stress their dislike or admiration for the Soviet Union.

The purpose of this book is to present as nearly as possible an objective description of the Soviet Union and of the people who live there. Since the geography and the history determine to a large degree the environment of a society, these topics are presented first. The literary heritage and the impact of the communist philosophy have also greatly influenced the outlook of the Soviet people, and these influences logically follow in this presentation. Current conditions play a large role in the attitudes of the people, and for this reason the next part of the book is concerned with recent history, the structure of the Communist Party and the Soviet Government, Soviet leadership, and various aspects of the economy and culture. The individual Soviet citizen and his role in the society are then discussed. It is hoped that this approach will help Americans to understand the attitudes of the Soviet people.

It is also hoped that what is written here will be recognized by Soviet citizens as a representation of their life. The author has intended to be as accurate as possible. Any misrepresentations have not been intentional.

In order to present an objective account the author has read widely newspapers, textbooks, reference books, and pamphlets concerning the Soviet Union from both the Soviet press and the American press. He has travelled extensively in the Soviet Union, and during the fall semester of 1972 he lived in Volgograd and taught English in the Pedagogical Institute there. His experiences at that time greatly increased the knowledge, which he had previously acquired as a teacher of the Russian language and of Russian Civilization in the United States. The author must admit, however, that his understanding is incomplete. He believes that no one can have a complete knowledge of so vast a subject, but he hopes that his contribution provides a comprehensive picture. He recognizes that any discussion of Soviet life is controversial. However, this work is written not to please or to challenge tenets of any viewpoint. It has been written to inform people and to encourage them to study and learn more concerning the peoples of the Soviet Union.

A problem of spelling names and places in the Soviet Union persists due to the lack of standardization of transliteration procedures. Common usage of many names and places also makes this problem more complex. The author has combined historical spellings (e. g. Alexius), current spellings (e. g. Moscow, Tchaikovsky, Yuri Gagarin, and Kirghiz Republic), and phonetic transliterations (e. g. Khrushchev, Tyumen Oblast, Krasnoyarsk Krai, etc.). This procedure may help identify persons and places for historians, Russian language students, and general readers.

Gratitude is extended to all of those, too numerous to mention, who have helped to make this work possible. Letters and printed materials from Soviet citizens have added much information which was not available from other sources. Questions from students have also inspired the author to seek for and find answers to a variety of problems. The opportunity to order books and reference materials through a research grant by the University of Missouri - Rolla has been a very valuable means for finding information which helped to fill important gaps in certain areas. It is hoped that a personal touch is also reflected in this work based on the travel experiences of the author in the Soviet Union.

CHAPTER I

THE GEOGRAPHY OF THE SOVIET UNION

An understanding of Russian civilization rightfully starts with a look at the geography of the Soviet Union. The wide expanse of the territory and its northerly location play a significant role in the lives of the Russian people. The great distances and the cold climate have caused the people to work together for survival. Collectivism was a part of their lives long before the ideas of Karl Marx came to Russia.

Human relationships in the Soviet Union tend to resemble more closely those in the United States than those in the smaller countries of Europe. The attitudes of friendliness and generosity, which are common among both the Russians and the Americans, may be traced at least partially to geographic conditions on the open plains.

The Russian Steppe is the widest expanse of level land in the world. The land varies in elevation only a few feet to a maximum of one hundred feet over a distance of roughly four thousand miles from Poland to the Ural Mountains. It is this area that has provided the homeland for the Russian people. It is "Mother Russia." Even now most of the population of the Soviet Union lives there.

VARIOUS REGIONS

The steppe is the heartland of Russia, but the Soviet Union today encompasses a great variety of natural regions. It is necessary to divide the territory into these regions in order to understand the complex geography of this large country.

Much of the northern part of the Soviet Union is frozen the year around. This area is known as the tundra or permafrost region. North of the Arctic Circle there is very little vegetation or animal life. Only the surface of the land thaws in the summer, and only grass and moss are available for the reindeer to eat.

South of the tundra there is a very dense forest which extends the full breadth of the Soviet Union. This tremendous expanse of forest, the taiga, is the largest reserve of timber in the world. The region is sparsely populated. Most of the people live along the major rivers, which serve as the main transportation routes. There are few railroads and almost no highways in this region, except for the southwestern part, which extends onto the steppe. Moscow and other large cities are located in this southwestern section of the taiga region. To the east of the Ural Mountains are the areas of Siberia and the Far East, both of which are in the taiga region. The economic development of these eastern sections also lies along the southern border of the taiga.

The steppe which lies south of the taiga in the western part of the Soviet Union is traditionally an agricultural area. The central and southern parts of the steppe are known as the "Black Earth Belt," because of the fertile soil. This area, which includes the Ukrainian Republic, is also referred to as "The Breadbasket of Europe." Wheat, barley, and rye are the major crops, and the grain production is the main concern of Soviet agriculture. The rest of the country is dependent on this area for most of its food products.

East of the Ural Mountains and south of the taiga is a large desert. The northern part of the desert region is actually a semi-desert, and it is the location of much new industry, which has been developed in the last thirty years. It is this area that is the new frontier of economic development. The central and southern parts of this region are an extensive desert. In these parts the population is sparse, except for the cities in the fertile valleys of the rivers which run through the desert. Efforts to utilize the desert have been concentrated along the rivers and canals, and the oases in this desert region now have become a major textile producing area. Due to the low elevation and the southerly location the Fergana River Valley has become the center for cotton production. The rapid expansion of the cotton industry here has made the city of Tashkent the fourth largest city in the Soviet Union.

East of the desert region is the Soviet Far East, which has become an important mining area. Agriculture has also become a major enterprise in this area. National defense, however, has been the main boon here. Vladivostok is the headquarters of the Far East Naval District, and Khabarovsk is a Soviet Army headquarters. These military and naval installations have brought many people to the Soviet Far East. The increased military significance of this area has influenced its industrial development and population growth.

MOUNTAINS

Traditionally the Ural Mountains have been considered the dividing line between Europe and Asia. These mountains are only

12

three to four thousand feet above sea level, but they form a natural barrier which influences the direction of the rivers and winds. The rivers west of the Urals run south to the Black and Caspian Seas; the rivers to the east run north to the Arctic Ocean. The prevailing winds cause the eastern slope of the mountains to be much colder than the western slope. For these reasons people have favored settling west of the Urals, and Siberia has remained sparsely populated.

The Ural Mountains are rich in mineral deposits. Iron mines have been very productive near Sverdlovsk and particularly at Magnitogorsk (Iron Mountain). In addition, lead, zinc, silver, copper, and other ores are abundant in the Ural Mountains. Uranium deposits are also mined north of Sverdlovsk. Recent oil and natural gas discoveries near Ufa (between the southern Urals and the Volga River) have brought even a greater economic significance to the Ural Mountains region.

The highest mountains in the European part of the Soviet Union are in the Caucasus Range, which is located between the Black Sea and the Caspian Sea. Several mountains in this range are over 14,000 feet high. Mount Kazbek is over 16,000 feet high, and Mt. Elbrus is over 18,000 feet. These mountains have served as a refuge for minority groups for centuries. The diversity of peoples in the Caucasus Mountains has given both cultural and economic contributions to the Soviet Union. The political contribution of Stalin, who came from this area, also has had a lasting impact. The economic contributions have been oil and gas from Baku, iron and steel products from Tbilisi, and wines and tea from Tbilisi and Erevan. The Caucasus are also important for the sportsman and the hunter. The writings of Turgenev and Lermontov have portrayed the beauty of this range of mountains.

The highest mountains in the Soviet Union are the Pamirs, which are located along the border of the Soviet Union and Afghanistan. The Pamirs are part of the Himalayan Range, the highest range of mountains in the world. Mount Communism (formerly Mount Stalin) is over 24,000 feet. It is the highest mountain in the Soviet Union. The Pamirs are the home of the Tadzhik people, who like the Iranians, are descendents of the ancient Persians. They are herdsmen of goats and sheep.

Another high mountain range with peaks up to 10,000 feet is that of the Verkhoyansk and Yabloni Mountains, which are located east of the Lena River. These mountains separate Siberia from the northern part of the Soviet Far East. The only population, except for scattered Eskimos, is located along the Lena River to the west and near the Pacific Coast on the east. The main economic products

13

are furs, reindeer, gold, and diamonds, the center of which is
Yakutsk on the Lena River. The importance of the coastal region is
national defense and fishing.

RIVERS, LAKES, AND SEAS

The Volga River, "Mother Volga", extends from the area
south of Leningrad and runs past Kalinin, Moscow, Gorky, Kazan,
Kuibyshev, Saratov, Volgograd, and on by Astrakhan to the Caspian
Sea. The Volga River has been a life line for these large cities and
to many, many more towns and settlements along its banks. It is a
transportation route for passengers and freight. It is supplier of
fish and caviar. More recently the Volga has become an important
source of electric power from the hydro-electric power stations at
Volgograd, Kuibyshev, Gorky, and Kalinin. History records the
stories of the Volga Boatmen, who hauled barges up the river to
bring products to the northern cities. The importance of the river
has by no means waned since that time, and the rapid industrialization of the country has given the Volga River a new significance.
The love for the river by the Russian people has inspired and will
continue to inspire songs, verses, paintings, and other forms of
artistic expression. "Mother Volga" is a part of Russian culture.
Two other rivers in the European part of the Soviet Union
are the Don River and the Dnieper River. They too have played
important roles in the lives of the people. The Don River area was
the home of the Don Cossacks who fought both against the Tatar and
Mongol invaders and against the autocracy of the tsars. The history
of the Cossacks and the tales of Stenka Ryazin and of Pugachev have
left imprints on the culture of the people who live by the Don River.
Also the writings of Mikhail Sholokhov, a foremost Soviet author,
has depicted the life of the Quiet Don. The Dnieper River also has
served as a trade route from the Scandinavian countries to the
Byzantine Empire more than a thousand years ago. It was the bap-
tismal waters for the early Christians at Kiev. The Dnieper River
is the river of the Ukrainians. It is still a source of food, a transportation route, a supplier of electrical power, and the location of
many good swimming beaches.
The Don River originates south of Moscow, runs southeast
to a point not far from Volgograd (formerly Stalingrad) on the Volga
River and turns southwest toward the Black Sea. The large cities
along its banks are Voronezh and Rostov-on-the-Don. In 1952 a
canal was constructed between the Don and Volga Rivers near

Volgograd. Now river boats cross over from the Volga and go to the Black Sea or cross over from the Don and go south to the Caspian or north to Gorky and beyond. This canal has connected a transportation link that unites the Russian people. It has been hailed as a tremendous step forward in the industrialization program of the Soviet Union. This transportation link runs through the Black Earth Belt. Much of the river freight is agricultural products.

The Dnieper River originates west of Moscow and runs south through Smolensk, Mogilev, Kiev, Cherkassi, Kremenchug, Dniepropetrovsk, Zaporozhe, Kherson, and on into the Black Sea. Hydro-electric power dams have been built at Kiev, Kremenchug, Dniepropetrovsk, and Kakhovka (near Kherson). The dam at Dniepropetrovsk was one of the earliest, large hydro-electric power dams, which resulted after Lenin's drive to "Electrify the Country." The Dnieper River continues to be a major transportation route and recreational area along with its contributions to industry. An island in the Dnieper River at Kiev is a recreational center with a swimming beach and boating facilities.

The major rivers east of the Ural Mountains are the Ob, the Yenesei, the Lena, and the Amur. They are all very long rivers. The Ob, the Yenesei, and the Lena run from the highlands near the borders with China and Mongolia and wind northward into the Arctic Ocean. The Amur River also starts in the same highland area, but it winds eastward along the border between the Soviet Union and China to the city of Khabarovsk, where it turns northward and runs into the Pacific Ocean near the Island of Sakhalin.

The Ob River drains all the western parts of Siberia from the many tributaries which run into it. The largest city on the Ob River is Novosibirsk, which has become a major scientific and industrial center. A hydro-electric power dam has been constructed on the river near Novosibirsk to provide power for the new industrial complex in this area. The largest tributary of the Ob River is the Irtysh River, which actually originates in China and goes north to Ust'-Kamenogorsk, Semipalitinsk, and Omsk before running into the Ob River. The main branch of the Ob is formed from tributaries which run together near Barnaul. The Ob then runs north beyond Novosibirsk to the Arctic. Other tributaries of the Ob come from Kuznetsk Basin and run into the Ob north of Novosibirsk. The large cities in this area are all on the southern branches of the Ob. However, there are many villages all along the Ob and its tributaries. The life of this whole area is dependent on this river system. Other than airways the river is the only means of transportation through the forests and swamps of Siberia. The river will also continue to be a source of the industrialization of this area.

15

The Yenesei River drains central Siberia. The largest city on this river is Krasnoyarsk. Even though the Yenesei is an unusually beautiful river there are few villages located along its banks. Hydro-electric dams have been constructed at Krasnoyarsk on the Yenesei and on a tributary, the Angara, at the new city of Bratsk. The hydro-electric power dam at Krasnoyarsk is the largest dam in the world. The construction of this dam has been another feat of the "Communist Construction", in which large numbers, including Soviet youth, participated. The Bratsk and Krasnoyarsk dams are now major points of pride for the Soviet people.

The Lena River originates near Lake Baikal. It drains eastern Siberia. It goes north along the western slopes of the Verkhoyansk and Yabloni Mountain Ranges and empties into the Arctic Ocean. The largest city on the Lena River is Yakutsk, which is important for the mining of salt, gold, and diamonds, and for the raising of reindeer. Other settlements are located along the Lena River, but there is little population in this remote area. There is talk, however, of changing the climate of this area by means of the construction of a large electric power station at the mouth of the Lena. By industrializing the Lena River Basin this area may become another Novosibirsk, but now the Lena River has the distinction of being the longest river in the USSR.

The Amur River has become important in several ways. The increased population in this area has come from efforts to improve agriculture, to industrialize the economy, to intensify the military defense of the Far East, and to conduct foreign trade. The largest cities on the Amur River are Blagoveshchensk, Khabarovsk, Komsomol'sk-on-the-Amur, and Nikolaevsk-on-the-Amur. The latter city is a port on the Pacific Ocean. The upper Amur River is the border line between the Soviet Union and China.

The major seas of the Soviet Union are the Black Sea and the Caspian Sea in the south of the European part and the White Sea and the Baltic Sea in the northwest. Except for the oceanic seas of the Arctic and Pacific Ocean areas, the other large bodies of water in the Soviet Union are the Aral Sea and Lake Balkash in Central Asia and Lake Baikal in the Eastern Siberia.

The Black Sea has long been a contested area between the Slavic peoples and the Turks. Today it is between the Soviet Union and Turkey, but Turkey still controls the outlet into the Mediterreanean Sea. Odessa, on the western part, is the largest Soviet city on the Black Sea. It is the location of the Black Sea Naval Fleet. Odessa is also an important shipping center. Other Soviet cities on the Black Sea are Sevastopol' on the Crimean Peninsula, and Novorossiisk, Sochi, Sukhumi, and Batumi on the eastern side. Each of these cities is a shipping center, and each location has swimming beaches and recreational facilities. The Black Sea coast, in general, is a rest and vacation area. In addition, there are many health resorts and sanatoria overlooking the Black Sea. The eastern shore of the Black Sea is favored with a semi-tropical climate. Oranges and lemons are grown there, and the forests are sprinkled with eucalyptus and cyprus trees. Many of the swimming beaches on the Black Sea have pebbles rather than sand, but this does not deter the people from sunbathing and swimming there.

The Caspian Sea has no outlet. It is a salty sea surrounded mostly by desert. The largest city on the Caspian Sea is Baku, which is a rich oil-producing area. Oil wells are both on the land and in the sea near Baku. This area has been one of the richest oil producing fields in the world. One can smell oil in the air as he goes along the coast line there. Near the mouth of the Volga River is located the Caspian's second largest city, Astrakhan. It is a shipping and fishing center. Caviar is produced here in large quantities. The great desert to the east of the Caspian has kept the population low, but there are a few settlements along that coast. The largest one is Krasnovodsk, which is connected by rail to Ashkhabad and Samarkand. The southern shore of the Caspian Sea belongs to Iran.

The White Sea is located in the northwestern part of the Soviet Union. It runs into the Arctic Ocean. Its importance to the country has been for the shipping of lumber, fish, and furs. It has also become important to a lesser degree for foreign commerce, particularly in war time. The White Sea has really been the only open sea port area that has not been restricted by foreign powers. However, the White Sea does freeze over, and the transportation has been from ice-free Murmansk south by railroad. During Stalin's time the White Sea Canal was constructed from the White Sea across land and through lakes to Leningrad for facilitating the shipping of raw products to the cities. Arkhangelsk, which is on the White Sea, has for a long time been an important lumber and fishing center.

The Baltic Sea has always been a Scandinavian sea, but with Peter the Great in the early 1700's the Russians obtained a "Window to the West" by building St. Petersburg (now Leningrad) on the Baltic Sea. Leningrad is now the main naval headquarters of the Soviet Union. It is also a commercial and cultural center. In addition, Riga and Kaliningrad are important shipping ports on the Baltic Sea. However, the Baltic Sea is still controlled by the Danes and Norwegians. In peace time though Soviet merchantmen and sailors freely use the Baltic Sea.

The Aral Sea, similar to the Caspian Sea, has no outlet and is very salty. It too is surrounded by desert, but the Amu Darya River and the Syr Darya River empty fresh water into the Aral Sea. Yet there are still few people in the area of the Aral Sea. Far from the Aral Sea these rivers have provided water for a tremendous canal project, the Kara Kum Canal, which provides water to desert regions. The Kara Kum Canal was started in the early 1950's, and it has been extended more than 500 miles long. It has followed old river beds, and with the use of locks makes a water transportation route, which is projected to go another 750 miles to the Caspian Sea.

Lake Balkash is another large body of water in the desert area toward the eastern part of the Kazakh Republic of the Soviet Union. It is in an undeveloped area, and the only city of more than 10,000 population in the area is Balkash, which is located on the northern side of the lake and is connected to the coal mining area at Karaganda by rail.

The most famous lake in the Soviet Union is Lake Baikal. It is a very large, fresh-water lake. It is more than a mile deep. Lake Baikal is located on the eastern end of Siberia and is considered to be the gateway to the Soviet Far East. It is a beautiful lake with its light blue water against the green background of the heavy forests and rolling hills.

On the west of Lake Baikal is the city of Irkutsk, which was first founded by gold miners. It is still a gold mining center, but now it also is a center for education, scientific research, and recreation. To the east of Baikal is Ulan Ude, the cultural center of the Buryat Mongolians in the Soviet Union. Lake Baikal is truly a bridge between peoples. Both cities, Irkutsk and Ulan Ude, are connected by rail to Vladivostok on the east and to the cities of Siberia and European Russia on the west.

ADMINISTRATIVE-POLITICAL SUBDIVISIONS OF
THE SOVIET UNION

The administrative-political subdivisions of the Soviet Union are based primarily on the nationalities of the people in the various geographic areas. The Soviet Union is divided into fifteen union republics, each of which is named after the predominant national group within that area. These union republics and their capital cities, going from the northwest along the western and southern borders are:

The Russian Soviet Federated Socialist Republic	Moscow
The Estonian Soviet Socialist Republic	Tallin
The Latvian Soviet Socialist Republic	Riga
The Lithuanian Soviet Socialist Republic	Vil'nyus
The Belorussian Soviet Socialist Republic	Minsk
The Ukrainian Soviet Socialist Republic	Kiev
The Moldavian Soviet Socialist Republic	Kishinev
The Georgian Soviet Socialist Republic	Tbilisi
The Armenian Soviet Socialist Republic	Erevan
The Azerbaidzhan Soviet Socialist Republic	Baku
The Kazakh Soviet Socialist Republic	Alma Ata
The Uzbek Soviet Socialist Republic	Tashkent
The Turkmen Soviet Socialist Republic	Ashkhabad
The Tadzhik Soviet Socialist Republic	Dushanbe
The Kirghiz Soviet Socialist Republic	Frunze

The Russian Republic is the largest one. It occupies more than two-thirds of the total territory of the Soviet Union and is called a federated republic because in addition to the Russian population it includes several minority national and ethnic groups and diverse geographic areas. This republic is a combination of parts of European Russia, Siberia, and the Soviet Far East.

The other union republics each have their own national group, which speaks a different language and has a different cultural history. These republics all border either the open sea or a foreign country and could, according to the Soviet Constitution, withdraw from the USSR and exist as independent countries.

The main administrative breakdown of a union republic is an oblast. An oblast is usually an area which is economically related to an important city. The size of an oblast varies considerably. On the average an oblast consists of about 20,000 square miles and has a population of 750,000. The Moscow Oblast has a population (including the city population) of more than twelve million in an area of about 15,000 square miles, whereas the Tyumen Oblast has a population of only 200,000 in a territory of 554,000 square miles.

Both oblasts and cities are subdivided into regions (rayony) for purely administrative reasons.

Other important subdivisions of the Soviet Union are autonomous oblasts, and national okrugs. An autonomous republic is an area which meets two of the three conditions necessary for being a union republic. Usually it meets the condition for having a separate ethnic population of sufficient numbers, but it does not have a common border with a foreign country or does not have a sufficiently strong economy. A Krai is a large territory with a sparse population. It is more an economic and administrative sub-division than a national or ethnic one. Autonomous oblasts are similar to other oblasts, but each has a separate ethnic group, which is too small to form an autonomous republic. A national okrug is usually a subdivision of a large oblast or krai in the Asiatic part of the Soviet Union. It has a large territory with a sparse population of a separate ethnic group.

THE FIFTEEN UNION REPUBLICS

The Russian Republic

The Russian Republic extends over 6,000 miles from Leningrad on the west to Vladivostok on the east, and it averages about 2,000 miles from north to south. It occupies about 65% of the territory and more than 50% of the population of the Soviet Union. Most of the people are Russians, but there are several other ethnic groups, e.g. the Tatars, Bashkirs, Karelians, Yakuts, Kalmyks, and Buryats. The densest population is in and near the large cities of Moscow, Leningrad, and Gorky.

Moscow is the capital city of the Soviet Union and the Russian Republic. It is the center of the government, the economy, and the culture. More than seven million people live in Moscow and its suburbs. Heavy industry, the Academy of Sciences, and educational institutions continue to attract more people to Moscow. Tourists in

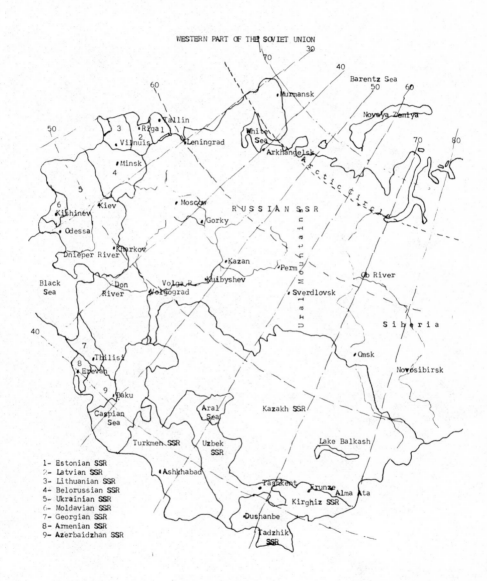

WESTERN PART OF THE SOVIET UNION

Barentz Sea

Novaya Zemlya

Murmansk

White Sea

Tallin
Riga
Vilnuis
Leningrad
Arkhandelsk

Minsk

Moscow
RUSSIAN SSR

Kiev
Gorky
Kishinev
Odessa

Kazan
Perm
Ob River

Kharkov
Dnieper River

Volga R.
Kuibyshev
Sverdlovsk

Black Sea
Don River
Volgograd

Siberia

Omsk

Tbilisi
Erevan

Novosibirsk

Baku

Caspian Sea

Aral Sea
Kazakh SSR

Lake Balkash

Turkmen SSR
Uzbek SSR

1- Estonian SSR
2- Latvian SSR
3- Lithuanian SSR
4- Belorussian SSR
5- Ukrainian SSR
6- Moldavian SSR
7- Georgian SSR
8- Armenian SSR
9- Azerbaidzhan SSR

Ashkhabad

Tashkent
Frunze
Alma Ata
Kirghiz SSR

Dushanbe
Tadzhik SSR

Ural Mountains
Arctic Circle

21

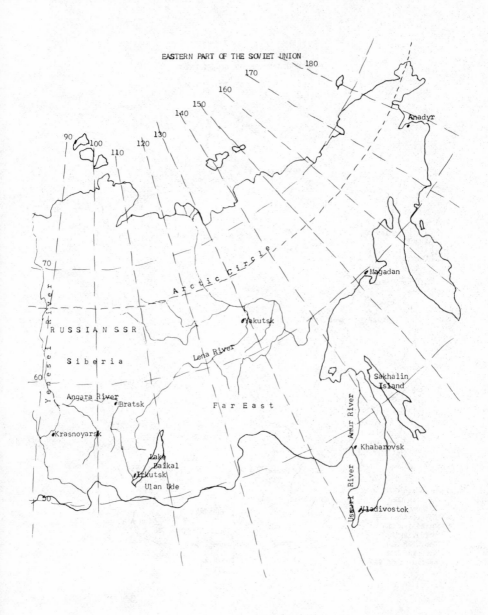

EASTERN PART OF THE SOVIET UNION

22

large numbers, both Soviet and foreign, visit Moscow, but the city
has had to restrict Soviet citizens from moving there, because the
growth has been faster than the building of housing, schools, and
facilities for the new residents.

Leningrad is the second largest city. Formerly the capital
city of Tsarist Russia, Leningrad (then St. Petersburg) is now also
a cultural center, naval headquarters, and industrialized city. It
was founded as Peter the Great's "Window to the West" and still is
an important commercial city. Leningrad has a population in excess
of four million people, most of whom are Russians.

Gorky is an industrialized city down the Volga River from
Moscow. It is the location of a large automobile and truck plant and
of other heavy industry installations. It is the third largest city in
the Russian Republic and has a population of more than one million
people.

The Volga and Don River systems and their cities of Voronezh,
Rostov-on-the-Don, Kuibyshev, Saratov, and Volgograd have played
important roles in the development of agriculture and commerce.
They too have become industrialized and are contributing agricultural machinery, electric power, and various consumer products to
the Soviet economy. Each of these cities has population in excess of
600,000. This area has the tradition of "Old Russia", which represents the peasants, fishermen, craftsmen, and traders. The people
are predominately Russian and preserve the Russian culture and
heritage.

The Russian Republic is more than Old Russia though.
Large numbers of Turko-Tatars and Finno-Ugrians still live along
the Middle Volga and on the western slopes of the Ural Mountains.
This area has been divided into autonomous republics within the
Russian Republic. Seven of the sixteen autonomous republics of the
Russian Republic are located in this area. Three of them are the
Tatar A. S. S. R. , the Bashkir A. S. S. R. , and the Chuvash A. S. S. R.
These people are descendents from the Turko-Tatars, and they
number more than eight million inhabitants. The Finno-Ugrian
peoples, who are related to the Finnish and Hungarian peoples,
inhabit the Admurt A. S. S. R. , the Mari A. S. S. R. , the Mordovian
A. S. S. R. , and the Komi A. S. S. R. These people number another
four million, and they live along the Volga and north toward the
Ural Mountains.

Formerly there was a Karelo-Finnish Union Republic, but it
has been reduced to the Karelian Autonomous Soviet Socialist Republic since the Russo-Finnish War of 1939-40. It is located along the
border with Finland. Its peoples are Finns and Karelians, who are

23

also descendents of the Finno-Ugrians. The population there is now about 700,000.

Along the western side of the Volga River south of Volgograd is a desert area occupied by a Mongolian tribe, the Kalmyks. They are descendents of the Genghis Khan tribes and have retained the Buddhist faith. The Kalmyk people are mostly herdsmen, and they number approximately 137,000.

Other autonomous republics are located in the northern Caucasus Mountain region. This area has traditionally been a refuge area for minority groups, and the northern slopes of the Caucasus is divided by ethnic groups into the Dagestan A. S. S. R., the Chechen-Ingush A. S. S. R., the Northern Ossetian A. S. S. R., and the Karbardino-Balkar A. S. S. R. The Dagestani and the Chechen-Ingushi are Caucasian or Indo-European peoples, but they are also distinct ethnic groups. The Northern-Ossetians are historically related to the Persians, and the Karbardino-Balkars are related to the Turks. But each group consists of many other minority groups who have fled to the Caucasus Mountains throughout history.

In Siberia and the Far East there are Altais, Buryats, Nenets, Evenkis, Lamuts, Eskimos, and other groups, some of which are distantly related to Finno-Ugrians, Turko-Tatars or Mongols and also others which have no known relationship.

Siberia is sub-divided, going from west to east, into the following sections; the major cities are shown with each sub-division.

Tyumensky Oblast	Tyumen
Khanti-Mansiisky national okrug	Khanti-Mansiisk
Yamalo-Nenetsky national okrug	Salekhard
Omsky Oblast	Omsk
Tomsky Oblast	Tomsk
Novosibirsky Oblast	Novosibirsk
Altaisky Krai	Barnaul
Gorno-Altaisky autonomous oblast	Gorno-Altaisk
Krasnoyarsky Krai	Krasnoyarsk
Khakassky autonomous oblast	Abakan
Taimyrsky national okrug	Dudinka
Evenkiisky national okrug	Tura
Tuvinsky Autonomous republic	Kyzyl
Irkutsky oblast	Irkutsk
Ust'-Ordynsky Buryatsky national okrug	Ust'-Ordinsk

The Soviet Far East is sub-divided, going west to east, into the following sections: The major cities are shown with each section.

Buryatsky Autonomous Republic	Ulan Ude
Yakutsky Autonomous Republic	Yakutsk
Chitinsky oblast	Chita
Aginsko-Buryatsky national okrug	Aginsk
Amursky oblast	Blagoveschensk
Khabarovsky Krai	Khabarovsk
Evreisky autonomous oblast	Birobidzhan
Sakhalinsky oblast	Yuzhno-Sakhalinsk
Primorsky Krai	Vladivostok
Magadansky oblast	Magadan
Chukotsky national okrug	Anadyr
Kamchatsky oblast	Petropavlovsk-Kamchatsk
Koryaksky national okrug	Palana

The Baltic Republics

Three union republics are located on the Baltic Sea. They are Estonia, Latvia, and Lithuania. Formerly they were a part of Tsarist Russia, but between the two world wars they existed as independent countries. During the Second World War they were annexed to the Soviet Union.

The Estonian Republic is located in the northern area not far from Leningrad. Its capital city, Tallin, is a port city on the Gulf of Finland and is important for shipping, fishing, machine building, textiles, and dairy products. The Estonian people are Finno-Ugrians, and their language resembles that in present day Finland. Yet they are a separate group of people. Historically they have been farmers and fishermen, but today the Estonian Republic has become industrialized. The population of Estonia is about one million three hundred thousand.

The city of Riga, the capital of the Latvian Republic, is a major port on the Baltic Sea. Shipbuilding, railway car construction, and the manufacture of electro-technical equipment have changed the emphasis of the economy from dairy farming. Dairy products and textiles are still important parts of the economy though. The people of Latvia are classified as Baltics, i. e. they are distantly related to European peoples, including German and Russian. But the Latvian, or Lettish language, as it is also called, is a

25

distinct language even from the Lithuanian language, which it most closely resembles. There are now about two million three hundred thousand people living in Latvia. Most of them are Latvians, but there are also large numbers of Russians, Germans, and Jews.

South of the Latvian Republic is the Lithuanian Republic. It has had an agricultural economy, but now the republic is becoming industrialized. Its major products are machine tools, turbines, electric machines, and building materials. The Lithuanian people are related to the Latvians, but the infusion of Poles and Germans has greatly influenced the language and culture. The Lithuanian language is a different language, but it is still classified in the Baltic group. There are over three million people in the Lithuanian Republic, including the Poles, Belorussians, and Germans.

Belorussia and the Ukraine

The Belorussians and the Ukrainians are Slavic peoples, who speak languages related to the Russian language. The languages differ from each other, but they do share many common words. Belorussians, Ukrainians, and Russians can with some difficulty communicate with each other while speaking their own languages because of these similarities. The Russian language, however, has become the official language of the Soviet Union, and today most Soviet citizens are able to speak Russian.

The Belorussian Republic has an agricultural economy. Its main industry is agricultural machinery. The land is a part of the wooded plain, but much of it has been cleared for raising potatoes, flax and hemp. Pigs, cattle, and poultry are also important contributions to the economy.

Minsk is the capital city of Belorussia. It has a population of almost one million people. Belorussian translated means "white Russian," but the name comes from the Polish and Scandinavian features of the people, who have intermarried for centuries, rather than for political reasons. At this point one should note that the Belorussians were not the "Whites", those who carried a white flag during the 1917 Revolution and 1918-1921 Civil War. Those "Whites" were loyal to the tsar or to the Provisional Government and were opposed to the "Reds."

The almost nine million people in the Belorussian Republic are separated from the Ukrainians by the Pripyat marshes, which have been a physical barrier between them.

The Ukraine is a rich, agricultural area. It has been known as the "Breadbasket of Europe" for its grain production. Kiev, its capital city, was formerly the capital of early Slavic principalities. It was the Prince of Kiev in 988 A.D. who first brought Christianity to the Eastern Slavs. Today Kiev is the third largest city in the Soviet Union. It has a population of 1,764,000 people and is a highly industrialized city. Machine building, food processing, and chemical enterprises are its leading industries.

Kiev boasts of its culture, education, and science. Songs and dances have been and still are associated with the colorful folk costumes of the Ukrainian people. A university, other higher educational institutions, and research institutes of the Academy of Sciences are located at Kiev. Kiev is also known as the "Green City" due to its great number of trees, shrubs, and flowers.

East of Kiev lies some of the best farm land in the Soviet Union. Farther east is the City of Khar'kov, a large railroad and communications center. Khar'kov is the sixth largest city in the Soviet Union with a population of 1,280,000 people. It also has a university, several research institutions, and many industrial enterprises. It is at the University of Khar'kov that the famous Yevsei Liberman teaches economics. Prof. Liberman proposed many reforms, which have helped increase the production and distribution of economic goods. His reforms have been widely accepted by the country's leaders and have been implemented on a large scale.

The Moldavian Republic

During the Second World War a part of Bessarabia, which was within the country of Rumania, was annexed to the Soviet Union. Formerly it had been a part of the Tsarist Empire. Moldavia, as it is now called, has a mixed population of Moldavians, Russians, Ukrainians, Jews, Gypsies, and Bulgarians. The majority of the people today in Moldavia are Moldavians, who are a branch of Indo-European language family.

Moldavia is primarily an agricultural area. On the hills of the Carpathian Mountains are grown grapes and fruit trees. Sheep raising has also been a major part of the economy. The industry specializes in food processing and wine making. There are about three and a half million people living in the Moldavian Republic. Almost 400,000 of them live in the capital city of Kishinev.

The Caucasus Republics

In the mountainous region between the Black Sea and the
Caspian Sea are three union republics; Georgia, Armenia, and
Azerbaidzhan. There are many, many different national and ethnic
groups in the Caucasus Mountains. These three republics are named
after the three largest groups.

The Georgian Republic is located in the northwestern part of
the Caucasus. Its capital city, Tbilisi, is an old city which was at
one time a fortress city of the Persian Empire. Later it became an
early Christian center, which predates the Roman Catholic and Eastern Orthodox split. The Georgian people are unique by historical
tradition, Christian worship, language, and culture. The Georgian
language does not belong to any other language group. It is different
as to vocabulary, grammar, and alphabet from any other language,
except possibly the Basque language.

It was not far from Tbilisi in the city of Gore, where Stalin
was born. The position of the Georgian Republic was favored during
the time of Stalin, and even today there remains a spirit of national
pride and self-sufficiency in the Georgian Republic.

Tbilisi is a large industrial city. Iron mines and iron works
are located not far away at Rustavi. Tbilisi itself prepares packaged
tea, wines, and bottled soft drinks. The population of the Georgian
Republic is over four and a half million people, of whom about 20%
live in Tbilisi. Tbilisi is the thirteenth largest city in the Soviet
Union.

In the Georgian Republic are also two autonomous republics,
both of which are located on the Black Sea. The Abkhazian autonomous republic is located in the northwest section, and its capital city
is the health resort and recreational city of Sukhumi. The Adzhar
autonomous republic is located in the southwest corner of the
Georgian Republic, and its capital city of Batumi is another health
resort. Batumi claims to have the best beach on the Black Sea.
The Adzhar autonomous republic has within its territory the Southern
Ossetian autonomous oblast, which has a capital city named
Tskhinvali. These autonomous sub-divisions of the Georgian Republic have minority ethnic groups, which are separate from the
Georgians and separate from each other. The 492,000 people in the
Abkhazian autonomous republic speak a language distantly related to
Turkish, but it is more closely related to the North Caucasian
languages of Adygei and the Kabardino-Balkars. The Adzhar people
number over 320,000. Their language is a peculiar one, which may
relate distantly to the Georgian language. The Southern Ossetians

number about 100,000 people, most of whom live in rural areas. Their language, as that of Northern Ossetians who live in the North Caucasus, is related to the ancient Scythian language.

The Armenian Republic is located in the south central Caucasus and borders both Turkey and Iran. The Armenians also have a very old culture. They were known as traders long before the time of Christ, and they too accepted Christianity from the very early missionaries. Like the Georgians, they have their own brand of the Christian religion.

Erevan, the capital city, is located in the mountains at the foot of Mount Ararat, where Noah's ark has been reported to have landed. Erevan now has a population of 818,000 people, who are mostly all Armenians. The city is a trading center for agricultural products, copper, wines, and cheese. The industrial growth includes machine building, chemical industry, textile production, and building materials.

The total population of the Armenian Republic is more than two and one half million people, including a few Russians, Georgians, Turks, and Persians.

The Azerbaidzhan Union Republic is located in the eastern Caucasus and faces the Caspian Sea. Oil has been the main product from this Union Republic, and its production is near Baku, both on the land and in the Caspian Sea. The economy is supported by the oil industries. The agricultural production is cotton, wheat, hay, and rice.

Baku is the fifth largest city in the Soviet Union and has a population of a million three hundred thousand people, which is compared with five million people in the whole republic. The Azerbaidzhan people are related to the Turks in language and culture. Large numbers of them live across the border in Iran. Their religion historically has been Moslem, and now they have operating mosques and minarets in Baku.

Most of the people in the Azerbaidzhan Union Republic are Azerbaidzhani, but there are also minority groups of Armenians, Georgians, Russians, and other small ethnic groups. The Nakhichevansky autonomous oblast is located separate from the rest of the Azerbaidzhan Republic and borders the Armenian Republic to the north and Iran to the south. Most of the people of this small (21,000) ethnic group live in the rural areas and occupy themselves with farming and livestock raising. The capital city, Nakhichevan, and a few smaller towns have together only about 46,000 people. There is also an autonomous oblast within the mountainous area of Azerbaidzhan. It is called the Nagorno-Karabakhsky autonomous

oblast, and its capital city is Stepanadert. These people number
about 150,000, and two-thirds of them live in rural areas. The
people there are mostly Armenians and smaller groups of people
related to different Turkish sub-groups.

Central Asia

Soviet Central Asia includes five Union Republics: Turkmen,
Uzbek, Kazakh, Kirghiz, and Tadzhik. The whole area is a large
desert with most of the population living along the river valleys and
in the mountains in the southern regions. This is an area where
Turks, Mongols, and Persians have met in the past, and the population there now is related mostly to one or more of these three
groups.

Kazakh Republic

The largest Union Republic in Central Asia is the Kazakh
Republic. The people there are a mixture of the Mongols and Turks
who fought over this territory more than 500 years ago. The territory stretches from the Caspian Sea to the border of China across
the northern part of all Soviet Central Asia. The capital city, Alma
Ata, which means "Father of Apples", is located in the extreme
southeast part of the Republic. It has a population of 776,000 people,
in comparison with the more than thirteen million people in the whole
Republic.

The northern part of the Kazakh Republic was the location for
Khrushchev's virgin land project, where he wanted to reclaim semi-
desert land and irrigate it for increasing the acreage of wheat, corn,
and rye. This project met with some success, but great difficulties
forced the drastic cut-back in the project. It was found that the dry
climate, which was subject to long droughts was poorly suitable for
grain crops. Irrigation also was hampered by the water soaking into
the dry land before it arrived to the fields.

The Kazakh people were historically nomads. They speak a
Turkish language, but it is distinct from that of the Turkmen,
Azerbaidzhani, and Uzbeks. Most of the people live in the northern
and eastern parts of the Republic. Karaganda in the east central
district is an important coal mining area, and Balkash on the northern shore of Lake Balkash is important for copper production. Semipalitinsk, Ust-Kamenogorsk, and Pavlodar along the eastern border

A young Buryat couple enrolling at the Polytechnical
Institute in Irkutsk.

Azerbaidzhan girls in Baku.

An Uzbek mother and young daughter at the table in the
yard in Tashkent. (The young lady is a tourist)

A Gypsy mother, her son, and baby in Tashkent.
(The man is an American tourist)

33

A Russian grandmother and her granddaughter at a collective farm near Rostov.

A Kazakh girl (on left) and an Uzbek
girl (on right) in Leningrad.

Russian mothers and their children at a sandbox in a Leningrad park.

Ukrainian men in folk costumes for a dance group in Kiev.

35

A Tatar man selling melons to Russians in Volgograd.

A Tatar woman selling melons to Russians in Volgograd.

and on the Irtysh River are industrial areas, which produce meat and agricultural products. They are also locations of scientific research institutions. Tselinograd and Pavlodar were the focus of attention during the height of the Virgin Lands Project, and both of them established plants for agricultural machine building. Ust-Kamenogorsk has lead and zinc mines, and there has been constructed a big hydroelectric station of the Irtysh River there.

The area between Semipalitinsk and Karaganda also is the location of the sites for launching rockets and sputniks as well as the former test areas for atomic explosions. This area is not far from the scientific research institutes in the cities of Novosibirsk, Akademogorodok, and Barnaul, which are in the RSFSR just east of the Kazakh Republic. This whole region is the location of a scientific-industrial complex.

The Uzbek Republic

The Uzbek Republic is the most populous part of the Soviet Central Asia. Its capital city, Tashkent, is now the fourth largest city in the Soviet Union with a population of over 1,461,000. It has become the main center of cotton growing and textiles mills in the country.

The Uzbek Republic lies south of the Kazakh Republic and north of the Turkmen Republic. A neck of land extends south between the Turkmen and Tadzhik Republics to the border of Afghanistan. The town of Termez near the border of Afghanistan has the hottest climate in the Soviet Union.

Most of the population live along the river valleys in the Uzbek Republic, which are in the heart of the desert. The Fergana River valley which includes Tashkent is the most populous area. Another river valley, that of the Zeravshan River, was the center of ancient civilizations. The old cities of Samarkand and Bukhara reflect the past with their mosques and minarets, which although partially in ruins still show the beauty of the ancient artistry. The largest rivers in the Uzbek Republic are the Amu-Darya and the Syr-Darya, and their valleys too support populated centers. They are the source of the water for electrical power and for irrigation as well as for the Kara Kum Canal, which is being constructed across the Uzbek and Turkmen Republics to the Caspian Sea.

The Uzbek people were historically Turkish Moslems who herded sheep and goats in this area. Many of them settled early along the river valleys and engaged in farming. They did not mix with the Mongols and today they constitute about three-fourths of all

37

the people in the Uzbek Republic. In Tashkent and Bukhara there are several minority groups, including Russians, Jews, Tadzhiks, and Armenians. The Uzbek people have their own branch of the Turkish language family, and the people resemble the long-faced Turks rather than the round-headed Kazakhs.

The total population of the Uzbek Republic exceeds twelve and a half million. This number includes the Kara-Kalpaks who live in the Kara-Kalpak autonomous republic in the area along the Amu-Darya River near the Aral Sea. The Kara-Kalpaks number 745,000 people.

In addition to the cotton farming and textile mills in the Uzbek Republic, there are industries which produce oil, sulphur, coal, and marble. Food products and agricultural machinery are also produced there. Astrakhan furs and wines are exported throughout the world from this Republic.

Tashkent is an educational and scientific center. The Central Asian State University is located there. Both the Uzbek Academy of Sciences and a branch of the Soviet Academy of Sciences are in Tashkent. These institutions have done research and collected ancient manuscripts for the library of the Institute of Oriental Studies. This collection has a tremendous value for historians, linguists, antropologists, and archeologists.

Museums, libraries, music schools, theatres, and art galleries contribute to the culture of the Uzbeks in Tashkent. Young people attend schools and institutions of higher learning in Tashkent, and many of them go to Leningrad and Moscow for more specialized learning.

The Turkmen Republic

The people in the Turkmen Republic most closely resemble the Turkish people in Turkey today both in appearance and in language. Turkmenia was the former homeland of the Turkish peoples. Today the population is sparse because of the vast desert. A large number of the people live along Iranian border near mountain streams. The capital city of Ashkhabad is located there. It has a population of 266,000. The whole Republic has two and a quarter million people. Other populated locations are along the Amu-Darya River, which runs near the border of the Uzbek Republic, and along the Murgab River, which runs north from Afghanistan and disappears in the sand in the south central part of the Turkmen Republic, near the ancient city of Mary (Merv).

Plans to increase industrial and agricultural production in the Turkmen Republic have only been partially realized. Oil fields have been discovered and developed near the Caspian Sea coast. Inland as far as Nebit Dag are located oil processing plants. Other petroleum products including chemicals are a major contribution to the economy. Agricultural products are cotton, wool, grains, vegetables, and melons. Machine building, building materials, and consumer products are also a part of the economic plans, which have started to show results.

The education and culture of the Turkmen Republic is centered in Ashkhabad and Chardzhou, where there are located institutions of higher learning and scientific research institutes. Ashkhabad boasts of a state university and its own academy of sciences.

The Tadzhik Republic

The Tadzhik people live in the mountain regions of the vast desert. The climate is colder than on the plains, but it is just as dry. There are few trees, except in the southern and eastern parts, which include the Pamir Mountain Range. The Tadzhik people are related to the Persians (Iranians) both in appearance and in language and culture. They claim the heritage of their ancient ancestors of the Old Persian Empire. Today these people, who are mostly herdsmen of sheep and goats, number over three million. About 65% of them live in rural areas. The only cities of any size are Dushanbe, the capital city with a population of 400,000; Leninabad, the second city with a population of about 80,000; and several smaller places-- Ura-Tyube, Kulyab, Kanibadam, and Kurgan-Tyube.

The eastern section of the Tadzhik Republic makes up the Gorno-Badakhshan autonomous republic with the city of Khorog as its capital. These people live in the highest mountains in the Soviet Union, the Pamirs. The highest mountain is Mount Communism (formerly Mt. Stalin), which is higher than 24,000 feet. The people in this autonomous republic speak different dialects of Persian languages, and they number about 92,000 people, ninety percent of whom live in rural mountain areas.

The Pamirs produce various minerals, including gold, flourspar, salt, sulphur, phosophorite, tin, and wolfram. Other than agriculture and mining though, the main economic production in the Tadzhik Republic is metal-working, building materials, and textiles.

The educational and scientific institutions are mostly in Dushanbe. There is an academy of sciences, a state university, and several specialized institutes.

The Kirghiz Republic

The Kirghiz Republic is south of the Kazakh Republic and north of China. Formerly the people in this area were nomads who moved back and forth between these national groups. They also mixed with them, and the Kirghiz people today have part Turkish and part Mongolian characteristics. Their language, however, is related to Turkish and very similar to the language of the Kazakhs.

The Kirghiz Republic is divided by the Fergana River. The northern part is lowlands with a dry climate, and the southern part is mountainous and not quite as dry. The Pamir Mountains extend into the Kirghiz Republic, and some of the mountains are over 18,000 feet above sea level. The highest mountain is Mount Pobeda, which is almost as high as Mount Communism.

The capital of the Kirghiz Republic is Frunze, which was named after a famous military general of the Civil War Period of 1918-1921. Frunze is a city with a population of 453,000, which is only a small part of the total 3,080,000 people who live in the Republic. About 38% of the people live in urban areas. Most of the people raise cattle, sheep, or goats or they grow wheat, cotton, sugar beets, and hay.

The main industries are processing of agricultural products and mining. Cotton gins, meat packing plants, grain storage, and wool and hides processors are the main agriculturally oriented industries. The mines produce coal, lead, antimony, and mercury. There are aslo several light industries, including building materials, textiles, and metal-working and machine-building products.

In Frunze there are a university, an academy of sciences, and several specialized institutes of higher learning.

MAJOR CITIES IN THE USSR

Soviet cities have been experiencing a phenomenal growth. Not only are the cities in European Russia growing rapidly, but also many small towns throughout the whole country have become large cities. This rapid growth and wide distribution of cities have been caused by the industrialization of the economy and the migration of rural people to the cities. There are now more Soviet citizens living in the cities than living in rural areas.

The following chart shows the twenty largest cities in the Soviet Union in order of their size and the growth which they experienced from 1956 to 1970.

City	1956	1970	from 1956 to 1970 % of Increase
Moscow	@ 5,000,000	7,061,000	40%
Leningrad	@ 3,000,000	3,950,000	33%
Kiev	@ 1,000,000	1,632,000	60%
Tashkent	778,000	1,385,000	70%
Baku	900,000	1,261,000	33%
Khar'kov	877,000	1,223,000	33%
Gorky	876,000	1,170,000	34%
Novosibirsk	731,000	1,161,000	47%
Kuibyshev	760,000	1,047,000	37%
Sverdlovsk	700,000	1,026,000	46%
Minsk,	412,000	916,000	120%
Tbilisi	635,000	889,000	40%
Donetsk	625,000	879,000	40%
Chelyabinsk	600,000	874,000	45%
Kazan	565,000	869,000	55%
Dnepropetrovsk	576,000	863,000	50%
Perm	538,000	850,000	32%
Odessa	600,000	822,000	37%
Omsk	500,000	821,000	64%
Volgograd	525,000	818,000	55%

Only four of the twenty largest cities are located in Old Russia: Moscow, Leningrad, Gorky, and Volgograd. Five of them are in the Ukrainian Republic: Kiev, Kharkov, Donetsk, Dnepropetrovsk, and Odessa. Minsk is located in the Belorussian Republic, and Baku and Tbilisi are located in the Caucasus Mountains. Tashkent is located in Soviet Central Asia, and Novosibirsk and Omsk are located in Siberia. Kazan' and Kuibyshev are located on the east bank of the Volga River in the area long under the control of the Tatars. Sverdlovsk and Chelyabinsk are located in the mining areas of the Ural Mountains, and Perm is just west of the Urals in the forest region north of the Tatar settlements.

The notable significance of this listing of major cities is their wide distribution across the map of the Soviet Union. An extension of this list to include ten more cities would further emphasize this point. The extended list would include Alma Ata in Central Asia and Krasnoyarsk in Central Siberia. The plan for rapid industrial growth includes this wide distribution for military purposes in case of attack and for economic reasons to develop the vast natural resources throughout the country.

Moscow is the "Mecca" of the Soviet Union. There is a proverb "Kto v Moskve ne byval - Krasoty ne vidal." (He who has not
been to Moscow has not seen beauty.) There is a great desire of
Soviet citizens to go to Moscow. It is the center of Soviet civilization. A tradition has been established for secondary school graduates
to come together with the classmates to Moscow to celebrate their
graduation. They stay up all night and see both the day's activity and
the night life of this great city.

Moscow has the Kremlin, Red Square, St. Basil's Cathedral,
GUM (the largest State Department Store), Lenin's Mausoleum,
Gorky Park, Bolshoi Theatre, Moscow State University, the Lenin
Stadium, the Park of Economic Achievement, and many more interesting places. The subway, too, is an attraction that everyone must
see. It is the cleanest and most beautiful subway in the world. Each
station differs from the next in the artistic work -- chandeliers,
mosaics, statues, stained glass, and stonework. Moscow is a tourist center for both Soviet citizens and for people from all over the
world.

Leningrad boasts of its culture. Many people prefer Leningrad. It was the capital city before the 1917 Revolution, and it was
the first to become a Soviet city. Also it retains cultural ties with
the West, because this city was the "Window to the West", which
Peter the Great created in his campaign to modernize Russia.

First of all, Leningrad has the Hermitage, the former Winter Palace of the Tsars. It now has one of the best collections of
art from Europe and Russia. The Hermitage has original paintings,
carved wood work, cut stone urns and figures, crystal chandeliers,
and all the best artwork for everyone to see.

Leningrad also has theatres, museums, parks, and fountains.
St. Isaac's Cathedral, Peter and Paul's Fortress, the Kirov Stadium,
the beach on the Neva River, a stature of Peter the Great riding his
horse on the crest of a wave, the zoo, and the intra-city canal system all add to the personality of Leningrad.

The subway in Leningrad was patterned after the one in
Moscow. Soviet citizens pack on the subways, ride to train stations,
and ride commuter trains to lakes and river banks to spend their
days off. The environs of Leningrad include many streams, lakes,
forests, and other beautiful spots.

Peter the Great selected one of these spots near the Finnish
Gulf to construct his Summer Palace. This park is now a great
tourist attraction. Peter the Great was a prankster, and he set up
trick fountains throughout the park to entertain his guests. Tourists
today hesitate at stone walkways while expecting a trick fountain to

The Soviet Hotel in Leningrad. This hotel caters primarily
to foreign tourists.

A "Spravka" (information bureau) in Leningrad. For a
few kopecks a person may have information about housing,
work, or almost anything.

A typical Soviet service station. This one is located in
Leningrad on the road to Moscow.

A Russian man selling milk in Kalinin. Bulk milk is sold this
way, and a person may buy it by the glass or by the liter.

GUM (The State Directorate of Stores) from Red Square
in Moscow. Almost anything that is sold in the Soviet
Union may be bought here.

The center aisle in GUM. The fountain, bridge-ways,
and the sky-light are hallmarks of this department store.

King Bell (Tsarskii Kolokol) in The Moscow Kremlin. The
size of the bell is indicated by the 11-year-old boy and
his 8-year-old sister (American tourists) who are standing
in the broken part.

The grave of Joseph Stalin near the Kremlin wall in
Moscow. The picture was taken before the bust was
erected in 1970.

The bombed-out mill in Volgograd. The only building
left standing after the Battle of Stalingrad.

Crystal chandeliers and the ceiling at a Subway Station
in Moscow.

Escalators in the Subway in Moscow.

49

Icons and gold-work in the cathedral at Peter and Paul's
Fortress in Leningrad.

St. Basil's Cathedral in Moscow.

St. Sophia's Cathedral in Kiev.

A statue to Yermak, the famous Siberian explorer, in his
home town of Cherkassk.

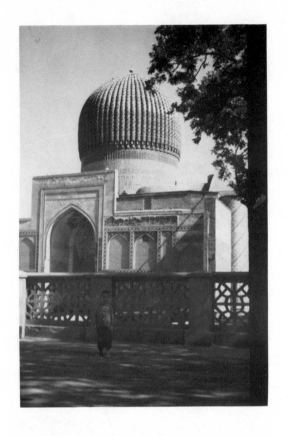

The Blue Mosque in Samarkand. The burial
place of Tamerlane.

A new apartment house (experimental architecture) in
Volgograd, 1971.

A group of Russians selling and buying flowers at a public
square in Novosibirsk.

Russian workers building a rock fence in Bratsk.

soak them. Children run in and out of an umbrella-like structure while trying to outguess the fountain. All of this is located in a park full of trees and flowers.

Kiev is also known for its beauty of nature. It is called "The Green City" because of the trees, vines, and shrubs. Vines grow up and around the statues of the former Ukrainian heroes.

The history of Kiev as the first capital of Slavic peoples and as the first center of Christianity among the Slavs is reflected in current attractions for visitors to the city. St. Sophia's Cathedral, the monastary, the statue of Prince Vladimir, and the catacombs all represent a part of the past culture.

The new, modern apartment houses in the growing areas of Kiev point to the future. The design of architecture seeks not only the practical but also the esthetic needs of the people. Verandas, windows, growing plants, and even the variety of paint colors are distinctive from the apartment houses in other Soviet cities.

The theatre in Kiev presents the culture of the Ukrainians. The colorful costumes of the Ukrainian dancing teams and the ample supply of flowers for the artists point out the attitudes toward beauty of these people in the Ukraine.

Memories of war also linger in Kiev. An island in the Dnieper River was restored not as the dwelling place for the children of those civilians who died there but as a park and beach for all the people of Kiev. The horrors of by-gone years are replaced by the beauty and happiness for today.

Tashkent is not a Russian city nor a Ukrainian city. It is a city of the Uzbeks, descendents of Turkish and Mongol peoples who accepted the Moslem faith. Today Tashkent has the wide streets, parks, fountains, theatres, and markets which are in all Soviet cities. It also has the mosques, minarets, and artistic walls of another culture. The Uzbek people wear different clothing. Many men wear skull caps on their heads. A few people still wear long robes rather than Western clothes. Most of the people though have adapted to Western customs. The women's veil is no longer worn, but the Uzbek culture still thrives. The music and art have an oriental influence.

Tashkent has become industrialized. The people have become educated, and the social environment has changed rapidly. Many non-Uzbeks, including large numbers of Russians, have moved to work in the cotton industry in Tashkent.

In 1966 Tashkent suffered severe earthquakes, but the damage was quickly reconstructed. The prosperity of Tashkent continues to grow in spite of this calamity. Due to their Moslem faith, which tells them to live close to the ground, and due to the earthquakes, many Uzbeks refuse to move from their clay homes in the "Old City of Tashkent" into the modern apartment houses of the new Tashkent. In this way, Tashkent is really two cities, one new and one old, with quite divergent cultures.

The Soviet film industry has made Tashkent its center. The warmer climate and the dry, sunny days make Tashkent the ideal location for filming movies. In 1968 Tashkent was the host for the first International Film Festival for the Countries of Asia and Africa.

As Moscow is a "Mecca" for Slavic peoples, Tashkent is becoming a "Mecca" for Asians. And as Slavic people throng to Moscow, so do Asians and many tourists throng to Tashkent. Tashkent has become a major attraction for world travellers.

Baku is still somewhat off the main tourist path. However, many tourists do come for short stays. Baku has still a different culture, which includes both Moslem and Russian contributions, but still retains Persian and Caucasian roots. The influence of the large oil industry in this city dominates the life of the people. The smell of oil permeates the air, and one can see oil derricks both on the land and in the Caspian Sea.

Baku is an ancient city. The old city wall still surrounds the heart of the city, and inside the walled section the narrow streets wind between tall stone buildings. Old mud-walled, one story, dwellings are being torn down and replaced by new, Soviet style apartment houses.

Mosques and minarets are not only tourist attractions, they are also used for religious worship by the people of Baku. Worshippers bring their rugs and place them on the floor of the mosque where they kneel and pray. Mosques are kept in good and clean condition.

For many years in the ancient past Baku was a Persian city with a Persian Fortress. Azerbaidzhani people have had their former homeland divided between Iran and the Soviet Union. The cultural and national ties still exist between the people of both areas.

On a high hill in Baku is a statue of Kirov, the early Communist leader of the Caucasus and who was shot by an assassin in the early 1930's. Also the Palace of Culture has statues of several of the early Communist heroes. The nearby park as in many Soviet cities has an eternal flame dedicated to the soldiers who died in battle.

Overlooking the Caspian Sea there is an open air theatre with an open backdrop for the stage. Beyond that is a modern restaurant, which appears like a flying butterfly. Both the stage and the restaurant are located in a park area which is full of trees, shrubs, and flowers.

Khar'kov is a Ukrainian city, but the Russian influence may be even greater than the Ukrainian one. Russian is spoken in all public places there. Khar'kov is an industrial city with railroad and communication centers.

Like other Soviet cities it has a large square bordered by government buildings, statues of Lenin, and a large hotel. It also has a children's railroad, which runs through parks to give rides to both children and adults. The trains, including the engines, and the tracks were constructed and are maintained by children under adult supervision. This activity is one of the youth enterprises which are maintained for recreation and training for the children of the workers.

Another interesting place in Khar'kov, though not distinctive to this city, is the Marriage Palace. After obtaining their marriage permits the young couples come to the Marriage Palace to officiate in the ceremony. They have to wait for the couples ahead of them, but when their turn comes they enter a large hall. They are accompanied into the hall with relatives and friends and approach a large table, behind which are seated three officials, a man and two women. The ceremony consists of statements of loyalty to each other and a pronouncement of marriage by the officials. The bride and groom kiss each other and proceed with their guests into one of the banquet rooms, where a wedding feast awaits them.

Khar'kov also has its own spring, where people congregate to obtain fresh spring water.

Volgograd is a re-born city, which is full of a new life. Formerly it was called Tsarytsin, later Stalingrad, and now is called Volgograd, the city of the Volga River. The destruction of Stalingrad came by the Nazi attacks and Russian counter-attacks during the Second World War. Today there stands one building, only the shell of the former structure, which remained in Russian hands throughout the battle and which stood almost alone among the ruins of the former city. The rest of the city is new - reconstructed or constructed anew with the rapid growth of the city.

Volgograd is a long, narrow city, which stretches more than twenty miles along the western bank of the Volga. It is an industrial city. It is also a frontier city, not of territory, but of time. Its clean streets, clean buildings, and fresh minds of its citizens reflect an enthusiasm for greater activity and productivity for the betterment of people. This attitude is further displayed on Mamaey Hill, a former battleground, where there have been constructed monuments honoring the past and looking forward to the future. But over-towering all is the statue of a young lady, who offers a sword to foes and peace and friendship to friends.

Volgograd can also be called "the friendly city", because the people do not have the reserve of big city people. They are open and hospitable. If the Russian word "prostoy" (genuine, sincere) does apply to the New Soviet Man, it certainly can apply to the people of Volgograd.

Each city in the Soviet Union has its own personality, and like cities everywhere they mean something different to each person who lives there or who comes as a visitor.

Rostov-on-the-Don, for instance, has the tradition of the Don Cossacks. Not far away is a Museum to Stenka Ryazin, the one time leader and hero of the Cossacks. Today living in Rostov is Mikhail Sholokhov, a foremost Soviet author, who has immortalized the Don River in his writings. Rostov is also an agricultural center. Seen in the city are new tractors, combines, and other farm equipment ready to be delivered to the farms. Even the concert hall was built to resemble a caterpillar tractor.

Pyatigorsk, another distinctive city, is located in the northern Caucasus Mountains. It honors Lermontov, who loved nature and wrote poems about life in the mountains and the book "Hero of Our Times", which portrays relationships among the people of the Caucasus. Today in Pyatigorsk is a statue to Lermontov, and his former home has been made into a museum dedicated to him.

But Pyatigorsk is also the city of the Eagle and of the Wind Gods. A statue of an eagle overlooks the city, and on the top of a peak is the Harp of Aiolos (the Greek Wind God), through the pillars of which the wind plays its song.

Sochi, on the eastern shore of the Black Sea, is yet another type of Soviet city. It is a recreational center. It is a vacation resort and a swimming beach. The climate is warm and sunny. Semi-tropical plants grow everywhere.

Sunbathing is more popular than swimming at Sochi. People come from all over the Soviet Union and from many foreign countries to relax and sun themselves. Along the beach is a walkway, and every so often there is a stack of boards, which people rent for a few kopecks to lie on the stony beach. The beach is covered with people stretched out on their sunning boards. Some go swimming, but they are mostly children. The small children wear no clothes, and the others wear very little. Rather than using bath houses to change clothes, most of the people have learned to keep covered while changing right on the beach. But even so everything appears proper and in order. Hugging or kissing is rarely seen on or near the beach.

Sochi is full of hotels, cabins, apartments, and even tents for the vacationers. Soviet citizens come usually by train and go to the housing office to find a place to stay. Young people usually come in groups and stay in cabins or tents. Families find a small apartment or a cabin, but individual adults usually stay in the hotels, which are close to the beach.

On the main street in Sochi is a calendar made of plants. Each day the blocks are changed so that it reads, for example: Sochi, June 14, 1972. The next day it reads: June 15, 1972.

There are also many other types of cities in the Soviet Union. On one hand are the industrialized cities, like Gorky, Sverdlovsk, or Magnitogorsk, and on the other are the new cities which have been built on open land, like Volzhky (near Volgograd) or Bratsk (near Lake Baikal). The industrialized cities have the apartment houses, the public buildings, the parks, and the statues, but what impresses one are the thousands of people going to and from the large factories. Gorky, for instance, to many people is the Gorky Automobile Plant, which in March, 1967, produced its five millionth automobile. Not only did this achievement help mark a milestone for the 50th anniversary of the Communist Revolution, it also put a focus on the life of the worker in an industrialized city. The setting is a long conveyor belt onto which each work section, and each individual, contributes only a small part toward the construction of complex machines. The belt has been compared with a flowing river into which tributaries of all sizes empty into the big river that goes on forever. The worker senses challenges of time and effort. Everything seems rushed, and everyone must keep working to stay in step with a giant industrial complex.

The new cities are in the wilderness, though. There are few apartment houses, one or two public buildings, and no parks or statues. Instead, there are masses of young people high on scaffolds and other groups walking here and yon through the mud and dust, depending on the weather, to take on their parts in the construction project. At the new site people are facing new experiences. Each day is different. Groups move from task to task, doing what they are told is necessary to complete the assignment. There is singing and laughing, but there is also a lot of hard work. One gets dirty, and people get hurt. In response to the question, "What are you doing here?", they answer, "We are building Communism."

Baransky, N. N., Economic Geography of the USSR, Moscow:
    Foreign Languages Publishing House, 1956, 413 pp.
Christian Science Monitor, Dec. 27, 1967.
Dewdney, John C., A Geography of the Soviet Union, Oxford:
    Permagon Press, 1965, 154 pp.
East, W. Gordon, The Soviet Union, Princeton, New Jersey: D. Van
    Nostrand Co., Inc., 1963, 136 pp.
Fitzsimmons, Thomas et als., USSR, its people, its society, its
    culture, New Haven: Hraf Press, 1960, pp. 590.
Izvestia, 10 Mar. 67; 2 Mar. 67; 1 Mar. 67.
Jorre, Georges, The Soviet Union: The Land and Its People, New
    York, John Wiley & Sons, 1967, 379 pp.
Law, David A., personal experiences and contacts with Soviet
    citizens, 1962, 1964, 1967, 1971, and 1972.
Lyalikov, N. I., Ekonomicheskaya Geografiya SSSR, Moscow:
    Gosudarstvennoye Uchebnoye Pedadgogicheskoye Izdatelstvo,
    Ministerstvo Proveshcheniya RSFSR, 1959, 343 pp.
Maxwell, Robert (ed), Information U.S.S.R., New York: Permagon
    Press, 1962, 982 pp.
Makhailov, N. N., Po Stopam Ispolina, Moscow: Izdatelstvo
    Politicheskoi Literatury; 1967.
Pravda, 27 May 1967:
Presidium of the Supreme Soviet of USSR, SSR Administrativno-
    Territorial'noye Deleniye Soyuznikh Respublik, Moscow:
    Presidium VS SSSR, January, 1965, 702 pp.
Shabad, Theodore, The Geography of the U.S.S.R., New York:
    Columbia University Press, 1951.
Tsentral'noye Statisticheskoye Upravleniye pri Sovete Ministrov
    SSSR, SSSR v Tsifrakh v 1971 Godu, Moscow: Izdatelstvo
    "Statistiki", 1972, 239 pp.
Tsentral'noye Statisticheskoye Upravleniye pri Sovete Ministrov
    SSSR, SSSR v Tsifrakh v 1967 Godu, Moscow: Izdatelstvo
    "Statistiki", 1968, 159 pp.
Tsentral'noye Statisticheskoye Upravleniye pri Sovete Ministrov
    SSSR, Narodnoye Khozyaystvo SSSR v 1965 g., Moscow:
    1966, pp. 910.
Vvedenskiy, B. A. et als., Ezhegodnik Bol'shoy Sovetskoy
    Entsiklopedii 1967, Moscow: Izdatel'stvo "Sovetskaya
    Entsiklopediya", August 1967, 623 pp.

CHAPTER II

THE HISTORY OF TSARIST RUSSIA

Kiev and Novgorod

Novgorod, in the north near present-day Leningrad, and Kiev, in the south, shared the early history of the Russian people. Both cities were principalities under the strict control of strong leaders. Their control extended throughout the cities and as far into the countryside as they could exert their influcence and collect taxes. Each principality also claimed authority over other principalities and nomadic tribes scattered upon the wide open steppe.

The people were Eastern Slavs, the ancestors of the present-day Russians, Ukrainians, and Belorussians. Their brothers, the Western Slavs, had long since settled in Eastern Europe in the lands now known as Poland, Czechoslovakia, Bulgaria, and Yugoslavia. Both Slavic groups sometime in the distant past had lived in the Northern Caucasus. Possibly they came from the ancient state of Urartu, the remains of which have been found in the areas of present-day Georgia and Armenia. Other archeological diggings show another former civilization which existed at Tripol'e, near the Dnieper River. Some of their ancestors could have also lived here. The early history, however, is not clear because the absence of written records and the unreliability of the few recorded mythologies. Therefore, this historical account starts in the ninth century with the leading principalities of Novgorod and Kiev, which claimed authority over the other Slavic tribes at Minsk, Smolensk, Vladimir, Suzdal' (near Moscow), and Ryazan.

These early people were pagans. They had three gods: Dazhd'bog, god of the sun; Stribog, god of the wind; and Perun, god of the storm. The seasons of the year were met with religious holidays. They also worshipped or prayed to dead ancestors.

The culture of the early Eastern Slavs was very primitive. The little writing that did exist was in cuneiform (wedge-shaped symbols, which were cut in stone). The people sustained themselves by hunting, fishing, herding cattle, and raising grain. Their weapons were made of metal (copper and iron), and their farming tools and implements were made of wood with metal tips. Rather than staying in one place, most of the tribes moved about to take advantage of new land for grazing and for farming. The knowledge of their skills and their understanding of life was passed from generation to generation by songs, stories, and proverbs. They also created and recited long epic poems, known as byliny, about the fantastic exploits of bygone heroes.

During the ninth century the principalities of Kiev and Novgorod were joined together under Prince Oleg, and Kiev became the capital city of all principalities. The new state was financed by taxes on the citizenry in order to defend itself against warring neighbors. There were also established guards to assist the prince in defending, governing, and taxing the people.

Oleg's successor, Prince Igor, is also known for his contribution for unifying and strengthening the principality of Kiev. His reign became a legend which was recorded in the early chronicles. Prince Igor was both loved and feared. He joined with his guards for the collection of taxes, and according to the legend he was killed while demanding excessive taxes from the peasants.

When Prince Igor was killed, his wife Olga, and later his son Svyatoslav ruled the whole principality with a strong hand. Prince Svyatoslav expanded the territory to the Volga River as far north as Kazan and south to the Caspian Sea. He also waged war against the Byzantine Greeks and later joined forces with them against Bulgarians. The respect which he gained in military battle helped him obtain favorable trade agreements with the Poles, the Hungarians, the Czechs, and the Byzantine Greeks. He established a powerful nation state.

His son Vladimir continued the progress by Kiev by establishing even closer relations with Byzantium and by adopting their religion, Christianity. Near the end of the tenth century Vladimir had the citizens of Kiev go into the Dnieper River and be baptized Christians. Christianity was then proclaimed the state religion. Today a statue to Prince Vladimir holding a cross stands on the bank of the Dnieper River in Kiev.

With the new religion came also the culture of the Byzantines. A new alphabet was adopted. This alphabet was made of Greek, Latin, Hebrew, and some original characters, and it is the forerunner of the present Russian alphabet. Churches were built, and they became centers of learning. Books were collected, and schools were opened. The chronicles and other records were kept in the new writing, and church books were translated into the Slavic language.

During the time of the next two princes, Yaroslav the Wise and his son Vladimir, the power of the nation-state and the culture of the people were greatly enhanced. Trade with other nations flourished. Yaroslav married a Swedish princess and gave his daughters in marriage to French, Hungarian, and Norwegian kings. His son

Vladimir married a Byzantine princess. These marriages greatly influenced the trade relations between the Kievan State and these countries. Novgorod became the main commercial center. Merchants came from as far away as Persia, India, and Afghanistan.

Yaroslav the Wise also increased the role of the church. He had constructed the St. Sophia's Temples in Kiev and in Novgorod. The acceptance of Christianity, however, still was not universal throughout the Kievan State. Even Vladimir, the son of Yaroslav, reverted to paganism in his youth and returned to Christianity only after his military contacts with European powers.

One of the most significant developments during the time of Yaroslav and his son, Vladimir, was the institution of a written legal code, which was called "Russian Pravda" (Russian Truth). This system of laws further strengthened the rule of the prince and his guards over the people. It also established monetary fines rather than corporal punishment for violations of the law.

After the death of Yaroslav and during the time of his son Vladimir's rule, the Kievan State weakened. There was a struggle of power between the sons of Yaroslav. Wealthy merchants had imposed foreign governors over Novgorod, and the local princes gained greater control over their own areas. This trend was also compounded by the Church schism between Constantinople and Rome in 1054. About this time the bishops of Kiev were trying to assert their independence from Constantinople. They named their own metropolitan, Ilarion (Hilarion). In addition, the attacks of eastern tribes, particularly the Pechenegs, had longed plagued the Kievan State. Later came the Polovtsy who ravaged fields and settlements alike. The decline of the Kievan State continued as struggles for succession took place in Kiev and as local principalities had to defend themselves against the attacks of nomadic peoples. For a short time during the rule of Vladimir Monomakh in Kiev in the early 1100's there was an attempt to restore law and order, but this attempt failed due to the fighting for succession among his heirs.

The Vladimir-Suzdal' Principlaity (near Moscow) became stronger as Novgorod and Kiev weakened. The city of Vladimir became the political center, and the city of Moscow was founded as a fortress by Uri Dolgorukiy in 1147. But neither Vladimir nor Moscow attained the former status of Novgorod or Kiev at that time.

Novgorod was also attacked by Swedish military forces. In 1240 the Swedish ruler established his troops on the bank of the Neva River. Prince Alexander of Novgorod was supported by both the guards and all the people of Novgorod in defending their city. Alexander led his forces against the Swedes and defeated them at the

Neva River. Henceforth he was called Alexander Nevsky and has been renowned as a military hero. Soviet authorities today refer to him as a forerunner of Communism, because with the support of the lower classes in Novgorod he defeated the Swedes, a powerful European nation. This defense has been considered as a popular uprising against foreign aggression.

Alexander Nevsky further brought recognition upon himself by his victory over the German knights in a battle on the ice of Lake Chudskoe (Peipus). He attacked the Germans broadside while they were crossing the ice and defeated them completely. His victories saved Novgorod from western attacks, and he has been eulogized in stories and in a Soviet film.

THE MONGOL AND TATAR INVASION

The invasion and occupation of the territory of the Eastern Slavs by the Mongols and Tatars lasted for almost 250 years, from 1237 to 1480. This defeat brought about the collapse of the Kievan State and the subjugation of the other Slavic principalities.

The Mongols under the leadership of Genghis Khan came from east of Lake Baikal and occupied the territory of Central Asia. They moved on to the Caucasus Mountains and defeated the Georgians, who had a powerful nation throughout the Caucasus Mountains under King David. The Georgian people were heavily taxed, and those who could not pay were taken into slavery.

The rulership of the Mongols was passed on to Baty, the nephew of Genghis Khan, and Baty continued the attacks further west. In 1236 Baty led his forces onto the steppe, and in 1237 he crossed the Volga River and destroyed the City of Ryazan. By 1240, while Alexander Nevsky was fighting the Swedes on the Neva River, the Mongols and Tatars had taken both Moscow and Kiev. Cities were burned, and the people were taxed or taken into slavery. By 1259 the Mongols faced Novgorod and subjected Prince Alexander Nevsky to their rule.

The Mongol Empire was known as the Golden Horde. Its capital city was established at Noviy Sarai on the lower Volga River. Among the Mongols were many Tatars, who had been included into the Mongol forces as the Mongols occupied their lands in Central Asia. The Tatars became front line soldiers and later servants for the Mongols. Gradually the Tatars were given additional administrative power and were used as tax collectors.

The Mongol leaders built a beautiful city at Noviy Sarai. The Khan collected wealth for the construction of palaces and gardens in his capital city. The Tatars became powerful in carrying out the strong will of the Khan. The city thrived with the production of craftsmen, who worked with metals and pottery. The craftsmen constructed lead and clay pipes for providing water for the city. Culture was brought into the city by writers and scholars who came to Noviy Sarai.

The influence of the Mongols on the Slavic peoples was less than that of the Tatars. The Mongols stayed near Noviy Sarai, and the Tatars were sent to govern the Slavs. The evidence of this relationship is apparent today in the locations of the descendents of these peoples. The Tatars now live mainly in the area between the Volga River and Ural Mountains. Kazan and Ufa are the capital cities of the two Tatar autonomous republics (Tatar and Bashkir). The Mongolian peoples live in the Kalmyk Autonomous Republic in the area near the former capital city of Noviy Sarai. As the power of the Golden Horde waned, the power of the Tatars increased for a time, but it was not until 1480 that the payment of taxes to the Tatars finally stopped. And it was not until 1552 that Russian troops under Ivan IV defeated the Tatars at Kazan and 1556 that they moved against the Tatars and Mongols to capture Astrakhan at the mouth of the Volga on the Caspian Sea.

The whole balance of political power was shaken by the Mongol invasion. The collapse of the Kievan State brought the Swedes, the Poles, and the Lithuanians into struggle for territory both as a buffer against the invading Mongols and as an annexation to their expanding spheres. The Swedes were stopped by Alexander Nevsky in the north, but the Poles and the Lithuanians moved deeper into the former Kievan State as the power of the Mongols and Tatars waned. Both Poland and Lithuania became powerful nations as a result. The Mongols also aroused the Turks in Central Asia, and the Turks too moved westward to occupy the land that is present-day Turkey. The Turks defeated Constantinople in 1453 and moved on toward Vienna. They also occupied the land on the North shore of the Black Sea.

For many years the territory of the Ukraine was occupied by Tatars, Lithuanians, Poles, and Turks. Belorussia also fell under the rule of the Lithuanians.

THE RISE OF MOSCOW

The defeat of the Swedes by Alexander Nevsky was a great achievement for the rising power of Moscow. Even though Novgorod did become subjected to the Golden Horde, it was far removed from Noviy Sarai and did not have the strong interference from the Tatars and Mongols. Moscow also shared in the advantages of less restrictions. As long as the tax money was paid, these regions were left to govern themselves.

Russian princes struggled among themselves to maintain local governments under the control of supervising Tatars. The princes collected taxes and paid their collection to the Tatars in exchange for securing their own political power.

Moscow benefited by Yuri, a son of Alexander Nevsky, becoming prince of the Moscow Principality and by the unification of the Vladimir and Moscow Principalities. A further advantage was that the Church Metropolitan from Kiev had been transferred to Vladimir at the time of the fall of Kiev. After the annexation of Vladimir to Moscow, then the Metropolitan moved to Moscow.

In 1325 Prince Ivan, a grandson of Alexander Nevsky, became prince of Moscow. He worked closely with the Tatars to enrich himself and to expand his authority. Due to his aggressive behavior he was called Ivan Kalita, which means Ivan "money bags." Ivan Kalita further improved his position with the Tatars by leading a military force against the city of Tver to punish the inhabitants for the murder of a Tatar emissary. For this Ivan Kalita was named a Grand Prince by the Mongol Khan in 1328. Henceforth, he was known as Ivan I.

Ivan I declared Moscow to be the political and religious center of Russia. He beautified the city and built the Uspensky Cathedral. The princes of other areas began to look toward Moscow for leadership.

When the Tatar leader Mamai recognized that Moscow was becoming a threat to Tatar rule, he planned to attack and destroy the city. Prince Dmitriy, a grandson of Ivan I, called on forces from Rostov (in the north), Yaroslav, and Belozer to help him resist the Tatars. Dmitriy led his forces against the Tatars and met them on a tributary of the Don River. He successfully attacked and defeated them only to have them attack Moscow later and destroy the city. His temporary victory against the Tatars earned him the title of "Dmitriy Donskoy."

For more than ten years Moscow was again in the control of the Tatars. People fled to Nizhniy Novgorod (now Gorky) and to Novgorod. But the Kingdom of Lithuania and Poland threatened Novgorod as the Tatars threatened Nizhniy Novgorod. Ivan III, a great-grandson of Dmitriy Donskoy, recognized the need to oppose these threats, and he gathered forces to fight in Novgorod. His successes there enabled him to re-establish the Moscow principality with Novgorod as a part of it. He then turned to the Tatars and met them in a stand-off near Tver. Neither army crossed the river, and both armies sat until finally after several months the Tatars retreated. This retreat marked the end of the Tatar control and the birth of the new Moscow State.

Ivan III returned to Moscow to rebuild his city. The Kremlin wall was built of stones to replace the old wooden fortress walls. The wooden Uspensky Cathedral also was replaced with a five-dome, stone structure. A Granite Palace was also constructed within the Kremlin walls as a reception center for foreign dignitaries.

Ivan III was honored by foreign emissaries from European countries. The Roman Pope referred to him as a Caesar, from which came the term Tsar. But neither Ivan III nor his immediate successor Vasili III was crowned Tsar. This honor was to await his grandson Ivan IV.

IVAN IV AND THE TIME OF TROUBLES

The power of the Moscow State was greatly strengthened by the marriage of Ivan III to Sophia, the niece of the Greek Emperor, Constantine XIII. This marriage gave through heredity to their grandson the power of the state from his grandfather as a descendent of Novgorod rulers and the power of the church from his grandmother as a relative of the Greek nobility. Ivan IV rightfully as heir of these powers was crowned as Caesar or Tsar of all Russian principalities. The government of Moscow then became the government of all Russia by the decree supported by both political and religious authority.

Not only did Ivan IV claim authority over all the local princes and boyars (nobility), but many of them respected this authority and voluntarily submitted to Moscow rule. In return they expected a guarantee of their rights to own land and to govern the peasants who worked on the land. They could also join their guards with the Moscow forces for defending the land from foreign aggression.

However, some princes resisted the supremacy of Moscow. Ivan IV sent his guards (oprichniki) to force them into submission.

The attacks of Ivan's forces against other Russian nobility and his ruthless demands on his own bodyguards for strict loyalty to him earned him the name Grozniy, which means "terrifying" or often translated as "terrible." In return for the diligence of his body guards Ivan Grozniy divided among them the land, which he had deprived from the disloyal boyars.

The line of authority, which had been based on heredity, was now broken. Authority stemmed from loyalty to Ivan Grozniy and no longer from princes or descendents of former nobility. To strengthen further the new regime Ivan Grozniy established a corps of riflemen (streltsy) to preserve unity both in the royal court and throughout the landed estates.

The change of local authority also created a new relationship between the peasants and the local land owners. There had been some freedom of the peasants to move from one landed estate to another, particularly after the crops were harvested in the fall. A special day, Yuri Day, was set aside for peasants to move, if they wished. However, difficulties arose during the transition of power in Moscow. Peasants would flee from cruel land owners to more favorable places. This running away occurred during other times of the year and frustrated the farming operations in many places. To prevent these disorders Ivan Grozniy froze the peasants to the land and completed the establishment of the feudal system in Russia. The peasants became serfs, who could be bought and sold, given in marriage, and physically punished according to the will of the landlord.

As the power of Russia became greater by the accession of more land and by the modernization of weapons according to European standards, Ivan Grozniy looked toward the east. He wanted to free the Russians who lived along the Volga River from Tatar control and to expand Russia to include all that territory. With 150 cannons and 150,000 soldiers he attacked the Tatar stronghold at Kazan. This force was no match for the Tatars who still relied on bows and arrows, spears and shields, and fast running horses. Kazan fell to the Russians in 1552, and four years later the Russian army had moved down the Volga River to Astrakhan on the Caspian Sea.

Additional territory was gradually seceded to Russia either voluntarily or by force until the Ural Mountains and Western Siberia were both included. The fertile farm land of the Kuban, in the Northern Causasus, was also annexed to Russia.

The expansion into the Ural Mountains and into Siberia was aided by the powerful Stroganov family, who owned more than two and a half million acres of land between Kazan and the Ural Mountains along the Kama River. The Stroganov's turned against their former rulers, the Tatars, and helped subjugate them to the Russian State. They further helped expand the territory by hiring Yermak, from the Don River valley, to lead detachments of 800 explorers into Siberia to subdue the Tatars there. Even though Yermak never returned, he is credited for annexing Siberia to Russia.

Ivan Grozniy at the same time was building Moscow to make it beautiful and elegant. The greatest landmark of Moscow, the St. Basil's Cathedral, was built in the late 1500's by the order of Ivan Grozniy. The nine towers topped by different types of cupolas of St. Basil's Cathedral on Red Square even today are acclaimed for their outstanding beauty.

The story of the construction of St. Basil's Cathedral is told today by Moscow Intourist Guides as almost a fantasy. They say that Ivan Grozniy hired Italian architects to design the most beautiful cathedral in the world. Then, according to the story, the architects came to him after the completion to receive payments. The Tsar praised them and asked them if they could build another one just as beautiful. Happy with his praise the architects agreed that they could and would. Since the Tsar wanted his new cathedral to be the one and only masterpiece, he put out the eyes of the architects so they could not build another one which might compete or detract from his. And so goes the story.

Also in the Kremlin today are seen the Bell-Tower Cathedral and King Cannon, both of which were built during the time of Tsar Ivan Grozniy.

Ivan Grozniy was cruel, even merciless. He destroyed many people, including members of his own family, who opposed his power. So jealous he was of his power and so fearful of subversion in his own ranks, he trusted neither relatives nor associates to take over his authority when he died. He left Russia many times larger, more powerful, both respected and feared at home and abroad, and elevated to a higher cultural level. Yet when he died there was no one to carry on for him.

The next thirty years was called the Time of Troubles or the time of dissension. It was marked with rebellions and various leaders who tried to assume power either because of popular support or because of stated rights of heredity. The popular rebellions were led by Ivan Bolotnikov, Ileika Muromets, and others, who had all suffered retribution by the former bodyguards of Ivan Grozniy. Among the nobility there was chosen another popular leader, Boris Godunov, who was the head of the government for a short while. But there was no lasting authority until 1613.

During this time of weakness other nations attacked. Mercenary soldiers under the King of Sweden attacked and took Novgorod and other Baltic areas. The Polish army took Smolensk and even held onto Moscow for a time.

Russian forces under the leadership of popular men, Minin and Pozharsky, attacked the Poles and drove them from Moscow in 1613. They also drove back the Swedish mercenaries and freed Novgorod in 1617.

THE BEGINNING OF THE ROMANOV DYNASTY

After the Poles were driven from Moscow in 1613 there was held in Moscow a council meeting of representatives of the boyars, the clergy, the landowners, and the merchants. At this meeting there was selected a new Tsar, Mikhail Romanov, who was a grand-nephew of Ivan Grozniy. He was yet a child, and the council wanted to rely on his recognized authority as a means of their governing Russia. The father of Mikhail Romanov interceded, however, and the power was gained by the Romanov family to last from 1613 to 1917, the time of the Communist Revolution.

Neither Mikhail nor his immediate successors, Alexei and Feodor, made any notable changes in the Russian society. Rather than trying to expand the territory, they defended their own land and consolidated power within the government and among the peasantry. The council, which had elected Mikhail as tsar, continued to function as an advisory body for the tsar. Representatives from the various sectors of the upper class did not assume any supremacy over the tsars, but they did retain great power within the court. The measures taken to consolidate power had the greatest effect on the peasants, about ninety percent of the population, who became virtual slaves of the landed gentry. The rift between classes became sharper. In 1649, laws were decreed which further defined the roles of the hereditary classes and which tightly bound the peasants to the service of the landowners. For disobedience to the landowners the peasants were severly punished, beaten with sticks, placed in jails, and deprived of food. Runaway serfs by law were liable for capture for five years, and upon capture they were left to the mercy of their landowner.

The enriched landowners sold their goods on the market and started new business and industrial enterprises. They made guns and tools from iron and cooper. In addition, they made utensils of various kinds to sell on the market. Foreign traders brought silk, linen, carpets, guns, sugar, and wine. Russian merchants traded for these products furs, wax, honey, potash, and resin. Commerce increased, and a greater distinction arose between peasants and the upper classes.

In the meantime changes were taking place in the Ukraine and in Belorussia. Unrest evolved into rebellions along the Don and Volga River valleys. The peoples in these areas were also in a state of unrest due to Polish domination from the west and Turkish domination from the south. Polish nobility came to the Ukraine and tried to institute serfdom similar to that in Russia. People fled from the land and joined in with cavalry groups known as Cossacks. The Cossack bands were made up of Tatars, Russians, Ukrainians, and others who were fighting against oppression.

In response to the Polish threat in the Ukraine, Bogdan Khemel'nitskiy organized a group of Cossacks and fought against the Poles. He drove the Poles across the Dnieper River and took Kiev but was unable to cross the river in other places. To maintain his position he appealed to the Russian Tsar Alexei for an alliance. They joined forces and drove the Poles back at Smolensk.

This agreement of 1654 between Khemel'nitsky and Tsar Alexei helped extend Russian power into the Ukraine. Today there is a statue in Kiev to Khemel'nitskiy as the liberator of the Ukraine from Poland as the unifier of the Ukraine to Russia.

Serfdom was brought into the Ukraine from Russia. This action and the attempts to extend serfdom along the Don and Volga River valleys brought renewed resistance. The pacification of these areas was to await another one hundred years.

In 1670, another rebellion evolved into an actual civil war. This war was waged by a Cossack, Stepan Ryazin. He sailed a river boat on the Don River and the Volga River. For a time he ruled these rivers from Cherkassk on the Don and Astrakhan on the Volga almost to Nighny Novgorod (now Gorky) on the Volga. He also controlled cities as far west of the rivers as Tambov, Temnikov, and Arzamas. These cities became sites of great battles against the forces of Tsar Alexei. Stepan Ryazin gained wide popular support from both the Tatars and Russians in opposition to the autocracy of the tsar. But the Cossacks were finally defeated. Thousands of people were hanged in Arzamas for their rebellion against the tsar. Stepan Ryazin was seized and taken to Moscow, where he was publically tortured and put to death.

Today, a statue of Stepan Ryazin is displayed in the Don Cossack Museum in Cherkassk, the same town where Yermak, the Siberian explorer, was born.

PETER THE GREAT

Peter the Great ruled from 1682 to 1725 and brought tremendous changes and reforms to the Russian society. He modernized Russia by introducing many western customs and techniques.

He waged war against the Turks in order to protect Russia's southern borders and to gain access to the Black Sea. Several attempts failed due to the strong Turkish fortress at Azov, near the mouth of the Don River.

War was then waged against Sweden to gain access to the Baltic Sea. Peter the Great wanted a "Window to the West". His troops fought a hard war against the Swedes and then his workers fought a hard war against the natural elements to construct a city on the Baltic. St. Petersburg was built on a swamp on the Finnish Gulf. Workers died of disease, the cold, and hunger. They worked standing up to their waist in water, but they built the city which became the new capital of Russia. St. Petersburg (now Leningrad) became a large port city and is now the second largest city in the Soviet Union.

Peter the Great had recognized the need for ships, but Russia had never had a navy. He personally went to Holland to gain actual experience in shipbuilding and to England to learn about navigation. Later he returned to St. Petersburg and directed the construction of ships for the navy.

After building a fleet he sailed from St. Petersburg to the Black Sea and attacked the Azov Fortress from the sea. This time he defeated the Turks and held this fortress to protect the southern border.

When Peter the Great built his new capital at St. Petersburg, he demanded that those in the royal courts adopt western customs. They had to bathe, shave off their beards, and wear western clothes. He brought in French and German tutors to teach them manners and refinement. Schools were established for the youth of the nobility, and he made schooling mandatory for them.

Prior to Peter the Great records were written in the Church Slavonic alphabet, which had been prepared by the Greek missionaries at Kiev more than 700 years before that time. Peter revised the alphabet by simplifying some letters and deleting others. He also started the first Russian newspaper, established the first theatre, set up a Naval Academy, and ordered the founding of the Academy of Sciences.

For governmental reorganization, he established a nine-man senate, which acted in place of the tsar, when he was away. In addition, he established a system of colleges or departments to supervise administrative matters, e.g., foreign affairs, military, naval, finance, etc.

Peter the Great was responsible for moving Russia forward in many ways. He made Russia a modern military power. He introduced industry and manufacturing and put Russia on a more competitive position with European powers. He gained the respect of world leaders and actually brought Russia into the modern era.

However, his reforms caused much opposition for all segments of the society. The moving of the capital from the traditional Moscow to St. Petersburg was the cause of not the least of this opposition. The regimentation of the whole country into governmental provinces with prescribed obligations for government officials and peasants alike caused great dissatisfaction. Peter's attack on the church was not accepted by church leaders or the people. He abolished the position of metropolitan and established a synod under government authority to direct the affairs of the church. The reorganization of the army along Western Europe lines also met with great opposition. Peter the Great had taken all authority upon himself to the complete disregard of tradition. He was also jealous of his authority and put to death his son Alexis, who had challenged Peter's power. When Peter the Great died, he left no heir, and the time that followed was a struggle for power among his descendents.

During the years that followed the death of Peter the Great the government was actually run by a Supreme Privy Council, which was established by Peter's widow and by regents who named successors, four in a row, who were either under age or unqualified to rule. But in 1741, Elizabeth, a daughter of Peter, conspired with the guards to assert her right to the throne. Elizabeth ruled then for twenty years trying to stabilize the domestic reforms of her father and to maintain an alliance with Austria and France against Prussia during the Seven Years War in Europe. Her armies did defeat the Prussian soldiers, but her victories did not guarantee the complete defeat of Prussia. Dissension in her own court and the events that followed her death brought about an alliance between Russia and Prussia.

The greatest contribution of Elizabeth was the continuation of the domestic reforms of her father. Great social and economic changes took place. The status of the local landowner had been raised to that of a government agent, and the status of the serf was reduced to that of chattel. Serfs became the property of the landowners and could be bought and sold separately rather than being bound to the land as before. However, the realignment of the society did produce economic advantages. Serfs were used as laborers on the farms, in the crafts, and in industry. These branches of the economy all prospered due to the supply of manpower provided by the reforms and also caused by the steady increase in the population. The demands for military goods and supplies and for economic goods for foreign trade stimulated increased production. Mining and metullurgy became important industries. The new Academy of Sciences greatly assisted mining and other industries. Textiles were produced in larger quantities, and cotton became an important product as well as linen. Local craftsmen produced household goods made of iron, copper, and lead. One of the greatest boons to the economy though was the production of wheat in the Black Earth Belt. Russia became a major exporter of wheat. Trade also flourished in furs, honey, wax, wood products, and pig iron.

Cultural changes were also taking place. The affluence of the upper classes and the educational and cultural institutions founded by Peter the Great brought about an enlightenment among the ever-increasing number of the nobility. The number of people who could trace their lineage back to royalty, both directly and indirectly, had become very large. These people all enjoyed special privileges in the society. They received instruction from French and other European tutors and had free time to pursue studies and cultural enjoyment of their own choosing.

A notable achievement was the founding of the Moscow University in 1755 by Mikhail Lomonosov, a son of a fisherman and shipbuilder who lived in a village near Arkhangel on the White Sea. At the age of 19, Lomonosov left home to seek an education. He studied languages at a Moscow academy and later went to Germany to study physical sciences. Upon his return to Moscow he was appointed to the Academy of Sciences and became an outstanding chemist and writer. He made many discoveries in chemistry, and he also contributed much to the standardization and enrichment of Russian literary language. He may even be called a forerunner of the Golden Age of Russian Literature. Lomonosov's work in initiating and supporting a university was rewarded by having the University of Moscow named after him by Tsarina Elizabeth. A one time, it was said that "Lomonosov is the Moscow University," because he was the only professor. But in 1755 the university was established with ten professors and three departments (philosophy, law, and medicine). Now it is one of the world's outstanding universities, and it is called the Moscow State University (imeni) of Lomonosov.

CATHERINE THE GREAT

At the death of Elizabeth her palace opposition gained control and named as tsar another person who was unqualified to assert his own rule. The new tsar was Peter III, who had married a German princess, Catherine. Peter III was not able to withstand the intrigue of the court, and Catherine took the opportunity to gain power for herself. Within a year she had gained favor with the Guards for the purpose of killing Peter and gaining power.

Then Catherine became ruler of Russia and assumed the title of empress. Dissatisfaction with the domestic reforms had already caused widespread unrest throughout the country. Many serfs were escaping and fleeing to join the Cossacks, who were still the main authority along the Don and Volga River valleys. The nobility and landowners were divided among themselves on policies of the reform, dissension in the church, and foreign relations. This dissatisfaction was further intensified by the naming of a German to be tsarina or empress.

Catherine continued her drive for power, however, on the international level. In 1764, she concluded a treaty with Prussia for military cooperation, which led to the partition of Poland in three stages--1772, 1793, and 1795. Catherine also sent her army against the Turks in the Balkans and along the Black Sea.

The defeat of the Turks was recognized as a victory for all of Southern Europe as well as for Russia. The Moslem Turks had long been a threat to Europeans and Christianity. Catherine was hailed for driving back the Turks and was given the name of Catherine the Great. Her greatness was exemplified by her selection of capable military leaders. She named Colonel Alexander Suvorov to lead the Russian army against the Turks and Admiral Feodor Ushakov to command the naval forces. Suvorov took his forces through the Balkans and south to the Black Sea taking the territory for Russia which is now a part of the Soviet Ukraine. Ushakov took his fleet from St. Petersburg to the Mediterranean and Black Seas and defeated both Turkish and French forces along the northern shore of the Black Sea.

With the annexation of land from Poland the areas of present-day Belorussia and Lithuania were added to Russia. Annexed land from Poland and also that previously under Turkish control moved the Russian border westward to establish the Ukrainian frontier.

The military victories, however, did not settle the unrest and dissatisfaction within Russia. Actually civil disturbances increased.

Tatars feared Russian domination along the Black Sea and on the Crimean Peninsula. As a result of this widespread dissatisfaction the numbers and the power of the Don Cossacks steadily increased.

Rumors started that Peter III was not really dead and that he would return to remove Catherine from power and to free the peasants from serfdom. A strong leader of the Don Cossacks, Emelyan Pugachev, fought against the Russian fortresses along the Volga River and recruited many peasants to join him. This uprising spread rapidly, and people started to call Pugachev their Tsar Peter III. Rumors continued to grow and Pugachev assumed the role as a liberator.

The whole Volga River valley from the Caspian Sea to Kazan was taken by Pugachev. In addition, his forces moved east and took the land of the Ural Mountains and beyond. Pugachev then turned to Kazan and in a major battle defeated this important fortress of the tsarist army.

As Pugachev turned south toward the fortress at Parepta, he was deceived by traitors and turned over to the tsarist generals. Pugachev was then put in chains and placed in a cage. He was taken in this cage to Moscow and displayed as a wildman or as an animal on Bolotnaya Square for all people to see. Finally he was tortured and killed as were also many of his followers.

Catherine the Great had with military force expanded the borders of Russia, gained respect of foreign governments, and quelled the uprisings throughout the country. Her achievements increased the power and prestige of Tsarist Russia, but the social ills of the country were far from being solved.

The first of the writers of the Golden Age of Russian literature, Alexander Pushkin, a member of the nobility who enjoyed special privileges in the society, has written the book "The Captain's Daughter," which portrayed Pugachev in a much more favorable light than that displayed in Moscow. His writings were the beginning of a new era of literary dissent, which lead to even greater opposition to the autocracy of the tsars.

Events abroad also became topics of discussion among scholars and writers. Both the American and French Revolutions took place during Catherine's reign, and the democratic ideals became a great influence on the thinking of many Russians.

After the sudden death of Catherine the Great, her son Paul was tsar for five years. His policies were confusing and irresponsible both on the domestic scene and abroad. Paul responded to the call of Austria and Italy to fight against Napolean. He sent General Suvorov to fight in Italy, but Paul's misunderstandings with the

Austrians caused General Suvorov to be stranded without Austrian support. Suvorov was forced to retreat over the Alps Mountains, where he and his men met tremendous hardships, but Suvorov managed to save his army. Due to the tragedies of the Russian Army, Paul blamed the Austrians for lack of support and broke off diplomatic relations with both Austria and England.

Opposition against Paul was very strong among Russian Government officials. A group conspired against him attempting to have him abdicate in favor of his son Alexander, and during the attempt Paul was murdered.

ALEXANDER I

As a young man Alexander was an idealist, and during the first few years of his reign he initiated many reforms. He freed many prisoners and relaxed civil regulations on censorship, bans on foreign travel, and prohibitions on improting foreign literature. He also proposed to make the Senate a separate legislative body. Serfdom was obnoxious to him, but he only attempted insignificant reforms for the peasants.

Having come to power in 1801, Alexander's major international problem was Napoleon. His main concern was peace, and he joined coalitions with Great Britain, Austria, and Sweden in opposition to Napoleon's aggression. In 1805, the Russian army fought against Napoleon's forces in Austria and in 1807 in Poland. Both times the Russians were defeated and had to retreat. It became necessary for Alexander to accept the Treaty of Tilsit with Napoleon to prevent a war with France. In this treaty Russia gained the territory of Finland and Bessarabia (Moldavia) in exchange for the recognition of Napoleon's right in Europe.

For the next few years Alexander toyed with democratic ideas for government organization, but no real reforms took place. His attention was again diverted by Napoleon, who was making preparations to attack Russia. Alexander staged a defense at Smolensk in order to prevent an attack on Moscow. The French army with three times as many soldiers as the Russian army had quickly attacked in June of 1812 and penetrated deep into Russia. Recognizing the futility of defending Smolensk against informidable odds, the Russian army retreated and saved its forces.

Napoleon's attack on Russian unified the country more than ever before. Colonel Mikhail Kutuzov, a popular military leader and a former student of Suvorov, was named to head the Russian army in defense of Moscow.

Kutuzov conducted a "scorched earth" and "retreat" policy. He conducted skirmishes against the French, but he did not want to meet them in a major battle. The peasants were told to destroy their crops, burn their fields, and kill their cattle to prevent the French from obtaining food and supplies. The peasants then fled into the countryside and formed partisan bands. Napoleon advanced rapidly, but he was frustrated by Russian policies. His supply lines and communications lines were lengthened, and he had difficulty feeding his troops. He could not meet the Russians in battle, except once at Borodino, which was a terrible slaughter for both armies.

As Napoleon's forces came to Moscow, the Russians evacuated the city. They took their possessions, their food, and their clothing. Again Napoleon was frustrated. He expected to sign a treaty and to have supplies for his troops. But he obtained neither. The city was vacant. He waited and continued to wait. Finally there was nowhere to go but to retreat. And it became necessary to retreat as the winter came on since he had neither food nor winter clothing for his troops.

The Russians rallied and followed the French soldiers in their retreat. They attacked sporadically but the real test for the French was the cold weather. The Russians had fur hats and fur coats, but the French could not withstand the cold.

Kutuzov gathered his army and chased the French across the border and beyond into Europe. Napoleon was defeated, and he lost most of his army. He entered Russia with 600,000 men and left with only 50,000 or less.

Even though the battle of Waterloo was the final blow to Napoleon, much of the credit was given to Russia and to Alexander I personally. At the Congress of Vienna in 1815, Alexander I participated as a major spokesman in settling the affairs of Europe after the Napoleonic Wars. In the same year, he also initiated the Holy Alliance with Austria and Prussia. Later this alliance was signed by other European powers, including France. Alexander I became the leader of the Holy Alliance, which was primarily a statement of support for Christianity and for the "Divine Right of Kings." It was directed against democracies, which like France's evolve into military dictatorships, and against the Moslem Turks in a pledge to keep them out of the Balkans. The Holy Alliance became an issue during a revolt in Greece in which American troops were involved, and in European interference in America. The Monroe Doctrine of the United States was a response to the Holy Alliance.

The more effective international organization, however, was the Quadruple Alliance of Austria, Great Gritain, Prussia, and Russia. It later became the Quintuple Alliance when France was admitted. Alexander's influence waned in this alliance, and greater power was assumed by Austria and Britain. Alexander I gradually lost the influential position which he held at the Congress of Vienna.

During the last few years of his life Alexander became reactionary. He recognized the needs for reform, but he assigned military leaders the task of freeing serfs gradually. This reform had little significance for the serfs. Alexander I strongly opposed the organization of secret societies, which were espousing greater reforms, and he sent Guards against them. His attacks were unsuccessful, and further opposition continued to grow. Alexander I could not reconcile his former ideals with the reality of the demands of the serfs and intelligentsia for immediate reform and abolition of serfdom on one hand and the vested interests of the landowners and nobility on the other. His sense of order was inconsistent with rapid change, and he feared uprisings and revolts. But he was not to find the answer to these problems nor to see the revolts. He suddenly died of an illness in 1825.

NICHOLAS I

The attempts of Alexander I to destroy the secret societies did no more than to divide them into two groups, the Northern and the Southern Societies with headquarters in St. Petersburg and Kiev, respectively. When Alexander I died, the resentment against his successor, Nicholas I, was already very strong, because he was known to be much more reactionary than his brother, Alexander I.

Within a few days after the death of Alexander I, revolts broke out in St. Petersburg and other locations. The major revolt in St. Petersburg was led by members of the Guards, who had been active in the secret societies. However, the revolt was supported by peasants, merchants, and the intelligentsia. This Decembrist Revolt, as it was called because of the month of the year, was poorly organized and hastily carried out. One purpose was to prevent Nicholas from taking power, but they also espoused abolition of autocracy, freedom for the serfs, and an end to military colonies. They also advocated freedom of speeck, freedom of the press, and freedom of religion. But they were destined to failure, because they were unprepared, poorly armed, and small in numbers. They gathered on Senate Square in St. Petersburg, but they were quickly dispersed by cannon shot. Their rocks and sticks were no match against the Tsarist soldiers, and many of the insurgents were killed.

Nicholas I reacted to this revolt by implementing strong measures to control the society. He formalized the institution of secret police, established strict censorship, and reorganized education to eliminate liberal and radical teachings. Many revolts continued to take place among different groups of people, and each revolt was put down with military and police action. It was this time that Siberia gained the infamous name of a prison camp or the so-called "salt mines." Many agitators were exiled to Siberia.

Serfdom became a problem not only for the serfs but also for the landowners. Inflation and indebtedness brought economic pressure on the landowners. Merchants were also caught in this economic bind. Instead of having any relief of this financial crisis, the landowners and merchants were met with increased taxation.

Unrest and dissatisfaction spread throughout all strata of the society. The landless nobility, which was composed of scholars, scientists, writers, musicians, and those less dedicated, became known as the intelligentsia. They enjoyed special privileges because of their birthrights, but they had little responsibility. It was from this group that many fine cultural contributions came. Many of them had studied abroad and brought back liberal ideas. The exchange of ideas among these people dealt with literature, music, religion, art, and politics. In spite of the censorship many of them were able to produce great artistic works. This time became the beginning of the Golden Age of Russian Literature. During the reign of Nicholas I there appeared such writers as Alexander Pushkin, Nikolai Gogol, and Mikhail Lermontov. Mikhail Glinka came forth as a great composer, and Alexander Ivanov gained renown as a great painter. Many of these artistic works reflected the spirit of the times and a hope for a release from the oppression. It is the questioning and the hope for a better life which help make these works unusually great.

On the international scene Nicholas I also sought for stability of autocracies and Christian orthodoxy. He wanted good relations with Austria, France, Prussia, and England, and he opposed the 1848 revolutions in Europe. He sent troops to assist Austria in putting down the Hungarian Revolt of that year. The fear of a Turkish revival in the Balkans caused him to invade this area to preserve Christianity against the threat of the Moslems. He expected support from his former allies, but to his sorrow England and France feared Russian aggression and refused to accept Nicholas I's design to partition Turkey. When Russian forces moved into the Crimea in 1853, the British and French took the side of Turkey in the Crimean War. This action was an affront to Nicholas I, and he was forced to accept the fall of Sevastopol and other Black Sea fortresses to the French and British. However, his death came before the peace treaty of that war.

ALEXANDER II

The coming of Alexander II to power marked a great change both in domestic and foreign policies. The Crimean War marked an end to further military action against the Turks. The British Navy stood in the way. Rather than looking to Europe, the Russian expansion gradually moved east into Central Asia by exploration and military conquest. It was during this time that Tashkent became a part of Russian territory.

The greatest achievements for Alexander II, however, were in domestic reforms. In February of 1861 he abolished serfdom by emancipating the serfs from their landlords and by granting them land to be purchased on long-term contracts with the government. The landowners would then be paid for their land, which had been taken for the peasants. In this Alexander II hoped to solve the problems without injury to the landowners, who were also allowed to keep approximately one-third of their land holdings.

In January of 1864, Alexander II introduced the Zemstvo System (Land Council System) of local government in the rural areas. This reform granted a measure of self-government, but the Zemstvo was subordinated to the Tsarist Government through local administrative officials. The peasants were permitted to participate in the Zemstvo through elections based on the amount of land they held. Since the previous landowners still held the largest areas of land, they were better represented in the Zemstvos. However, this was a dramatic change for the peasants.

The real problems for the peasants came later. Their inability to make payments on the land kept them over-obligated to the government. Conditions worsened, and they could not even pay the interest on their government obligations. Some of the peasants fled from the land to escape the financial burden and to seek employment in new industries, which were rapidly growing in the cities. This action resulted in a government decree to freeze the peasants and their descendents to the land until the land was paid for. This situation was unbearable for the peasants, but thanks to the need for industrial workers in the city this decree was not always enforced. Many young peasants left their homes to live and work in the cities.

Alexander II announced further reforms, including reforms in the cities. In 1863 he modernized university education by granting professors freedom on administrative and curriculum affairs and by removing the class barriers for student admission to universities. In 1864 he introduced an independent judicial branch of the government to provide greater justice in the courts and to free the courts from autocratic abuses. In 1870 he organized municipal councils for city government through elections based on tax payments. These reforms benefited primarily the upper classes, but the poorer people also gained new opportunities. The growth of industry was benefited by tax reforms, and workers were needed in great numbers.

The whole new atmosphere was advantageous to the intelligentsia, and the Golden Age of Literature came into full bloom with Leo Tolstoy, Ivan Turgenev, Feodor Dostoyevsky, Alexander Goncharov, and Nikolai Nekrasov. The theatre also came to fore with Alexander Ostrovsky, and music reached a new level of expression through Modeste Mussorgsky, Alexander Borodin, Nikolai Rimsky-Korsakov, and Peter Tchaikovsky. The St. Petersburg Free School of Music, which was founded in 1862, has gone on to produce some of the world's greatest music. The reforms of Alexander II took off the lid of latent cultural expression, and Russia established a new culture of its own. Today Leningrad enjoys the tradition of this culture and boasts of its contribution to the world. The works of most of these artists are produced in opera, ballet, or stage plays in the theatre of both Leningrad and Moscow as well as by travelling troupes throughout the Soviet Union.

But the enlightenment and the great progress of the reforms during the time of Alexander II did not effect all people equally. The poor peasant and the industrial worker produced more than ever before, but he did not share in the benefits. He was still unable to attend schools, to learn to read and write, and do more than hard physical labor. Even though there were enough exceptions to this statement to indicate a betterment for them, the fact is that 85% to 90% of the population still lived in poverty and ignorance. The contrast between the rich and the poor continued to plague the whole society, and these sharp differences were the subjects of much of the great literary work. The demands for change became even stronger. The intelligentsia, including school teachers who had been hired to teach at the new schools which had been established by Alexander II, continued to express feelings of discontent and dissatisfaction. They obtained the writings of French, American, British, and German writers. These works were translated into Russian and were read by the educated people.

Among the writings received in Russia and translated were those of Karl Marx. Members of the intelligentsia had already read and translated the writings of Jacques Rousseau, Thomas Paine, Thomas Jefferson, and other advocates of democracy. But the Communist Manifesto and Das Kapital of Karl Marx and Friedrich Engels were brought to Russia and translated during the time of Alexander II. But the social and political impact of these writings did not develop into political parties until the reign of Alexander III.

In 1881, Alexander II worked on further reforms in the legislative branch of government. He was considering elective representatives from the Land Councils (Zemstvos) and the City Councils to make up a State Council. Movement toward a constitutional type of government was beginning to take place, but this was ended by the assassination of Alexander II on March 13, 1881. Revolutionaries were still demanding greater and quicker reforms.

ALEXANDER III

Alexander III came to power in 1881 after the death of his father. He was greatly distrubed by his father's assassination and believed that the reforms had caused more problems than they solved. His reaction was to curtail or to reverse all of the reforms. He re-instituted censorship, restricted education to the upper classes by raising the fees, denied Jews the right ot vote for representatives to local councils, and placed the land councils (zemstvos) under the control of provincial governors.

The situation for both the peasants and the industrial workers deteriorated. Even with the increase of tillable land, the peasants had less and less land to farm each generation due to the rapid increase of rural population. Land payments and high taxes continued to keep them in a financial squeeze. Attempts by the peasants to acquire more land were thwarted by restrictions on credit. Peasants became less acceptable for industrial jobs, due to their illiteracy and lack of training. Even those who did become industrial workers continued to experience economic difficulties. They worked long hours under difficult circumstances, and their pay was low. Attempts to organize labor for better conditions were met with legal prohibitions and police action. In spite of their illegal status labor organizations did grow, and strikes took place at many industrial sites. Government legislation to reduce working hours and to protect child labor was poorly carried out by the employers. The whole situation became even worse in the middle 1880's when there was a market decline causing widespread unemployment.

Alexander III reacted to the dissension and unrest as the result of agitation of non-Russians, both the Russian Jews and foreigners. Greater restrictions were placed on all publications, which became subject to a pre-publication censorship. Foreign ideas were rejected as subversive, and Alexander III held to the concepts of nationalism, orthodoxy, and autocracy. He believed that the true Russian should be a loyal subject to the tsar. He completely rejected the concept of a constitutional form of government that his father was considering just before his death.

Political organizations had existed since the time of the Northern Society and the Southern Society of the Decembrist Revolt days. A populist (narodniki) movement became active in the 1770's, but its illegal status caused it to be taken over by extremists and terrorists. Political parties in the democratic sense could not develop, even though the intelligentsia supported this idea.

After the writings of Karl Marx, the Communist Manifesto and Das Kapital, were translated into Russian in 1872, one of the Populists (Narodniki), Georgi Plekhanov, was inspired by Communist teachings and became a leader of the Communist movement in Russia. He organized Communist organizations in Russia and abroad. His activity and writings greatly affected a young man, Vladimir Ulyanov, who became known as Lenin and the leader of the 1917 Communist Revolution.

Lenin was the son of a school teacher in Simbirsk (now Ulyanovsk). He was an excellent student in school and entered the University of Kazan. However, he was expelled, not because of his activity but rather that of his brother. Alexander Ulyanov was a participant in the illegal People's Will (Narodnaya Volya) group, which carried out terrorist activities. Because of this membership he was arrested and executed. Young Vladimir Ulyanov (Lenin) became incensed over this execution and dedicated his life to the overthrow of the autocratic government. He re-entered the University of Kazan after several requests and finished with a law degree in a very short time. While practicing law, he became acquainted with the writings of Plekhanov and then those of Marx and Engels. His life then became dedicated to the Communist movement.

Alexander III only lived to serve as tsar for fourteen years. In 1894 the rule of Russia went to his son, Nicholas II.

Nicholas II, the last of the Russian tsars, tried to follow in the steps of his father, but he was not as capable. As the difficulties increased he became frustrated and leaned heavily on advisors. At first his greatest dependence was on his father's reactionary advisor, Constantine Pobedonostsev. This reliance on Pobedonostsev helped to maintain the old policies, which were constantly becoming more difficult for the Russian people.

Foreign affairs were at low ebb for Tsarist Russia. Russian influence in European power circles was limited to France and Albania. Neither Alexander III nor Nicholas II were able to restore the prestige that was enjoyed by their predecessors. However, expansion to the east had steadily progressed so that Siberia, Central Asia, and the Far East were all a part of Russia. Russian possessions in North America had been sold to the United States in 1867, but Russian still possessed a large unexplored frontier. Alexander III had contracted with France for loans to enable him to construct a railroad across Siberia, and this construction started in 1891. New foreign relations were being established between Russia and Japan. Territorial disputes arose between Russia and Japan in the Far East.

Territorial disputes in the Far East led to the Russo-Japanese War of 1904-05. The Russian army did not expect any serious resistance from the Japanese, but they met defeat after defeat. Neither country was prepared for a long war, and it was necessary to have the differences mediated by a neutral power. President Theodore Roosevelt of the United States provided this mediation service at Portsmouth, New Hampshire, in 1905, and settled the differences with a setback for Russia.

Opposition to the Russo-Japanese War added to the dissatisfaction and the unrest in Russia. Strikes continued in industries, and different political parties began to form. The largest group was the Social Revolutionaries, which included various factions with different concepts of revolution and of the new government. They advocated the overthrow of the Tsar, and they were supported by the Communists. There was also an agrarian group, which arose from the Zemstvos (land councils). This group also included members of the intelligentsia, who urged the establishment of a constitutional government. Later this group became known as the Constitutional Democrats. The SR's (Social Revolutionaries) and the KD's or Kadets (Constitutional Democrats) gradually became powerful political opposition to the tsarist government.

Working conditions in the factories continued to become worse, and the number of strikes increased from year to year. In January of 1905, under the leadership of a Russian Orthodox liberal, Father Gapon, a number of workers marched to the Winter Palace in St. Petersburg to appeal to Tsar Nicholas II for greater reforms and better working conditions. This group was joined by others so that it totalled approximately 200,000 persons. Since it was on a Sunday, many people came out to see the "parade," and the crowd appeared as a real threat to the Guards. As the crowd gathered on the square in front of the Winter Palace, children climbed into the trees to have a better view. The marchers were not armed and had not planned a riot. They only wanted to submit a petition to the tsar. However, the Guards feared an attack on the Winter Palace, and they fired shots over the heads of the crowd as a warning to stay back. Unfortunately, they did not know about the children in the trees, many of whom were shot and fell to the ground. The crowd became enraged and picked up sticks and stones to throw at the Guards. The march then became a riot, and the Guards drove over the people with their horses. Many, many people were killed. Sunday, January 9, 1905, became to be called "Bloody Sunday" and has also been referred to as the "First Russian Revolution."

Demands for representation in the national government increased sharply after Bloody Sunday. Uprisings occurred in Moscow and in other cities. The protestors were joined by large numbers of persons, even soldiers and sailors. In the Black Sea there was a mutiny aboard the battleship Potemkin.

In October of 1905, Tsar Nicholas II started to made concessions. He asked his prime minister to announce the formation of a national legislative body, the Duma. Along with this announcement came statements of civil rights and greater suffrage. The Duma was to have the right of approving all laws.

For a short time there was some acceptance of the Duma, but as it was seen that the Duma had no real power, there were more demands for a genuine constituent assembly. Reshuffling appeared in the political parties. The Social Democrats, an off-shoot from the Social Revolutionaries, had already divided into two groups--the Bolsheviks and the Mensheviks. The Social Revolutionaries also splintered again, as did the Constitutional Democrats. But those who supported the Duma were quickly dissillusioned, when in 1906, the Duma was dissolved by the tsar.

With the appointment of a new prime minister, Peter Stolypin, in 1907, there were elected representatives for a second Duma. This Duma became more effective under the more liberal Stolypin. He announced a land reform, which reduced and later abolished the land payments that the peasants had for so long been burdened. This action also granted personal freedom to the peasants and gave them the right to own land. They were also permitted to leave the land and move to new locations. The reform was fully acceptable to some representatives in the Duma, but others demanded nationalization of the land. Further disputes arose concerning voting rights, and the Duma again was abolished.

Tsar Nicholas II did not want to give real power to the Duma, and it remained an advisory body, which he dissolved at will. The following Dumas were short-lived and never again did they become as powerful as the second one under Stolypin.

In the family of Nicholas II there occurred a tragedy. Their son, Alexius, was a hemophiliac, for which there is no known cure. They had heard of a religious mystic who could cure illnesses, and they called on him. This man, Gregory Rasputin, was a peasant from Siberia, who had gained a reputation as a healer. Some people accepted him as a messenger from God even though his life was completely immoral. Somehow, though, Rasputin was able to stop the bleeding and help Alexius over several very difficult times. For this almost miraculous help, the Tsar Nicholas and his wife, Alexandra, owed him an unpayable debt. Especially Alexandra almost worshipped him and asked her husband to seek his advice on matters of state.

Stolypin strongly opposed Rasputin, but after the death of Stolypin, Rasputin became a terrifying force in the government. He caused many leaders to be discharged and recommended policies that were harmful to Russia. Until his death in 1915, Rasputing virtually controlled the government and made the Duma completely impotent.

During this time Nicholas II was faced with even a more difficult problem. The First World War caught him unprepared, but Russia's alliance with France and her concern for the Balkans brought Russia into the war in 1914 on the side of the Allies. He immediately sent a massive infantry against the Germans, but they were no match against the well-trained and well-equipped German army. Peasants and industrial workers, with practically no training and insufficient arms, were slaughtered in great numbers. The Russians were forced to retreat, and morale fell both in the ranks and at home. Dissertions became a major problem, and discipline broke down in the ranks.

The need for leadership became apparent not only on the military fronts but also on the home front. The diversion of men from the farms and from the factories for military service caused a decrease in the production of food and equipment. The food shortage was further increased by military priorities, and there became a famine particularly in the cities.

Attempts by the tsar to revive morale were fruitless. His personal appearance among the troops temporarily inspired the men, but this was no substitute for guns and ammunition. Revolts broke out at the front, and food riots took place in the cities.

Authority was being taken by local councils (soviets) due to the lack of leadership and order. The Duma also asserted more power and demanded that the tsar abdicate. Due to the complete chaos, Tsar Nicholas II had no choice, and in March, 1917, he abdicated in favor of his brother, Mikhail, but Mikhail, in turn, abdicated in favor of the Duma.

The abdication left the governmental authority divided. On the national level the Duma became a Provisional Government, but regional and local affairs were assumed by the city and land councils (soviets). The Petrograd (St. Petersburg) Soviet also contested the Provisional Government for national authority. This division was also based on political party differences. The Constitutional Democrats largely controlled the Provisional Government, while the soviets were made up of Social Revolutionaries. At this time the Social Democrats had boycotted the Duma, and many of the leaders, including Lenin, were in exile abroad.

The Provisional Government issued legislation on civil rights, universal suffrage, and amnesty for political prisoners. It also made preparations for a constitution and planned an election in October.

In June of 1917, there was called an All-Union Congress of Soviets, which was controlled by the Social Revolutionaries but was also well represented by the Social Democrats of both factions, Mensheviks and Bolsheviks, with the Bolsheviks in the minority. At this Congress there were organized a Central Committee and a Presidium to represent the soviets throughout the country.

By July of 1917, Alexander Kerensky had become the most powerful man in the Provisional Government. He organized political commissars to restore discipline in the army, but this action was only temporarily successful due to another defeat. General Laurus Kornilov, who just been named Commander in Chief of the Russian Army, accepted Kerensky's authority in exchange for his support of a general reorganization of military discipline.

Also in July, the Bolshevik wing of the Social Democrats attempted to overthrow the Petrograd Military Garrison in an attempt to take over the government. General Kornilov reacted to this action with an attempt to establish a military dictatorship in Russia. These events caused a further polarization of power, so that the Bolsheviks were gaining strength from the Mensheviks in the Social Democrats, and the military was gaining strength within the more liberal Provisional Government's Constitutional Democrats. Kerensky ordered the dismissal of General Kornilov and arrested him after Kornilov's unsuccessful military attack on Petrograd. Kerensky received the full support of the Social Democrats in the repulsing the Kornilov forces.

In the fall, Lenin returned to Petrograd in a sealed box car, which had been prepared by the Germans for adding further confusion to the Petrograd situation. Rather than causing a full collapse, however, Lenin was able to rally the Communists. He stressed the slogans of "peace, land, and bread" (immediate peace, land to the peasants and factories to the workers, and food distribution to the people) and "all power to the soviets."

With the support of peasants, workers, and soldiers, Lenin's forces were able to take over the Winter Palace, which housed the Provisional Government, on October 25, 1917, (November 7, new calendar) and announce the establishment of a Socialist Government. There was little resistance to the attack, and few lives were lost. Similar attacks took place in Moscow and other cities, and the power structure came into the hands of the Communists.

The first acts of the new government were to carry out the promises of the slogans. The peasants were told to take their land. It was now theirs. The workers were told to take the factories and operate them on elections of a factory soviet. All power was vested in the soviets on the local level, and the national power was in the All-Union Congress, executive committee, and presidium. Food was distributed to the people from store houses, and the troops were told to come home. A representative, Leon Trotsky, was sent to draw up a separate peace treaty, at almost any price, with the Germans and to end the war.

Foreign debts were repudiated, and foreign assets were nationalized. All the acts and agreements of the Tsarist Government and of the Provisional Government were declared invalid. The power was now in the hands of the people as represented in the soviets.

A new society had been established--a new socialist government. The Revolution was a success, and all that was left was to consolidate the position and build anew.

Alekseev, S. P. & Kartsov, V. G., Istoriya SSSR, Moscow,
Gosudarstvennoye Uchebno-Pedagogicheskoye Izdatel'stvo,
1960, 159 pp.

Clarkson, Jesse D., A History of Russia, New York: Random House,
1961, 857 pp.

Ellison, Herbert J., History of Russia, New York: Holt, Rinehart &
Winston, 1964, 644 pp.

Florinsky, Michael T., Russia--A History and An Interpretation
(Vol. 1 & 2), New York: Macmillan Co., 1953. (Vol. 1 & 2,
1511 pp.)

Florinsky, Michael T., Russia: A Short History, New York:
Macmillan Co., 1964, 653 pp.

Maxwell, Robert (Ed.), Information U.S.S.R., New York: Permagon
Press, 1962, 982 pp.

Mazour, Anatole G., Russia--Tsarist and Communist, Princeton,
New Jersey: D. Van Nostrand Co., Inc., 1962, 995 pp.

Nechkina, M. V. & Fadeev, Istoriya SSSR, Moscow:
Gosudarstvennoye Uchebno-Pedagogicheskoye Izdatel'stvo,
1961, 239 pp.

Pares, Bernard, A History of Russia, New York: Alfred A. Knopf,
1966, 611 pp.

Vernadsky, George, A History of Russia, New Haven: Yale
University Press, 1961, 512 pp.

Walsh, Warren Bartlett, Russia and the Soviet Union, Ann Arbor:
University of Michigan Press, 1958, 640 pp.

CHAPTER III

THE GOLDEN AGE OF RUSSIAN LITERATURE

Early in Russian history there were folk songs, fables, stories, and proverbs, which were sung or recited and passed from generation to generation. There were also created long epic poems, byliny, about the heroes, both real and mythical, of the by-gone days.

Great literary works, however, did not appear in Russia before the 19th Century, and almost suddenly there appeared a time which became known as the Golden Age of Russian Literature. In the latter part of the 18th Century Mikhail Lomonsov was credited for contributing much to the standardization and enrichment of the Russian literary language during his association with the Moscow State University. But Lomonosov did not create any literary masterpieces.

The great Russian writers are Pushkin, Lermontov, Gogol, Turgenev, Dostoyevsky, Tolstoy, and Chekhov, who all lived in the 19th Century. Their works have had and still do have a great influence on the Russian people and on most of the civilized world. Soviet citizens are proud of these great authors, and among the most common questions that they ask foreign tourists are questions concerning their works. The writings of these great authors have much to do with the way the citizens of the Soviet Union think today.

KRYLOV

Ivan Krylov was a prolific writer and should be included here because he collected many of the old stories from Russian folklore and from the old folklore of other countries and wrote them in Russian for his posterity. Today he is to the Russians what Aesop is to the Greeks, Western Europeans, and Americans. In fact, many of their stories are the same or very similar.

Ivan Krylov lived from 1769 until 1841. He wrote over 200 fables, many of which reflected events in Russian history. Since his stories and poems could be easily understood by everyone, even children, his sayings have become a part of the language of the people. In this way he too enriched the language and contributed much to the learning of the people.

Some of Krylov's best known fables are The Wolf and the Crane, The Fox and the Grapes, The Monkey and the Looking-Glass,

The Elephant and Moscow, The Curious One, and Martyshka and Her Eyeglasses. The first of these is a story of a crane helping remove a bone which was stuck in the wolf's throat. The Fox and the Grapes is the story of the fox which could not reach the grapes by jumping and decided that the grapes must be sour anyway. The Monkey and the Looking-Glass is the story of a monkey criticizing his own reflection in a mirror. Each of these fables is a simple, humorous story, which is loved by children.

PUSHKIN

Alexander Pushkin, who lived from 1799 to 1837, may be called the father of Russian literature. At least, he was one of the first authors during the time of the Golden Age of Russian literature. He wrote many poems, some novels, and a play. His works became a standard by which others guided their writings because of the quality of his style, the richness of his expressions, and the clarity of meaning. Many of his writings portrayed real events in his own life or in the history of Russia. Pushkin questioned these events and introduced his own views.

Alexander Pushkin had the distinction of being the grandson of an Abyssinian princess and a Russian nobleman. He received a good education from a French tutor and in a lyceum at Tsarskoye Selo (the tsar's residential village, which is now called Pushkin after the author). Pushkin spent many years in exile, not because he was a negro but because he was critical in his writings of the tsarist autocracy and serfdom. For several years during his exile he lived on the Black Sea coast and in the Caucasus Mountains. Later he returned to St. Petersburg and lived under close supervision of Tsar Nicholas I. However, his writings and his life continued to be controversial. His romances caused him to be challenged to several duels, and in 1837 he fought his last duel.

Among his poems is Uznik (A Prisoner), in which he compares life in exile with that of a young eagle in a cage. He portrays the attempts and the great desire of both to gain freedom. In another poem, v Sibir' (to Siberia), Pushkin sympathizes with his friends who were sent to Siberia as a result of the Decembrist Uprising.

His play, The Tragedy of Boris Godunov, as the title implies, concerns the Time of Troubles and the short reign of Boris Godunov. He praises Godunov as a popular leader and a good ruler. The historical value of this play has been recognized because Pushkin used

the language and the customs of Godunov's time which he learned by
reading the old Chronicles. Pushkin was particularly capable of
describing people's positions in life by the speech patterns he gave
them.

Pushkin's novels are also valuable for their historical and
social contributions. Eugene Onegin is a poetic novel concerning
the life of the nobility, which Pushkin explains and criticizes. In
Dubrovsky Pushkin depicted the life of the peasantry in the early
19th century. This novel was based on actual lives of a nobleman
and the serfs on the estate. Pushkin brings out very clearly the
character traits of the people and provides a vivid insight into their
relationships.

One of the most remarkable works of Pushkin is the short
story, The Captain's Daughter. This story follows the life of a
young officer, Peter Grinev, who is assigned to a small fortress
during the time of the Pugachev Rebellion. Grinev falls in love
with the captain's daughter, Maria Ivanovna Mironova, before the
attack on the fortress by Pugachev's forces. During the attack both
the captain and his wife are killed. The story here portrays vividly
the horrors and atrocities that occurred in these battles. Grinev
becomes acquainted with Pugachev, and they gain a personal respect
for each other. Grinev is allowed to go to Orenburg, the nearby city
fortress, and the command of the local fortress goes to Grinev's
antagonist, who joins Pugachev's command. Maria Ivanovna remains
in the custody of the local fortress chaplin. While at Orenburg
Grinev receives a letter from Maria Ivanovna in which she rebels
against her forthcoming forced marriage to the new fortress commander. During the attack on Orenburg Grinev once again meets
Pugachev and makes arrangements with him to free Maria Ivanovna
from her plight. Having collaborated with Pugachev for the successful rescue of Maria Ivanovna, Grinev placed himself in jeopardy
with the Russian army. After the war Grinev is arrested and tried,
but by the intervention of Maria Ivanovna to Tsarina Catherine,
Grinev is exonerated and marries Maria Ivanovna.

The relationships between the nobility and their servants,
between the army officers and Pugachev's men, and between the
nobility and the tsarina are very clearly portrayed throughout the
story. The language and behavior patterns of the different groups
are carefully prescribed to the characters in such a way to show how
well Pushkin knew people and to make the reader understand their
roles.

A main theme of The Captain's Daughter is the great gulf of
misunderstandings and differences that existed between the common

people and the nobility at that time. Rather than condemning whole groups of people, Pushkin singles out the good and bad traits of various people in different groups. The story is a study of people as well as a report on the great historical events.

This story and his other works help set a precedent that marked the beginning of a new era of literature in Russia. His example was noted carefully by those who followed him.

This literary precedent also greatly influenced the artistic expressions of other great Russian artists in opera, ballet, and painting. The love story of Ruslan and Ludmila was first composed as a long poem by Alexander Pushkin, but it is better known as the outstanding opera set to music by Mikhail Glinka, who in turn is known as the father of Russian composers. Peter Tchaikovsky, probably one of the greatest composers of all times, also selected Pushkin's works, the novel, Eugene Onegin, as the base for an opera by the same name. Painters also looked to Pushkin's works for inspiration. Karl Bryullov interpreted Pushkin's verses, entitled The Fountain of the Bakhchirsarai, which depicts the luxurious life of the Crimean Tatar nobility, in his famous painting, which he also calls The Fountain of Bakhchirsarai. And Modest Mussorgsky gained his fame as a composer by the music he set to the writings of Pushkin on The Tragedy of Boris Godunov.

Pushkin also wrote for children. His verses entitled A Tale about a Fisherman and a Fish is a children's classic. It is a story of an old fisherman and his wife. She pushed him too hard to catch fish and provide for her wants. When he is fishing he catches a gold fish, which pleads to be released into the water in exchange for wishes. The fisherman releases the fish and returns to tell his wife, who dreams of riches, power, and splendor. Each time a wish is granted, she asks the fisherman to return to the fish for even more. Finally the wife wants to be ruler of the whole sea and of the fish, and the fish replies by returning the fisherman and his wife to their original condition of poverty.

LERMONTOV

Lermontov greatly respected Pushkin. His first literary work was dedicated to Pushkin. He called this poem Death of a Poet and expressed his love for the "marvellous genius." Like Pushkin, Lermontov also lived part of his life in St. Petersburg, spent several years in exile in the Caucasus, and died in a duel.

Mikhail Lermontov lived from 1814 to 1841 and spent his adult years during the repressive reign of Nicholas I. His father was an army officer and encouraged Mikhail to serve as an army officer. During his youth Mikhail had lived with his grandmother in a village far from St. Petersburg in the present Penza Oblast. There Lermontov learned to love nature, and later during his exile in the Caucasus Mountains he developed an unusual appreciation for natural beauty.

Even though Lermontov's actual writing career lasted only five years he did write many poems and a novel. Unfortunately he died in a duel at the age of 27 years in 1841.

Today at Pyatigorsk in the Caucasus Mountains there is a statue to Lermontov and a museum, where he lived and worked during his few years of writing. Pyatigorsk means "five mountains," and it was here in this scenic place that he received much of his inspiration to describe the beauty of the Caucasus.

At first Lermontov wrote anonymously to avoid persecution. In his praise for Pushkin he also took a stand against popular opinion and for greater freedom. In a second poem, Clouds, Lermontov talks about the freedom of the clouds, saying that they know no fear and no suffering, that they are cold and free, and that since they have no country they have no exile.

But in another poem, Native Land, Lermontov expresses his love for his country. However, this love is for the beauty of nature, the steppes, the forests, and the rivers, not for the social order and political system.

Lermontov wrote two long poems which represent the strong desire that man has to express himself and to live life fully. One of these is Mtsyri (Novice), which is about a young man who leaves a monastery to return to his native land in the Caucasus. In his adventures Mtsyri climbs the high cliffs, goes through the forest, and experiences dangers, even fighting a wild leopard, but to him this is the life that gives him satisfaction. In the Demon Lermontov depicts the workings of the mind of a rebellious man who is anxious for a fight. The thoughts of this man, however, are not put into action. They represent a protest that cannot be expressed. These two poems, as well as Lermontov's other writings, show a great frustration in the mind of Lermontov in not being able to live a natural life.

Another example of this longing for freedom is his poem, Parus (A Sail), in which he envies a sail because it is free in the wind, it is not seeking or fleeing anything, and it does not have to find an inner peace.

Probably the best known of Lermontov's works is the novel, A Hero of Our Time. Actually this novel is a collection of several stories, but there is one character, Pechorin, who is in every story. The stories take place in the Caucasus Mountains, and they depict the beauty of nature, the rivalries between men,and the lives of the common people in the mountains. It is a love story, an adventure story, and a psychological study of man's behavior. This novel was written simply and directly so that it can be easily understood both as to its description of people and places and as to its meanings of people's total personalities.

A Hero of Our Time is also a valuable historical contribution because of its description of the life and customs in the Russian Army at that time. The accuracy of his accounts are largely based on his own personal experiences and his own acquaintances during his time in the army and the Caucasus Mountains. The story could almost be considered as an autobiography as to its presentation, and part of it is presented as a personal diary. But the real value is the depiction of types of people rather than the historical account of the author's own life.

GOGOL

Nikolai Gogol offered a new contribution to Russian literature. He was not a member of the higher nobility. His father was a land owner in the Ukraine. His life had a close tie to the Russian steppe, and his later years in St. Petersburg gave him little satisfaction. He lived for several years in Rome, but he was drawn back to Russia by his longings for a more meaningful life. Gogol considered himself to be patriotic and religious, but the realities of life frustrated his basic beliefs. In his writings he described people and events in an attempt to give them a philosophical or religious meaning. His realistic descriptions proved to be greater, however, than his explanations, which tended toward fantasy. As a result he wrote satires, which became very popular at the time and which have been recognized as great literature.

Gogol lived from 1809 to 1852. He attended school in Poltava and received higher education in Nezhina. It was not until 1828 that he came to St. Petersburg, where he intended to work in a government position. Later he tried to be a dramatist, but gradually his writings were more successful than his work in the theatre.

His writings about life on the steppe and among the Cossacks reflect his early life. A short story entitled An Evening at a Farm near Dikan'ki was published in a reader in 1831 and started him to consider writing more seriously. This story presents various characters at a Ukrainian farm - a funny devil, a wicked old woman, a simple peasant, and a wandering Gypsy. It is rich in humor, but its greatest value is in the realistic description of the people and their feelings. Gogol's greatest writing concerning the steppes, however, was Taras Bulba, a long narrative about the life of the Cossacks of the 16th century. Taras Bulba is a Cossack leader who experiences peace and battle, joy and sorrow, and a turbulent life and a heroic death. The historical value of this story is probably its best contribution. It has been recognized widely and made into an American film.

The best known of Gogol's writings is probably Revizor (The Inspector General). It has been translated into many languages and has been made into movies. It is a story of the constant checking and double checking in a society to prevent corruption, but it is shown that those who do the inspecting are as corrupt, if not more so, than those whom they are inspecting. The story is a satire, which Gogol directs to all places and times, but it takes place in Russia in the 1800's. All the deceit, false pride, bribery, theft, and other social evils that can be found in a small town are exaggerated to the ridiculous. The whole town prepares for the coming of the inspector, but instead an imposter comes and makes a fool of everyone, even himself. Gogol tries to tie in his view of right and wrong by ending the story with the understanding that all the characters will now meet the real inspector. However, the value of the story has already been presented in the exposure of the shortcomings and vices of the people.

Dead Souls was to be Gogol's masterpiece in presenting the great evils of man with a follow-up for leading mankind out of the hell he is in. He completed the first parts in depicting various evil persons, but he tore up or burned his succeeding drafts and never completed the whole task. But the first parts are satires on the most repulsive persons, whom Gogol keeps referring to as a dog, a swine, or other animal.

The main character of Dead Souls is a schemer who buys dead bodies. His advantage is to be able to list his ownings of serfs for prestige purposes. The advantage to the seller is to avoid the tax on persons on his estate. The situation is caused by the long delay in record keeping by the bureaucracy so that people are listed as living usually for a long time after they have died. The whole plot depicts the horrors of serfdom and the inhuman values that are taken on by selfish and profit-seeking persons.

A less morbid and lighter comedy by Gogol is <u>Shinel'</u> (<u>The Overcoat</u>). This story is about one man, who is a poor government official trying to improve his position or at least his reputation. The man works very hard and saves his money to be able to buy an overcoat. Finally, after a long time, he buys the coat. Now he can put the coat on over his ragged clothes and walk down the street as a gentleman. He has reached a point of respectability. But on the first night the coat is stolen, and he is back where he started. The story points out the futility facing the poorer people, even those who were working for the government. One plot of the story ends at this point, but Gogol tries to justify the class differences by continuing the story beyond the death of the poor worker. His ghost then returns to steal the coat from the man whom he envied all of his life. In a way this second plot was to reaffirm Gogol's concept of justice.

TURGENEV

Ivan Turgenev was a naturalist, a philosophy professor, and a writer. He was born and raised in the present-day Orlovskaya Oblast, which is about halfway between Moscow and Khar'kov. His father was a wealthy land owner, and the landed estate of the Turgenev family was a refuge for Ivan even later during his adult life. He was educated in Moscow, St. Petersburg, and Berlin. Much of his life was spent in Berlin and Paris, but he returned often to Russia and to the farm lands near Orel. He loved to hunt and spent many days out with nature. Probably his greatest work was his notes, which he kept while on these hunting trips. He published them first as articles in a magazine and later in book form.

Turgenev lived from 1818 to 1883. He was more of a storyteller than a novelist. He described scenes of nature and people as he saw them rather than trying to criticize them or to reform society. But his descriptions do illustrate many of the problems and weaknesses of the society. The result of censorship and his being exiled from St. Petersburg did effect his writings though, and in his later works he did portray evils of the class structure and advocated the abolition of serfdom.

His <u>Notes of a Hunter</u> (<u>Zapiski Okhotnika</u>) received wide acclaim both in Russia and in Western Europe. This book has been translated into many languages and is greatly appreciated for the beautiful descriptions of nature. It is also revealing of the personalities of people, both serfs and noblemen, who lived in Central Russia. <u>Notes of a Hunter</u> is not just one story. Actually it is a collection of stories with a wide panorama of scenery, people, and events. The careful use of adjectives in describing everything and everyone presents colorful pitures in the minds of those who read this work.

Turgenev could have been writing about himself in his short novel, Rudin. Rudin was an idealist, who never achieved any of his ideals. Rudin studied first in Moscow and then in Germany, as did Turgenev, but his education did not motivate him to positive action. Rudin could enthuse others, but they too could not realize their dreams. Even in love Rudin failed. His girl friend, Natal'ya, loved him, and he loved her, but her mother said that she would rather see her dead than married to Rudin. They respected the mother and were never married. So it was with many of the other people in the story. They had high hopes, but these hopes could not fit into the reality of Russia in the 1830's and 1840's.

Ottsy i Deti (Fathers and Sons) was one of Turgenev's later works, in which he did philosophize on the political and social problems of the reign of Nicholas I. However, this book was not published until 1862, which was during the reign of Alexander II and after the abolition of serfdom.

Fathers and Sons might be called a study of the generation gap. Actually Bazarov, the father, was a progressive thinking man, a democrat and an intellectual. He was an ordinary, hard-working man. He was self-educated and believed that others could do as he had done. But the youth did not follow in his foot steps. His chief antagonist was Pavel Petrovich Kirsanov, who was an aristocrat, the cream of the nobility. Pavel was lazy and irresponsible. He preferred the English culture over the Russian. He wore cologne and had nothing to do with the common people. Turgenev referred to Pavel as a Nihilist. Another type of youth, Pavel's brother Nikolai, was a dreamer and a sentimentalist. Nikolai liked poetry, music, and the beauty of nature. But he did fill the role of a land owner and did behave as a baron. He recognized the contributions of others, but he did not contribute much himself. Another brother, Arkadii, tried to follow the pattern of Bazarov, but he had no strength of his own. He was a follower rather than a leader. Arkadii only became a hard-worker after his marriage to Katya, who inspired him and encouraged him to become a progressive and responsible person.

The relationship between Bazarov and the youth presents a problem, which appears in every generation. Fathers and Sons has been acclaimed for its universal truths. It has been translated into many languages and has been produced in plays and films.

Turgenev also wrote a sentimental story about Gerasim, a deaf and dumb serf. The story, Mumu, is both a heart-warming and a heart-rending account of a kind man who had been displaced from his farm environment to the city home of a noble woman. Gerasim was exceptionally strong. He worked hard for the baroness, but he was lonely. The one serf girl who befriended him was married off to a scoundrel by the command of the baroness. Gerasim found a stray dog for a pet and for his only friend. This happiness was also destroyed by the baroness, who disliked the dog barking. Gerasim does many good things for the baroness and for others, but he receives very little for himself. Finally, in complete dissatisfaction he leaves everything in the city and returns to his country home.

DOSTOYEVSKY

Feodor Dostoyevsky was almost a fanatic on religious mysticism and psychological intrigue. His writings differ from those of other Russian writers, and he has not been recognized as a really great writer by Soviet standards. However, he has been acclaimed in Western countries for his insight into the workings of man's mind. He was obsessed with the role of evil in life, and he questioned its relationship to religion.

Dostoyevsky was born in 1821 in Moscow. As a young man he was arrested for his membership in a secret discussion group, sentenced to death, and after a commutation served for several years in a Siberian prison camp. Most of his works were written in St. Petersburg, after he returned from the prison camp, until his death in 1881.

His best known work is probably Crime and Punishment, in which he explores reasons for people's behavior. The main character, Rodion Raskolnikov, a former university student, observes and experiences all kinds of social evils, which cause him anxiety, depression, and confusion. In his quest for his identity and for the meaning to his life Raskolnikov perceives the personification of evil in a landlord, Svidrigailov, who seeks self-satisfaction, and the personification of good in a girl, Sonya, forced by poverty into prostitution to provide for her family. Raskolnikov, however, sees both good and evil in his own life. He wants to consider himself good, but he is lead by evil forces to act in ways that he cannot understand or explain.

As a student, Raskolnikov lived in a small, closet-like room in a boarding house. He did not have enough money for rent and was

forced to pawn his silver watch, but he becomes very disturbed that
he had to do this. While pondering his conditions, he stops for a beer
at a basement tavern. At the tavern he meets a former government
official, Marmaledov, who had been dismissed from work for drunkenness. This man relates the sad story of his decline and of the poverty in his family. He tells of his daughter, Sonya, who became a
prostitute as the only available means for supporting the family.
When Raskolnikov responds to this man's request for help to get home,
he sees the squalor, where the family lives, and the ridicule of the
man by his wife. The situation depresses Raskolnikov, but he is
tempted to see Sonya, whom he respects for her helping the family in
this predicament.

The next day Raskolnikov receives a long-awaited letter from
his mother, who tells him the problems of his family at home. His
sister, Dunya, had been working as a governess for the Svidrigailov
family. The father in that family kept propositioning Dunya, whom
his wife blamed for her husband's actions. The wife spread rumors
and almost destroyed the Raskolnikov family, but when she learned
the truth she tried to compensate for her actions by finding a husband
for Dunya. Dunya, then, prepared to marry this man and bring
status to the family.

Rodion Raskolnikov became even more disturbed about the
problems in his own family and walked the streets of St. Petersburg.
He sees a teen-age girl, who is drunk, being pursued by a middle-
age man, but he is unsuccessful in warning the girl or in dissuading
the man. This incident further dejects Raskolnikov. He then goes
to eat something and to drink a glass of vodka. Before going home
he takes a nap on a lawn and has a bad dream about some men beat-
ing a horse to death. As he walks from there home he passes some
shops and overhears some people talking to Lizaveta Ivanovna, the
retarded sister of the lady to whom he pawned his watch, and recalled a story students had told him about the old woman who had lots of
money and mistreated her retarded sister. His recollections
included their talk of murdering her for her money. Raskolnikov
goes home and sleeps with all these thoughts on his mind.

He is awakened late the next day, and half in a stupor he
plans to kill the old woman, whom he considers to be evil, and to
take her money. The night before he had overheard that her sister
would be gone, so he plots a time to do this act while the old woman
is alone. With a kitchen ax, which he borrowed on the way, he proceeds to the pawnbroker's home and kills her. While looking for the
money, he hears the retarded sister come in, and he is compelled
to kill her too. But he is able to find no more than a gold watch and

a few other items. Noises scare him away, and he returns unnoticed to his room, after cleaning the ax and putting it in its proper place.

These events are the first part of the story of Crime and Punishment. The rest of the story is based on Raskolnikov's reactions to his behavior and to his relations with his family, Sonya, and Svidrigailov.

After the murder Rodion Raskolnikov becomes ill and delirious. He cannot understand himself why he killed the pawnbroker. His delirium turns into an obsession after he recovers from the illness. Admitting to himself that he had not killed her to get money to meet his expenses or to help his family, he accepts that he killed to show his own power that he was more than an ordinary man. He had wanted to prove to himself that he could determine the course of events rather than being subject to events. But after the murder he realizes that he has not attained this. Contrarily, he finds that he is subjected to his past behavior. He hates himself and feels estranged from his own family. Raskolnikov cannot approach his mother or sister because of his own guilt and because of the feeling that he might contaminate them. But he could not live alone. He needs someone and goes to Sonya to confess his crime.

During his confusion and ramblings of mind he tries to sort out his values. He takes Sonya to Siberia in a self-imposed exile, and there he finds love for her and directs his hatred toward Svidrigailov. His love for Sonya causes him to identify her with his love for God and the principles of Christian faith - meekness, unselfishness, and self-denial to serve others. Svidrigailov, on the other hand, represents all the evils in society - self-gratification, indulgence in lust, lack of feelings and concern for others, rejection of responsibility, and reliance on reason. Raskolnikov experiences a nightmare, in which he sees the world infested with microbes which make men mad and convince them that their own thoughts are life's truth. In this nightmare he sees the future portrayed as a time the world is governed by reason, rather than emotions, and is being destroyed by greed, lust, and murder.

But Raskolnikov believed that he has found his own redemption through his confession of the murder and by his love for Sonya.

Dostoyevsky had previously written a novel, which is more typical of the other Russian authors of that time and of English and American novelists. This book was, Poor Folk, which portrays the simple love of a poor man and his loss of his sweetheart to a wealthy landowner. Makar and Varvara are brought together by letters. Both of them are poor, but he sacrifices what he has to help her. But Varvara realizes that he does not have the ability to provide for her and decides to marry for security rather than love. Even yet Makar tries to help her prepare for this marriage.

But a better love story is Dostoyevsky's novel, The Idiot, which personifies love and goodness in the main character, Prince Myshkin. The prince is really not an idiot in the ordinary sense, but he does not understand reality and keeps asking why things are as they are. He is the epitome of everything good, kind, and sincere. Myshkin accepts only the good in people and does not even pretend to understand evil or where it comes from.

Prince Myshkin is loved by women for his kindness and devotion to them. And he prefers Nastasia, because she needs him. She also loves him, but they know that marriage is out of the question due to his infirmity. Nastasia then is forced to marry another man, who is a hard-working miller, but this man is mean and evil. Myshkin accepts the marriage because he thinks that Nastasia will be happy, but when she complains about her unhappy married life, Myshkin consoles her. The miller does not like his wife confiding with Myshkin, but he cannot blame an idiot. Instead he blames his wife and beats her. In a fit of anger the miller kills his wife. All that Prince Myshkin can do is ask why. He cannot condemn the miller, but he weeps as a result of the tragedy.

The Possessed, on the other hand, is a diatribe of hatred toward atheism, liberalism, and socialism. His main characters, Verkhovensky and Stavroghin, are possessed by demons. They rely on force and deceit to achieve their goals, but Stavroghin cannot take such a life and commits suicide. The good of man is represented only by minor characters in the story.

Dostoyevsky's The Brothers Karamazov was his last novel and was a culmination of his preceding work. It presents a panorama of many types of characters, but carried through the story are the questions of crime, punishment, religion, and politics. It represents the span of Dostoyevsky's thinking during his life.

TOLSTOY

Leo Tolstoy was the greatest author of the Golden Age of Russian Literature, and his work, War and Peace, is acclaimed around the world as one of the best works of literature of all time. Tolstoy was a prolific writer, and the writings represent the change of beliefs that he had during his life. He wrote with a wide breadth of understanding people and events, and it was not until near his death that he became disillusioned.

105

Tolstoy lived from 1828 until 1910. He was born at Yasnaya Polyana, which is south of Moscow near Tula. It was here that he lived and worked, and today Yasnaya Polyana is a cultural center, dedicated to the memory of Leo Tolstoy. Tolstoy's parents were wealthy land owners. His father was a count and his mother a countess. They both died while he was young, and he inherited an estate with over 300 serfs. But he was not satisfied with the life as land owner and enlisted in the Russian Army to serve in the Caucasus Mountains. He was following the pattern of his father, who had served as an officer in the war against Napoleon. Tolstoy also had battle experience, first against the mountain tribes in the Caucasus and later at Sevastopol during the Crimean War. He was wounded in the Caucasus and nearly died. During his recovery he began to write, and after the Crimean War he came to St. Petersburg where he continued to write about his early life and his experiences in the army. Tolstoy then went abroad to France, Switzerland, Italy, and Germany, but he returned to Yasnaya Polyana, where he opened a school and taught peasant children. While teaching he studied various methods of education and established a system of freely conducted discussions, which emphasized individual instruction. From this experience he published an educational journal called "Yasnaya Polyana". Opposition to his teaching methods brought about the destruction of his school by government gendarmes, and Tolstoy became embittered.

His marriage to Sophia Andreevna Bers brought a new inspiration into his life, and he worked arduously for almost six years in writing War and Peace. He taught again for a few years and then returned to writing.

War and Peace is not just one story but many stories which intertwine during the events of the Napoleonic Wars. From a historical view point it reveals the attitudes, the customs, and the actions of the people during the war and afterwards. It asks questions concerning loyalty both to country and to one's loved ones. It probes the meaning of hostilities and the morality of the Russian social system.

The main character is Pierre, half French and half Russian, who is the illegitimate son of a wealthy nobleman. Pierre is accepted into society because of his claim to nobility, but he is rejected because of his illegitimacy and his reserved and awkward behavior. He stands between controversial issues and has a perspective that is closed to those on one side or the other.

Pierre does not fight in the war. He hesitates to know which side he should support. He views the battles, the misery, the destitution. His friends go to war. Some are killed. Others are injured. To him the war seems ridiculous, wasteful, and destructive. Patriotism seems much less important than the happiness and good welfare of the people. He hates the atrocities, but he cannot bring himself to kill those who are said to be responsible for them. Instead he tries to help the unfortunate, wounded, and the deprived.

Love also leaves Pierre confused. Upon the death of his father he inherits a lot of money. A beautiful girl, the belle of the ball, becomes his wife. He has admired her for a long time, but she all at once takes a liking to him. But there is no real romance. She is soon unfaithful to him, and he is left in a quandry. Pierre is forced into a duel, and only by accident does he seriously wound his rival and win the duel. He then feels sorry for him and blames his wife more than he does the man.

Later on he admires a younger girl, Natasha, and they become good friends. He is concerned for her future and tries to help her, but she too becomes the victim of a promiscuous lover, in this case the brother of Pierre's former wife. Pierre does not blame the girl, but he tries to help her. Only long after time does a love develop between them and they become happily married.

War and Peace is great for its emphasis on human values and the patient tolerance Pierre has toward antagonists. And Pierre's part is only the intertwining thread through a wide panorama of people, events, and time. The book is a series of episodes, each a story in its own right.

One of these episodes is the departure of Andrei to the war and his leaving behind of his beautiful and lovely wife, who is expecting a baby. The love of Lisa for her husband is tender and devoted, but Andrei disregards her and thinks only of his honor as a military officer, which has been instilled in him all during his youth by his father, a respected army officer. Andrei advises Pierre not to marry until he is old and stresses that women are weak and stand in the way of what a man should do. He advises Pierre to enjoy life while he is young but that he should not mix in with the wild crowd at Kuragin's. Pierre respected Andrei, but he lacked his own self respect. When Andrei wanted to talk more about Pierre's future, Pierre responded that he had no future, he had no fortune, and he had no status, because he was illegitimate. But Andrei demanded a promise from him that Pierre would not go to the Kuragin's. But after Pierre departed from his friend, his weakness overcame him and he went to the Kuragin party. This party was a drunken brawl. A detailed description is given of men taking wagers to see who could stand in an open window high above the ground and drink a

whole bottle of rum without falling out the window. With great gusto
one of the men successfully accomplishes this feat. Having drank too
much, Pierre also wanted to try, but he was easily restrained by his
friend, Anatoly Kuragin.

This episode fully establishes the personalities of Lisa,
Andrei, Pierre, and Anotoly, four of the main characters of the
novel. It also depicts their basic concerns, their characters, and
their regard for others, not only for the sense of the following
episodes but also as people anywhere or any time facing a threat of
war.

Another episode concerns the introduction of Natasha, the
future wife of Pierre, when she was a teenager, and her cousin,
Boris. The scene depicts the young love, first kisses, and romantic
foolishness of young teenagers. A more serious aspect of the same
scene is the romance between Nikolai and Sonya, who were a few
years older than Natasha and Boris. This short episode is a refresh-
ing interlude in the pomp and ceremony of the aristocratic soirees
and their contrived arrangements to marry for economic or political
reasons. This interlude also is oblivious to the war and political
controversies.

There are too many such episodes in War and Peace to sum-
marize here, but to mention a few there are the duel of Pierre with
the lover of his first wife, the visit that Pierre takes to the battle on
the outskirts of Moscow, the view that Pierre has from a secret
hiding place as French troops march into Moscow, the visit of Pierre
to Andrei's father's home in the country, and finally Pierre's discussion with Nikolai after the war is over.

In this last episode Pierre philosophizes about the war and
about peace. He states that if evil men can conspire to carry out
evil purposes, then good men can also work together for good purposes. Pierre also states that there should not be a secret society
and that the people should join hand in hand with the one purpose of
general welfare and general security. But Nikolai, who was an officer in the war, squirms in his chair, and Natasha, Pierre's wife,
demonstrates love for her husband without revealing her thoughts
about his over-simplicity and lack of understanding. But they all
listen to Pierre with respect and love.

Tolstoy leaves the reader to decide who is right concerning
the issues of war and peace, but it is evident that Pierre's words
are the thoughts of Tolstoy. Not only is this book enjoyable historical fiction, but it carries messages of strong political and religious
convictions of its author, Leo Tolstoy.

Anna Karenina also stands out as exceptionally good literature. Tolstoy again probes the question of love. Anna Karenina is a beautiful woman who is married to a successful landowner. Her husband devotes his life to his work, and Anna feels neglected. She tries to gain more of his attention, but she becomes lonely and dissatisfied. Her desire for love is accepted by another man, and she thinks that she has found happiness. The question arises in her mind as to the meaning of happiness, love and morality. But her husband is hurt by her immoral behavior both as to his self pride and as to the damage to his professional reputation. Anna then loses her self respect. She want to rebuild the love with her husband, but she is rejected. Her answer then is to take her own life, and she throws herself in front of a train. Her husband then feels absolved of the sin. The reader is left to judge their guilt.

Tolstoy wrote many short stories, but there is one more novel which should be specially noted. That novel is Resurrection, which is another study on immorality and illegitimacy. But the emphasis is on the new life that the girl builds after having been immoral. She has a difficult time in overcoming her past. However, the man is able to recant and regain a good position, i.e. to be resurrected. This novel indicates a change in Tolstoy's thinking, and he tries to give more religious and political answers than he tries to seek truth and justice. This was his last major work.

Tolstoy can be accepted by all groups for his broad tolerance and also because of his changes of views during his life. Even his disillusionment from his former ideals is recognized by many as his final realization of the truth. He lived longer than the other authors of the Golden Age, and his writings will also probably outlive all theirs.

CHEKHOV

Anton Chekhov was the last great Russian author who lived and died before the 1917 Communist Revolution. He was born in 1860 and died in 1904. He is best known for his short, humorous stories.

Chekhov's early home was at Taganrog near the Sea of Azov. His father was a merchant, and young Chekhov worked with his father in the store. Due to this hard work as a lad Chekhov has said "In my childhood I had no childhood." He continued to work part time at the store while attending school, and for three years he remained alone in Taganrog to finish school after his family moved to Moscow. When he came to Moscow he entered the University of Moscow and studied to be a medical doctor. For several years he wrote short stories to support himself while he was in school and for a time after he started practicing medicine. He treated poor people and received little or no pay, and he continued to write. In 1886 he published his first book, Pyostriye Rasskazy (Assorted Stories).

In addition to the many short stories he wrote, he also wrote plays and even a book about the Island Sakhalin, after a trip he made across Siberia to Sakhalin.

Poprygun'ya (The Grasshopper) is one of Chekhov's novels, which is liked both in the Soviet Union and abroad. It is a story which relates closely to Chekhov's life, in that it is a story of the wife of a medical doctor. It reflects Chekhov's adversion to pomp and ceremony. The doctor's wife in the story is the grasshopper, because she is continually jumping from one thing to another. She is not impressed with the work of her husband and does not try to understand it. Instead she takes interest in music, painting, and other arts. She invites musicians or painters to her house to honor them for their achievements and to help her with her current fad. She respects them, entertains them, and feeds them. Her husband is considerate for her interests in arts and for her friends, but he continues to work on his medical profession. As she changes from one interest to another, she meets new and interesting people. One painter becomes particularly interested in her and invites her to go with him to paint landscapes. This trip evolves into a love affair, but she still longs for her husband. Her lover learns to dislike her as a person, and they return home. Even though the doctor finds out about the romance, he tolerates his wife and wants her to be happy. He is never angry and always good to her, but she does not realize his devotion to her or his success in his work even when he calls it to her attention. Only when he is on his death bed for having contracted a serious disease during his work at the hospital does she notice the respect that others are giving to her husband. She hears that he is a great man, and she is astonished. But it is too late. The doctor dies, and she goes on jumping.

The Cherry Orchard is a play by Chekhov, and it was first produced on the stage of the Moscow Art Theatre in 1904, the year he died. It is a comedy with three themes. The first theme is the downfall of a nobleman's estate due to the decline in the economy and the attitudes of the nobility. The second theme is the victory of the Lopakhin family over the Gayev and Ranevsky families in a business deal. The third theme was a view into the future of Russia. All three themes are satires on the people and their do-nothing attitudes.

Chekhov criticizes the pretense, the pomp, and the ceremony and points to the youth as the hope for tomorrow. The heroes are a young, hard-working student, Petya Trofimov, and Anya Ranevskaya, a seventeen year old girl.

Chekhov made a character study in his novel, Three Sisters. It points out the different characters of the three sisters and explores the meaning of their attitudes. In this exploration the concepts of beauty and love, goodness and love, and loneliness and love are discussed. It is also a comedy and a satire.

One could go on and on mentioning the stories of Chekhov. They are very numerous. But the main theme is a comedy for amusement primarily, but each of them also has an underlying satirical meaning aimed at persons, institutions or customs.

Bocharov, G. K. , Rodnaya Literatura, Moscow, Uchebnoye
Pedogogicheskoye Izdatel'stvo, 1961, 352 pp.
Bocharov, G. K. & Belen'kiy, G. I. , Rodnaya Literatura, Moscow:
Izdatel'stvo "Prosveshcheniye", 1964, 352 pp.
Davies, Ruth, The Great Books of Russia, Norman, Oklahoma:
University of Oklahoma Press, 1968, 397 pp.
Dostoyevsky, Feodor M. , Izbrannye Sochineniya, Moscow:
Gosudarstvennoye Izdatel'stvo Khudozhestvennoy Literatury,
1946, 483 pp.
Florinskiy, S. M. , Russkaya Literatura, Moscow, Uchebnoye
Pedogogicheskoye Izdatel'stvo, 1964, 296 pp.
Golubkov, V. V. et als. , Rodnaya Literatura, Moscow: Izdatel'stvo
"Prosveshcheniye", 1965, 254 pp.
Mal'tseva, K. V. & Zhdanov, N. S. , Literaturnoye Chteniye na
Russkom Yazyke, Moscow: Gosudarstvennoye Uchebnoye
Pedigogicheskoye Izdatel'stvo, 1958, 288 pp.
Shevchenko, P. A. & Florinskiy, S. M. , Rodnaya Literatura,
Moscow, Gosudarstvennoye Uchebnoye Pedigogicheskoye
Izdatel'stvo, 1961, 430 pp.
Slonim, Marc, An Outline of Russian Literature, New York: The
New American Library, 1958, 176 pp.
Tolstoy, Lev, Voina i Mir, Moscow: Gosudarstvennoye Izdatel'stvo
Khudozhestvennoy Literatury, 1960, volume 1, 2, 3, & 4,
1238 pp.
Turkevich, Ludmilla B. , Masterpieces of Russian Literature,
Princeton, New Jersey: D. Van Nostrand Co. , Inc. , 1964,
791 pp.
Vasys, Anthony et als. , Russian Area Reader, New York: Pitman
Publishing Corp. , 1962, 484 pp.
Zerchaninov, A. A. & Raykhin, D. Ya. , Ruskaya Literatura,
Moscow, Uchebnoye Pedigicheskoye Izdatel'stvo, 1964,
344 pp.

CHAPTER IV

COMMUNISM

Communism means so many different things to different
people. Some people believe that it is the culmination of all evil, and
others believe that it is the only hope for the future. However, no
matter what one's attitude is toward communism, he should try to
understand it as it really is.

Materialism

First of all, communism is a philosophy based on materialism. That means that communists believe that all reality consists
of material things. In other words, matter is the basis of all existence. This concept denies the existence of anything which cannot be
perceived by man and cannot be subjected to scientific analysis.

Materialism has historically been opposed to idealism, which
considers the basis of all existence to be ideas. The extreme idealists believe that matter is only a manifestation of ideas and that matter by itself does not exist. Communists strongly oppose idealism,
because they believe that ideas can only be derived from man's perception of material things. To communists idealism is only a
fantasy.

Religious concepts are also rejected by the communist definition of materialism. They believe that there is no Supreme Being
or God. They also deny the existence of spirits, a life beyond death,
and communication between man and a Creator. To them these
beliefs are only superstitions, which have persisted due to the ignorance and fear of man.

This conflict between the supremacy of matter or ideas is by
no means new with communist philosophers. Nor is it strictly a
religious controversy. Many people throughout history and even
today among non-communists disagree concerning the relationship
between ideas and matter. Plato and Hegel were idealists. Religious people tend more to accept idealism, at least partially, and
non-religious people tend more to accept materialism, at least
partially. However, many non-communists today refer to themselves as realists and accept both material things and ideas as parts
of reality. Even the communists call themselves realists, but they
continue to contend that matter is the only reality and that ideas are

only abstractions from material things. They say that matter is objective, i. e. it exists outside of man's mind. And they add that ideas are subjective, i. e. they exist only in man's mind.

Materialism in this sense does not mean to be materialistic. It is not related to money or finances. To be materialistic, mercenary or selfish is opposed stronger in the Soviet Union than it is in the United States.

Materialism in the eyes of a communist is a liberating concept. This belief frees him from superstitions, prejudices, and artificial restrictions. To him it means that he is free to become the master of his destiny. By learning the laws of science and society and using them for the benefit of man, he believes that he can build a better society and make life happier for everyone.

Dialectics

Dialectics is a process of interaction between opposites. It is the process of a debate or of judicial proceedings. When any ideas or forces clash against each other, this action is called dialectics.

The concept of dialectics was used by Plato in his book, The Republic. He used dialectics or discussion as the means for defining justice. One person stated his definition, and another stated an opposing definition. They continued to discuss and to refine their own definitions. Finally they resolved a definition, different from either the first or the second, which they could both accept. They both recognized that this new definition was nearer the truth.

Plato called the first definition or view the thesis. We might call it a statement or a proposal. The second or opposite definition or view is called the anti-thesis or antithesis. The product of the discussion or the new definition is called the synthesis.

The process of dialectics does not stop with the snythesis though. The synthesis becomes the new thesis, which is met by another opposing idea or force. The new thesis and the new anti-thesis then continue the interaction of resolving their differences and form yet another newer and better synthesis. And this process of dialectics goes on and on.

The German philosopher, Hegel, applied dialectics to his idealist philosophy. He believed that opposing ideas and their evolution to new ideas determine the course of history.

Karl Marx studied Hegel's works, but he could not accept idealism. He turned the philosophy upside down by replacing materialism for idealism, but he did accept the concept of dialectics. Marx called his contribution dialectical materialism.

114

Dialectical Materialism

Marx recognized matter rather than ideas as the substance of reality. He did not believe as Hegel that ideas determine the course of history. He contended that the opposition between material things and the forces of matter determine the course of history.

Dialectical materialism is the concept that matter is the substance of all reality and that dialectics is the process which brings about the changes in matter. This concept recognizes that all matter is in motion and that motion is caused by the opposing forces in matter. Dialectics is the name given to the process or the interaction between those opposing forces. Dialectics is the moving force. It puts life into matter.

The combination of the substance (materialism) with the process (dialectics) provides the communist explanation of reality. They say that all reality is moving matter. It is matter in motion, and the motion is caused by dialectics. This concept is substantiated by the evidence of opposites in everything. They exist everywhere, and these opposites continue to interact against each other. Some of these opposites are hot and cold, light and dark, wet and dry, positive and negative, male and female, and right and wrong. Everything has its opposite.

Dialectical materialism explains that these opposites by their struggling against each other keep all matter in motion. They are the motive power of all existence. This concept denies the existence of any outside force, which creates or which governs either the matter or the motion. It denies the existence of God and the influence of God on the lives of men.

Dialectical materialism then is the governing force of nature and of society. It is the cause of all action in both physical and social affairs. Dialectical materialism governs the relationships between men. It is the belief that opposing material forces and their evolution into new material forces determine the course of history.

The Class Struggle

Applied to society and the relationships between people dialectical materialism becomes a struggle between classes of men. In social and political relationships throughout history the fighting and warring among peoples are attributed to the struggle between classes of people - those who rule and those who are ruled, those who have material things and those who have not. It is this continued struggle between classes that causes the progress in society. The rulers or property owners have fought to maintain their status, and those have-nots have fought to gain power and wealth for themselves.

History substantiates changes in social orders, and communists attribute each change to dialectical materialism, i.e. the class struggle. The patriarchial order of early civilizations was a society in which the father or clan leader ruled the whole tribe. The children and grandchildren were subject to him. The patriarch was one class, and the rest of the tribe was an opposing class, which struggled for more rights and for property. Sons sought leadership and took the power from their father or elder brother so that they could have a share in the land, property, and rights. This struggle gradually evolved into a new society, in which several persons, sons or older grandsons, became princes over their own principalities. The government became a group of princes who shared power with a grand prince. This new society was the synthesis, which was the product of the class struggle.

This synthesis became a new thesis. The princes and the grand prince were members of one class (the thesis), and the rest of the population made up the other class (the antithesis). As the leadership role was divided, the other members of the clan obtained a lower position in the society either as serfs or as slaves. This institution was called serfdom. The serfs then began to fight for the power and wealth of the lords. But the princes and lords enriched themselves at the expense of the serfs. The increased wealth brought about crafts and merchants. Industry and commerce were introduced into the society. Serfdom was a higher type of society than the former patriarchial order. But as the society changed, the serfs became stronger in their struggle against the princes and lords. Some serfs were able to gain wealth and power. They became craftsmen and merchants. A new distribution of wealth was taking place, and a new type of society was being formed. The princes and lords lost their positions as rulers of the society. In their place came the industrialists and financeers. A new society was a synthesis of the struggle between lords and serfs. The new society was capitalism.

Capitalism then becomes the new thesis and is challenged by its antithesis, the working class. The working man was hired by the capitalists and was subject to them for his livelihood. But the working men organize into unions in order to increase their strength in opposing the industrialists and financeers. As the working man continues his opposition to the capitalists he causes a redistribution of the wealth. But the new distribution of wealth takes place only by taking it from the capitalists, because they will not give it up without a struggle. At this level of society the class struggle evolves into a revolution for bringing about a new order. The revolution forces the capitalists to share their wealth and power with the working man. The dialectical process then forms a socialist society.

The class struggle begins at this stage of history to take on a new form. The class struggle was for a new distribution of the power and wealth. Each change in society was a quantitative change in which the amount or quantity of power and wealth is distributed more equally among the members of the lower class. With the establishment of socialism the total quantity of wealth and power becomes the property of all people and there is only one class. The class struggle has been fulfilled, but the dialectical process continues in a different form. It changes from a quantitative struggle between opposites and becomes a qualitative struggle for a better and enriched society. In this way socialism leads on to communism, the highest level of social development, when there is an equal distribution of great wealth and power among all peoples of the society.

The whole evolution of society is based on the substance of reality (matter or material property) and on the process (dialectics or the class struggle). It is material forces in motion. It is the course of history according to communism.

Determinism

The concepts of matter and motion are basic parts of communist philosophy, but they are incomplete in explaining the course of history. The examples concerning the class struggle imply a direction of the course of history. This direction is not determined merely by motion, and the question is left as to what determines that direction. Since communists reject any outside force, it follows that the force for the direction is inherent in the moving matter. It lies in the nature of matter and its relationship to other matter. It is a cause and effect relationship between different kinds of matter.

In social relationships some types of matter have properties which are valuable to man. They have an economic worth. It is this economic worth of matter that determines man's relationship to that type of matter. The class struggle is over the matter or the power derived from that matter which has an economic worth to man. That is why the communists say that economics or ownership of the means of production determines the direction of history. So when communists say determinism they mean economic determinism.

117

Economic determinism must be distinguished from other types of determinism in order to understand it fully. It is not a concept of fatalism or predestination. Communist reject a set course of history which was predetermined by some outside force. That is one of the quarrels that they have with some religions. Determinism to communists is the relationship between men and property. The men not the property are the key to the direction of history. In past societies some men have used property to control other men, but in the communist society men are to use property not to control others but for the common good. Man then becomes the captain of his future. Man is in the driver's seat, but he cannot drive until he gains command of physical properties and the laws which regulate them. That is why communism emphasizes science, so that man can learn to take command of all nature. For man's relationship to nature is the determinant of his course in history, and progress comes as man gains greater control over the elements of the earth.

The Communist Party

Man is a collective being according to communist philosophy. He does not exist alone. He cannot control nature by himself. It is necessary for people to work together to accomplish the common good. They must determine the direction of their activity and be constantly aware of the direction they are going. This understanding means organization and cooperation. And organization and cooperation imply leadership.

The leadership of the communist movement and the vanguard of the working class in a society moving toward communism is the political organization. It is the Communist Party.

The Communist Party consists of those persons who have learned dialectical materialism, who know the direction of the course of history, and who have proved their ability to lead and direct the people. They become members of the Communist Party because of their dedication to the principles and because of their training through practical experience to assume the role of leadership in the society.

The Communist Party then is not initially a political party consisting of the large masses of people. It is a select group for guiding the people. The power of the working people is vested in the party to carry out the responsibility of political leadership.

In the class struggle the role of the Communist Party is particularly acute. The struggle is a revolutionary war against the old society for building a new society. Unified leadership is necessary, and the leadership must have strict discipline over the people in order to be effective against the powerful opposition. The Communist Party must be more powerful than its opposition in order to lead the working people to victory. Therefore the Communist Party must be a leadership group that has total power with the support of the people.

It is this relationship between the Communist Party and the people that is called the Dictatorship of the Proletariat. The proletariat is the working people, and they vest their power, their total power, in the hands of the Communist Party to carry forth the program. This power is dictatorial power since it is total power. However, it is dictatorial in relationship to the opposing forces, but within the communist society it is democratic. The leaders of the Communist Party are selected and supported by the working people. The will of the people is given to the Communist Party through conferences and elections, and the Communist Party carries out this will with dictatorial force against the opposition.

Dictatorship of the Proletariat is necessary in a young communist movement in order to guarantee the protection of the people from the opposition both within the country and outside. As the communist power is established the dictatorial power is replaced with a more democratic structure.

The Dictatorship of the Proletariat in the Soviet Union was replaced by the All-Peoples Government in 1962 as the Soviet Union approached closer to communism. The All-Peoples Government does not do away with the Communist Party. Rather it is expanded to include more people into leadership positions. It broadens the base of power. As the communist society is fully formed, the Communist Party will evolve into an All-Peoples Party.

Democratic Centralism

According to communist philosophy the Dictatorship of the Proletariat is based on the concept of Democratic Centralism. This relationship exists between the Communist Party and the society. It is the relationship within the society which is protected outwardly by the Dictatorship of the Proletariat.

Democratic Centralism is a two-way street between the people and the government. It is democratic in the sense that all the people participate in forming the policy and in selecting leaders. Each leader is an elected representative, who is responsible to the electorate. The centralism concept is the unification of the people's will in the central government and the carrying out that will with complete authority. It prevents a few people from violating the will of all the people. As the policy-making goes one way on the street, the enforcement of policy goes the other way. Democratic Centralism according to communist philosophy is the only true concept of democracy.

The ingredients of the democratic concept include full participation of the citizens of the society. The citizens not only vote and run for office in the society, but they also take on responsible positions and assignments. The organization of the society includes organized groups (collectives) on every level of the society and in every school, enterprise, factory, and farm. All people belong to their local collective and participate in the activities for building and strengthening the society.

In the first grade in school the students are taken in a group to clean the snow from the school yard. They work together with shovels, brooms, and wagons to clean the snow off the yard. When the group is through with the work, the teachers tell them that they are a "collective". She explains that the work would take one grown man all day but that the children completed the whole task in an hour. She points out that a collective activity is more productive, more fun, and better all around than individual activity.

This concept of the "collective" permeates the whole communist society. The full participation in physical, mental, social, and cultural activities promotes the welfare of the whole group and each individual in that group. This method is also true with economic and political activity according to communist philosophy.

The total effort is called by some people a totalitarian democracy. It may also be called a comprehensive government. The communists call it an All-Peoples Government.

Surplus Value

No discussion of communism is complete without mentioning the concept of surplus value. Actually all the foregoing discussion is abstract concerning the meaning of communism. It is not until one discusses surplus value that he gains a clear distinction between economics in a communist society and economics in a capitalist society.

Surplus value is nothing more than the mark-up on the sale of goods over and above the cost of production. In a capitalist society, it is the profit. To a communist it is a form of exploitation. It is a form of economic slavery over the working class because it deprives the worker of his just wage and increases the cost of his purchases. It is an amount of money that is not earned by the capitalist but which goes into his pocket.

Going back to matter, it is presumed by communists that all matter in its natural form is common property. It belongs to nobody. Therefore it belongs to everybody. No individual or group of individuals has the right to take the property from the whole society or if they do take it they have no right to sell it. That is exploitation.

Value of economic goods then is not the price put on raw materials. The value lies only in the labor used to extract or obtain the raw materials and the labor necessary to produce or refine them. Also any price placed above the cost of labor after production is exploitation. Both types of exploitation are surplus value, which is highly condemned by communists.

Surplus value also appears in rents and in service charges in a capitalist society. Communists do not begrudge the charging for the actual labor involved, but unearned profits separate people into economic classes.

In the communist society any additional mark-ups in the costs of goods does not go into the pockets of individuals or groups of individuals. This money goes into the public treasury for the common good. Actually there are mark-ups on many goods which are sold in the Soviet Union, but this money helps finance education, medical care, cultural programs, housing, transportation, and national defense.

Truth, Freedom, and Democracy

Most discussions of communism do not become any more concrete than the previous sections of this chapter. A person is still left in a difficult position to say what communism really is. One should also look at communism from a different perspective. The communists emphasize the concepts of truth, freedom, and democracy, and it is worthwhile for a careful examination of communism to look at their concepts of these principles.

Truth is defined in Soviet reference books as the correct reflection of the material world in the mind of man. By this definition one sees that truth is a relationship between matter (basic reality) and man. The words "correct reflection" are used to indicate that there is no distortion. Neither is there any addition or subtraction from reality. In other words, truth is an objective view of reality as seen by man. Of course, this concept of reality includes only material things. The definition also implies that man receives this view or reflection into his mind, where he interprets the sensation and produces an understanding. However, the communists do not say that the interpretation or understanding of each man is truth. But they do say that truth starts from the sensations in the minds of men.

A fuller understanding of the communist view of truth goes on into methods of interpretation and analysis. They use science as the primary method. They also use abstractions in mathematics and logic, but they say that all truth must be concrete, i. e. it must be perceptible and understandable. They also add that all abstractions, theories, or hypotheses must be verified in human practice to be accepted as truth. The final acceptance of truth is experience or practice.

This concept of truth includes methods of scientific inquiry, but it rejects subjective thinking, religious faith, myths, superstitions, and legends. It differs primarily with American views of truth in that it shatters many traditional beliefs, particularly in the area of religion. It also differs in that there is one approach to truth in the communist view and that the Americans use several approaches and accept different possibilities and different answers. However, both societies profess the value of a democratic vote and agree that all the people know better than some of the people. But each society demands additional evidence for substantiating truth. Communists outline a series of steps in determining what is true. The first step is human experience and practice in one's environment. This means that a person receives sensations from his interaction with material things and that these sensations are recorded in his mind. The second step is the arranging and organizing of these thoughts in one's mind. It includes the discipline of scientific experiments: observing the situation carefully, examining and studying the evidence, and drawing conclusions based on that evidence. The third step is the taking of these conclusions, determining their relationships, and establishing generalizations or theories. This step includes logic, intuition, and imagination, but these procedures must be directed by a materialistic outlook. The final step is putting into practice those generalizations or theories. Actual practice in concrete situations is the real test of truth. Communists maintain that truth is proved by practice rather than by logic or by one scientific experiment.

These steps start with human experience and practice, and they end with human experience and practice. This emphasis on the source of truth is parallel with their emphasis on the common man. The total experience of the working people is the criteria for general truths. This total experience represents the true will of the people. It is this basic belief that causes communists to put so much faith in the common men and to rely on their history as the guide to the future.

Freedom is not as clearly defined in communist publications. However, they do state that freedom cannot be separated from obligations and responsibilities. Also freedom is closely related to truth. The disregarding the truth, obligations, or responsibilities is not freedom from the communist viewpoint. Freedom is the adherence to the truth and the fulfilling of obligations and responsibilities.

An example for explaining freedom is a story about a man lost in a forest. His way out is compared with truth. If the man wanders aimlessly he remains lost in the forest and does not learn the way out. In other words, he does not learn the truth and does not gain freedom. Only when the man follows an outlined course; by the stars, lay of the land, a stream, or other sign, does he find his way out and gain his freedom. Freedom, therefore, is the learning of the truth and living according to that truth.

Opposition to natural or social laws from the communist viewpoint can lead neither to truth nor to freedom. An individual or a society can gain freedom only by learning laws and obeying them.

Communists reject the concept of free will, in that there is a will in each man which he must exercise to express his freedom. They deny any God-given freedom in man. Instead man must overcome the problems of nature and of society to gain his freedom. The whole history of mankind is a struggle for man to gain his freedom, and each social change brings greater freedom for more people. Finally, freedom for all the people will come only in a communist society.

Freedom, democracy, and socialism converge together in communist philosophy. There cannot be one without the other two. True freedom and democracy are possible only in a socialist society. Democracy and socialism are based on certain freedoms.

In defining democracy, which is equated with socialism, the communists say that democracy is the rule of the people, all of the people. They add that democracy consists of economic, political, and social freedoms, which in turn, are balanced with obligations and responsibilities.

Economic freedom is based on the right to work and the right to rest. It means that everyone must observe these rights and

123

obligations. It also means that everyone must receive a just wage. There is no exploitation or discrimination. Women as well as men enjoy this right with equal compensation. Since no exploitation exists, there are no landlords and no capitalists. All property is owned by the society, and everyone is employed by the society. No one makes a profit from a person's work except for that person and the whole society. In addition, each worker enjoys favorable working conditions, short hours, rest periods, and paid vacations. Democracy does not exist, according to communist teachings, without this economic freedom. It is a basic difference between Western democracies and democracy in a socialist state.

Political freedom is based on the right to vote, to run for office, and to participate in political affairs. There is no discrimination. It is both a right and an obligation. Nearly all people participate in Soviet elections. They are given released time from work and directed to voting places. Everyone over the age of 18 can vote, except for mental incompetents. People at this age can also run for local offices, and a few years later can run for regional and national offices. Not only do people vote and run for office, but they all can participate through public meetings in discussing political issues and in nominating candidates for office. They also can recall officials from office. The elected representatives are responsible to the electorate, and they express the will of the people who elect them. Elected officials are replaced at new elections so that new people can be brought in and can share in the experience of government. The concept of an All-Peoples Government is based on the idea that everyone will have the opportunity to serve for at least one term in a local government office. This full political participation is the basis of political freedom and is a necessity in a socialist democracy.

Social freedoms consist primarily of learning the truth and living by it. The first aspect is education. Education in the Soviet Union is free and compulsory. Everyone has the right and the obligation to attend schools and become educated. Soviet citizens boast that they have increased literacy in the Soviet Union from about 15% in 1917 to almost 100% now. Not only has the Soviet Union built up a great system for elementary and secondary education, but they have also established an extensive higher education system and comprehensive adult education program. Everyone has the right to participate in the adult education program to increase his capabilities so that he can advance in his work or to learn new ideas or skills so that he can change his employment. Workers can be released from work for two hours and attend an institute for four hours a day. The costs are paid by the enterprise. There are institutes for practically every type of knowledge and skill. But education goes farther. Culture is also stressed. In fact, to be considered uncultured (nekul'turniy) is an insult and a disgrace in the Soviet Union. There are theatres, ballet, opera, movies, the zoo, and parks of culture and rest. Cultural attractions are presented everywhere, and people attend them in large numbers. The drive for learning; which is noticed by foreigners as they watch Russians reading books on trains, busses, airplanes, in parks, and everywhere; is social democracy in action.

Social freedom also include the casting away of superstitions, myths, fantasies, and religions. It does not include the persecution of those who believe in these ideas, but it does include the helping of these people to learn the truth and to live by the truth.

Social freedoms also exclude any type of persecution, discrimination, and inequality. It excludes exploitation and other actions which degrade man.

Democracy in the full sense must include these economic, political, and social freedoms. This democracy then becomes socialism.

Democracy in the communist viewpoint can also be understood through a comparison with other political philosophies. It differs from these philosophies in several ways. For the comparison the term communism will be used to distinguish between Western or American democracy and fascism. Communism differs from fascism even to a greater extent than it does from American democracy. This can be seen better in chart form.

Comparison of Political Systems

Communism	American Democracy	Fascism
1. rule of the working class	1. rule of all the people	1. rule of the upper class
2. one political party	2. two political parties	2. one political party
3. representation by population and national groups	3. regional representation by population	3. corporate representation
4. all-peoples ownership of property	4. private ownership of property	4. corporate and state ownership of property

5. belief in social revolution	5. belief in legislated change	5. belief in maintaining order
6. defined rights and responsibilities	6. guaranteed rights and liberties	6. defined duties
7. full popular participation in government	7. voluntary popular participation in government	7. restricted participation in government
8. guaranteed full employment	8. high employment-some unemployment	8. high employment-much employment
9. low income, low taxes, low costs	9. high income, high taxes, high costs	9. low income, high taxes, high costs
10. no religion	10. freedom of religion	10. state religion
11. free, compulsory education	11. free, compulsory education	11. limited educational opportunities
12. one large social class, few rich or poor	12. large middle class, some rich and some poor	12. small elite class, large poor class
13. five-year plans	13. free enterprise and large corporations	13. monopoly controls

Rule of the Working Class

Since the people in the Soviet Union are considered to be workers, the term rule of the working class means a rule of all the people. However, the saying of Karl Marx that "he who does not work does not eat" still applies. People can be deprived of their right to participate in the rule of the government if they do not carry out their obligations. Rights and obligations are not separated from each other.

Soviet citizens do participate actively in the political processes. Almost 100% of the qualified voters do vote in each election. There are also many public discussions of political issues in every town and village. But according to the concept of Democratic Centralism, the decisions of the people are vested in the government. In addition, the Communist Party is in effect a super government, which is the "Dictatorship of the Proletariat" and the "Vanguard of the People." The result of the participation of the citizens in the political processes then becomes a ratification of decisions previously made by the Communist Party.

If one equates the Communist Party with the working class, then the concept of the rule of the working class is valid. However, if one does not do this, the rule in the Soviet Union is that of the Communist Party.

Actually, there are few opportunities for a Soviet citizen to initiate policies, to choose between alternative candidates or policies, or to dissent from proposed legislation. The strict censorship also prevents people from having free access to information on which they could make alternate choices. The lack of consumer goods and the low priority placed on correcting social (not political) problems are evidences that the party and government are not "for the people." In fact, the party and government control and regulate the citizens rather than serving them. Hence, the phrase "rule of the working class" means the "rule of the Communist Party leaders."

One Political Party

One political party is said to be more representative of a one-class social system. Two parties mean two groups or two classes. In a unified society there is no room for divisions and dissension. The choice in a socialist (communist) vote is either for or against the candidate. It is more like sustaining a selection or the ratifying a choice than an election. The element of democratic participation comes first in the nominating procedure. It is in the nomination process that the choice is singled out in a one-party or even in a two-party system. It is at that level where democracy is tested. In the Soviet Union public meetings are held on each level of the society for the naming of candidates. The persons attending the meetings may speak for or against the nominees. The nominees must also speak both for and against their own candidacy. In this way both the strengths and the weaknesses of the candidates are learned, and the selected candidate is placed on the ballot. If the voter opposes the candidate, he may vote against him. The candidate could be defeated, and a new election could be called for the new candidate. But the nominating processes eliminate those nominees who are not dedicated and who would not carry out the will of the working people (the Communist Party). The candidates then have the support of the Communist Party and are generally voted into office. After an election there is no organized group which opposes the government officials, and individual citizens are expected to support them. The society remains united with the one party system, where there is no opportunity for effective opposition, while this is not true for a two or more party system.

Representation by Population and National Groups

On every level of the society there are soviets (councils) which represent that level of government. That is how the Soviet Union received its name. These soviets are organized with the responsibility to represent the citizens in local, regional, and national affairs. Each unit of society forms its own local soviet under the direction of the Communist Party and sends representatives to the higher soviets and on to the Supreme Soviet, which is the national legislative body. Representation is based on population counts and on ethnic groups. These national representatives come from many different occupations and from every geographic region. On all levels of government there are among the representatives young people, women, non-party people, and members of the Communist Party.

These soviets are the center of government of each level. From them are elected an executive committee to carry out the decisions of the soviet representatives. The local soviet functions on the basis of democratic centralism, which means that it represents both the people in the local area and the whole society through cooperation with the soviets on other levels of government.

All-People's Ownership of Property

All-peoples ownership of property is a basic concept of communism. Communists say that private property leads to exploitation of man by man. One form of such exploitation comes through rents and leases of property to other persons. Since land and natural resources are not products of man's labor, they should not belong to any individual or any one group of individuals. They should belong to the whole society. Then no one can enrich himself at the expense of another person. Another form of exploitation comes through hiring others to work so that an employer can make a profit from the labor of his employees. When private enterprise owns the means of production, the employees do not receive their share of production. The surplus value or the profit goes into the hands of the owners, the

128

management, or the stock holders. When the means of the production are owned by the whole society, the profits either go to the employee as wages or go into the public treasury for the whole society so that the whole society can benefit from the use of the property and from man's labor on that property. In the communist philosophy public ownership is the way to eliminate man's exploitation of man.

But all-people's ownership or public ownership actually means government ownership. The citizens work for the government, and the relationship of the employer versus the employee exists in a manner similar to a company town. The government, as the company town, sets both the wages and the prices. The government also rents housing to citizens. Some public services are inexpensive, but wages are low, and many prices are high. Soviet citizens may consider the gap between wages and prices to be compensated for by the inexpensive public services. But the large government investment in heavy industry and in military defense is an exploitation by the government, when one considers the low priority placed on consumer goods.

Belief in Social Revolution

In a country where private enterprise exists, the ownership of the property inevitably becomes concentrated in the hands of a few. Monopolies form and control the wealth of the society. Communists point to capitalist societies to show evidence of this trend. When the laboring class sees that the rich are becoming richer at their expense and when the people want to gain a fairer share of the nation's wealth, they must struggle with the upper classes to do so. The upper classes will not voluntarily give up their wealth, their power, and their privileges. That is why communists say that revolution is inevitable. The transition from a capitalist society to a socialist or communist society is based on revolution for the very reason that the rich and the powerful will fight against a more equal distribution of the wealth. The only way the working people can have this redistribution of the wealth is to fight and win the revolution.

Communists have been called war mongers because they believe that revolution is necessary in order to found a communist society. But communists say that they are opposed to wars of aggression. They favor only wars of national liberation in which an oppressed class of peoples is fighting for its independence from a foreign power or from economic exploitation in its own country. Communists point to the American and French Revolutions as examples of that type of war, and they say that that type of war is just and necessary. But communists oppose wars between the major powers. They say that these wars are based on economics and that their purpose is to extend the colonial territory or to form international monopolies for increasing the wealth of a few. Communists reassert that they are opposed to war. This opposition is particularly strong in the Soviet Union, where so many people were killed during the Second World War. But the communists believe that the dignity of man depends on his right to liberate himself from oppression, from persecution, and from exploitation. For this reason communists favor wars of national liberation.

Defined Rights and Responsibilities

When a socialist society forms, it must establish a government to protect the rights of its citizens. The political power of the government must be able to defend the people from both external and internal enemies. In order to provide this protection and to guarantee the freedom of the people, the society needs the cooperation of the people. In this sense obligations and responsibilities cannot be separated from rights and freedoms. They go hand in hand. Each stated right then carries with it the stated responsibility. The right to work means that a person will find employment and he will work. The right to vote means that a person has the opportunity and the obligation to vote. The right of national defense carries with it the obligation to serve in the military forces. And so it is with all rights. For this reason the Soviet Constitution defines the rights of Soviet citizens and specifies the obligations which guarantee those rights.

Full Popular Participation in Government

The concept of full popular participation in government is both a right and an obligation. This participation is necessary in order to insure a democracy. Democracy means the rule of the people. If some people do not participate, then the democracy falls down. Full participation is the only way to learn the will of the people and to have fair representation. People in the Soviet Union are organized into collectives so that they may be guaranteed their rights and so that their responsibilities and obligations are carried out by group efforts. These collectives are organized in schools, at places of employment, and at every work location. Every individual belongs to a collective. The communists are proud of the fact that there are no disassociated people in their society. An example of their collective action is the process of voting. The work group or collective is released from work and transported together to the voting place. After voting they return together and resume working. Another example is the enlistment into the military service. All the 19-year-old men in a group report at the same time for the draft call. An announcement is made that on such a day they will report. A big ceremony takes place in the community, and all 19-year-old men from one community go to the same training camp. These examples are typical for attending school, for conducting summer work projects, for recreational activities, and for political discussions. Full participation is both provided and required. Social pressure more than legal sanctions keep a person participating, not just because he has to, but because he is motivated to want to participate. Such participation, it is said, decreases delinquency and crime. It keeps people doing constructive activities and prevents destructive activities.

But participation in the political affairs of the Soviet Union is limited to rendering support. Real participation implies an opportunity to contribute one's own ideas and to have some of them accepted. The presence of censorship and the absence of privately-organized groups make such contributions impractical. Soviet citizens are kept so busy with political activity which supports Communist programs that they could believe that they have real participation, but they really have no avenue for dissent.

Guaranteed Full Employment

The guarantee of full employment is parallel to the full participation concept. A person is motivated to want to work, and opportunities are provided for everyone. Graduating students are assigned to work locations where they are obliged to work for a year or two. Later they may change jobs and change locations, if they desire. Job opportunities are posted at all enterprises, and public offices help people find employment. A person carries a work booklet, which shows where he works and when he started. This booklet is a basic document, which enables the worker to find housing, to attend adult education programs, to enjoy trade union benefits, and to change jobs. If a person works and has an up-to-date work booklet, he enjoys his economic rights. The saying that "he who does not work does not eat" is a reminder that a person must work. However, the greatest incentive to work is the motivated desire that one wants to work. This desire is taught in schools and in youth work projects. The whole program of building communism is a challenge to all people to work so they can enjoy the benefits of that labor for themselves and for their children. This desire then is met with government planning, organizing, and providing work opportunities for all.

Low Income, Low Taxes, and Low Costs

The redistribution of the wealth in a society requires a minimum wage and a maximum wage with a relatively small range between them. Communism is not based on a leveling concept so that all people are equal. That concept is not consistent with reality. But it is based on an attempt to provide a floor and a ceiling on earnings so that there will not be great wealth on one hand and poverty on the other. A division of the gross earnings of a country into the number of working people does not produce a high wage for everyone. Appropriations for wages are decreased more by the necessary social expenses, which must be channeled through the public treasury, e. g. national defense, education, building factories, etc. Therefore, the wages are not high in the Soviet Union, but neither are the taxes high. The state income comes from the production, a part of which is diverted to the public treasury for government operating expenses, rather than from taxes. Since there is no private enterprise and no need to make a profit on every item, the production and distribution of consumer goods and services are based on the consumer needs in comparison with public needs. The costs of consumer goods then are not determined by supply and demand, but there does remain some relationship to the cost of production. Many services are free or very inexpensive. Education and medical care are free. Housing is based on ten percent of one's income. Transportation is quite inexpensive. Some goods are inexpensive. Luxury goods are more expensive. There is little direct comparison of costs between the Soviet Union and other countries. Costs are based on plans and the fulfillment of plans rather than on a market quotation. But the average citizen lives comfortably. He has the necessities, and now he enjoys some luxuries. Since the Soviet citizen does not buy land and does not invest his money, he does not need large bank savings. He does not have to save for "a rainy day", because he has security with medical care and old age benefits. The distribution of the wealth prevents extreme luxury. It also prevents poverty. It is believed that the citizen is better served by the society when income, taxes, and expenses are all low. Eventually, the communists say, there will be no money in the communist system. The work booklets will become their passes for free goods and services. It is not the monetary relationship which becomes important in the communist society. Labor, goods, and services need not be based on a separate value system when everyone participates "from each according to his ability and to each according to his needs."

No Religion

Religion is viewed as a superstition in the Soviet Union. Religious freedom does not mean "freedom of religion." It means "freedom from religion and superstition." It is believed that religions have been used by the upper classes to dominate, control, and exploit the lower classes. Religion, in this viewpoint, has been an instrument of the governing classes to frighten the masses of people into submission to their will. Freedom for a communist then means the removal of these artificial regulations, which have been imposed by religions. A person then becomes free when he can learn the truths of natural and social laws and use these laws for the betterment of the whole society. The materialistic outlook of communists denies the existence of God, of the soul of man, and of a life beyond death. They say that these concepts are unknowable by man and have been contrived by man for the benefit of a few, who extract offerings and services from the many for their own enrichment. Therefore, religion of any type is discouraged. Church members are not punished, but attempts are made to re-educate them. Believers in religion are not full participants in the "collectives", and, therefore, they cannot take full advantage of the opportunities. This statement does not mean that people are denied anything due to persecution. It takes the form of a self-denial because they withdraw from some activities. Church members in this way are restricting their own freedom by a adhering to vestiges of the past and by not accepting the scientific truths and living by them. Communists believe that freedom only comes by obeying natural and social laws, as determined by science.

The lack of religion in the Soviet Union has left a void though. The Communist Party has partially filled this void by the almost deification of Lenin, the almost canonization of Lenin's writings, and the shrine-like monuments and eternal flames dedicated to those who were killed in the Second World War. The Soviet citizens take off their hats, may weep, and listen to organ music. Such devotion to dead heroes is almost a religious or spiritual experience, which is accepted often as people return to thse monuments.

The comradery and the moral precepts which can be obtained in church are partially provided in the collectives at academic institutions or work enterprises. But the close association with peoples of different age groups and of different occupational interests which one meets in an American church cannot be found in the Soviet collective.

Free, Compulsory Education

Education is a paramount principle of communist philosophy. Since past generations have been prevented from learning, it becomes necessary to educate everyone in the society. Not only was it necessary to teach almost 85% of the people to read and write in the Soviet Union after the Communist Revolution; it was also necessary to teach them work skills, more positive attitudes, and a whole new philosophy. People had to unlearn many beliefs. Not only did people profess a religious belief, but they also believed many old myths, superstitions, and rumors. The Soviet Union has attacked ignorance on all sides. Now the Soviet Union can boast of near 100% literacy, universal education, and a large number of highly educated scientists and scholars. Culture, too, is a part of this educational drive. Palaces of Culture have been constructed in every town and on many collective farms. In these Palaces of Culture there are plays, operettas, ballet, variety shows, folk dances, and lectures. These stage presentations are inexpensive, and all education is free, even higher education. Elementary and secondary education is compulsory, and higher education is available to all through adult education programs in the evenings. Soviet citizens are encouraged to become educated and cultured, and the Soviet Union has made great strides in this direction.

One Large Social Class, Few Rich or Poor

These principles are summarized by the belief in a classless society. There are few extremes of wealth or poverty. Since everyone works, he receives wages and participates in social benefits. They have these social services in schools, clinics, hospitals, rest homes, and sanatoria, which provide security from destitution that may come from accidents or disease. There is just one class with few exceptions, and there are no disassociated persons in the communist society.

But wealth and poverty are relative terms. It is true that there are no wealthy persons, even including top Communist Party officials, according to American standards. But by these same standards the whole society is poor. The lack of adequate housing, automobiles, consumer items, and stylish clothing is an indicator of a low standard of living. Even the television, piano, and the furniture in the Soviet home, which to them are marks of economic well-being are also in the homes of many of the American poor.

It is not fair, however, to compare with American standards. When comparing the standard of living in the Soviet Union at the present time with that of twenty-five years ago, there is seen a substantial improvement. And since there are not the extremes of wealth and poverty in comparison with the average standard of living in the Soviet Union, it is fair to say that there are few rich and few poor there.

Five Year Plans

A planned economy is another basic feature of the communist system. The contention is that both goals and means for attaining those goals are meaningless without planning. Without plans the result is chaos with periods of inflation and depression. A stable economy can only be assured by preparing and following a unified plan.

In the preparation of the plan the resources and the capabilities for production are considered at each plant, factory, farm, mine, or other enterprise. The figures are tabulated and compiled by the State Planning Commission. The needs for each level of production and the needs for the whole economy are then compared with the potential to fulfill those needs. Based on this preparation a five year plan is compiled and distributed throughout the country. Within the plan are categories for each type of production and sub-categories for one year, six months, and one month.

The unified plan becomes the law of the land and is enforced. In addition, incentives are built into the plan to encourage the workers to fulfill and over-fulfill the plan.

In such a way the needs of the country regulate over-production in some areas and under-production in other areas. Priorities are established so that goods and services will be provided, even though in another system these goods and services may not be profitable ventures. Profits in some types of production compensate for subsidies to other types of production.

Communists believe that the system of planning is the scientific way to operate an economy. They believe that it is fair and just to the producers, the government operations, and the consumers. The plan is an essential part of socialism or communism.

But the Soviet Union has not perfected these plans. Even though there are some contingency funds built into the plan, there are still problems in the concept of a planned economy. When construction stops in September and has to wait until January for more funds to proceed, there is a great waste of manpower. Possibly better administration or better planning could overcome such problems, but they persist from one plan to the next. On a smaller scale there are also times when funds for supplies, repairs of equipment, and new purchases are lacking. Of course, such problems may also occur in the budgets of a capitalist society. The cause, however, is central planning, which is removed from the actual work situation.

Reaction to Communism

Non-communists have reacted to communism in many ways. There are the violent anti-communists, who teach that communism is the culmination of evil. These people refer to communism as a disease, the power of the devil, or a threat of destruction to morality and social orders. To them communism is a grave danger.

Refugees from communist countries and victims of military action during revolutions or other hostilities usually have a very negative attitude toward communism. These negative attitudes are very prevalent in many non-communist societies. Communist Parties have been outlawed in some countries, and they are considered to be subversive in other countries.

Communists say that this opposition is spawned by the upper classes who see communism as a threat to their wealth, their power, and their special privileges. It is this opposition that makes revolution a necessity when establishing a communist system.

An objective look at communism must include some of the reaction to the existence and expansion of that system. Some weaknesses or at least differences are apparent in the foregoing paragraphs, but another look at some concepts may bring them into a clearer perspective.

The controversy between religion and atheism is probably the greatest dispute between non-communists and communists.

Unfortunately, this misunderstanding cannot be resolved by science or by debate. It is a difference in the major premises. Acceptance of religion or of atheism can come only by a complete change of attitudes and beliefs. It is interesting to note that religion persists on a rather large scale in the Soviet Union and that atheism and agnosticism are widespread in non-communist countries. Religious persons may continue to oppose communism, but they also oppose people of other religious faiths. The differences between Moslems and Christians or between Catholics and Protestants have also caused controversies. Wars have been fought and people have been persecuted over religious differences. It is probably in this area that people should learn to become more tolerant of opposing beliefs. Controls on religions have fluctuated in the Soviet Union. As people learn to recognize the true spirit of religious freedom and the personal nature of basic beliefs, religious tolerance should increase both in non-communist countries and in the Soviet Union. Democratic societies have largely rejected the concept of religious wars. Even though people strongly believe in religion or in atheism, they are probably better off for themselves and for other human beings not to insist that this difference is a reason for hostilities.

Free enterprise and public ownership could also be classified as the major difference between capitalism and communism. Americans believe that free enterprise, private property, and competition are the basic reasons for the productive economy and the free society of the United States. But at the same time they have to recognize that government controls on monopolies and government services in non-profitable enterprises have indirectly contributed much to the greatness of the country. Government subsidies and tax benefits to industry have added strength to the economy. Income taxes and federal monetary regulations have stabilized financial crises. The interaction between free enterprise and government has proved to be beneficial. But the United States denies a trend toward communism. Also the Soviet Union denies a trend toward capitalism as it institutes greater competition between collectives, profit incentives for enterprises, and expanded ownership of consumer goods (including automobiles). The great difference in the economy persists in the basic approaches in the two systems, but the average individual citizen need not be concerned with these differences. The emphasis on private ownership or public ownership only becomes of a great significance when people are concerned with personal ownership. Whether the factory, institution, or farm is owned by the state or by a large, impersonal corporation is of little consequence to the individual worker as long as he receives a wage commensurate with a decent standard of living. If that worker can identify with the corporation by owning shares or with the government by participating in the collective, he still sees himself as a small part of a large industrialized society. The question here evolves to individualism versus collectivism. But this question also becomes theoretical in an industrialized society with a very large population.

The real threat to mankind, which one finds in communism, can also be found in other societies. This is the threat against the dignity of man by violating human rights. This is the threat of destruction of man, both in the physical and in the moral senses. This is the threat of violence, deception, and coercion. It is the use of force and threats of force, either overtly or covertly.

This threat is the one seen by many refugees, by victims of oppression, and by witnesses of atrocities. This threat existed in the time of Militant Communism following the 1917 Communist Revolution. It also existed during the purges by Stalin in the 1930's and during the Second World War. To some extent it has persisted in the Soviet Union, but few people, even Soviet citizens, know the extent of it.

Of course, this threat is not peculiar to time or place in the history of man. But it is this fact of communism that is publicized outside of the Soviet Union. It has also been and is the face of many governments, both dictatorial powers and so-called democracies. It can also be a threat in the United States, and to the degree it does exist in the United States it is magnified and reported in the Soviet Union. This threat, no matter where it comes from, is the real enemy of man and should be opposed by all men, both non-communists and communists.

The de-Stalinization Campaign in the Soviet Union was a drive against this type of inhumanity of man to man. The advocacy of Peaceful Coexistence was also an attempt to reduce this threat to mankind which grew during the so-called Cold War. This danger to all mankind has been greatly reduced, but still it exists in all nations, both communist and non-communist, where the dignity of man is not respected.

The concept of the dignity and the worth of man in the Soviet Union is not the same as that in the United States. Life just does not have the same value in the Soviet Union. Wars and revolutions are considered to be a part of life, and the death of many is considered necessary for preserving and building the communist society. Human values are also given a lower priority for the living. This is evident in the do-nothing attitude toward the long lines that people have to wait in to buy consumer goods. It is also evident in the poor quality of work on houses, buildings of all types, streets, and particularly on public toilets. The Soviet Government may make some effort to simulate a government of the people and by the people, but there is little effort to make it a government for the people. On the contrary, the people study, work, and contribute much time for the building of the communist society. They have to dedicate their total effort for this goal. Children are exempt from this great pressure to some extent, but adults work hard and long to achieve the goals of the government and have little time and opportunity for their own self-enlightenment. And for all this time and effort they receive low wages, inadequate housing, and shortages in personal possessions.

A Soviet Youth's View of Communism

When a Soviet Youth is asked what communism means to him, he has quite a different answer from all the foregoing paragraphs in this chapter. His story will go something like this:

Communism is building a new and better society. It is the electrification and industrialization of our country. It is the creating of a new Soviet man. Just look at the achievements of the Soviet Union over the last fifty years. That is communism in action. See how illiteracy and unemployment have been completely eliminated. See how the Soviet Union has become the second largest industrial and military power in the world from one of the most backward nations of last century. See how the Soviet Union sent the first sputnik into space. These are the products of communism. Communism is progress and happiness for all. Communism is the way of the future.

SOURCES FOR CHAPTER IV - COMMUNISM

Bol'shaya Sovetskaya Entsiklopediya (2nd ed.),
    Demokratiya, XXXIII, 655
    Istina, XVIII, 614-16
    Patriotism, XXXII, 236
    Svoboda, & Svoboda i Neobkhodimost', XXXVIII, 267
Galitskaya, I. A., Mysli o Religii, Moscow: Gosudarstvennoye
    Izdatel'stvo Politicheskoy Literatury, 1962, 255 p.
Hulicka, Karel & Hulicka, Irene M., Soviet Institutions, The Individ-
    ual and Society, Boston: The Christopher Publishing House,
    1967, 680 pp.
Konstantinov, F. V., Filosofskaya Entsiklopediya, vols. 1-4,
    Moscow; Gosudarstvennoye Nauchnoye Izdatel'stvo "Sovetskaya
    Entskilopedia", 1960, 504 p. 584 p., 591 p.
Konstantinov, F. V., Osnovy Marksistkoy Filosofii, Moscow:
    Izdatel'stvo Politicheskoy Literatury, 1964, 667 p.
Lenin, V. I., Khrestomatiya po Marksisko-Leninskoy Filosofii, vol.
    2, Moscow: Gosudarstvennoye Izdatel'stvo Politicheskoy
    Literatury, 1961, 759 p.
McClosky, Herbert & Turner, John E., The Soviet Dictatorship, New
    York: McGraw-Hill Book Co., Inc., 1960, 657 p.
Marks, K., Engels, F., & Lenin, V. I., Khrestomatiya po Mark-
    sistsko-Leninskoy Filosofii, vol. 1, Moscow: Gosudarstven-
    noye Izdatel'stvo Politicheskoy Literatury, 1961, 771 p.
Rozental', M. M. & Yudin, P. F., Filosofskiy Slovar', Moscow:
    Izdatel'stvo Politicheskoy Literatury, 1963, 544 p.
Shaffner, Harry G., The Soviet System in Theory and Practice,
    New York: Appleton-Century-Crofts, 1965, 480 p.
Shakhnazarov, G. Kh. et als., Obshchestvovedeniye (4th ed.),
    Moscow: Izdatel'stvo Politicheskoy Literatury, 1966, 384 p.
Shakhnazarov, G. Kh. et als., Obshchestvovedeniye (9th ed.),
    Moscow: Izdatel'stvo Politicheskoy Literatury, 1971, 366 p.
Voronov, D. M. et als., Marksistskoy-Leninskaya Filosofiya -
    Istoricheskiy Materializm, Moscow: Izdatel'stvo "Mysl'",
    1968, 367 p.
Vostrikov, A. V. et als., Marksistko-Leninskaya Filosofiya -
    Dialekticheskiy Materializm, Moscow: Izdatel'stvo "Mysl'",
    1968, 367 p.
Whiting, Kenneth, The Soviet Union Today, New York: Praeger,
    1966, 423 p.
Yaroslavskiy, E., Bibliya dlya Veruyushchikh i Neveruyushchikh,
    Moscow: Gosudarstvennoye Izdatel'stvo Politicheskoy
    Literatury, 1962, 408 p.

CHAPTER V

HISTORY OF THE SOVIET UNION

The turmoil in Tsarist Russia since Bloody Sunday in 1905 and during the First World War made a dramatic change in the government inevitable. Tsar Nicholas II had no choice and was forced to abdicate in March, 1917. The power of the Duma, which became the Provisional Government, was not much stronger than that of the tsar. A vacuum existed, and the people of Russia demanded leadership. The attempts of Alexander Kerensky to rally people around the Provisional Government did not unify the people. The abortive coup of General Lavr Kornilov to seize St. Petersburg also was not an acceptable answer. Even if this coup had been successful, the people would have rebelled again against a military dictatorship.

The Social Democrats (re-named Communists) were not numerous, but their slogans were popular. They promised rapid change. They called for "Peace, Land, and Bread." Governmental power was to be given to the people. The slogan, "All Power to the Soviets", meant that their local city and land councils (soviets) would become the new government.

The war against Germany had been a catastrophe for Russia, and a call for an immediate, separate peace could not help but receive a strong response. The need for a land reform had been intensifying since the 1861 Emancipation of the Serfs. The peasants were heavily in debt for very meager plots of land. Starvation had become acute, particularly in the cities. The food distribution system had broken down, because priority for first deliveries was to the soldiers on the front. The slogan "Peace, Land, and Bread" was a welcome sound.

People had lost faith in the government. What faith people did have in national authority was based on their religious belief that the tsar was a representative of Christ on earth. When the tsar abdicated, this belief could not be transferred to the Provisional Government or to a military dictatorship. The alternative was for the people to assume governmental power for themselves. The slogan "All Power to the Soviets" offered this opportunity.

When Lenin returned from Switzerland and provided charismatic leadership for these popular causes, he met little resistance in staging and conducting the October, 1917 Revolution. The take-over of power from the Provisional Government, which was located in the former Winter Palace of the Tsars, was almost bloodless. Similar action took place in Moscow and other Russian cities.

All at once the revolutionaries were not fighting against auto-cracy, orthodoxy, and nationalism as they had done for years. Now they had become the government. They had to meet the demands of the people. Lenin immediately proceeded to carry out his promises.

Official announcements declared an end to the war, and Leon Trotsky was sent to Brest-Litovsk in Poland to sign a separate peace with the Germans. This peace was achieved at a great sacrifice to Russia, but at least it was achieved. The land reform and the star-vation problem were both settled by the announcement that the land, the food, the industry, and the natural resources belonged to the people and that the people should take this property from the capital-ists, the exploiters, and the land lords. Large land holdings were immediately subdivided, and the former owners were removed. This transferral of ownership did not take place smoothly. Chaos resulted for a time, but the problems of land and bread were being solved for the peasant. All financial obligations for land had been cancelled.

The councils (soviets) held a national conference and estab-lished the new central government. It was the Council of People's Commissars (Sovet Narodnikh Kommissarov), and Lenin was named chairman. The headquarters were then moved from St. Petersburg to Moscow, and the Soviet Government was established in the Kremlin. The local power remained in the local soviets in coordination with the Council of People's Commissars. The government had been estab-lished in the soviets. All power was given to the soviets and coordi-nated by the national soviet, The Council of People's Commissars.

RUSSIAN CIVIL WAR

Of course, there was not immediate unity in the new Soviet Republic. The power of the former rulers had to be completely removed. At the same time those persons who retained some power and who opposed the new regime attempted to use that power to re-gain control. The revolution was not really over. It took another three years to consolidate the power in the Soviet Republic.

The time of 1918 to 1921 is referred to as the time of the Russian Civil War or the time of Militant Communism. It was the time for putting down the resistance in Russia and consolidating power.

The first and strongest opposition to the new regime became known as the "Whites" because they carried a white flag. The govern-ment forces carried a red flag, and they become known as the "Reds."

The "Whites" became organized around those persons who were still loyal to the tsar or to the Provisional Government. They were also supported by other persons who opposed communist power. The "Whites" were strongest in European Russia.

The new Soviet Republic had greatly aggravated its allies of the First World War. The international commitments, both political and financial, of the Tsarist and Provisional governments had been repudiated. This meant that the pledge not to have a separate peace with Germany had been broken. Also the foreign debts had been cancelled, and all property of foreigners in Russia had been nationalized. Russia's former allies--England, France, United States and the exile government of the Czech people; all reacted to this violation of international treaties. The governments of these countries considered the Soviet Republic to be temporary, and they aided in the opposition against it.

The Peace Treaty at Brest-Litovsk between Russia and Germany took place in March, 1918. This act was followed by immediate attacks on the Soviet Government by England, France, United States, and the Czechs. England landed forces in Murmansk and attempted to proceed toward Moscow. France came from the south through the Black Sea. Both the Americans and the Czechs came from Japan into Siberia.

Other independent groups also organized to fight. Some of these were political powers, and they carried green or yellow flags. Others were less organized and less politically motivated. Some of them were just armed bandits, who killed and plundered only for their own gains.

The foreign intervention in some ways was beneficial to the Soviet Government. The Russian people quickly responded to fight against the foreign invaders. A spirit of patriotism encouraged many people to participate in or support the Red Army. In addition, the drive of the foreign powers was short-lived, because World War I ended in November of 1918 before they had penetrated very far into the territory of Russia. With the end of the war with Germany, the appeals for the soldiers to come home had to be heard. Within a short time the foreign intervention had ended. This change of events was a victory for the Soviet Government.

The Soviet Government also had many advantages over the "Whites" and other opposition forces. The control of the central government and the two largest cities, Moscow and St. Petersburg, gave the Soviet forces the advantages of stored equipment and supplies and short lines of communication and transportation for delivering that equipment and supplies to the troops.

The Red Army was formed out of the old Tsarist Army. Officers were recruited, and they brought with them the men under their command. They also brought with them military equipment and the know-how for using it. Many former deserters re-joined the army and were welcomed into the Red Army as loyal citizens. The old army had been re-vitalized.

Many people saw the fulfillment of the promises by the Soviet Government as their justification to support the new regime. Others also could look at the Soviet Government as the only legitimate government, because it was based on the soviets. They felt the need for loyalty to their government and their native land.

The Red Army was the most successful in stopping the armed bandits and in restoring order where there had been chaos. The "Whites" continued to offer strong resistance, and there was fierce fighting between the "Reds" and the "Whites." Many people were killed, and there were many atrocities. Large groups of the former aristocracy fled the country into Western Europe and to America. Alexander Kerensky was in one of those groups. Other former leaders were sought out and killed. Nicholas II and his family were among those people who met this fate. Communists also suffered great losses. Even Lenin was severely wounded.

Order was not restored until after the defeat of Admiral A. V. Kolchak in April of 1920. Admiral Kolchak left his former command on the Black Sea and organized an army to fight with the foreign powers against the Red Army. His army had become a strong force which gained wide control in Siberia, and the defeat of this army by General Mikhail Frunze of the Red Army was a final victory for the Soviet Government.

During the rest of 1920 and on into 1921 the Soviet Government established territorial control over the heartland of Russia, the Ukraine, the Caucasus Mountain region, and Siberia. Soviet power had been firmly established.

In spite of the Civil War the Soviet Government was able to make further gains in the society. In November, 1917, Lenin had proclaimed a Declaration of Rights for the people of Russia. This declaration was followed in July, 1918, by a new constitution for the Russian Socialist Federated Soviet Republic. The 1918 Constitution further provided basic freedoms of speech, press, and religion, and it stated that the power of the government was vested in the All-Union Congress of Soviets and its interim Executive Committee. The Declaration of Rights and the Constitution, however, could not immediately guarantee these rights and freedoms. The war and the internal chaos had to be ended first.

144

In December of 1920 Lenin took the initial steps for the industrialization of the country. He announced a massive electrification program, which became known as GOELRO (The State Commission on the Electrification of Russia). Lenin said: "Communism is Soviet Power plus the electrification of the whole country." His plan consisted of the construction of thirty large electric power stations near Moscow, in the Ukraine, and along the Volga River.

THE NEW ECONOMIC PLAN

The Russian Civil War had weakened the economy even further than before. Drastic measures had to be taken to produce food and clothing for the people and at the same time to industrialize the country. At the conference of All-Union Congress of Soviets in December, 1920, Lenin announced his New Economic Plan.

In a sense this plan was a reversal to capitalism. Lenin had said that it is necessary sometimes to take one step backward in order to take two steps forward. This was his explanation for instituting free enterprise for farming, small businesses, craftsmen shops, and small industry. He said that this measure was temporarily necessary in order to supply the food, clothing and consumer goods to the people. This action also relieved the state economy and allowed it to concentrate on the industrialization of the country. The Soviet Government maintained control and direction of the heavy industry, all banking and financial institutions, and all foreign commerce. This plan would enable the rapid growth of industry and the fulfillment of the electrification program.

The New Economic Plan was initiated in 1921. The Civil War had ended, and people were now able to work with few restrictions for satisfying their economic needs. Civil authority had been established, and the chaos, killing, and plundering had stopped. Farming and food distribution through private markets relieved the hunger. Craftsmen and small shops provided goods for their other needs.

Consistent with the plan to industrialize the whole country was the need for greater unity in the government. With the annexation of the Ukrainian Republic, the Belorussian Republic, and the Trans-Caucasian Republic to the Russian Republic there became the need for a union of these republics. In 1922 these republics were united into the Union of Soviet Socialist Republics, and gradually other republics were added until 1929 the Tadzhik Republic was added. The formation of the USSR was followed in 1924 with the adoption of a new constitution, which recognized this union and extended the rights of the people to the other republics.

The rapid industrialization program met against the problem of the illiteracy of the workers. Education had been a great concern of the new government. Lenin's wife, Nadezhda Krupskaya, worked closely with the Commissar of Education, Anatoly Lunacharsky, in establishing a nine-year school system for the youth. Many innovations had been instituted, but the program was not extensive enough to satisfy the need of all the youth of the country and not directed to satisfy the need of the illiterate adults. In December, 1923, a new education program was set up on a crash basis to attack the problem of illiteracy.

All education efforts were directed toward a four-year program for everyone, including all adults. Teachers were recruited from every walk of life. The basic requirement was that they knew how to read and write.

The progress of the New Economic Plan was interrupted, however, by the serious illness of Lenin in 1922, as a result of his earlier wound, and by his death in January of 1924. This unforeseen circumstance brought a new problem, that of succession of power.

STALIN AND TROTSKY

During the organization of the Soviet Government Joseph Vissarionovich Dzhugashvili (Stalin), a Georgian, became the Commissar of Nationalities, and Leon D. Bronstein (Trotsky), a former Menshevik, became Commissar of Foreign Affairs. Both were also right hand men to Lenin in the affairs of the Communist Party. Stalin had become head of the Party Secretariat. Trotsky was also a close advisor to Lenin, and it is said that he was favored over Stalin as his successor. But no firm arrangement had been made before Lenin's death.

Just before Lenin's death in April of 1923 the Twelfth Party Congress was convened under the directorship of a three-man executive committee. This committee consisted of Stalin, Zinoviev, and Kamenev. During Lenin's serious illness and for a while before his death this committee continued to function in Lenin's place as the leading power of the country. Trotsky was not included, and he attacked the policies of this group. Stalin, in turn, used Zinoviev and Kamenev to oppose Trotsky.

The policy differences consisted of Trotsky's program to extend revolutions to capitalist countries and to have a world revolution and of Stalin's program for communism in one country. Stalin wanted to solve the peasant problem and to collectivize agriculture.

146

In December of 1925 Stalin reasserted his leadership by attacking Trotsky's policies and by alienating both Zinoviev and Kamenev. At the Fourteenth Party Congress the majority backed Stalin in opposition to Trotsky, Zinoviev, and Kamenev. The counter attacks of these three against Stalin were met with further opposition. In 1926 all three of them were expelled from the Politburo, and in 1927 Trotsky was exiled. Stalin had gained leadership of both the Communist Party and the Soviet Government.

THE FIVE YEAR PLANS

During the struggle for power in the Politburo Stalin had already started introducing plans to alter the New Economic Plan. Stalin proved to be dedicated to the establishment of socialism not only in heavy industry and in banking but also in agricultural and commerce. His policy for "communism in one country" was carried out in dramatic actions.

Stalin introduced the system of Five Year Plans, which has continued since 1928. These plans are comprehensive plans for the whole economy. They are based on the potential of production for every enterprise, institution, and farm and on the projected needs of the country over the five year period.

The first Five Year Plan was a continuation of the industrialization and electrification of the country. It also initiated the collectivization of agriculture. The first Five Year Plan marked the end of the New Economic Plan. This plan lasted from 1928 to 1933. The second Five Year Plan started in 1933 and continued into 1937 with the main purpose of collectivizing agriculture.

These years from 1928 to 1937 marked a great transition in the Soviet Union. Stalin ruthlessly carried out his plans and thoroughly established socialism. Among the industrial achievements were the large hydro-electric power dam at Dniepropetrovsk on the Dnieper River in the Ukraine, the tractor plants at Khar'kov and Stalingrad, the automotive factories in Moscow and Gorky, the steel plants in Magnitogorsk and Stalinsk (Kuznetsk Basin), and the farm implement factories in Saratov and Rostov. Large numbers of people were transferred to industrial jobs. Youth groups were assigned to work on construction jobs both to help do the work and to set energetic examples for the other workers. The Stakhanovite Movement or shock workers movement started to show by example how the workers could increase their production.

Agricultural production was planned in the same fashion. The land was to be collectivized, and farms would follow the industrial pattern. There were established both collective farms and state farms. The state farm was operated as an industrial farm, where the workers received wages for their work. They did not share in the ownership and profits of the farm. The collective farm, on the other hand, was a reorganization of old land estates into community projects. The farm workers would retain their own house, their furniture and household goods, and a garden plot. They could also keep a few chickens, a cow or two, and a limited number of other livestock and fowl. But the fields were collectivized, and the farmers worked on them together. They shared in the profits after fulfilling the quota on the Five Year Plan, and these profits were usually taken in produce.

The collectivization of agriculture was a very difficult task. It meant a reversal of the New Economic Plan, which the farmers had grown accustomed to. It also meant that the farmers had to turn over to the collectives the land, the cattle, the farm equipment, and all the wealth that they had accumulated since 1921 or earlier. This action of the government appeared to them as outright theft. Some places the collectivization process went rather smoothly. People accepted that they were still owners on a collective basis in the new arrangement. But the more wealthy land owners became enraged and fought to retain their property. These people became known as kulaks (fists) because of their fighting and resistance. In some places the fighting took on the proportions of rebellion, and government forces were required to put it down.

Kulaks, in many cases, burned their fields and killed their cattle rather than turning them over to collectives. This destruction of property caused the Soviet Government to declare war on the kulaks. Many people were killed, and the destruction of agricultural products brought about a famine in some of the best agricultural lands.

But by 1936 agriculture had been collectivized. The kulaks had been defeated, and collective farms were organized. During the collectivization process it was necessary to provide agricultural machines, equipment, and tools through Machine Tractor Stations. Since there was not enough machinery to provide all farms with an adequate amount, the Machine Tractor Stations rented this equipment to the farms on a rotation basis. These Stations also helped to supervise the farming activities as a means of increasing production.

In 1936 Stalin announced that socialism had been achieved in the Soviet Union, and he authorized the preparation of a new Constitution of the Soviet Union. The 1936 Constitution incorporated the principles of the Declaration of Rights and also the principles of socialism. It stands today, as amended, as the Constitution of the Soviet Union.

In 1937 Stalin continued to push for more production in both industry and agriculture. The third Five Year Plan was then to extend into the Second World War.

THE PURGES

Dissatisfaction in the Soviet Union extended from the farms into industry, the government, the army, and even into the Communist Party. The pace of Stalin's industrialization was considered by many to be too fast, and the collectivization seemed to many people to be unnecessary and wasteful. The reaction by the Commissar of Internal Affairs (the internal police) to put down the dissatisfaction, the opposition, and riots was too harsh. Rumors of secret arrests, mass murders, and mass exiles spread through the country. Violence broke out against the kulaks and against other disloyal persons, and these persons fought even harder.

In 1934 Sergei Kirov, a member of the Politburo, who had been the Liberator of the Caucasus and who was then Party leader of Leningrad, was assassinated. This assassination immediately intensified the suspicion, the dissatisfaction, and the government reaction. Stalin blamed this assassination on a conspiracy to overthrow the government. To prevent this overthrow he ordered a purge of the Communist Party and an attack on the conspirators.

The purges of the 1930's have been condemned throughout the world and in the Soviet Union itself during the de-Stalinization program of Khrushchev after 1956. Stories of mass murders, prison camps, secret arrests, and atrocities have been told by people who witnessed and who suffered the arrests and punishment. It was said that Stalin reacted only on suspicion and that many people died or suffered even though they were completely innocent. It was a time of horror.

During this time many of the military leaders, former officers of the Tsar's Army, were removed from office. Other leaders during the 1917 Revolution found that they too were removed from office, arrested, and punished. Court trials convicted many people and sentenced them to death.

The responsibility of this fight against conspiracy was given to the Commissar of Internal Affairs (NKVD), Nikolai Yezhov. He carried out his assignment with great vigor, even to excess. Finally, Stalin had him removed from office and subjected him to the same fate as his victims.

After the 1917 Communist Revolution the former allies of
Russia were slow to extend diplomatic recognition to the Soviet Union.
Antagonism against the Soviet Union and communism was strong
throughout the world. The intervention by England, France, United
States, and other powers did not help establish a favorable attitude in
the Soviet Union either.

The separate peace treaty with Germany was recognized by
Germany. This act did help establish some international legitimacy
to the Soviet Government. But the defeat of the Kaiser's army
brought about a new government in Germany. However, it was that
New German Government that extended the first hand of friendship to
the Soviet Union. In 1922 the two countries signed the Treaty of
Rapallo, which cancelled Russian debts to Germany and Soviet war
damages claims against Germany. This treaty was later followed by
trade agreements and declarations of neutrality if war started.

Great Britain was the first of Russia's former allies to recognize the Soviet Union. After the Labor Party won the British election
in 1924, the Prime Minister Ramsey MacDonald extended diplomatic
recognition to the Soviet Union. But this recognition was severed in
1927 due to a change in British Government and the activities of the
Communist International and of the British Communist Party.

The Soviet Union and China had already negotiated agreements
in 1923 for extending military aid to the Chinese Nationalists. But the
relationships with China were also unsteady. Chiang Kai-Shek established an anti-communist policy in China. This action caused friction
between him and the Soviet Union.

In 1929 the Soviet Union established again better foreign rela-
tions by signing disarmament agreements with Latvia, Poland,
Rumania, Estonia, Lithuania, Turkey, and Persia. Also in 1929
Great Britain resumed diplomatic relations with the Soviet Union.
But the best ally to the Soviet Union was still Germany.

The coming of Hitler to power in Germany in 1933, however,
substantially changed the role of the Soviet Union in world affairs. In
1933 and 1934 the Soviet Union established diplomatic relations with
the United States, Poland, France, Czechoslovakia, and Romania.
Also in 1934 the Soviet Union gained a permanent seat in the League
of Nations.

Maxim Litvinov became the Soviet delegate to the League of
Nations. His appeals for disarmament and his personal friendliness
greatly improved the image of the Soviet Union among other nations.

Of course, the threat from Nazi Germany also caused the Western Powers to look toward the Soviet Union as a potential ally.

As the Nazi Army moved into Austria and Czechoslovakia in 1937 and 1938 the position of the Soviet Union greatly fluctuated. The Soviet Union did not want to get involved in another war. The Soviet Army was not ready for conflict. The economy of the country also could be destroyed. In fact, the whole Soviet cause could be lost.

In 1939 Stalin felt compelled to establish a Non-Aggression Pact with Hitler. This pact was followed by the Soviet Union building a buffer zone along the western border. The areas annexed had formerly been in the Russian Empire--Latvia, Estonia, Lithuania, and Moldavia. Parts of Finland were also annexed to the Soviet Union.

THE SECOND WORLD WAR

In June, 1941, Hitler turned his forces against the Soviet Union in complete violation of the Non-Aggression Pact. Even though preparations and training had greatly increased the Red Army's ability to fight, the Nazi forces moved quickly across the plains of the western farmlands. A three-prong attack was aimed at Leningrad, Moscow, and Kiev with the greatest force initially directed toward Leningrad in hopes of taking the city quickly with blitzkrieg tactics.

Leningrad was subjected to attacks and to a blockade that lasted for two and a half years, but Leningrad never sumitted to Nazi control. Since the initial attacks failed, the Germans turned a greater force toward Moscow. But Moscow, too, under the leadership of General Georgi Zhukov, was defended.

Nazi attacks were more successful in the Ukraine. Forces were drawn from the Leningrad and Moscow battle zones for a greater push into the interior of the country in the south. Kiev fell in September, 1941, and the Germans fought on toward Khar'kov and later Stalingrad.

Soviet forces had rallied to the defense of their native land. The tactics used against Napoleon over a hundred years before were used again. Fields were burned and cattle were killed so that the Germans could not have food supplies from the land. Auxiliary forces were formed to help the Red Army both at the front and behind enemy lines. These forces were called Partisans, and they consisted primarily of young people, both young men and girls. The Partisans conducted espionage and sabotage against the Germans. They established radio contact with Red Army units and provided them information about deployment and movement of the Nazi forces. The deeds of these young people have been highly praised for their contribution to the war effort. Alexander Fadeyev later wrote the book, The Young Guards, about the hardships and the exploits of the Partisans.

Suffering was very acute during the war. Deaths reached staggering proportions. The story of the defense of Leningrad is almost beyond the belief of the possible endurance of man. Starvation and deprivation lasted for so long during the blockade that the people ate dogs, cats, wild birds, and anything that had food value. They even boiled leather goods, wall paper, and books to make soup. The starvation drove people to fight among themselves over even the smallest scrap of food. Most of the population of the city starved to death, but a meager existence remained possible because of blockade runners across the ice of Lake Lagoda.

Property damage throughout the whole western and southern parts of the Soviet Union was hard to calculate. Much of the industrial equipment and whole factories around Moscow were dismantled and moved to the Ural Mountains. Many people carried what they could on their back and walked a thousand miles to the east.

The turning point of the war took place at Stalingrad. The Germans had hoped to take Stalingrad and then to move south along the Volga River to take the oil fields of Baku. They struck with lightning force against Stalingrad in July, 1942. Stalingrad was an industrial and river port city. It stretched about twenty miles north and south along the western bank of the Volga River. The Nazi forces expected to take Stalingrad quickly. But the Russians fought back ferociously. For more than six months the fighting went back and forth. The Germans gained ground and buildings and then lost them to the Russians. The greatest fighting took place on a Mamayev hill which exchanged hands over and over again. But the Russian forces stood their ground and defended the city. Actually they had to fight. They could not retreat. They had no means of crossing the mile-wide Volga River, and they were backed up to its very banks.

By February, 1943, the Second Front in Europe was still more than a year away. The allies had sent some supplies through the ice-free port at Murmansk, and other aid was sent across Iran into Central Asia. But the victory at Stalingrad was a victory of the Red Army. The Nazi forces had extended their supply lines across the steppes of Russia and left themselves in a vulnerable position. General Zhukov was able to take Red Army Forces from Moscow, which had been secured, and cut through the German supply lines.

The persistent fighting at Stalingrad and the successful attacks of
General Zhukov turned the battle in favor of the Soviet Union. The
Nazi Forces had to retreat.

Today in Volgograd (formerly Stalingrad) there stand memorials to that heroic battle and victorious achievement. This action
was the beginning of the turning point of the whole war not only for
the Soviet Union but also for the West. In Volgograd there is now an
obelisk and an eternal flame to honor the unknown soldier of the Battle
of Stalingrad. Also in the city there has been a perforated shell of a
building, which used to be a mill. This building was left as it was
after the battle to remind people of the horrors of war. It was one of
the very few buildings which remained in Russian hands during the
entire battle and was not completely flattened. In 1973 this old mill
was being replaced by a new war memorial museum to add even more
respect to those people who fought and died there. But the greatest
memorial to the Stalingrad Battle is on Mamayev Hill, the highest
point in Volgograd. This hill had changed hands many times during
the battle, and for years afterwards the soil there was replete with
fragments of human bones. Now on this hill stands probably the tal-
lest statue in the world, a large retunda, a reflection pool, and a
variety of monuments and stonework, which tell the history of this
heroic victory and commemorate those who died. This whole memorial complex is like a holy shrine, to which pilgrims come to pay
their devotion.

After the Battle of Stalingrad there was one more major
attempt of the Germans to advance. A fierce tank battle took place at
Kursk to turn the stem of the German retreat. But this battle was
the final blow to the Germans when the Russians were again victorious.
Historians are now saying that this battle at Kursk was even more
decisive than the one at Volgograd in defeating the Germans. But the
result is the same. The Soviet Army was driving the invaders back.

The retreat of the Germans from the territory of the Soviet
Union took still another year. The Red Army continued fighting to
drive them back to Berlin. Kiev was re-taken in December, 1943,
and in December, 1944, all of the Soviet Union was free from Nazi
forces. But the Soviet soldiers did not stop there. They drove on
under the command of General Zhukov to liberate Eastern Europe
from Nazi domination. Berlin fell in April, 1945, and the Red Army
met its allies from the West. The war was over.

The impact of the war was a terrible loss to the Soviet Union. Estimates of between seven and thirty million people had lost their lives, and several million more were wounded. Almost everyone had lost a close relative and several friends in the war. The losses in life, property, and time were an appalling setback to every aspect of civilization.

The general mood in the country as a whole was for peace and isolation from international affairs. The concept of socialism in one country was reasserted, and the foreign policy was one of building greater defenses and establishing buffer zones along the borders of the Soviet Union. Friendly Liberated areas were assisted in establishing socialist democracies which were friendly to the Soviet Union.

In the Soviet Union itself the theme was "socialist realism." The works of great men in the 1930's were acknowledged. These men were recognized as examples of "socialist realism," which means relating all aspects of life to the Materialistic outlook of communist Philosophy.

Maxim Gorky was honored for his literary works, especially The Lower Depths, which portrays the oppressed lot of the exploited poor. It carries the theme of economic determinism and shows the degraded life of those who have been deprived of material goods.

Konstantin Tsiolkovskiy was praised for his construction of a metallic dirigible and his contribution to aviation. His discoveries were recognized also for their value to further the study of inter-planetary flights.

Socialist realism was personified in a man named Ivan Michurin. He applied this approach to horticulture. By changing the environment and selecting the more hardy fruits, vegetables, grains, and flowers, he was able to produce new strains which were resistant to frost and which were much more productive as to size and quantity. The city Kozlov was renamed Michurinsk in his honor.

Rather than giving credit to the common people or even the Communist Party, though, Stalin attributed all successes, even the war victory, to his personal leadership. A period of autocracy, which has been called the "Deification of Stalin" or later referred to as the "cult of the personality," held sway for several years. When contro-versies arose in literature, mathematics, and biology among the leading men in those fields, Stalin stepped in with an official statement which resolved those differences. The most sensational was the pol-icies of Trofim Lysenko, which were supposed to revolutionize biology. Stalin sided in with Lysenko against other Soviet biologists and also

Western biologists to support the concept that environment of the parents rather than heredity determines the characteristics of the offspring of animals. Lysenko went on to contend that acquired characteristics would be passed on from one generation to the next. Stalin saw the practical value of these theories and awarded Lysenko by naming him Minister of Agriculture.

The autocratic role of Stalin also caused the demotion, imprisonment, and execution of people who opposed him. This effect was felt both within the Soviet Union and in the Soviet foreign affairs. One of the persons demoted was General Georgi Zhukov, the defender of Moscow, the leader of reinforcements to Stalingrad, and the hero at the fall of Berlin. In foreign affairs the policy of isolation and noncooperation intensified hostilities between the Soviet Union and the West, which Winston Churchill called "The Cold War."

Opposition to Stalin became very strong throughout the world and in the Soviet Union. The first successful resistance came from Tito's Yugoslavia in 1948 after Tito had refused to be intimidated by Stalin and refused to participate in the Soviet-sponsored Cominform. Tito was alienated by the Soviet leadership of the international communist movement. He refused to let Soviet advisors come into Yugoslavia and broke off trade agreements with the Soviet Union.

Andrei Zhdanov, who was a member of the Politburo and the Party Boss of Leningrad, became the leader of the newly formed Cominform (Communist Information Bureau). He advocated closer cooperation with the Eastern European countries and plotted against Stalin for the organization of an Eastern European Republic, which included Leningrad and the Eastern European countries. But Zhdanov died suddenly in July, 1948, and a suppression in Leningrad followed. "The Leningrad Affair" caused major shakeups in the top party organization and in the Leningrad city government. Stalin removed from power those persons who had been loyal to Zhdanov and replaced them with his own supporters.

Since before the Second World War the Communist Party of the Soviet Union had not held a party conference, which is supposed to be held every three or four years. It had been thirteen years before the Nineteenth Party Congress was called for October, 1952. Stalin was already seriously ill, and he had named his successor, Georgi Malenkov, to direct the conference.

Suspicion and fear began more and more to motivate the actions of Stalin. The opposition to his autocratic methods had grown stronger, but people dared not oppose him openly. Sensing this opposition Stalin staged a program against cosmopolitanism. This program was directed against all groups of people with international connections. Isolationism had reached its peak.

The culmination of the program against cosmopolitanism came in January, 1953, with the announcement of the "Doctor's Plot" to kill Stalin. Some of these doctors were Jews, and Stalin blamed them for trying to kill him medically. These doctors were arrested and also charged with having killed Zhdanov. But Stalin grew weaker and died in March, 1953.

THE RISE AND FALL OF KHRUSHCHEV

Georgi Malenkov became the new leader of the Soviet Government, but his power was shared with the Minister of Foreign Affairs, Vyacheslav Molotov, and the Minister of Internal Affairs, Lavrenti Beria. One man rule was replaced by a collective leadership. The position of General Secretary of the Communist Party was given to a Politburo member from the Ukraine, Nikita Khrushchev.

Malenkov was an administrator rather than a political leader. Both Molotov and Beria tried to gain control of the government and to direct the activities of Malenkov. Beria used his position with the police and the military to try to establish a military dictatorship, but his plot was stopped before it even started. Beria was arrested and shot. His "police organization" was divided into a Ministry of Internal Affairs and a Committee of State Security in an attempt to prevent a reoccurrence and to strenghten the Communist Party leadership.

Soon a conflict arose between Malenkov and Khrushchev. Malenkov proposed changes in industrial production to allow for increases in consumer goods and for increased military preparations. Khrushchev reacted to the drastic decrease in grain production of 1953 and advocated a crash program to develop the virgin lands of Northern Kazakhstan for grain production. Malenkov, having come to power from the Moscow Oblast Committee, relied on the Moscow industrialists to support his program. Khrushchev, who had been the First Secretary of the Ukrainian Party organization, relied on the agricultural interests of the country for his support. In 1955 Nikolai Bulganin replaced Malenkov as Chairman of the Council of Ministers, and this action was a major step in Khrushchev gaining the leadership role. Khrushchev, in his position as General Secretary of the Party, also effected a major shake-up in the party membership in order to strengthen his support.

In February of 1956 the Twentieth Party Congress convened in Moscow. Bulganin was still the head of the government, but the congress was directed by Nikita S. Khrushchev. He gave a major address, which was closed to the public, concerning the "cult of personality." In his address Khrushchev enumerated the mistakes of Stalin during the years of the collectivization of agriculture, the purges of the 1930's, and the Second World War. Khrushchev severely criticized the one-man-rule of Stalin. He also followed this denunciation with major changes in both domestic and foreign policy.

Khrushchev was beginning to assert his leadership role and gradually to replace Bulganin. His criticism of Stalin was also an indirect criticism of Molotov, Kaganovich, Shepilov, and other Moscow supporters of Stalin and Malenkov.

Khrushchev's approach has been called "The Thaw." He advocated "peaceful co-existence" with foreign powers, including capitalist countries. His emphasis on agriculture and increased foreign trade reflected the economic interests of his Kiev and Leningrad supporters. Khrushchev also changed the emphasis on heavy industry by reducing it in favor of light industry and consumer goods. Also in opposition to the Moscow industrialists was his reorganization of the ministries in the Council of Ministers which, in effect, removed Stalinists and replaced them with men from his own faction.

The news of the de-Stalinization campaign spread rapidly throughout the world, and it was interpreted as a relaxation of Soviet controls in Eastern Europe. The first response was the election of Wladyslaw Gomulka, who had been demoted and arrested during Stalin's time, as the First Secretary of the Communist Party in Poland. This election was accompanied with demands by the young people for more freedom.

The relaxed atmosphere in Poland was not challenged by Soviet authorities. In October, 1956, attempts for liberalization in Hungary at first followed the pattern of Poland, but these attempts were supported by people who wanted not only to reform the society but to overthrow the government. The Soviet Government looked with alarm at this uprising and felt compelled to intervene. But there was the pressure of world opinion and the threat of reaction by Western Powers.

At the same time the Western Powers became involved in the Suez Crisis. Fighting between the United Arab Republic and Israel and the nationalization of the Suez Canal by the U.A.R. conflicted with the interests of England and France. Upon the refusal of American forces to cooperate in a venture against the Arabs, England and France went ahead and attacked the canal area.

The action at the Suez Canal was the signal for Soviet Forces to move into Hungary to put down the rebellion. If England and

France could use military force to further their interests, they could not object to the Soviet Union using force to stabilize the Hungarian Government.

Khrushchev's actions and the reactions in Eastern Europe disturbed some of the leaders of Party Presidium (Politburo) and caused them to try to oust him. When Khrushchev was in Leningrad in June, 1957, a secret meeting of the Party Presidium voted against Khrushchev. But Khrushchev returned immediately to Moscow, convened a meeting of the Party Central Committee, and expelled Malenkov, Molotov, Kaganovich, and Shepilov from the Party Presidium. They were each demoted and assigned to other work. Malenkov was assigned to head a power station in the Soviet East.

On October 4, 1957 the Soviet Union surprised the world by launching the first successful artificial satellite, Sputnik I, which circled the earth for twenty-one days. This event was the beginning of a series of successful space explorations. In November, 1957, Sputnik II carried a live dog, Laika, into space, and in January, 1959, the Soviet Union sent the first rocket to by-pass the moon. The Soviet Union lead the world in space exploration.

In September, 1958, Khrushchev was formally announced as the First Secretary of the Communist Party and the Chairman of the Council of Ministers of the Soviet Union. These positions gave him the top power in both the Communist Party and in the Soviet Government. He now held the same positions, if not the same power, which Stalin had.

Since the Second World War the Five Year Plans had been directed toward the reconstruction of war-damaged areas and toward the establishment of a strong military defense. The fourth plan lasted from 1946 to the end of 1950, and the fifth one continued into 1955. The sixth plan (1956-1960) was now able to aim toward increased production, but the emphasis was still on military goods.

Khrushchev started to change the direction of the economic production as he consolidated his position in power. He tried to increase production by reducing the work day from eight to seven hours and by increasing wages so as to encourage workers to produce as much or more during the shorter day. He also established regional economic councils for encouraging better coordination between industries on the local level. He then pledged to give a much greater emphasis to the production of consumer goods.

In January, 1959, Khrushchev called the Twenty-First Party Congress and announced a new program. He terminated the sixth Five Year Plan and replaced it with a Seven Year Plan to last through 1965. Khrushchev re-emphasized the mistakes of Stalin, many of which still persisted in government administration. The new plan was to mark a substantial change in the economy by increased industrial production and by a much greater emphasis on housing and consumer goods. He wanted to expand the labor forces by increasing the recruitment of young people into industry. He also advocated the development of Siberia and the Soviet Far East. Khrushchev envisioned catching up with the United States in industrial production by 1970 through the extensive use of man power and natural resources.

Reforms were announced in all aspects of Soviet life. Reorganization spread through the government administration for putting greater responsibility on local leaders and work crews for increased production. He abolished many administrative controls on the economy and gave greater authority to local committees and public organizations of the workers themselves. In addition, the courts were required to reduce the penalties for minor crimes, and prisoners were pardoned and released.

At the Twenty-First Party Congress Khrushchev also announced changes in foreign policy. He initiated peace petitions, which were later circulated through the whole society and abroad. He talked of "peaceful co-existence" with the capitalist world and challenged the West to an economic competition. He wanted to replace the "Cold War" with an economic race, which could relax international tensions and at the same time inspire the Soviet citizens to greater production. "Peaceful Co-existance" and "Peace and Friendship" became slogans that appeared everywhere in public places. Khrushchev left the congress with a feeling that he could reform the whole society. He kept this same spirit as he toured the Soviet Union making speeches.

Economic reforms included a re-evaluation of Soviet currency to make it more on par with other nations and to increase the purchasing power of Soviet citizens. These reforms were accompanied by a substantial increase in foreign trade. In addition, tourism was greatly expanded. The few foreign tourists, who had been allowed into the Soviet Union since 1956, became large crowds. The isolation period of Stalin had ended. Some Soviet citizens were also allowed to travel abroad.

In September, 1959, Nikita Khrushchev travelled to the United States, addressed the United Nations, toured America, and had private talks with President Eisenhower. He also visited the Roswell Garst Farm in Iowa and learned about the "corn and hog cycle" in American agriculture. Khrushchev left the United Sates with the confidence of incorporating American technology and practices into Soviet agriculture and of maintaining peaceful relations with the United States. Both he and President Eisenhower spoke of the "Spirit of Camp David," which was the spirit of peace and friendship.

Further space exploration continued through 1959. In September of that year the Soviet Lunik II hit the moon, and in October Lunik III circled the moon and took pictures of the opposite side. Even though the United States was also exploring space by this time, these two Soviet achievements were mankind's firsts.

A Summit Conference for world leaders was scheduled for May, 1960. Khrushchev talked of expanding the "Spirit of Camp David" to other countries and of improving relationships with the United States. He also continued to inspire his own people in the Soviet Union to catch up and surpass the United States production.

But the Summit Conference failed. A few days before the conference an American U-2 spy plane was shot down near Sverdlovsk in the Ural Mountains. The pilot was captured and interrogated. This plane had not been the first to fly over Soviet territory, but it was the first one to be captured by the Soviet Government. Accusations came from the United States stating that the Soviet Union purposely used this time to shoot down an unarmed reconnaisance plane in order to break up the conference. The Soviet Union blamed the United States for talking peace at Camp David and conducting military actions over Soviet territory. This event not only ruined the conferences; it also weakened Khrushchev's position for advocating peace with the United States. General Rodion Malinovsky, the Soviet Minister of Defense, accompanied Khrushchev very closely at the Geneva Conference. Khrushchev appeared to be under guard. He gave a very strong verbal attack against the United States.

Milhail Suslov, who had gained a leadership position in the Moscow faction of the Party Presidium (Politburo) threatened Khrushchev's position. Several of Khrushchev's appointees to government and party positions were removed from office. But Khrushchev stayed in power and maintained control.

The fall of 1960 and the spring of 1961 were the beginning of a real push in space exploration and of the reaping of great successes. A test probe was sent to by-pass Venus in February, 1961. In April, 1961, Yuri A. Gagarin became the first man to ride into space in an artificial satellite. This event was followed by Gherman Titov in August, 1961. Since the American spaceships were accomplishing similar feats with John Glenn in February, 1962, and Scott Carpenter in May, the Soviet Union sent Andrian Nikolayev and

Pavel Popovich into space in August in separate spacecrafts. The space race with the United States was in full swing.

The Twenty Second Party Congress was convened in October 1961, for the outlining of a program for building communism in the Soviet Union. It went much further in reforming the economy and improving living conditions. It outlined three steps for building communism: (a) the creation of a material-technical base, (b) the moulding of communist social relationships, and (c) the creation of a new Soviet man through education. Socialist competition was again stressed to increase production so that the Soviet Union could catch up and surpass the United States. Khrushchev announced that the people at the congress would see the establishment of communism. He declared an end to the Dictatorship of the Proletariat. Its role had been fulfilled. The new society would be an All-People's Government in which everyone has the opportunity to participate in government leadership positions on a rotation basis. He said that at each election at least one-third of the representatives in the soviets will be new members. In addition, Khrushchev announced the increased production of consumer goods. He inspired the Soviet citizens to "build communism."

The Twenty Second Party Conference marked the peak of Khrushchev's program both for changing the mistakes of the past and for forging on to a new era. The process of de-Stalinization eliminated all references to Stalin. His body was moved from the Lenin Mausoleum and buried near the Kremlin wall. Statues of Stalin, which had been in practically every city, were by this time replaced with statues of Lenin. Cities which bore the name of Stalin were renamed. Stalingrad became Volgograd, Stalino - Donetsk, and Stalinabad - Dushanbe. Stalin's name was practically eliminated from school textbooks. Soviet citizens were to forget a large share of their past and to look forward to a life under communism.

International relations did not improve, however, and Khrushchev's position was challenged again by the more conservative members of the Party Presidium. His talking was louder than his achievements. He tended to exaggerate and to live recklessly.

American threats against Cuba caused Soviet anxiety over the new ally in the Western Hemisphere. Raids by Cuban exiles from American bases caused the Cubans to expect an attack by the United States. In response to a Cuban request the Soviet Union provided arms and missiles to Cuba. What the Soviet Government termed defensive the United States called offensive. There developed a confrontation, which became known as "The Missile Crisis." In

October, 1962, use was made of the "hot line," a direct teletype line between the United States and the Soviet Union for preventing an accidental war. Nikita Khrushchev and President John Kennedy used this line to make agreements to avoid war. Apparently these secret agreements were a pledge by the United States not to attack Cuba in exchange for a Soviet withdrawal of the missiles from Cuba. The threat subsided, and a third world war was prevented.

Mikhail Suslov immediately attacked Khrushchev's leadership, and some of Khrushchev's close associates in top positions were replaced. But Suslov also met with new difficulties. He had tried to improve relations with the Chinese People's Republic. Mao Tse Tung had been attacking the new Soviet policies and calling them revisionism. But the conflict became more serious than verbal attacks. In 1963 Suslov went to China to patch up the differences. But his mission failed. The rift split even wider. When Suslov came home he became ill, and his personal threat to Khrushchev weakened.

As differences with China grew worse the relationship with the United States began to improve. Continued efforts to prevent a nuclear war resulted in a multi-lateral Nuclear Test Ban Treaty, which was signed in Moscow in 1963 by delegates of the Soviet Union, United States, and Great Britain with the United States and the Soviet Union as the main sponsors. This agreement prohibited the testing of nuclear weapons in the atmosphere. By this time both the United States and the Soviet Union had conducted several series of such tests. The Soviet Union had developed the atomic bomb in 1949 and the hydrogen bomb in 1953. Both nations had large stockpiles of nuclear weapons. This agreement marked a recognition by both countries that either one had the potential to wage a nuclear war and that great efforts must be made to prevent it.

But Khrushchev did not regain a strong control over the Communist Party in the Soviet Union. People grew tired of Khrushchev's blundering and the rivalry between factions in the Kremlin. While Khrushchev was vacationing at the Black Sea in October, 1964, the Party Presidium (Politburo) called a special meeting of the Central Committee. A unanimous decision of the Central Committee removed Khrushchev from power. He was officially retired, and two of his own appointees became the new leaders. Leonid Brezhnev became First Secretary of the Communist Party, and Alexei Kosygin became the Chairman of the Council of Ministers.

An era of rapid change had been checked but not stopped. Khrushchev was criticized not for his aims but for his boasting,

his crude talking, and his unrealistic planning. The events of the
U-2 flights of 1960, the Cuban Crisis in 1962, and the rift with
China all pointed to failures in his foreign policy, but the decline
in economic production, particularly in agriculture, was probably
the final blow. The shortage of food in 1964 caused not only long
lines at the food stores but also public protest. In Novocherkassk
and in Tbilisi there were food riots. Even though these riots were
put down quickly, they undoubtedly were a major cause for Khrushchev's removal.

In 1963 and 1964 the exploration of space had continued.
Cosmonauts included the first woman to go into space, Valentina
Tereshkova, who was launched into space in June, 1963. Then in
October, 1964, Voskhod I carried the heaviest load, almost six
tons, including three cosmonauts in one space ship.

In spite of the failures, the Khrushchev era did bring about
great improvements in the living conditions in the Soviet Union,
spectacular achievements in space, improved relations with the
Western World, and a recognition of the threat from China. Khrushchev must be commended for his attempts to reduce tensions both
within the Soviet Union and abroad. The relaxation of censorship,
the opening of the borders to foreign travel, and the slogan for
"peaceful coexistence" marked a significant change for the better
in Soviet policy.

THE 50TH ANNIVERSARY

Both the domestic and foreign policies became more stable
under Brezhnev and Kosygin. Major problems and even crises did
occur, but their solutions were less sensational and more realistic. They recognized that catching up and surpassing the United
States could not happen within a few years. But they did not cut
back an effort for building communism.

An attempt to improve relations with China in November,
1964, brought the Chinese Premier, Chou En Lai, to Moscow for
consultations. However, the talks were unsuccessful, and relations with China continued to deteriorate.

The space effort continued to produce outstanding results.
Voskhod II in March 1965, marked the first time a man, Alexei
Leonov, walked in space. The ability to leave the space ship and
to re-enter while out in space was a great step toward the landing
men on the moon or other planets. In February, 1966, Luna IX
furthered this progress by providing the first soft landing on the

moon.

In April of 1966 the Twenty Third Party Congress convened, and the formulated policies of Brezhnev and Kosygin were announced. These policies were incorporated into a new Five Year Plan for 1966 through 1970. They included a proposed 40% increase in the national income, a 50% increase in industrial income, and a 25% increase in agricultural income. The emphasis was on the increased production of consumer goods, including automobiles, television sets, washing machines, and refrigerators. Re-adjustments were made in the wholesale prices to increase the incentives for greater production. Retail prices were lowered, and wages were increased. Better living conditions were assured. The housing shortage had been alleviated. Now a new campaign to supply higher quality housing could replace the crash drive for quantity.

The plan of Professor Yevsei Libernam of Khar'kov University was adopted in major factories. Profit-sharing was established between the regional councils and the factories and their work crews. Bonuses were set up on the basis of goods sold rather than on goods produced so that the production was keyed to consumer needs. Fashions and styles in clothing became popular. There was a noticeable change in the whole orientation of consumer goods. Shortages had almost completely disappeared.

These policies were also introduced into agriculture. Socialist competition was adopted on the farms, and the workers received bonuses for increased production.

Increased production in both industry and agriculture was brought about by continuing the local policy-making authority, but coordination of these policies was also strengthened by increased central controls and enforcement.

There was no fundamental change in the teachings of Marxism-Leninism, but there were some efforts to tone down Khrushchev's policies. These changes were for building a strong communist society. A major reduction of the de-Stalinization campaign was noticed. Stalin was given credit for industrializing the country and for winning the war, but he was not restored to full status. No names of cities were changed back, and no new statues were constructed, but neither was the campaign inflamed again. The names of the First Secretary of the Communist Party and the Party Presidium were changed back to the General Secretary of the Communist Party and the Politburo, respectively. There was also an increased effort to

re-establish "socialist realism" in the literature and arts.
The criticism of artistic expression became stronger as
the result of two writers, Andrei Sinyavsky and Yuli Daniel, who
had anti-Soviet literature published abroad under pseudonyms.
These two writers were arrested and sent to correctional labor
camps for their subversive activities.

But society remained open for more criticism within the
guidelines of social order. Dissent was controlled rather than
prohibited. The society was to regulate itself within prescribed
guidelines. "Socialist realism" was still considered to be that
basic guideline.

Relationships with the West continued to improve. Foreign
tourists came in even larger numbers. Exchange of students,
delegates to conferences, and artistic performers also increased.
Scientific reports and other scholarly publications were both sent
abroad and received from other nations. Foreign trade continued
to increase approximately 10% per year from 1965 through 1968.

The first bi-lateral treaty between the Soviet Union and
the United States was signed in March, 1967, to provide consulates in addition to the embassies in each other's countries.

In June, 1967, Premier Alexei Kosygin travelled to
America to address the United Nations General Assembly on the
Arab-Israeli conflict. He also met with President Lyndon Johnson
at Glassboro, New Jersey for two days in June. They discussed
the Arab-Israeli conflict, the Vietnam War, and nuclear weapons.
These discussions led to other agreements between the Soviet
Union and the United States. In 1968 both countries agreed at
the negotiations at the Committee on Disarmament in Geneva,
Switzerland to limit the spread of nuclear weapons. Further
discussions continued on means of limiting the construction of
antiballistic missiles and of restricting the use of nuclear weapons
on the ocean floor.

In March, 1967, the Soviet Union opened its Northern Sea
Route through the Arctic Ocean along the northern boundaries of
the Soviet Union to all nations. Then in 1968 a mutual agreement
with the United States provided for direct flights of Soviet and
American jet planes between Moscow and New York.

At the time of the Fiftieth Anniversary in 1967 Brezhnev
and Kosygin were still feeling their way cautiously. The deteriorating relationship with China and the improving relationship
with the United States were a new problem of knowing how far the
Soviet Union could go in these directions. The extent of personal
freedom and regulating restrictions also presented a problem of

165

maintaining a balance. Reforms in industry and agriculture which included both local autonomy and central controls were another dilemma for the Soviet leaders. They wanted to keep building and progressing, but at the same time they wanted to preserve the structure and system which had been built over a period of fifty years.

The Fiftieth Anniversary marked a time of great achievement. The Soviet Union had come from a backward, predominately agricultural, and undeveloped country to an advanced, highly industrialized, and powerful nation. Illiteracy and poverty had been replaced with a near 100% literacy and full employment. Not only did everyone attend school and go on to productive employment, but the society had become a top leader in education, science, and culture. In 1957 the Soviet Union had opened the way to the exploration of space and had continued to lead and produce many firsts in this exploration. The Soviet Union had also attained a military defense capability on par with or superior to any other military power in the world. At the same time the Soviet people were as happy, healthy, and dedicated to social improvement as any people on earth.

The future looked brighter than ever before. The Revolution had fully succeeded, socialism had been achieved, a war had been fought and won, serious mistakes had been corrected, the society was inspired with enthusiasm, and all the citizens were well on their way to build a new communist world.

The celebration for this achievement was going on all year with its culmination on November 7, 1967. All across the Soviet Union, and especially in Moscow, the victory was celebrated with parades, singing, dancing, cheering crowds, posters and streamers, balloons, and fireworks.

The non-Communist world along with the allies of the Soviet Union gave a special recognition to this occasion. Journals throughout the world carried pictures and stories. Public meetings and scholarly conferences discussed the pros and cons of the Soviet achievement, which could no longer be referred to as an experiment.

But the hands of the clock moved on. The society and its leaders were faced again, similar to those who succeeded in taking the Winter Palace in 1917, with the problems of carrying on. This success did not imply rest and relaxation.

Trouble with China persisted. In the Middle East a war had taken place again between the Arabs and the Israelis in the summer of 1967, and tension and skirmishes still continued. The prolonged war in Vietnam, which was a drain on the Soviet economy for aiding the revolutionaries, went on and on. The situation in Eastern Europe was also deteriorating.

Dissent within the Soviet Union continued among writers and artists. Protests and petitions against the arrest and conviction of Sinyavsky and Daniel became more numerous. Other writers continued to write anti-Soviet literature. In 1968 Yuri Galanskov and Alex Ginsburg were arrested and sentenced to terms in correctional labor camps. These arrests were followed by even more protests.

But not all critical writings were considered subversive. Vladimir Dudintsev wrote in 1956 a book, entitled "Not by Bread Alone", in which he criticized socialist realism as not the only means of expression. Alexander Solzhenitsyn in 1962 wrote the book, "One Day in the Life of Ivan Denisovich", which exposed the horrors of Stalin's prison camps. In addition, the poet, Evgeny Yevtushenko, was able in the middle 1960's to recite his controversial poetry to tremendous crowds in the Soviet Union.

In August, 1968, major changes were taking place in Eastern Europe. Reforms in Czechoslovakia were threatening the socialist political structure. These events were interpreted by the Soviet Government as a result of West German influence in the internal affairs of Czechoslovakia. This occurrence also posed a threat to the Soviet Union. Good relations between the Soviet Union and the Czechoslovak Government were considered necessary for the defense of the Soviet Union against a possible re-birth of German Naziism. Czechoslovakia served as a buffer from a military point of view and as a supplier of manufactured goods from an economic point of view. It was considered to be in the Soviet best interest to intervene and to prevent the changes from taking place in Czechoslovakia. Even at the risk of alienating other communist nations and of inciting the American sponsored North Atlantic Treaty forces, the Soviet Union used military force to restore order to Czechoslovakia. Even though little blood was shed in this action, the verbal response to the Soviet Union mostly condemned this action. But the Soviet Army units and the units of other Warsaw Pact nations invaded and occupied the territory of Czechoslovakia. The leadership of Czechoslovakia was shuffled, and a group more friendly to the Soviet Union was installed as the new government.

Protests against the arrest of the writers were increased by adding the protest against the Czechoslovakian invasion. One of these protestors was Pavel Litvinov, the grandson of Maxim Litvinov (the Soviet delegate to the League of Nations in the 1930's).

Pavel Litvinov publicly criticized the Soviet involvement in Czechoslovakia. He was also accompanied by the wife of Yuli Daniel. The arrest of these two people tended to prevent further public protests.

In 1968 the Soviet space efforts decreased but did not discontinue. But in 1969 there was a new emphasis placed on the space program. In January, 1969 Vladimir Shatalov, was sent into orbit around the earth to gain data in preparation for establishing earth-orbiting space stations for inter-planetary space travel. Also in January there was a link-up of Soyuz IV and Soyuz V in space and the transfer of two spacemen, Yevgeny Khrunov and Alexei Yeliseyev, from one space craft to the other. The two men also stayed in space for more than an hour to show the possibility of rescuing people in space. These events were televized both in the Soviet Union and abroad. In May, 1969, two spacecraft were landed on the planet Venus and relayed information back to the earth. The Soviet Union had transferred interest from the moon to other planets, but the Venus probes revealed that human life is not possible on Venus because of the very high heat and the lack of oxygen.

In June, 1969, a Communist Summit Conference was held in Moscow, and representatives of 71 Communist Parties attended. The Chinese Communist Party and its allies and the independent Yugoslav Communist Party did not attend. The purpose of the conference was to unify the communist movement in its opposition against imperialism. Even though there had been an agreement not to attack other Communist Parties, a verbal attack against the Soviet Union by the Chinese News Agency caused Brezhnev to reply. He quoted the Chinese attack as saying that China advocated a nuclear war against the Soviet Union to destroy it. Brezhnev continued to deliver a very strong blast against China. The major emphasis of the conference then turned to reprimand the Chinese Communist Party. The rest of the conference dealt with the problem of unity among the Communist Parties and the problem of relative independence among them. Some opposition to the Russian intervention in Czechoslovakia was expressed by the Rumanian delegates. The conference concluded by calling for a new and bigger conference against imperialism. The new conference would include all anti-imperialist forces, including non-communists.

The differences between the Soviet Union and China became border disputes in the Far East, not far from Vladivostok, and in Central Asia along the Sinkiang and Kazakh border. Military attacks in these regions were reported both by the Chinese and Soviet news agencies. It was claimed that raids from both sides killed civilians as well as military personnel. Both countries expressed great concern over the possible attack and invasion by the other.

The Soviet Government delivered a statement to the Chinese Embassy in Moscow suggesting talks in Moscow during the latter part of the summer of 1969. Until then talks were to proceed at Khabarovsk to reduce the fighting and to prepare for the Moscow talks.

Brezhnev and Kosygin continued to try to maintain a balance both in foreign affairs and in domestic policy. Relations with the United States had improved, but the Czechoslovakian interference had strained these new relations. The Chinese situation was becoming worse, but hopes for a settlement were continually professed. The living conditions within the Soviet Union were better than ever, but the dissent, even though temporarily quietened, was becoming more widespread among the scientists as well as among writers and artists. There was also evidence of discontent among the military officers. The Politburo appeared to be unified. Time was yet to tell whether the balancing acts of Brezhnev and Kosygin would be more beneficial to the Soviet Union than the Blustering charges of Khrushchev. But the country, as a whole, was stronger than ever before, and the Soviet people too were still working hard to build communism.

THE BREZHNEV ERA

During 1970 and 1971 the collective leadership of Brezhnev, Kosygin, and Podgorny gradually became a power supremacy by Leonid Brezhnev without any change in the positions of Kosygin and Podgorny. Kosygin remained the Chairman of the Council of Ministers, and Podgorny retained his position as President of the Supreme Soviet. Yet the power of Brezhnev was seen in his public appearances, policy changes, and the opposition by a minority group within the Politburo.

Evidence of Brezhnev's ascendancy came in the spring of 1971, when he seemed to dominate the public scene. Also at this time rumors of a change within the Kremlin spread due to reported illnesses of Kosygin, Podgorny, and Suslov. Further evidence came by way of criticism by Suslov, Brezhnev, and Mazurov of Brezhnev's and Kosygin's economic results for 1969. But officially the Kremlin denied any Politburo change.

Major policies changes took place in the summer of 1970. The 24th Party Congress of the Soviet Union was postponed to

March, 1971. The formulation of the 1971-1975 Five Year Plan was scheduled for ratification at that postponed time. Then in July, 1970, a new Labor Code was published, which improved pension rights and other benefits for workers.

The continued attack against dissidents by the Soviet Government and the placing a granite bust of Stalin at his grave site near the Kremlin Wall shed light on another aspect of Brezhnev's policies. On the 25th Anniversary of VE Day the Minister of the Armed Forces, Andrei Grechko, praised Stalin for his contributions in defending the Soviet Union against fascism.

An increase in the production of economic goods and the exchange of these products in foreign trade for bolstering the economy were also a part of Brezhnev's policies. In April, 1970, he spoke at Khar'kov for introducing substantial changes in the structure of industrial management. During the spring of 1970 the Soviet Union increased its purchases of flour, wheat, butter, rubber, copper, tin, cocoa, beef, and mutton from the foreign markets in exchange for Soviet diamonds, furs, nickle, and sugar. Prices paid by the government for agricultural products were also increased as an incentive for greater production.

The Soviet Union placed a greater effort toward the production of automobiles and trucks. The production of the Zhiguli automobiles at the Fiat Plant at Tol'yatti, near Kuibyshev on the Volga River, started in the fall of 1970. Negotiations with American firms to build a plant for assembling trucks also began in 1970, first with Ford Motor Company and in 1971 with General Motors.

New efforts in space exploration gave indications of yet another aspect of Brezhnev's policies. In September, 1970, Luna-16 made a soft landing on the moon, and two months later Luna-17 delivered to the moon Lunokhod-1, a vehicle for travelling and exploring the surface of the moon. Lunokhod-1 remained on the moon and relayed information by instruments back to the earth.

Another venture in space to place a laboratory space station in orbit around the earth was accomplished in April, 1971. This space station, Salute-1, which weighed more than 17 tons, was left to orbit in space, awaiting further construction. On June 6th Soyuz-11 with three men aboard was launched to unite with Salute-1. The joining together of these space craft increased the weight to more than 25 tons. Dobrovolsky, Volkov, and Patsaev stayed in space on this laboratory station longer than any men had remained in space - nearly 23 days. On June 30th they returned to earth, having accomplished their mission, but due to a freak accident in their decent, all three men were killed. A hero's ceremony was given to these men at the Kremlin, and their cremated remains were placed in the Kremlin Wall. Brezhnev went on to say, however, that their accomplishments would not be halted and that the exploration in space would continue.

The major event of the initiating of the Brezhnev era, however, was the 24th Party Congress and the ratification of the new Five Year Plan in March, 1971.

Brezhnev gave major policy speeches. It was apparent that he was in firm control of the Party apparatus. He stated that a US-USSR Non-Aggression Pact was being studied by the Soviet Union. He also recommended a 6-point plan for banning the use of nuclear, chemical, and bacteriological weapons. This plan proposed a world conference to consider disarmament and a move toward dissolving NATO and the Warsaw Pact and working for collective security.

On the second day of the 24th Party Congress Brezhnev spoke concerning the growth of the Communist Party of the Soviet Union. He stressed the doubling of party membership from 7 million to 14 million persons in the preceding 14 years. But the heart of his talk pertained to the relationship of democracy and party discipline within the party organizations. He criticized those party members who were not diligent in their work and told them that there would be an exchange of party cards to strengthen the party and to increase the activity and party discipline of party members. He inferred that only the diligent and active members would remain in the party.

Kosygin read the new Five Year Plan at the 24th Party Congress. The Plan was printed in Soviet newspapers in February and had been discussed widely since that time. Kosygin read the whole plan, incorporating a few minor changes, for discussion at the Congress. On the last day the Five Year Plan was again presented and ratified by the Congress.

The 1971-1975 Five Year Plan provided for an increase in the production of economic goods and an improvement in the living conditions of the Soviet citizens. The rates of increase and improvement varied, but power (electricity, oil, gas, and coal), and basic building materials (steel and cement) ranged from 25% to 50% increase over the 5 year period. Agricultural products were scheduled to increase in production from 10% to 20%. Average wages for workers were to increase about 20%, and the fund for social needs (education, medical care, etc.) would be increased about 40%, which reflected the expected increase in the national income.

Major changes in the Communist Party leadership did not take place at the 24th Party Congress. Four people were added to the Politburo membership but no one was removed, even though Pelshe was 72 and Suslov was 69 years old. Three of the new members, Victor Grishin, Dinmukhamed Kunayev, and Vladimir Shcherbitsky, were previously candidate members of the Politburo, and the fourth Feodor Kulakov, was a secretary of the Central Committee. Naming them to the membership of the Politburo probably strengthened Brezhnev's position, but no dramatic change in intra-party policies was apparent. Such a change could become apparent when members lose their positions from the Politburo, but for two years following the Congress no members lost their positions.

Brezhnev was no longer maintaining a balance between the conservatives and the liberals in the Kremlin leadership. He had taken positions on the major policies of the country. His position was more realistic for economic growth than that of Khrushchev, but Brezhnev still advocated rapid increases in production without claiming obviously impossible goals. He asserted himself as the leader of a major world power and maintained a strong position in face of China, Israel, and the United States, while advocating disarmament and collective security and while building up Soviet defense capabilities.

Differences with the Chinese People's Republic had been decreased by the agreement in April, 1970, for the withdrawing troops from their common border and for establishing a joint commission to survey and define the 4000 mile border. The problem of world leadership of the Communist movement had not been resolved, but attention was being directed toward Soviet and Chinese cooperation in the Vietnam War against the United States.

Tensions decreased in the Mediterranean area. The Soviet Union had built up its naval forces in the Mediterranean Sea as a part of its aid to the United Arab Republic against the threat from Israel. But after the death of President Nasser, the new president, Anwar Sadat, worked through the United Nations for the reduction of tensions in the Middle East. This action was followed by a 15-year friendship and cooperation treaty between the Soviet Union and the United Arab Republic.

Relations with the United States of America were primarily directed toward the conflicting policies in regard to the Vietnam War, which was declining in scope, but which was not being settled.

In the fall of 1971 both the Soviet Union and the United States sent top leaders to several countries to gain support in the face of a re-alignment of countries in the international chess game of power politics. Canadian Prime Minister Trudeau had come to the Soviet Union in the summer of 1971, and the Soviet Chairman of the Council of Ministers, Alexei Kosygin, repaid the visit to Canada in October of that year. Brezhnev visited Yugoslavia and greatly improved the relations between those two countries. And Podgorny went to North Vietnam to reaffirm the Soviet position of aid. The American President, Richard Nixon, announced his visit to the Chinese People's Republic. Then in February, 1972, President Nixon made that visit, but he followed it by coming to Moscow in May of that year.

The meeting between top Soviet leaders and President Nixon's delegation in Moscow resulted in marked changes in Soviet-American policies. The major accomplishment was the signing of the SALT (Strategic Arms Limitation Talks) agreement to limit nuclear arms. Agreements were also made on foreign trade, rules of the road for military ships and planes, and plans for joint ventures in scientific research and space exploration. These agreements were followed by a foreign trade agreement to purchase wheat, oats, corn and other grains from the United States and by agreements on the details of cooperation in scientific and technological areas in July, 1972.

Brezhnev advocated and worked for improvements in the living conditions of Soviet citizens. An increased production of consumer goods and higher wage scales were the bases of his domestic policies. Yet Brezhnev kept firm in regard to dissidence. He considered cosmopolitanism to be a social evil. Even though he announced the end of anti-semitism in December of 1969, he could not tolerate Zionism and an attempt to high-jack a plane to Israel. He showed though that his bringing dissident Jews to trial in the Soviet Union was for their illegal activity rather than for their race or religion. Other forms of dissidence in literature, petitions, and public disturbances met criticism and court sentences. Brezhnev re-asserted the policy of socialist realism in the arts and the need to maintain law and order in the society.

The problem of Soviet Jews continued to arise. Large numbers of Jews made requests to emigrate to Israel. It had long been contrary to Soviet policy for its citizens to emigrate, and these requests at first were refused. But both internal and international pressures influenced the Soviet Union to allow some of the Soviet Jews to go to Israel. By the end of 1971 about 14,000 Jews had emigrated to Israel from the Soviet Union, and in 1972 more than 30,000 more Jews joined this list. However, the Soviet Union resisted this emigration by placing a high fee for an exit visa. It was said that a person had to pay for his free education, if he did not remain and work in the Soviet Union. This meant that the better educated persons were in effect being refused an exit visa. But Soviet Jews, particularly those in the Georgian U.S.S.R., raised money by fasting and other sacrifices to help their friends to emigrate to Israel.

Space flights did continue in 1972 and 1973. Several satellites for meteorological purposes were launched in 1972. Then in January, 1973, another moon rover (Lunokhod 2) was placed on the moon by the Soviet space craft Luna 21. The moon rover remained on the moon for analyzing soil samples, measuring temperature changes, taking pictures, and returning data back to earth. Also the first of a new series of space craft, Molniya I, was launched February 4th for aiding in telephone and telegraph communications.

The 55th anniversary of the Communist Revolution on November 7th and the 50th anniversary of the Formation of the Soviet Union on December 27th were times of re-asserting the program for building communism and the fulfillment of the goals of the 24th Party Congress. But 1972 was a bad year for agriculture in the Soviet Union. The harvest for grains and potatoes was particularly bad. There was no rain in parts of the Russian Republic and of the Ukraine from the first of May until the first of September. This drought destroyed many of the crops in those regions. The lack of snow cover in January, 1973, caused damage to winter wheat by frost also. To counter these problems wheat was imported from America, and a crash program was set forth to increase meat production during the winter of 1972-1973.

A few changes took place in top leadership positions. A 49-year old man, Vladimir Dolgikh, who had been the director of a metallurgical combine at Norilsk in the Soviet Far East, replaced Vasili Mzhavandze, a 70-year old man, as a candidate to the Politburo in December, 1972. This action took place at a meeting of the Central Committee and was probably a routine change. But in February, 1973, the Minister of Agriculture, Vladimir Matskevich, was removed from his position and replaced by Politburo member, Dmitri Polyansky. This change was connected with the decline in agriculture production, for which Matskevich was being removed. But it was unclear what this change meant or could mean for Dmitri Polyansky, who had been a First Deputy of the Chairman of the Council of Ministers. These changes could point toward a further shake-up in Soviet leadership.

Relations with other countries improved in late 1972 and early 1973. The President of Chili, Salvador Alliende, came to Moscow for talks with Brezhnev in December, 1972. Brezhnev had just returned from talks he had with Yanos Kadar in Budapest, Hungary. Then in January the ministers of foreign affairs of Hungary, East Germany, Poland, Czechoslovakia, Bulgaria, and Rumania all came together to Moscow for talks with Brezhnev. But the greatest improvement in international relations came with the Cease-Fire in Vietnam on the 28th of January, 1973. The official signing of that agreement between the United States, North Vietnam, the National Liberation Front, and South Vietnam marked the way for continued improvement in better relations for the United States and the Soviet Union. This event was followed by a delegation from North Vietnam coming to Moscow, where they received promises for further aid and support.

But dissension in the Soviet Union continued, not only from the Jews but also from Latvians, Georgians, and Russians. In the Baltic Republics there were people who committed self-sacrifices by burning themselves to death to demonstrate their protest against the Soviet Government. At the Central Committee meeting in December, 1972, the Communist Party announced amnesty for good behavior to those prisoners who had short terms, to women and children, and to older people. But there was no let up in censorship and arrests of those who distributed propaganda against the Soviet Union. The restriction of the free flow of information continued to be a thorn in the side of the Soviet leadership. On Constitution Day, December 5, 1972, a group of people stood on Pushkin Square in Moscow with their hats in their hands to protest these restrictions. Underground newspapers (so-called Samizdat literature) continued to be passed from hand to hand.

While making preparations to make official visits to West Germany and the United States, Brezhnev consolidated his position as leader of the Soviet Union. In April, 1973, he removed Peotr Shelest and Gennady Voronov from the Politburo and named Andrei Gromyko, Minister of Foreign Affairs; Andrei Grechko, Minister of Defense; and Yuri Andropov, Head of the Committee of State Security, as members of the new Politburo. Having done this, he was ready to visit Chancellor Willy Brandt in West Germany in May, 1973, and President Richard Nixon in the United States in June. Both of these visits were marked by substantial trade agreements and a general improvement in the relations between these countries and the Soviet Union. Probably the highlight of these visits was the agreement with President Nixon to work together to prevent nuclear war, the next thing to a non-agression pact.

Brezhnev's position was neither a return to Stalinism nor an endorsement of Khrushchev's de-Stalinization program. He gave some credit to both Stalin and Khrushchev, but he embarked on his own program for building communism. Generally, his program was one of improved foreign relations but increased restrictions in internal affairs. He continued to stress the obligations of the society for building the new society and for maintaining party discipline.

Alekseyev, S. P. & Kartsov, V. G., Istoriya SSSR, Moscow:
 Gosudarstvennoye Uchebnoye Pedagogicheskoye Izdatel'stvo,
 1960, 159 p.

Clarkson, Jesse D., A History of Russia, New York: Random
 House, 1961, 857 p.

Ellison, Herbert J., History of Russia, New York: Holt, Rinehart
 & Winston, 1964, 644 p.

Florinsky, Michael T., Russia - A History and an Interpretation,
 (Vol. 2), New York: Macmillan Co., 1953, 629-1511 p.

Gunther, John, Inside Russia Today, New York: Pyramid Books,
 1962, 604 p.

Mazour, Anatole G., Russia - Tsarist and Communist, Princeton,
 New Jersey: D. Van Nostrand Co., Inc., 1962, 995 p.

Monakhova, N. D. et als., Putevoditel' po Volgogrady, Volgograd:
 Nizhne-Volzhskoye Knizhnoye Izdatelstvo, 1966, 165 p.

Mints, I. I. & Karev, D. S., Istoriya SSSR, Moscow: Gosudarstvennoye Uchebnoye Pedagogicheskoye Izdatel'stvo, 1962,
 336. p.

Pares, Bernard, A History of Russia, New York: Alfred A. Knopf,
 1966, 611 p.

Pravda, Moscow, 1967-1973.

St. Louis Post-Dispatch, St. Louis, Missouri: 1967-1973.

Salisbury, Harrison, The 900 Days: The Seige of Leningrad, New
 York: Harper & Row, 1969.

Shakhnazarov, G. Kh. et als., Obshchestvovedeniye, (4th ed.),
 Moscow, Izdatelstvo Politicheskoy Literatury, 1966, 384 p.

Vernadsky, George, A History of Russia, New Haven: Yale
 University Press, 1961, 512 p.

Walsh, Warren Bartlett, Russia and the Soviet Union, Ann Arbor:
 University of Michigan Press, 1958, 640 p.

Whiting, Kenneth, The Soviet Union Today, New York: Praeger,
 1966, 423 p.

THE SOVIET GOVERNMENT AND THE COMMUNIST PARTY

The basis of the Government of the Soviet Union is the soviet (council). During the time of the tsars local government was based on land councils in the farm villages and urban councils in the cities. These councils (soviets) retained this authority after the abdication of Tsar Nicholas II, and the national authority was assumed temporarily by the Duma, which became the Provisional Government after March, 1917. The rivalry between the soviets and the Provisional Government in the summer of 1917 caused the soviets to organize a national All-Russian Congress of Soviets. It met for the first time in June and the second time in November, just after the Revolution. Between June and November the slogan "All Power to the Soviets" was proclaimed to abolish the Provisional Government and to replace it with the All-Russian Congress of Soviets made up of representatives from the rural and urban soviets. When this slogan was realized in November, 1917, the second All-Russian Congress of Soviets met and formed a new government. This congress continued to meet periodically and direct the affairs of the government. At the tenth All-Russian Congress of Soviets session in December, 1922, it was proposed to unify the soviet republics into the Union of Soviet Socialist Republics. Henceforth, the congress was called the Congress of Soviets of the USSR until 1936, when it became known as the Supreme Soviet of the USSR with the adoption of the 1936 Constitution. It was from the organization of this system of soviets that the government became to be called the Union of Soviet Socialist Republics.

THE SUPREME SOVIET

The Supreme Soviet is the highest organ of state power in the Soviet Union. It is both a legislative and executive body. The Supreme Soviet consists of two chambers, the Soviet of Nationalities and the Soviet of the Union. The Soviet of Nationalities consists of representatives from the national or ethnic groups in the Soviet Union. Representatives number twenty-five from each Union Republic, five from each Autonomous Oblast, and one from each National Okrug. The Soviet of the Union is based on the population count. There is one representative from each 300,000 persons, and these representatives are elected by election districts. The election of both types of representatives is supervised by the local soviets. In 1970 there was a total of 1517 representatives in the Supreme Soviet, 750 of which are in the Soviet of Nationalities and 767 of which are in the Soviet of the Union.

Each chamber of the Supreme Soviet has several standing commissions and special committees. The standing commissions are the same in each chamber:

The Commission on Planning and Budget
The Commission on Industry, Transportation, and Communication
The Commission on Building and Industrial Building Materials
The Commission on Agriculture
The Commission on Health and Social Security
The Commission on Public Education, Science, and Culture
The Commission on Commerce and Public Services
The Commission on Legislative Proposals
The Commission on Foreign Affairs

Most of the legislative work is done in these standing commissions and special committees. The Supreme Soviet meets regularly only twice a year for about two weeks each session and occasionally in special sessions. Legislative proposals may be initiated by members of either chamber, but it requires a majority vote in both houses to pass the legislation. The proposals are submitted to the appropriate commission, coordinated through the Commission on Legislative Proposals, and presented for public discussion before convening the sessions of the Supreme Soviet. Controversial proposals are given wide distribution through the newspapers and through public discussions in social organizations so that the differences of opinion can be expressed before their adoption. In this manner the proposals are refined, and the representatives become aware of the public reaction. This process reduces the time necessary for the passage or defeat of the proposals during the legislative sessions. Since the issues have already been widely discussed, the votes during the sessions are usually a support or ratification of the previous work. This method enables the Supreme Soviet to finish its session within a two-week period.

Representatives also work in their regular vocations between sessions so that they can know the opinions of the people on these issues. The representatives come from many different occupations and positions. Many of them are not professional politicians. There are both men and women and both party members and non-party people. In 1970 more than two-thirds of the representatives were elected to the Supreme Soviet for the first time. More than 30% of them were women, and about 27% of the total were not members of the Communist Party. About one-third of the representatives were industrial workers, roughly 20% were from farms, and the others were mostly from professional positions, e.g. teachers, physicians, writers and artists, military personnel, scientists, trade union workers, and government workers. Eighteen and one-half percent of the elected deputies were young people under 30 years of age. More than half of the total number of representatives had received higher education, and approximately 18% had finished secondary schools.

The Supreme Soviet and each chamber elects its own officers and commission members. The Supreme Soviet in joint session also elects the members of the Presidium, which assumes the executive authority when the Supreme Soviet is not in session. It also names the members of the government administration and other officials. These officials include the Chairman of the Council of Ministers, who is the Premier of the Soviet Union, and all the ministers (department heads) in the Council of Ministers (cabinet).

All of the power and authority comes from the people through the soviets. The Supreme Soviet delegates the national power and authority to other organs of the government, including both the administrative and judicial powers. But representatives of the Supreme Soviet can be recalled by the people in the election districts.

THE PRESIDIUM

The Presidium is delegated the executive power of the Supreme Soviet. It is an interim body which can exercise fully this delegated power when the Supreme Soviet is not in session. It can also call the Supreme Soviet into special session. The members of the Presidium numbered thirty five in 1970. This number includes one chairman, fourteen vice-chairmen, one secretary, and twenty regular members. Decisions are made by majority vote in the Presidium. The Chairman of the Supreme Soviet and of its Presidium is the titular head of the Soviet Government. He is in charge of ceremonial affairs and receives foreign dignitaries. His main function, however, is to preside over the

Supreme Soviet and its Presidium.

Since the Presidium has a small number of members, who maintain executive offices and who meet together often, it actually executes more power than the Supreme Soviet. However, its authority by law is subordinate to the Supreme Soviet.

Yet the USSR Constitution also gives very broad powers to the Presidium. It can, among other things, issue decrees, interpret laws, annul decisions of the administration, appoint or recall military commanders, declare war, ratify or renounce treaties, and even dissolve the Supreme Soviet (but only in cases of unreconcilable differences between the two chambers) and call new elections.

The routine work of the Presidium is closely connected with that of the legislative commissions when the Supreme Soviet is not in session. When the proposals are prepared by one commission in connection with the Commission on Legislative Proposals, they are then submitted to the Presidium for distribution to the other representatives and to the newspapers and public organizations for further discussion. In this capacity and in other routine affairs of the Supreme Soviet the Presidium fulfills the role of an administrator with a large staff.

The Presidium in coordination with the representatives of the Supreme Soviet also acts as a "watch dog" over all government functions. It works closely with the Politburo of the Communist Party and with the Chairman of the Council of Ministers, who actually exercise on the principle of "collective leadership," the total power of the government. This "collective leadership" was formerly the Dictatorship of the Proletariat and is now referred to as the All-People's Government.

THE COUNCIL OF MINISTERS

The administrative functions of the whole society of the Soviet Union are delegated to the Council of Ministers from the Supreme Soviet. The officers and the responsibilities are determined by the Supreme Soviet, but the work is supervised and conducted by the Council of Ministers and its ministries.

The officers consist of a chairman, who is premier of the government; two first vice-chairmen, and nine vice-chairmen. In 1972 these officers were:

Chairman - Kosygin, A. N.
First Vice-Chairman - Mazurov, K. T.
First Vice-Chairman - Polyansky, D. S.

181

and Vice-Chairmen - Baibakov, N. K.
                    Dymshits, V. E.
                    Kirillin, V. A.
                    Lesechko, M. A.
                    Novikov, V. N.
                    Novikov, I. T.
                    Smirnov, L. V.
                    Tikhonov, N. A.
                    Shelest, P. E.

Four of these vice-chairmen also serve as chairmen of important committees in the Council of Ministers. These committees and their chairmen were:

The State Planning Committee - Baibakov, N. K.

The State Committee of Material-Technical Supplies - Dymshits, V. E.

The State Committee on Science and Technology - Kirillin, V. A.

The State Committee on Affairs of Construction - Novikov, I. T.

These important committees and other committees in the central government have supervisory functions over the ministries and the whole economy. For example, the State Planning Committee coordinates and enforces the Five Year Plans.

Each ministry in the Council of Ministers has a particular function. These functions include both the political-government functions, e.g. foreign affairs, defense, foreign trade, etc., and the economic functions of the country, e.g., the gas industry, the meat and milk industry, etc. These ministries, however, are divided into two groups on a different basis. The All-Union ministries are those ministries which are directly responsible to the Council of Ministers. The Union Republic ministries have dual responsibility to the Republic Council of Ministers and also to the All-Union Council of Ministers.

The All-Union ministries and their ministers as of 1972 were:

Ministry of the Aviation Industry - Dement'ev, P. V.
Ministry of the Automobile Industry - Tarasov, A. M.
Ministry of Foreign Trade - Patolichev, N. S.
Ministry of the Gas Industry - Orudzhev, S. A.
Ministry of Civil Aviation - Bugaev, B. P.
Ministry of Machine Building - Bakhirev, V. V.
Ministry of Machine Building for the Light and Food Industries and Consumer Appliances - Doenin, V. N.

182

Ministry of the Medical Industry - Gusenkov, P. V.
Ministry of the Naval Fleet - Guzhenko, T. B.
Ministry of the Oil Industry - Shaskin, V. D.
Ministry of the Defense Industry - Zerev, S. A.
Ministry of General Machine Building - Afanas'ev, S.A.
Ministry of Making Instruments, Means of Automation, and
        Control Systems - Rudnev, K. N.
Ministry of Communications Routes - Beshechev, B. P.
Ministry of the Radio Industry - Kalmykov, V. D.
Ministry of Medium Machine Building - Slavsky, E. P.
Ministry of Machine Tool Building and Instruments
        Industry - Kostousov, A. S.
Ministry of Construction, Road, and Public Machine
        Building - Kortunov, A. K.
Ministry of the Ship Building Industry - Butoma, B. E.
Ministry of Tractor and Agricultural Machine
        Building - Sinitsyn, I. F.
Ministry of Transportation Construction - Kozhevnikov, E. F.
Ministry of Heavy Engineering, and Transportation Machine
        Building - Zhigalin, V. F.
Ministry of Chemical and Oil Machine Building -
        Brekhov, K. I.
Ministry of the Chemical Industry - Kostandov, L. A.
Ministry of the Cellulose and Paper Industry -
        Galanshin, K. I.
Ministry of the Electronic Industry - Shokin, A. I.
Ministry of the Electrical Engineering Industry -
        Antonov, A. K.
The Union Republic Ministries within the Council of Ministers
and the ministers in 1972 were:
Ministry of Internal Affairs - Shchelokov, N. A.
Ministry of Higher and Secondary Special Education -
        Elyutin, V. P.
Ministry of Geology - Sidorenko, A. V.
Ministry of Procurement - Nuriev, Z. N.
Ministry of Health - Petrovsky, V. B.
Ministry of Foreign Affairs - Gromyko, A. A.
Ministry of Culture - Furtseva, E. A.
Ministry of Light Industry - Tarasov, N. N.
Ministry of the Lumber, Cellulose, Paper and of Wood
        Working Industries - Timofeev, N. V.
Ministry of Land Reclamation and Water Resources -
        Alekseevsky, E. E.

Ministry of Assembling and Special Construction
Works - Yakubovsky, F. B.
Ministry of the Meat and Milk Industry - Antonov, S. F.
Ministry of the Oil Refining and Oil Chemistry
Industry - Fedorov, V. P.
Ministry of Defense - Grechko, A. A.
Ministry of Food Industry - Lein, V. P.
Ministry of Industrial Construction - Tokarev, A. M.
Ministry of the Building Materials Industry -
Grishmanov, I. A.
Ministry of Education - Prokof'ev, M. A.
Ministry of the Fishing Industry - Ishkov, A. A.
Ministry of Communications - Psurtsev, N. D.
Ministry of Rural Construction - Khitrov, S. D.
Ministry of Agriculture - Polyansky, D. S.
Ministry of Construction - Karavaev, G. A.
Ministry of the Construction of Enterprises of Heavy
Industry - Goldin, N. V.
Ministry of Commerce - Struev, A. I.
Ministry of the Coal Industry - Bratchenko, B. F.
Ministry of Finance - Garbuzov, V. F.
Ministry of Ferrous Metallurgy - Lomako, P. F.
Ministry of Non-Ferrous Metallurgy - Kazanets, I. P.
Ministry of Electric Power and Electrification -
Neporozhy, P. S.
Ministry of Justice - Terebilov, V. I.

Each of the Chairmen of the 15 Union Republic Council of
Ministers is also an Ex Officio member of the All-Union Council
of Ministers. Their responsibility is to coordinate the administrative activities between the Union Republics and the central
government. As of 1972 they were:

The Russian SFSR - Solomentsev, M. S.
The Ukrainian SSR - Lyashko, A. P.
The Belorussian SSR - Kiselev, T. Ya.
The Uzbek SSR - Khudaiberdyev, N. A.
The Kazakh, SSR - Ashimov, B.
The Georgian SSR - Dzhavakhishvili, G. D.
The Azerbaidzhan SSR - Ibragimov, A. I.
The Lithuanian SSR - Manyushis, I. A.
The Moldavian SSR - Paskar', P. A.
The Latvian SSR - Ruben, Yu. Ya.
The Kirghiz SSR - Suyumbaev, A. S.

184

The Tadzhik SSR - Kakharov, A.
The Armenian SSR - Muradyan, B. A.
The Turkmen SSR - Orazmukhamedov, O. N.
The Estonian SSR - Klauson, V. A.

Other independent directorates, and committees are also
responsible directly to the Council of Ministers. They are as
follows:
The Central Statistical Directorate - Starovsky, V. N.
The Administration of the State Bank - Shveshnikov, M. N.
The Committee of State Security - Andropov, Yu. V.
The Committee of People's Control - Voronov, G. I.
The State Committee on the Affairs of Publishers, Poli-
graphy and Book Sales - Stukalin, B. I.
The Committee on Problems of Labor and Wages -
Volkov, A. P.
The State Committee on Prices - Sitnin, V. K.
The State Committee on Standards - Boitsov, V. V.
The State Committee on Foreign Economic Relations -
Shachkov, S. A.
The State Committee of Timber Resources - Vorob'ev, G. T.
The State Committee on Professional-Technical
Education - Bulgakov, A. A.
The All-Union Confederation of Unions of Agricultural
Technology - Ezhevsky, A. A.
The State Committee on Television Transmissions and
Radio Broadcasting - Lapin, S. G.

The Council of Ministers has gone through many changes and
a tremendous growth of responsibilities and power. At the Second
All-Russian Congress in November, 1917, it was organized as the
Council of People's Commissars. It has had the administrative
power of the government since that time, but with the industrialization of the Soviet Union the functions and organizations increased.
By 1936 there were fifteen commissariats (ministries) and by 1946
that number had increased to sixty. Also in 1946 the Council of
People's Commissars was renamed the Council of Ministers, and
the commissariats were renamed ministries.

Changes since then have been internal re-organizations for
both economic and political purposes. After the death of Stalin
in 1953 the functions were again divided among fifty ministries to
de-centralize authority in 1956 as an economic reform, but in 1958
the functions were re-combined into seventeen ministries during
Khrushchev's attempt to remove Stalinists from top positions.

185

In 1958 there were seven All-Union Ministries, ten Union Republic Ministries, and seventeen committees or other independent organizations. By 1962 the expansion of functions were indicated by the addition of twelve more independent committees. The general re-organization of the Council of Ministers, after Khrushchev, increased the number of ministries back to fifty three. In 1972 there were twenty seven All-Union Ministries, thirty one Union Republic Ministries, and seventeen committees, including administrations and directorates. This increase is the result of the de-centralization and the expansion of functions. The great expansion has also increased the work and responsibility of the Council of Ministers.

Under the ministries and the committees there are many subordinate organizations, which have been established both on geographical and functional breakdowns. The geographical breakdown usually follows the Union Republic and Oblast lines. The functional breakdown follows the logical division of work responsibilities. A typical line of authority goes from a ministry to a directorate, from a directorate to a department (otdeleniye), and a department to a section (otdel).

It is difficult to comprehend the complexity of the bureaucracy under the Council of Ministers. It is also difficult to manage. For this reason Khrushchev organized the Regional Economic Councils to coordinate the work and to give greater autonomy to local authority. In addition, the local soviets have been given greater responsibility to help guide and direct the affairs on the local level.

The People's Control Committee, which is an arm of the Communist Party and of the Government, also works as an independent regulator on each administrative breakdown of authority. It reports both to the Council of Ministers and to the Central Committee of the Communist Party.

But the Council of Ministers, as a collective body, supervises and controls all the work of the government, both executive and administrative. In addition, it submits many legislative proposals to the representatives of the Supreme Soviet. The Separation of Powers concept of American Government does not apply to the Soviet Government. The concept of Collective Leadership is one of shared responsibility rather than divided authority.

THE SUPREME COURT

The Supreme Court is the highest judicial body in the Soviet Union. It consists of a chairman, two vice-chairmen, nine judges, and several lay judges, who are all named by the Supreme Soviet for a five year term. The Supreme Court is divided into three collegia: civil, criminal, and military. They try both appellate cases and significant original cases.

In addition, the Supreme Soviet names a Procurator General for a seven year term. He is independent from the Supreme Court and serves as a prosecuting attorney. He also serves as an advisor on legal matters for both the Supreme Court and for the lower courts.

The trials are supervised by a judge and two lay judges. There is no jury. But the defendant does have a defense lawyer. The judges study the presented facts of the case as well as the case history of the defendant. The purpose of the trial is not only to determine the innocence or guilt of the defendant but also to determine the causes of the crime so as to prevent a reoccurence.

The procurator in a trial upholds the laws and enforces adherence to them. In this way he serves also as a supervisor over the court as well as over the defendant.

Defendants can appeal from the lower courts to the Republic Supreme Court and on to the All-Union Supreme Court. But the Supreme Court meets in session every three months or oftener to determine whether the lower courts acted in violation of the law. The main responsibility here is to review the procedure of the lower court rather than to review the facts of the case.

At the periodic sessions the Supreme Court also issues instructions for the whole Soviet court system. In this way the Supreme Court supervises justice in the whole country.

THE GOVERNMENT OF THE UNION REPUBLICS

The Government of the fifteen Union Republics is practically a duplication of the All-Union Government. The Supreme Soviet of a Union Republic has only one chamber, because a Union Republic is not a multi-national government like that of the USSR. Also the Union Republic Council of Ministers has two types of ministries. One of these is for those functions which parallel those of the Union Republic Ministries of the All-Union Council of Ministers. These Union Republic Ministries have dual responsibility and accountability to the All-Union Council of Ministers. The other ministries are for local specialized functions, e.g. the Ministry of the Cotton Industry of the Uzbek Republic.

The Union Republic has the other branches of government which are partly autonomous and partly responsible to the All-Union counter parts. These branches include the Presidium of the Supreme Soviet and the Supreme Court. The Procurator on the Republic level is appointed by the Procurator General of the USSR and is responsible to him rather than to the Union Republic Supreme Soviet.

This pattern of government is the outline of the government for all levels of government in the USSR. See the chart:

THE GOVERNMENT OF THE SOVIET UNION

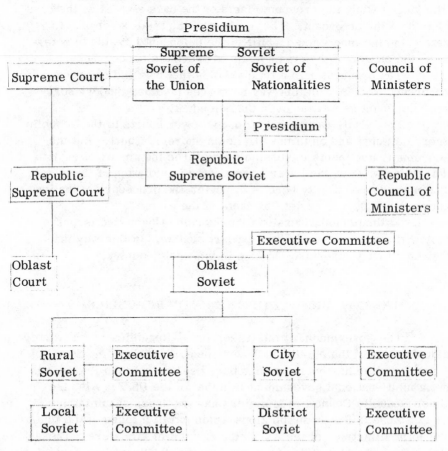

LOCAL GOVERNMENT

The main sub-divisions of a Union Republic are the oblast and the krai. They each have a soviet, which is the center of the local government. The oblast or krai soviet is responsible both to the Supreme Soviet of the Union Republic and to the Republic Council of Ministers. Representatives of the oblast or krai soviet are elected every two years at a regular election, and there are on an average about two hundred representatives in each of these soviets.

The oblast or krai soviet is responsible for all activity — economic, cultural, social, and political — in the oblast or krai. The rural and city soviets and their subordinate local soviets are directly responsible to the oblast or krai soviet.

All of the local soviets, including the oblast or krai soviets, have an executive committee, which has parallel authority of both the Presidium and the Council of Ministers on the upper levels of government. The executive committee of an oblast or krai soviet is a very powerful organization. It consists of a chairman, three to five vice-chairmen, and a secretary and also from nine to fifteen members, all of whom are elected from the oblast or krai soviet.

From the oblast or krai soviet are also elected twelve to fourteen standing commissions, each of which consist of ten to twenty representatives. The types of standing commissions vary from area to area, but typical standing commissions are: the budget and finance commission, the commission on commerce and public eating places, the commission on public services, the commission on communal economy and services, the commission on housing construction, the commission on public education, the commission on culture, health, and social security, the commission on road construction, the commission on welfare, and the commission on socialist legality. The standing commissions coordinate the economic, social, and cultural affairs of the oblast or krai. Their authority is primarily legislative and advisory.

The executive committee is the executive and administrative authority of the oblast or krai soviet. It also has subdivisions, which have administrative and quasi-executive authority. These units are sections and directorates. The typical sections are: a finance section, a public education section, a health section, a social security section, a communal economy section, a section on construction and architectural affairs, and a section for accounting for labor resources. The typical directorates are on: agriculture, local industry, public services, the food industries, the building

189

materials industry, the fuel industry, the butter and milk industry, the building and repair of highways, commerce, culture, motion pictures, preservation of social order, and planning. There may also be other directorates depending on the local economy and other local conditions. These sections and directorates work very closely with the enterprises and institutions within the oblast or krai and help support their administration.

In addition, in the soviet or in its executive committee are general sections: complaints section, legal consultant section, the organization-instruction section, the secretariat section, and several other auxiliary services. These general sections support the work in the soviet and in the executive committee, and they also serve the public.

The overall responsibilities of the soviet and the executive committee are: to plan the development of the local economy and of the social cultural work, to coordinate activities within the area, to establish the budget for the oblast or krai and assist the subordinate soviets in formulating their budgets, to maintain a financial control on area enterprises and organizations, to organize and to re-organize the structure of enterprises and organizations, to oversee the fulfillment of area plans, to set prices on produced goods, and to supervise and to guarantee legal protection for all social, cultural, and educational functions within the area.

The comprehensive nature of the Soviet Government is most apparent on the oblast or krai level. All governmental, economic, and social activities fall within the realm of the soviet and its executive committee. In this sense the soviet and its executive committee are both regulators and public servants. They are the focal point of civilization, all aspects of it. But the individual citizen is not only a benefactor, he is also a participant. His involvement is welcomed and rewarded.

The soviet must meet in public session at least four times a year, and the executive committee must meet at least twice a year. At these meetings there is conducted a review over the work since the last meeting. The commissions, sections, and directorates must account for their activity, their funds, and their time. But prior to these meetings the representatives of the soviet must conduct public hearings for discussing the activity within the oblast or krai. The discussion is also printed in the newspaper and broadcast over the radio. Full discussion beforehand is a requirement for the soviet. Public response must be heard.

Yet the participation of the individual is not only in being informed and in responding to his representatives. The participation also takes place through his collective — his social organization or his trade union unit. The sections and directorates are supported by an "aktiv", which is the participatory support of individuals through their collective activity. A group of individuals form a social or labor volunteer unit to work on special projects — public service projects of all kinds. This participation with the section and directorate members also increases the respect of these officials for the group and the individual. This respect helps the individual and his group to be heard at the public discussions. It is also through this type of participation that an individual can increase his chances for being elected to the soviet for the next term. This opportunity is greatly increased by the decision that at least one-third of the 200 representatives must be new each two years.

An understanding of local government requires a look also at the local soviet or at the city district soviet, because it is at this level that the public services are directly handled by the soviet. The sections of the local soviet are usually sub-divisions of the oblast or krai soviet, but they also carry out service functions. The local housing office, the local savings bank, the local registry office (for vital statistics), the local police department, and other local public services are administered by the local soviets through the executive committee and its sections.

Every local enterprise, every public service, every institution, and every group activity is coordinated with the local soviet. It is in this sense that there is no private enterprise and no disassociated person in the Soviet Union. Every person is a part of a "collective", and that "collective" is supervised by the local soviet.

The Soviet Government is a comprehensive government. Is it a participatory democracy or is it a totalitarian dictatorship? The answer to this question depends on one's background and point of view. Soviet citizens contend that the full participation and the full recipiency are the culmination of the people's rule or democracy. To them a government that is not all inclusive of the people can not be a democracy, because it does not give equality to all. They add that the Soviet people are free because they govern themselves.

But this claim brings rise to a question about the Communist Party. The Soviet answer is that the Communist Party is the leader and the organizer, but they add it does not exclude anyone from participation in government. Even the representatives are not all members of the Communist Party. Also the members of the Council of Ministers are largely non-party people.

A closer look at the Communist Party helps to clarify its role in the Soviet Government and in the lives of the people.

THE COMMUNIST PARTY OF THE SOVIET UNION

The basis for the organization of the Communist Party of the Soviet Union is the Party Congress, which by party rule meets at least one time in five years. The Party Congress consists of delegates from all units of the party, and in 1971 at the 24th Party Congress there were 4,740 voting delegates. This large body hears reports, approves party programs, and elects members for an interim body, the Central Committee, which actually wields the greatest authority in the Party.

The Central Committee is the locus of authority of the whole Communist Party of the Soviet Union. However, it too is a large body. In 1971 there were 240 members and 155 alternate members. But it does exercise its power at regular semi-annual meetings and at special meetings. In addition, the Central Committee has standing commissions, which supervise the activities of all party organizations, direct the work of the government and public organizations, and select party leaders and other functionaries.

The organization of the Communist Party parallels that of the Soviet Government, and the Party works very closely with the Government. Many members of the Central Committee also hold top government positions, and as in other countries the political leaders are also the government officials. In 1966 there were 167 out of 195 members of the Central Committee who were representatives in the USSR Supreme Soviet. In 1971 there were 17 of the 36 members of the Presidium of the Supreme Soviet who were also members of the Central Committee. Also in that year the chairman and the 11 vice-chairmen of the Council of Ministers were all members of the Central Committee, and about half of the ministers were members of the Central Committee. It can be seen that the Communist Party through its Central Committee has a strong leadership role in the top government positions.

The Central Committee elects the members of the Politburo to direct the work of the Central Committee when it is not in session. It also maintains a Secretariat for handling its administrative work. Even though both of these organizations are very powerful, they are still responsible to the Central Committee.

Evidence of the strength of the Central Committee was seen
in 1957 when Khrushchev reversed a decision of the Politburo (then
called the Party Presidium) for ousting him by calling a meeting of
the Central Committee. The Central Committee retained him in
power and ousted Molotov, Kaganovich, Shepilov, and Malenkov.
The Central Committee delegates authority to the Politburo, but
it can recall this delegated authority at any time. The removal of
Khrushchev in 1964 by the Central Committee is further evidence
of this power.

The Central Committee is accountable for its actions, primarily financial, to the Central Auditing Commission, which is
elected by the Party Congress. But the Central Committee oversees the affairs and accounts of other party organizations through
its supervision of the People's Control Committee. Members of
this commission are elected by the Central Committee.

The Politburo, even though responsible to the Central
Committee, actually exercises more power than any other organization of the Communist Party. It is the political leadership of both
the Communist Party and the Soviet Government. The sixteen
members of the Politburo are elected from and by the Central
Committee. These sixteen men are spokesmen for the party and
for the Soviet Government. They hold most of the top positions in
the Soviet Government. The chairmen of the Politburo, who is
called the General Secretary of the Communist Party, is the most
powerful person in the Soviet Union. He can speak for the party
and for the government, even though he may not hold a leading
government position. But his position must rely on the support of
the other members of the Politburo and of the Central Committee.

The Secretariat is the administrative office for the Politburo
as well as for the Central Committee. It is supervised by the
Politburo when the Central Committee is not in session. In addition
to its administrative power, the Secretariat maintains the party
records, both membership lists and financial records, and can use
this information for exerting great influence on party and government officials. During the transfer of power from one leader to
another the person or persons who have the closest connection
with the Secretariat have used information for their advantage.
Stalin and Khrushchev both followed this path to leadership.

Even though the Communist Party of the Soviet Union denies
the existence of factions within the party leadership, there is much
evidence to indicate otherwise. These factions were most apparent
during the time of Khrushchev. The use of the party records for
advancing a particular faction is possible by compiling information

on individuals and their relationships to other party members. Since membership and assignments in the Communist Party are based on recommendations of other party members, lines of loyalty develop between those who recommend and those who are recommended. Knowledge of these lines of loyalty is important when depending on other people for political support. It is in this way that those in charge of the Secretariat can further their political interests.

The pattern for the Communist Party organization on the Republic, Oblast, and local levels is the same as that on the All-Union level. The following chart illustrates the pattern and the relationships.

On each level there are congresses or conferences which are convened at least once in two years. These bodies elect their respective committees and respective auditing commissions in the same manner as on the All-Union level. The committee, in turn, elects from its group a bureau, which serves as an interim body as does the Politburo on the All-Union level. The Union Republic Central Committee also elects a Secretariat, but on the lower levels the secretarial duties are done in the local bureaus. The People's Control Committee has regional and local offices, which parallel the party structure, but they are independent from the congresses and conferences on that level. This committee is responsible to the All-Union Party Congress through the All-Union Central Committee.

Republic Central Committees meet once every four months in plenary session. They direct all the economic and cultural work in the Republic and govern all party affairs in the Republic. The Republic Central Committee also names the heads of departments within the committee and the editors of party publications.

The committees on the lower levels meet every three months in plenary session and conduct the same type of business on their respective levels. When they are not in session the bureau continues to direct the affairs of the party.

In enterprises, stores, farms, institutions of all kinds, and research institutes there are organized local party cells to coordinate the work of the party in these locations. The party members work at the job and work with the administrators to direct the work there.

The basic tasks of members of the Communist Party of the Soviet Union are:

1- to teach communist ideology and ethics and instill loyalty to the cause of building communism,

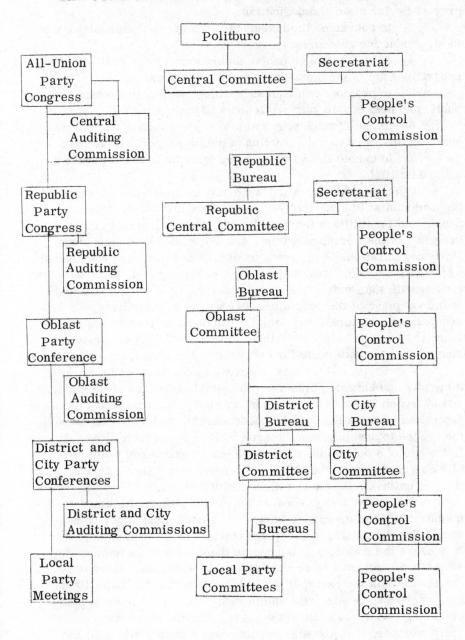

2- to apply the communist teachings to practice and help prevent revisionism and dogmatism,

3- to guarantee the leadership role of the Communist Party in all productive enterprises,

4- to help organize people and resources for fulfilling the program of the Communist Party and the five-year plans,

5- to promote communist teachings among the general public and help people gain proficiency in their work,

6- to be a "watch dog" to prevent violations of the law and guard against waste or destruction of public property, and

7- to uphold the moral code by example in one's personal and public life.

Other organizations in the Soviet Union are also directed by the Communist Party. Party organizations are set up for young people and for military personnel. These organizations are branches of the Communist Party and are guided by them. Non-Party organizations, e.g. trade unions, cooperatives, professional organizations, etc., are subject to party regulations, and they work closely with the Party. The Comntunist Party of the Soviet Union is the vanguard of the people in every aspect of their lives, occupational, cultural, and social. It helps everyone to improve himself so he can better contribute to the building of communism and can make a better life for everyone in the society.

Any Soviet citizen may become a party member by working diligently and adhering closely to the strict discipline of the party. Not everyone wants to become a party member, because it is a dedication of one's life to political leadership and a denying oneself the chance to specialize in the arts, sciences, or technology. It is the life of a politician, or it may even be compared to the life of a church minister, but it is really more strict then either of those counter-parts in a non-Communist society.

Only about five percent of the Soviet citizens become members of the Communist Party. It is not because they do not accept the communist ideology and ethics. Most of them do. It is because the majority of the people there as well as in any society does not want to accept leadership positions. More of them could join the party, if they wished, and as the Soviet Union has progressed in education and in industrialization more people percentage-wise have joined the party. But the percentage of party members will probably not increase substantially until the party changes from a leadership party to a mass organization.

Sociologists point out that in most societies that about five percent of the people are the top leaders, another five percent are in supporting positions, and the other ninety percent are followers. Whether this is the result of the nature of men or the nature of societies, one may argue, but it is a fact which probably largely determines the size of the Communist Party of the Soviet Union.

Party members usually come up through the youth organizations, where they learn and prove themselves. A person may be accepted into the Party at the age of eighteen. He or she must be recommended by three members of the Communist Party who have known him well for at least a year. The individual, after a public hearing, may then be accepted as a candidate member and serve a probationary period before being accepted as a regular member. A member must pledge to obey the party rules, to carry out the program, and to live a moral and patriotic life. When he is accepted as a party member, he then enjoys all the rights and privileges of other party members. He can vote and be elected to office, attend meetings, and speak at party meetings.

But becoming a party member is not just a formality. Anyone is eligible to become a member, but it is a great personal achievement to be accepted into the party. It is a selective process, and one really has to prove himself by being an outstanding worker and a dedicated servant to the cause of building communism.

Being accepted as a candidate member or even as a regular member is no guarantee that a person will always be a member of the Communist Party. A candidate member may never receive full membership, and he may soon be dropped as a candidate member. A party member may also be removed from party rolls for violation of party rules, moral codes, or public laws. He may be discharged for the lack of discipline or the lack of dedication. Party membership is a great responsibility, and the individual must always be worthy of his position.

The process of criticism and self-criticism at party meetings keeps one "humble" as well as steadfast. Any party member may be publically criticised by any other member when both are present. The accused party member does not defend himself. He must admit his errors. But he can criticise others. However, these criticism periods must be conducted on a constructive basis. The purpose is to increase one's dedication and loyalty. Party members have the responsibility to expose weaknesses of others and of themselves for the purpose of overcoming mistakes and working harder to carry out the assigned tasks. They help each other in correcting errors. Destructive criticism or personal rivalry in the party is said to be foreign to the conduct of a party member.

The relationship of a party member to a non-party person should also be one of brotherhood and friendship. A party member should work along with others and help them. He should be a positive example in his leadership role.

The relationship between the Communist Party and the Soviet Government should also be a friendly and comradely one. Leadership of the Party in Government affairs should be done by persuasion rather than by command. The Soviet citizens continue to stress that there is a democratic relationship between the Party and the Government. The Party has the obligation to guarantee equal and democratic rights for both members and non-members. Government workers, however, recognize and respect openly the role of the Communist Party. The ordinary Soviet citizen says that party members and non-party members are working together to build their new society.

CITY OR OBLAST PARTY COMMITTEE

A City or Oblast Party Committee directs the economic, political, and social life of the region. To coordinate and to supervise the administrative organizations the Party Committee has three sections: 1) the Propaganda and Agitation Section (five or more members); 2) the Organization Section (five or more members); and 3) the Industrial Section (15 or more members). The twenty-five or more party officials are also organized into a General Section for coordinating their work.

The local Party Committee is primarily concerned with the programs for building Communism and for achieving the goals of the Five Year Plan. It oversees the activities of the local Soviets, economic enterprises, and public organizations and institutions for carrying out the decisions of the Central Committee and the Politburo. The functions of the Party leaders include promotional work and investigations to verify the fulfillment of assigned tasks. Local leaders of the Soviets, economic enterprises, and social institutions are all accountable to the Party Committee.

The Propaganda and Agitation Section resembles an advertising agency, which promotes action. It posts banners, displays signs, and recruits people for demonstrations and group promotional activities. This section is also an educational institution, which distributes literature, provides speakers, and tries to instruct the public through publicity campaigns. People who work with this section form a para-political group, known as an aktiv, which does the routine tasks of the promotional work. The aktiv consists of party and non-party members who are leaders in other organizations. They play a supporting role to the local Party Committee in order to gain wide acceptance of the programs and policies of the Central Committee. One method of their work is to present speakers in public places, e. g. in the Park of Culture and Rest, to explain the party's position and to answer questions.

The Organization Section is the personnel section of the Party Committee. It recruits and trains people, both party members and non-party members, to assume leadership positions in the community. This section is an educational institution, which conducts classes and provides in-service instruction for Soviet, enterprise, and party officials. By means of personnel records and periodical reports the Organization Section also reviews of the work of these officials in order to maintain party discipline, which means that all leaders must adhere to the program, policies, and directives of the Central Committee and the Politburo.

The Industrial Section is the key section of the Party Committee for building Communism. It supervises, instructs, and checks the leaders of both local and large industries. By working through the director, manager, or leader of these industries, the Industrial Section helps implement the program of the Communist Party. This section may recommend the removal of an enterprise director, but the director is also responsible to the local Soviet (in the case of a small industry) or to a Ministry (in the case of a large industry). With the concurrence of the other authority the Party Committee may remove the director, or if a difference exists, the decision is referred to higher authority in the Communist Party. It is seen that the authority of the Industrial Section of the Party Committee supersedes that of the industrial leadership. But the procedures require the Industrial Section to work with the enterprise director and through him to his subordinates rather than undermining his position.

The General Section of the Party Committee meets at least once a month or oftener when considered necessary. It reviews the activities of the other sections and establishes local policies for their future work. At these meetings sessions of criticism and self-criticism are held as a means of increasing the dedication and enthusiasm of all members of the Party Committee. The head of each section reports the work of his section and recommends action. The decisions are made collectively by a vote after the reports have been thoroughly discussed.

Each Party Committee also has an executive bureau, which consists of the Secretary, the Section Heads, the newspaper editors. This executive bureau is the interim authority of the Party Committee between meetings of the General Section. The Secretary, as the top political leader, and the Section Heads, as the Secretary's direct associates, form the focal point for the decisions of the Party Committee and hence the major decisions in the local Soviet and local enterprises and institutions. The executive committee meets daily, and its decisions are made by a majority (often unanimous) vote of its members.

A typical local Party Committee is housed in a two-story building with individual offices, a library, and conference rooms. Each member of the Committee has an office with his name on the door, and each office is only large enough for individual work, e.g. correspondence, study, and report-writing. The library is six to ten times larger than an office, and it consists of a room of shelves of reference books. It is a storage area rather than a study area. One conference room is large enough for the whole Committee to meet. It has a large oval table around which the members sit. The entrance into the large conference room has double doors, which are padded for soundproofing. The small conference room is really a consultation room, which is large enough for a meeting of a section. The library is on the first floor, and the conference rooms are on the second floor. The building is not constructed for much direct contact with the public. The receptionist is on the second floor near the office of the Secretary rather than in a position readily available to the public. There are no barriers to restrict entrance into the building. A guard may be posted, but he only answers questions and gives directions.

The local Party Committee is responsible to higher party committees and finally the Politburo in Moscow. It is also responsible to the local Party Conference, which is a meeting of all Communists in the region. This Conference meets periodically (once in two or three years) to elect the members of the Party Committee and to establish the general policies. In theory the Party Committee has dual responsibility. Participation of the Party members is quite meaningful on the local level, but Party directives from the Politburo are supreme to all local decisions.

The average Soviet citizen has regular contact with local administrative authority. Public services are administered by agencies of the Oblast or City Soviet. The Oblast and City Committees of the Communist Party also perform various other functions which directly effect him. In addition, the enterprise where he works also has administrative rules which regulate his behavior.

Not only does the average citizen have these three lines of authority. Each enterprise has varying degrees of the same responsibility. Local industry and smaller enterprises are primarily responsible to the local Soviet. Large factories or institutions are usually responsible to a Republic or All-Union Ministry, which is in turn responsible to the Supreme Soviet. But all enterprises or institutions coordinate with the Communist Party Organizations.

A Radio and Television Station

Radio and television stations are directed from the State Committee on Television Transmissions and Radio Broadcasting of the Council of Ministers of the USSR. But the local administration comes through the Directorate on Television Transmissions and Radio Broadcasting of the Executive Committee of the Oblast Soviet. This directorate supervises all the work of radio and television stations in the Oblast. Its chairman is a representative of the Oblast Soviet and his position is confirmed by the Oblast Soviet. The chairman has two assistants, and they meet monthly with the head producer of the station and his chief editors. The Directorate confirms the monthly and quarterly work plans.

At the radio and television station there are three editorial offices, each of which is headed by a chief editor. These offices are: Art, Social-Political, and Program and Transmission. In these offices are several sections, e.g., Social-Political, Information and Sports, Industrial, and Agricultural. Each section is managed by a senior editor who is responsible for maintaining accurate and high-quality work. The senior editor also consults regularly with the chief editor and with the chairman of the Directorate.

The Art Editorial Office has a Youth-Children's Section, a

Literary-Dramatic Section, and a Music Section. It prepares programs for radio and television and has opportunities for creative and artistic work.

Every Monday there is a general staff meeting to evaluate the week's work. Here any worker may participate in the discussion, state his own opinions, and ask questions concerning policies.

In addition to the internal administration of the radio and television stations, a meeting of the station administration is held with the trade union organizations once a month. At these meetings the activities of the offices and sections are discussed and analyzed. The discussion topics of these meetings are then taken to the trade union meetings and to the meetings of the other social organizations.

A Pedagogical Institute

A pedagogical institute is subordinate to the Ministry of Education of the USSR and to the Ministry of Education of the Union Republic. But the administrative work is directed by the Standing Commission on Public Education of Oblast Soviet and by the Directorate of Public Education in the Executive Committee of the Oblast Soviet. The Executive Committee names a rector who is in charge of the administrative and educational work at the institute. The Executive Committee also names three pro-rectors (assistants to the rector) who are in charge of education work, scientific-research work, and administrative-business problems.

The internal governing body of the institute is the education council which consists of the rector, the pro-rectors, department chairmen, and the representatives of various social organizations.

The education council meets twice a month to discuss the problems related to the educational program, the distribution of education time, and the scientific-research work. Candidates for department chairmen and applicants for teaching positions are interviewed and given competitive examinations by the education council. The approval and acceptance of people for these positions is conducted by a special examination commission which excludes the rector. The education council also establishes requirements for the scientific-research work for all teachers at the institute.

Once a year the pedagogical institute has a Scientific-Research Conference at which teachers, teaching assistants, and graduate students present reports. These conferences promote research work and aid in the publishing of the reports of the conference.

Within the pedagogical institute there are also student organizations, i.e., the Komsomol (youth organization of the Communist Party), a trade union committee, and a student club. These organizations conduct educational and scholarly activities, sport competitions, music festivals, and art shows. They also help students by providing incentive trips to recreational areas and resorts and by rendering assistance to those who have had misfortunes.

In the summer the students from the pedagogical institute can participate in the student club and go on passes for a few rubles to a recreational camp for two or three weeks.

The students also have their own scientific-research society. It directs scientific-research work and organizes student conferences. This society also publishes the students' works.

A Polytechnical Institute

At the head of a polytechnical institute is a rector who is responsible to the Ministry of Higher and Secondary Special Education of the USSR. He directs the institute in its educational and research programs. Directly subordinate to him are three pro-rectors (assistant directors) who are in charge of the educational work, the research work, and the administrative work, respectively. These executive officers of the institute are selected from the faculty and they collectively form a rectorate (executive council).

Under the rector's direct authority is organized a scientific council of the institute which is known as the Bolshoi Soviet (the Grand Council). It consists of the rector, the pro-rectors, the deans, the professors, several lecturers, representatives of the social organizations, and representatives of enterprises which receive institute graduates. The Grand Council examines and plans the daily operations of the institute. It also conducts the defense sessions for higher degrees, and with the approval of the Ministry it awards degrees of doctors of science.

In the institute are several departments each of which are headed by a dean. At a polytechnical institute there are departments of radio engineering, electrical engineering, mechanical engineering, machine building, civil engineering, shipbuilding, metallurgy, and chemical engineering. The dean acts as chairman of a department council which directs the educational and research work in the department under the supervision of the Grand Council.

The departments, in turn, have sections for the various disciplines within the department. These sections are headed by a professor who is a doctor of engineering. The section staff includes lecturers, assistant lecturers, graduate students, and laboratory assistants.

The rector, pro-rectors, dean, and section heads are all elected for five-year terms by secret ballots within the Grand Council and are assigned with the approval of the Ministry of Higher and Secondary Special Education. Other faculty members, lecturers, assistant lecturers, etc., are also elected by secret ballot at the Grand Council sessions, but their appointments do not have to be approved by the Ministry. These assignments and appointments cannot be overruled after they have been accepted by a majority vote in the Grand Council.

A Tractor Plant

A tractor plant is directly subordinate to the Ministry of Tractor and Agricultural Machine Building in Moscow. Its director is appointed by the Minister, and he is responsible to the Ministry. The Oblast and City Soviets work with him, but their roles are strictly advisory. They do provide service functions to the plant, but they cannot countermand decisions of the director. On the other hand, the Oblast and City Party Committees do have supervisory roles. They do transmit directives to the plant director from central party authority and verify the fulfillment of these directives. The plant director must answer both to the Ministry and the Communist Party.

Within the administration of the plant on the staff level is an assistant director who directs the training of plant personnel. There are also three deputies to the director: 1) economics, 2) engineering, and 3) capital construction. These deputies are assisted by a chief construction engineer and a chief engineer in charge of development and technology. The chief engineer also has deputies for sales and for preparation.

Directly subordinate to the plant director are the chiefs of each section along the assembly line. These chiefs act as foremen over the workers and check the work in progress. Neither the section chiefs nor the workers have much voice in the general operation of the plant. They are encouraged to speed up and increase the production of the plant by directives from the director and by signs and slogans displayed throughout the plant. Some signs refer to the obligations of individual workers to carry out their responsibilities as soviet workers or as builders of communism. Other signs show figures of production and projected goals. Within the plant administration and within the work force are members of the Communist Party who work closely with the industrial section of the Party Committee. However, the Communist Party members work under the Industrial Section Chief of the Party through the director of the plant. As workers in the plant they have dual responsibility to the Party and to the plant director for carrying out the policies delegated to them.

SUMMARY

The concepts of democratic centralism, collective leadership, accountability, and popular participation are all evident on every level of Soviet administration. There is broad involvement of the personnel in the enterprise or institution staff meetings and in the committee meetings of the Soviet and Communist Party organizations. The dual lines of responsibility through government and party channels ensure some degree of collective leadership. All officials are accountable to higher authority. The organization charts and the official statements all indicate a democratic society.

But the pretense of democracy is not carried out in practice. Soviet citizens do not have the opportunity to contribute new ideas or to dissent from official policies. The Communist Party is in effect a super government, which directs the administration of affairs on every level of society. Participation is not extended to decision-making. It is limited to promoting and carrying out previously made decisions. In some senses it may be said that the Communist Party and the Soviet Government are "by" and "of" the people, but they are not "for" the people. They do not serve the people nearly as much as they regulate them.

The chief executive officer of an enterprise or institution has full responsibility for supervising all functions, for which he is accountable. Yet his actual work is constantly planned and reviewed by representatives of the Party Committee and the Soviet or Ministry. He can not deviate from the Party Program or the approved plans. And he may be removed from his position at any time.

SOURCES FOR CHAPTER VI

THE SOVIET GOVERNMENT AND THE COMMUNIST PARTY

Bannykh, M. P. (ed.), Organizatsiya Raboty Deputata Mestnogo
Soveta, "Yuridicheskaya Literatura", 1971, 62 pp.
Barabashev, G. V., Oblastnoy, Krayevoy Sovet Deputatov
Trudyashchikhsya, Moscow: Izdatelstvo "mysl'", 1967, 37pp.
Bauer, R. A. et als., How the Soviet System Works, Cambridge,
Mass.: Harvard University Press, 1964, 274 pp.
Chairman of the Industrial Section of the Bratsk City Party Com-
mittee, personal interview, Bratsk, July 22, 1971.
Deputaty Verkhovnogo Soveta SSR, Sed'moy Sozyv, Moscow:
Izdatelstvo "Izvestiya Sovetov Deputatov Trudyashchikhsya
SSR", 1966, 551 pp.
Ezhegodnik Bol'shoi Sovetskoi Entsiklopedii 1972, (16th ed.),
Moscow: Izdatelstvo "Sovetskaya Entsikolopediya", 1972,
623 pp.
Feifer, George, Justice in Moscow, New York: Dell Publishing
Co., Inc., 1965, 353 pp.
Genkin, D.M. & Kunik, Ya. A., Sovetskoye Grazhdanskoye Pravo,
Moscow: Izdatelstvo "Vysshaya Skhola", 1967, 559 pp.
Izvestia, Moscow 1969-1973.
Konstitutsiya (Osnovnoi Zakon) Soyuza Sovetskikh Sotsialististicheskikh
Respublik, Moscow: Izdatelstvo "Izvestiya Sovetov Deputatov
Tryudyashchikhsya SSR, 1971, 31 pp.
Pravda, Moscow: 1969-1973.
Programmy Pedagogicheskikh Institutov - Teoreticheskiy Kurs
Fonetiki Sovremennogo Angliiskogo Yazyka, Moscow:
Izdatelstvo "Prosveshcheniye", 1966, 56 pp.
Public Relations Officer of the Volgograd Tractor Plant, personal
interview, Volgograd, August 10, 1971.
Puzhin, A. V., Administrativno-territorial'noye Ustroystvo Sovet-
skogo Gosudarstva, Moscow: Yuridicheskaya Literatura,
1969, 1971 pp.
Rules of the Communist Party of the Soviet Union, Moscow: Foreign
Languages Publishing House, 1962, 32 pp.
Soviet Civil Legislation and Procedure, Moscow: Foreign Languages
Publishing House, 1962, 175 pp.
Spravochnik Partiynogo Rabotnika, Vypusk Sed'moy, Moscow:
Izdatelstvo Politicheskoy Literatury, 1967, 445 pp.
Spravochnik Partiynogo Rabotnika, Vypusk Shestoy, Moscow:
Izdatelstvo Politicheskoy Literatury, 1966, 523 pp.

Twenty-Third Congress of the Communist Party of the Soviet Union, Moscow: Novosti Press Agency Publishing House, 1966, 440 pp.

Ustav Kommunisticheskoi Partii Sovetskogo Soyuza, Moscow: Izdatel'stvo Politicheskoi Literatury, 1971, 61 pp.

Vasenin, V. K., Deputat Mestnogo Soveta, Moscow: Izdatel'stvo "Yuridicheskaya Literatura", 1967, 78 pp.

Vedomosti Verkhovnogo Soveta, No. 16 (1414) Izdatel'stvo Verkhovnogo Soveta, Moscow: 17 Apr. 1968, pp. 203-209, 234-238.

Vvedneskiy, B. A., Ezhegodnik Bol'shoi Sovetskoy Entsiklopedii 1967, Moscow: Izdatel'stvo "Sovetskaya Entsiklopediya", 1967, 622 pp.

Whiting, Kenneth R., The Soviet Union Today, New York: Frederick A. Praeger, Publishers, 1966, 423 pp.

SOVIET LEADERSHIP

Leadership in the Soviet Union may be compared to a comet flying through space. The direction is determined not only by the leaders themselves but also by the total mass of the comet (the society) and its relationship to natural and social forces. Communist doctrine does not accept the concept that one man or a small group of men can lead society without the support of the whole society. Rather it is said that the common man, the ordinary working man, makes history, because the masses of working men collectively change the course of history by their labor or by revolution.

The contention that all human society is moving toward communism because of the natural and social forces is the basis of the communist concept of leadership. The top leaders, or the individual leader as in the case of Stalin, can try to take society in a different direction, but society moves ahead in spite of the leadership and will gain new leadership which is representative of social progress. The old leadership is brushed aside as the society forges ahead.

The Communist Party of the Soviet Union has become the leader or the vanguard of the working people. According to communist philosophy the Party represents the will of the people. This will is determined by the Party leaders who study and apply the knowledge of natural and social forces in order to predict the direction of society's progress and to guide the people toward the fulfillment of their will. But the Communist Party leaders must always be on the lookout for dogmatism and revisionism in order to prevent a too rigid or a too flexible interpretation of the course of history. The proper interpretation is maintained by relying on broad participation in collective leadership roles and by having periodic sessions of criticism and self-criticism among the leaders.

The main leadership role is vested in the Central Committee of the Communist Party, which is a group of approximately 240 persons elected to their positions at All-Union Party Congresses. These 240 persons also have important government or other party positions where they exercise broad influences on national policies. However, the greater power lies in the Politburo, which is a group of sixteen men, who are appointed by the Central Committee to provide the executive leadership between the sessions of the Central Committee. Actually, the Politburo has become the center of political power and leadership in the Soviet Union.

The Central Committee also names several Candidate Members (alternates) to the Politburo and a group of secretaries, who form the Party Secretariat. These Candidate Members to the Politburo and Secretaries of the Central Committee have leadership roles, which are second only to that of the members of the Politburo. It is from these two positions that new members of the Politburo are usually selected.

It must be acknowledged that the Central Committee has much power and that it plays a very important leadership role. It was the Central Committee that blocked Khrushchev's ouster in 1957 and again supported his ouster in 1964. But the main individual leaders in the Soviet Union are in the Politburo or serve as Candidate Members or Secretaries of the Central Committee.

This study of Soviet leadership is therefore limited to these most powerful twenty-five men in the Soviet Union.

The Politburo consisted of eleven members from 1961 to 1971, when that number was increased to fifteen, and then in 1973 the membership was again increased to sixteen. There has been an unsteady balance between two factions of the Party. Khrushchev had replaced Stalinists with his own supporters during his rise to power. But more conservative members of the Politburo, who were led by Mikhail Suslov, tried to keep a check on Khrushchev by maintaining an even number of their own followers.

In addition to the natural trend of any group of human beings to divide itself into conservative and liberal factions there are several reasons that have helped to solidify these differences. One group, which was led by Khrushchev, was held together in its drive to displace Stalinism in the country. This group also favored "peaceful co-existence" with the West and an increased emphasis on agriculture and consumer goods in the national economy. These people were mostly from Leningrad and Kiev who represented the commercial and agricultural interests of their local economy. Leningrad and Kiev were also traditionally opposed to Moscow because of their former positions as the national capitols and of the long time of preference given to Moscow during the Stalin era. The other group represented the industrial power of Moscow, which controlled both the political and economic power due to the location of most of Soviet industry within a short distance of Moscow. Moscow interests resisted change and the innovations of Khrushchev. The Leningrad-Kiev group, on the other hand, gave

Khrushchev the necessary strength to maintain his position for several years.

The first open conflict between Khrushchev and his opposition came in 1957 when Molotov challenged Khrushchev and tried to oust him from power. Khrushchev was in Leningrad at the time, but he quickly returned to Moscow, called a meeting of the Central Committee and ousted Molotov, Shepilov, and Kaganovich from the Politburo. These people were then replaced by followers of Khrushchev. This move put Khrushchev in a strong position, but his opposition continued to struggle under the capable leadership of Mikhail Suslov, who has been considered to be the Party theoretician.

The next major contest came during the U-2 fiasco in 1960. Suslov attacked Khrushchev's leadership, and several of Khrushchev's followers were replaced. But Khrushchev maintained his position by giving some concessions to the conservatives. Again in 1962, during the Cuban Crisis, Khrushchev met another attack by his opposition. He suffered losses again, but he still kept control of the Politburo and the Central Committee. However, the power of Suslov had greatly increased.

In 1963 and 1964 the situation changed substantially. In the summer of 1963 Suslov went to China on a mission to help improve relations with that country. Not only did his mission fail, but he also suffered a reversal in his health. Then in October, 1964, the Central Committee ousted Khrushchev, but the leadership went to Brezhnev and Kosygin rather than to Suslov.

Leonid Brezhnev and Alexei Kosygin had come to power through the influence of Khrushchev and had supported his policies of peace and friendship and of the increased production of agricultural products and consumer goods. But they were now interested in bridging the gap between the factions and maintaining stability in the Soviet Union.

At the time of the ouster of Khrushchev the Politburo consisted of eleven members, six were old members and five had been added since 1957. Problems of age, sickness, and death required a re-organization, and in 1965 the new Politburo was formed as follows:

Brezhnev, Leonid	Suslov, Mikhail
Kosygin, Alexei	Voronov, Gennadi
Kirilenko, Andrei	Polyansky, Dmitri
Mazurov, Kirill	Shelepin, Alexander
Podgorny, Nikolai	Shelest, Pyotr
Mikoyan, Anastas	

Nikita Khrushchev had been ousted, Otto Kuusinen had died, Frol Kozlov had suffered a stroke, and Nikolai Shvernik was retired due to old age. The new members were Andrei Kirilenko, Pyotr Shelest, Kirill Mazurov, and Alexander Shelepin. The following year Anastas Mikoyan was also retired for old age, and he was replaced by Arvid Pelshe.

The new and more stable Politburo had a more conservative image than that under Khrushchev. Kosygin, Kirilenko, and Podgorny were the most liberal. Brezhnev, Mazurov, and Pelshe have been moderate, and Suslov has retained his leadership of the conservatives, which now included Shelepin, Polyansky, Shelest, and Voronov. Brezhnev changed his title from First Secretary of the Communist Party to General Secretary of the Communist Party. The de-Stalinization program slowed down, and there was a new attack against dissident writers in the Soviet Union. The conservative trend in Soviet policy was even more apparent during the 1968 intervention in Czechoslovakia. The Brezhnev-Kosygin attempt for stability was changing on several fronts to a position of instability.

During 1969 and 1970 differences grew among the members of the Politburo concerning the 1968 intervention in Czechoslovakia by Soviet troops, the decline in agricultural production in the Soviet Union, disputes and fighting at the Soviet-Chinese border, the changing situation in Soviet-United Arab Republic relations, the Vietnam War, and the Soviet-American talks on the limitation of strategic missiles. A Warsaw Pack Summit Conference was called in March, 1969, and a Moscow Communist Summit Conference in June of that year to gain support of Soviet policies. By the summer of 1970 these differences had not been resolved, and Brezhnev announced the postponement of the 24th Party Congress and the 1971-1975 Five Year Plan to the following March. This delay in resolving these differences caused speculation of shifts in the Soviet leadership. An increase in the activity of Nikolai Podgorny in speeches in the Soviet Union and in trips to foreign trouble spots caused some talk concerning his ascension to power at the expense of Kosygin and possibly Brezhnev, but there were no changes in any of these positions.

By March, 1971, though these differences became less apparent as Leonid Brezhnev affirmed his position as top leader in the Soviet Union and as Alexei Kosygin was the spokesman for the new Five Year Plan at the 24th Party Congress. However, it was also apparent that Nikolai Podgorny was accepted as an active participant in the top "collective leadership" role. The stability of the Soviet leadership was re-affirmed at this Congress by not removing any members from the Politburo and by adding four more members from among the Candidates to the Politburo and the Secretaries of the Central Committee. A year later there had still been no changes, even though Arvid Pelshe was 73 and Mikhail Suslov was 70, both beyond the age that Nikita Khrushchev was retired.

The leadership roles of Brezhnev, Kosygin, and Podgorny were further demonstrated by their world-wide travelling in the fall of 1971. Brezhnev went to Yugoslavia, Kosygin to Canada, and Podgorny to China and North Vietnam.

The new members of the Politburo in 1971 were Vladimir Shcherbitsky, Viktor Grishin, Dinmukhamed Kunayev, and Feodor Kulakov. Kulakov was a Secretary of the Central Committee, but the other three had previously been Candidates to the Politburo. Shcherbitsky and Kunayev were First Secretaries of the Ukraine and of the Kazakh Republic, respectively. Grishin held the position of First Secretary of Moscow. On the basis of their past affiliations it appeared that Shcherbitsky and Kulakov had more liberal leanings than those of Grishin and Kunayev.

In the spring of 1973 it could have been suspected that any further changes in the Politburo would include the retiring of Arvid Pelshe and Mikhail Suslov. But that was not the case. Instead two younger men, Gennady Voronov (age 63) and Peotr Shelest (age 65) were retired. It was reported that these two men had had differences with Brezhnev over improving relations with West Germany and the United States. In their place three men were added to the Politburo—Yuri Andropov (age 59) was elevated from being a Candidate to the Politburo; Andrei Gromyko (age 64) was retained as Minister of Foreign Affairs and named to be a member of the Politburo; and Andrei Grechko (age 70) was retained as Minister of Defense and named to be a member of the Politburo. To replace Andropov as a Candidate Member was Grigori Romanov (age 50), who had been the First Secretary of the Leningrad Oblast Committee of the Communist Party.

The spring of 1973 was further marked by a re-newed emphasis on improving international relations. Brezhnev visited Czechoslovakia, Poland, the German Democratic Republic, West Germany, and the United States of America. Kosygin visited Iran, where he promised Soviet help in building a metallurgical plant in Iran, and Sweden. Podgorny visited Finland and Afghanistan. In addition, several official visitors came to Moscow, among which were United States Senators, President Alvarez from Mexico, and leaders from North Vietnam. Negotiations were taking place for establishing diplomatic relations with West Germany and with Japan.

These events pointed further toward the moderate policies of Brezhnev and the strengthening of his position as General Secretary of the Communist Party. Brezhnev had gained greater power than Khrushchev ever had. He named an even number of membership in the Politburo and stressed unity, which left some doubt concerning the continuation of factions. But he had gained this broad support by relying on both conservatives and liberals in a way that emphasized personal loyalty rather than ideological differences.

In order to understand better the political leanings of the Soviet leadership and to look beyond for future events, it is necessary to look closer at the members of the Politburo, the Candidate Members, and the Secretaries of the Central Committee. This need has become even more important since the establishment of the All-People's Government at the 22nd Party Congress in 1961 and with the expansion in the membership of the Communist Party and the Politburo. This importance is further increased by the policy to strengthen discipline within the Communist Party by a purge of inactive members through the issuing of new party cards as announced at the 24th Party Congress in 1971 and carried out in 1973. There has become a wider base of support within the top leadership roles by including people from different areas and different backgrounds. The one-man dictatorship of Stalin was replaced by the "collective leadership" of Brezhnev, Kosygin, and Podgorny, but Brezhnev's power was far greater than the other two. Factionalism in the Politburo was replaced by an appearance of unity. But there are still many differences of opinion remaining among the leaders of the Politburo, and further changes in policy and top leadership were inevitable.

The main indicator of future changes were the ages of the top leaders. Several of them had reached the age of 70 or would soon reach that age. It must be recalled that Khrushchev was retired for old age at the age of 70.

The following charts showing the membership of the Politburo, the Candidates to the Politburo, and the Secretaries of the Central Committee give such indications. More details concerning each of these leaders follow the charts and provide some further understanding of their future roles.

MEMBERS OF THE POLITBURO 1975
(Listed according to age)

Name	Birth	Nationality	(1)	(2)	Occupations and Positions
Pelshe, Arvid	1899 Latvia	Latvian	1915/66		Union leader & teacher. Chr. of Control Comm.
Suslov, Mikhail	1902 Moscow	Russian	1921/52 & 55		Professor & Sec. of Central Comm.
Podgorny, Nikolai	1903 Kiev	Ukrainian	1930/60		Mech. engr. & Chr. of Supreme Soviet
Grechko, Andrei	1903 Ukraine	Ukrainian	1928/73		Army Marshall & Min. of Defense
Kosygin, Alexei	1904 Leningrad	Russian	1927/49 & 60		Teacher & Chr. of Council of Min.
Brezhnev, Leonid	1906 Ukraine	Russian	1931/60		Metallurgy engr. & Gen. Sec. of Communist Party
Kirilenko, Andrei	1906 Voronezh	Russian	1931/65		Electrician, aircraft engr. & Sec of Central Comm.
Gromyko, Andrei	1909 Minsk	Russian	1931/73		Ambassador to U. N. & Min. of Foreign Affairs
Kunayev, Dinmukhamed	1912 Kazakh	Kazakh	1939/71		Mining engr. & 1st Sec. of Kazahk UR
Mazurov, Kirill	1914 Mogilev	Belorussian	1921/65		Railroad tech. & 1st V-Chr. of Council of Min.
Grishin, Viktor	1914 Serpukhov	Russian	1939/71		Railroad depot deputy chief & 1st Sec. of Moscow
Andropov, Yuri	1914 Yaroslavl	Russian	1939/73		Telegrapher & Chr. of State Security
Polyanski, Dmitri	1917 Kharkov	Ukrainian	1939/60		Komsomol leader & Min. of Agri.
Shelepin, Alexander	1918 Voronezh	Russian	1940/65		Historian & Komsomol leader, Chr of Trade Unions

Shcherbitsky, Vladimir	1918 Dnepropetrovsk	Ukrainian	1941/71	Chem. engr. & Chr.of Ukrainian Coun. of Min.
Kulakov, Feodor	1918 Penza	Russian	1940/71	Agronomist & Komsomol leader, Sec. of Cen.Com.

CANDIDATES TO THE POLITBURO 1975
(Listed according to age)

Name	Birth	Nationality	(1) (2)	Occupations and Positions
Ponomarev, Boris	1905 Ryazin	Russian	1919/72	Historian, Chr. of Foreign Affairs Comm.
Ustinov, Dmitri	1908 Kuibyshev	Russian	1927/65	Civil engr. & Deputy Chr. of Council of Min.
Solomentsev, Mikhail	1913 Leningrad	Russian	1940/72	Factory director & Chr. of Comm. on Leg. Proposal
Rashidov, Sharaf	1917 Samarkand	Uzbek	1939/62	Teacher & ed., 1st Sec. of Uzbek Republic
Demichev, Peotr	1918 Kirov	Russian	1939/64	Chem. engr. & Sec. of Central Committee
Masherov, Peotr	1918 Vibetsk Belorussia	Belorussian	1943/65	Teacher & 1st Sec. of Belo- russian Rep.
Romanov, Grigori	1923 Leningrad	Russian	1944/73	Civil engr., 1st Sec. of Lenin- grad

(1) Party member since.   (2) Candidate since.

(Listed according to age)

Name	Birth	Nationality	(1) (2)	Occupations and Positions
Suslov, Mikhail	1902 Ulyanovsk	Russian	1921/47	University Prof. Politburo mem.
Ponomarev, Boris	1905 Ryazan	Russian	1919/61	Historian. Chr. For. Affairs Committee
Brezhnev, Leonid	1906 Ukraine	Russian	1931/63	Metallurical eng. Gen. Sec. Politburo member
Kirilenko, Andrei	1906 Voronezh	Russian	1913/66	Aircraft eng. Politburo mem.
Ustinov, Dmitri	1908 Kuibyshev	Russian	1927/65	Civil engineer Candidate to Politburo
Solomentsev, Mikhail	1913 Leningrad	Russian	1927/65	Civil engineer Candidate to Politburo
Kapitonov, Ivan	1915 Ryazin	Russian	1939/65	Civil eng., Sec. Man. of Party Org. Work
Kulakov, Feodor	1918 Penza	Russian	1940/65	Agronomist. Politburo mem.
Demichev, Peotr	1918 Kirov	Russian	1939/62	Chem. engineer Cand. to Polit.
Dolgikh, Vladimir	1924 Irkutsk	Russian	1942/72	Metallurgist. 1st Sec. of Krasnoyarsk Krai
Katushev, Konstantin	1927 Gorky	Russian	1952/69	Draftsman. Mem. Comm. on Const. & Ind. Bldg. Mat.

(1) Party member since. (2) Secretary since.

eonid Brezhnev   Andrei Gromyko   Viktor Grishin

Andrei Kirilenko   Alexei Kosygin   Feodor Kulakov

Nikolai Podgorny   Dmitri Polyansky   Mikhail Suslov

Dinmukhamed Kunayev

Kirill Mazurov

Arvid Pelshe

Andrei Shelepin

Andrei Grechko

Vladimir Shcherbitsky

Yuri Andropov

Peotr Demichev

Peotr Masherov

218

Grigori Romanov   Sharaf Rashidov   Dmitri Ustinov

Boris Ponomarev   Mikhail Solomentsev   Ivan Kapitonov

Konstantin Katushev   Vladimir Dolgikh

Leonid Brezhnev was born in the Ukraine. His parents were Russian industrial workers. He also started to work in the metallurgical industry, and by 1935 he had graduated from the metallurgical institute in his home town. At the institute he became a Communist Party organizer and continued this work while serving in the Red Army until 1937. When he returned from service he worked in the Dneprodzerzhinsk city and oblast party committees. Later he became a section chief in the Dnepropetrovsk Oblast Party Committee. During the Second World War he was re-assigned to the army as a political leader in the Ukraine and in the Caucasus Mountains. Brezhnev received special recognition for his participation in the defense of Tuapse in a battle against the Germans. As the Germans retreated he took part in the liberation of Hungary, Poland, and Czechoslovakia.

In 1946 Brezhnev returned to political work and became the First Secretary of the Zaporozhe Oblast Committee. A year later he was appointed by Nikita Khrushchev, who was then First Secretary of the Ukraine, to be the First Secretary of the Dnepropetrovsk Oblast Party Committee. He remained in that position and proved himself during the re-construction of the Dnepropetrovsk Hydro-Electric Power Dam. In 1950 he was appointed by Stalin to be the First Secretary of the Moldavian Republic, where he had the opportunity to use his knowledge as an agriculture specialist and his political ability. His successes in organizing collective farms in Moldavia gained him further recognition, and Khrushchev recommended him to work in Moscow. At the 19th Party Congress in 1952 Brezhnev became a Candidate Member of the Politburo only to lose that position during the reorganization of the Communist Party leadership after the death of Stalin in 1953. He worked for a short while in Moscow for the Soviet Navy. But when Khrushchev gained power, he assigned Brezhnev to head the Virgin Lands Project in the Kazakh Republic. Fortunately for Brezhnev, the weather was favorable that year and his work resulted in a bumper grain harvest. At the 20th Party Congress in 1956 he had received the Order of Lenin and a reputation of being successful. This achievement enabled him to be re-appointed as a Candidate Member to the Politburo and as a Secretary of the Central Committee. From 1956 to 1960 he went on official delegations to Korea, Finland, Africa, Yugoslavia, China, and Czechoslovakia. He has also been regularly elected to the USSR Supreme Soviet since 1950. In 1960 he became a full member of the Politburo under the sponsorship of Khrushchev. At that time he also became the Chairman of the Presidium of the Supreme Soviet and made that office much more than a titular position. Brezhnev participated in major responsibilities and decisions and gained the ability, reputation, and support to become the First Secretary of the Communist Party upon the removal of Khrushchev in 1964. Since then he has increased his support and assumed the title of General Secretary of the Communist Party.

Leonid Brezhnev has enjoyed a happy married life. His wife, Victoria Petrovna, has been a great support for him in his work and his climb to power. He attributes his success to her. They have two children, a daughter (Galina) and a son (Yuri), who are both married and have children of their own.

Brezhnev is considered to be a realist. His experience in the Ukraine and association with Khrushchev has made him more liberal in his views than some members of the Politburo, but Brezhnev has criticized Khrushchev for his unrealistic boasts and bungling in policy decisions. Brezhnev has been accused of returning to Stalinism, but his major interest is in maintaining stability both in domestic and foreign affairs. The support he gave to the Soviet intervention in Czechoslovakia in 1968 caused that policy to be called the "Brezhnev Doctrine". His critical remarks and policy decisions against dissent in the Soviet Union and his tempering down the de-Stalinization program of Khrushchev have gained him labels of conservatism and even neo-Stalinism, but he also is called a "revisionist" by the Chinese Communists and by some of the more conservative members of the Politburo. This latter label has largely come to him by his criticism of Chinese policies and his improved relations with the United States on the international scene and by his emphasis on agricultural production and an increase of consumer goods on the domestic scene.

Alexei Kosygin has been a new type of government official and party leader. His career started as an administrator in the textile industry. His strength was based on his exceptional capability as an administrator and as an executive rather than as a politician. However, he also proved himself as a competent political leader. Kosygin represented the Leningrad faction of the Communist Party and the commercial interests there. He has been a strong force in tempering the conservative powers both in the government administration and in the Politburo.

Kosygin was born in St. Petersburg (Leningrad) in February, 1904. His parents were Russians, who worked in industry. Kosygin attended the Leningrad Textile Institute and graduated from there in 1927. For several years after serving in the Red Army he worked in industrial management in Siberia. In 1935 he returned to Leningrad and worked as a director of a textile mill. He has also worked in party affairs since his joining the Communist Party in 1927. In 1938 he became the Chairman of the Executive Committee of the Leningrad City Soviet, and the next year he was named Commissar of the Textile Industry of the Soviet Union. In 1940 he was named Deputy Chairman of the Council of People's Commissars (Ministers), and also served as Chairman of the RSFSR Council of People's Commissars from 1943 to 1946. During the war he worked for the State Committee of Defense.

Kosygin's career was not adversely affected by the Blockade of Leningrad during the war or by the "Leningrad Affair" of 1948 and 1949. He continued to work in the Council of Ministers and serve as Minister of several ministries— Ministry of Finance, Ministry of Light Industry, and the Chairman of Gosplan (The State Planning Commission). During this time he was also a Deputy Chairman of the Council of Ministers, and in 1960 he became First Deputy Chairman of the Council of Ministers under Khrushchev.

Since 1946 Kosygin also held top party positions. He was a candidate member of the Politburo from 1946 to 1949, when he became a full member until Stalin's death. He again became a member of the Politburo in 1960 and has continued to serve in that position.

When Khrushchev was retired in 1964, Kosygin became the Chairman of the Council of Ministers. His experience in administrative and executive work has qualified him well for this position.

Kosygin is a mild-mannered man and has had a stabilizing influence in the Politburo. Possibly his experiences during the war have made him a proponent of peace. At least he has played a more pacifist role than some of his counterparts. He resisted initially the Soviet intervention in Czechoslovakia in 1968. During the Chinese border conflicts he advocated restraint, and he has urged for the limited disarmament agreements with the United States. On the domestic scene he has continued to advocate the spirit of Khrushchev's reforms, but he is much more practical than his former mentor. His main economic interest is that of increasing the production of consumer goods. Kosygin can largely take credit for the improvement of the standard of living in the Soviet Union during the last ten years. However, Kosygin is not striving for more power, and it is doubtful that he will take over Brezhnev's position.

The balance between Brezhnev and Kosygin was thought to be a temporary arrangement and that one of them would take over both positions within a short time. This belief was not valid. Neither Brezhnev or Kosygin could do as well as the other in the other's position. Brezhnev was a politician, and Kosygin was an administrator. The concept of collective leadership or that of separation of powers which was practiced by Brezhnev and Kosygin unified the party and strengthened the economy. But a balance of philosophy still persisted. Brezhnev tended to be more conservative both in domestic affairs and foreign policy than Kosygin. Change in the leadership must come, but that change would probably not take the form of one replacing the other. That change must come from others.

The most challenging individual for leadership was Nikolai Podgorny. He had become the Chairman of the Supreme Soviet in 1965. He also had been accepted into the Politburo by Khrushchev in 1960. His strength lay both in administration and politics. But he is three years older than Brezhnev and becomes less of a contestant for top positions each year Brezhnev remains strong and well.

Podgorny was born in 1903. His parents were Ukrainians, who worked in industry. Podgorny attended school in Kiev, and in 1930 he graduated from the Institute of the Food Industry there and also joined the Communist Party. He then became an engineer in the sugar industry. In 1939 he was named a deputy chairman of both the Ukrainian Commissariat of the Food Industry and the USSR Commissariat of the Food Industry. During the 1930's he also worked in the regional committees of the Communist Party in the Poltava Oblast of the Ukraine.

In 1942 Podgorny was assigned as director of the Moscow Technological Institute of the Food Industry, where he worked during the war. After the war he became the Ukrainian representative in the Council of Ministers of the USSR.

After 1950 he advanced rapidly in the Communist Party of the Ukraine. He became First Secretary of the Kharkov Oblast Committee, and by 1957 he was the First Secretary of the Central Committee of the Ukrainian Communist Party. In 1960 he became a member of the USSR Politburo and has continued to serve there. He was given additional work as a secretary of the Central Committee from 1963 until his appointment as Chairman of the Supreme Soviet in 1965.

Podgorny has travelled abroad on several occasions. He came to the United Nations with Khrushchev in 1960. He has also gone as a Soviet emissary to Czechoslovakia, East Germany, Rumania, Yugoslavia, Canada, China, and North Vietnam.

Podgorny was closely associated with Khrushchev. His political philosophy has been even more liberal than Kosygin's.

After the Czechoslovak Affair in 1968 Podgorny asserted himself in
Party leadership and increased his influence as Chairman of the
Supreme Soviet to a greater level of responsibility than his predecessor, Brezhnev, had done. During the 1969-1970 time of decisions he contested the views of Brezhnev causing some rumors that
he was striving for Brezhnev's position. Podgorny is a dynamic
person, but he was more concerned with improving international
relations and preventing war than in gaining more power for power's
sake. Podgorny has had the responsibility of consulting the Chinese
and the North Vietnamese in regard to the Vietnam War. Several
times he has travelled to the capitols of these countries. In 1972,
if not before, he urged the North Vietnamese to come to terms with
the United States and the Saigon Government at the Paris Peace
talks.

One of the oldest members of the Politburo is Mikhail Suslov.
He is the only one, except for Kosygin, who has been in the Politburo during Stalin's era. Suslov is a Stalinist. He strongly opposed
Khrushchev and tried several times to have Khrushchev removed
from power. Suslov also believed that he could resolve the differences between Khrushchev and Mao Tse Tung. In 1963 he headed
a delegation to China in an attempt to do that, but he was unsuccessful. For years he had lead the opposition of the Moscow faction
against Khrushchev, but in 1963 and 1964 his power decreased. In
1963 he became seriously ill, and in 1964 Khrushchev was ousted
from power. The position of Suslov since then has fluctuated, but
he continued to contribute a conservative influence in the Politburo.

Mikhail Suslov was born near Ulanovsk in 1902. His parents
were poor farmers. From 1918 to 1920 he worked in the Komsomol
organization in Saratov and served on the Poverty Relief Committee.
In 1921 he became a member of the Communist Party and continued
his education. After graduating from an institute in 1928 he began
to teach in the Moscow University. In the 1930's he was assigned
to work in the Urals and in the Chernigov Oblast of the Ukraine in
Communist Party activities. In 1937 Suslov became a secretary of
the Rostov Oblast Committee, and in 1939 he became First Secretary
of the Stavropol Krai Committee of the Communist Party. During
the war he continued to work in the Northern Caucasus and headed
the Stavropol Headquarters of the Partisan Divisions. After the
war he worked as Chairman of the Bureau for Lithuania within the
Central Committee of the USSR Communist Party. While in Lithuania he conducted purge trials.

Since 1947 Mikhail Suslov has been a secretary of the Central
Committee. In 1952 he was named to the Politburo, but after

Stalin's death he was dismissed. He continued to work as a representative in the Supreme Soviet and became Chairman of the Commission on Foreign Affairs in the Soviet of the Union. In 1955 he was again named to the Politburo. When Molotov and others were removed from the Politburo in 1957, Suslov became the leader of the conservative faction. From that time until the ouster of Khrushchev he continually attacked Khrushchev's policies.

Suslov has travelled widely in Eastern Europe and in Asia, but he has never been to the Western Hemisphere. He opposed the moves of Khrushchev and later of Kosygin to improve relations with the United States. But the differences between the Soviet Union and China weakened his pro-Chinese position.

The possibility of Suslov gaining top power in the Soviet Union has been greatly reduced. He has remained a strong conservative, and his influence in the Politburo continued to affect Soviet policy decisions. Yet his health, his age, and the change of the international scene have weakened his position. In 1972 he was 70 years old and was due for retirement. But there was no indication that he would be retired. Arvid Pelshe, also a member of the Politburo, is two years older, and there is no mention of his retirement. Suslov asserted himself again in the 1969-70 as the leader of the conservative wing of the Party, but as before his role was to advocate military preparedness and security rather than his own ascension to power. Suslov appears to be a quiet, easy-going person, but he continues to wield much influence in the Politburo due to his reputation as the party theoretician and to his seniority in the Party and in the Politburo.

Dmitri S. Polyansky was believed by many Westerners to be a potential successor of Khrushchev during the early 1960's. At that time he was the youngest member of the Politburo and had had a phenomenal rise in political power. He had come from the position of First Secretary of the Crimean Oblast Committee in 1955 to Chairman of the RSFSR Council of Ministers in 1958 and to a Deputy Chairman of the USSR Council of Ministers in 1962. During the shuffle of the Politburo after the U-2 Affair in 1960 he was added to the Politburo membership. But even with his appointment as First Deputy Chairman of the USSR Council of Ministers in 1965 there have been few indications of a continued rise in power. Yet he does stand in a strong position and could compete with others for Kosygin's position some time in the future.

Polyansky was born near Kharkov in 1917. His parents were poor Ukrainian farmers, but Polyansky had the opportunity to attend the Kharkov Agricultural Institute and the Higher Party School. He joined the Communist Party in 1939 after working as a section manager in the Kharkov Oblast Committee of the Komsomol. He had also worked on a State Farm while he was studying at the institutes.

When the war broke out, Polyansky served for a while in the Soviet Army, but he continued to carry out his party responsibilities. He was assigned to the Altai Krai as a chief of the political section of a Machine Tractor Station in 1942 and later became the First Secretary of a regional committee of the party in the Altai Krai. After the war he was reassigned to the Ukraine, where he worked as a secretary in the Crimean Oblast Party Committee. In the early 1950's he was named chairman of the Executive Committee of the Crimean Oblast Soviet and First Secretary of the Crimean Oblast Party Committee. From there he moved into positions as First Secretary of the Orenburg Oblast Party Committee and later as First Secretary of the Krasnodar Krai Party Committee before becoming Chairman of the RSFSR Council of Ministers and a member of the Politburo.

Polyansky did come to the United States in 1960 as the head of a Soviet delegation, but his foreign travel has not been extensive. Since his appointment to the Politburo he has remained most of the time in Moscow. He did make a few trips to party conferences within the Soviet Union, e.g. one in Novosibirsk in 1967. His responsibility has been directly connected with a project to increase agricultural production.

After the drought of 1972 there was a poor harvest, particularly for grain and potatoes. Polyansky was asked to help promote agricultural production for the next year, and in January, 1973, he was named Minister of Agriculture for the USSR. Speculation that this was a beginning for his removal from the Politburo did not prove to be right. Instead Polyansky has maintained a solid position in the Politburo. It is more probable that he will some day be a successor to Brezhnev.

Andrei Kirilenko was born in 1906 in the Voronezh Oblast. His father was a Russian handicraftsman. Kirilenko worked as an electrician and a locksmith when he was young. He also worked in a coal mine in the Donetsk Basin. In 1931 he joined the Communist Party and started attending the Rybinsk Aviation Institute. He became a secretary of the Zaporozhye Oblast Committee before the war. During the war he was a member of the Military Soviet of the army and helped in the State Committee for Defense in an aircraft plant.

After the war Kililenko became the First Secretary of Oblast Committees, first at Nikolaevsk and then at Dneipropetrovsk. From

1955 to 1962 he was the First Secretary of the Sverdlovsk Oblast Committee, and then he was assigned to be the First Deputy Chairman of the Bureau for the USFSR in the Central Committee. He was added to the Politburo in 1965.

Kirill Mazurov was born in 1914 near Mogilev in Belorussia. His parents were poor Belorussian farmers. As a young man he worked as a technician on highway construction and served in the Soviet Army from 1936 to 1938. He was active in the Komsomol and became a secretary of the Gomel City Committee of the Komsomol in 1939. In 1940 he joined the Communist Party. He graduated from an Automobile-Road Technical Institute and also the Higher Party School.

During the Second World War he continued to work as a Komsomol leader. He was sent behind enemy lines to organize the Partisans. For his work he became a secretary of the Central Committee of the Komsomol of Belorussia, and in 1946 he was named First Secretary of that organization. In 1947 he was also selected to be a Deputy Manager of a section of the Belorussian Central Committee of the Communist Party. Later he became the First Secretary of the Minsk City Committee and then the First Secretary of the Minsk Oblast Committee. In 1953 he was named the Chairman of the Council of Ministers of the Belorussian Republic, and since 1956 he has been the First Secretary of the Communist Party of the Belorussian Republic. In 1965 when Mazurov was chosen to be a Politburo member, he was also assigned to be a First Deputy Chairman of the Council of Ministers of the USSR along with Polyansky.

Mazurov accompanied Brezhnev in a Soviet delegation to Bulgaria in 1967. He also has been assigned by the Council of Ministers to speak in various cities in the Soviet Union.

Mazurov has an excellent record, and the future looks promising for him.

Alexander Shelepin is one of the youngest members of the Politburo. He was born in 1918 in Voronezh, but he has spent most of his life in Moscow. His parents were Russian railroad workers. But Shelepin went to Moscow as a youth and graduated there from the Moscow Institute of History, Philosophy, and Literature. He joined the Communist Party in 1940.

Before the war Shelepin served in the Soviet Army, and he was sent to fight with the cavalry on the Finnish Front. He was assigned political work in the army. From 1940 to 1943 he returned to Moscow and worked as an instructor and a manager of a section and as secretary in the Central Committee of the Komsomol, and by

1958 he was the First Secretary of the Komsomol Central Committee and a manager of the Party Organization Section of the Central Committee of the CPSU. Also from 1958 through 1961 he was the Chairman of the Committee on State Security of the USSR.

Shelepin was released from other positions in 1961 and assigned as a secretary of the Central Committee of the CPSU. From 1962 he served both as a Deputy Chairman of the Council of Ministers of the USSR and as Chairman of the Committee on Party-State Control (now the Peoples Control Committee). When he was selected as a member of the Politburo in 1965, he lost his government positions, but he remained a secretary of the Central Committee. In September, 1967, Shelepin was also released from his position as a Central Committee secretary because he had been assigned the position of Chairman of the Trade Unions in July of that year. Since 1967 he has been active visiting various plants and enterprises in connection with his trade unions work.

Shelepin may be the first one to lose his position from the Politburo. His abilities have seemed to be better directed toward teaching and supervisory work than toward leadership and executive work. However, Shelepin is an intelligent man and still has youth in his favor. His future could also depend heavily on other changes in top leadership positions. He has been one of the more conservative members of the Politburo. He could work easily with Suslov or Polyansky.

The oldest member of the Politburo is Arvid Pelshe. He was selected to replace Anastas Mikoyan, who retired in 1966. Mikoyan had been a moderating influence in the Politburo. He had lasted through the times of Stalin, Khrushchev, and Brezhnev and appeared to be loyal to each at the proper times. Possibly Pelshe has been able to assume this same role, at least temporarily. Pelshe was already 67 at the time of his appointment to the Politburo.

Pelshe was born in Latvia in 1899. He joined the Communist Party in 1915, and he came to Petrograd (Leningrad) during the 1917 Revolution. He participated in the first congresses of the early soviets. During the Civil War he was assigned to work in Archangelsk as a leader of the transportation workers trade union. Later he worked as a political agitator in the Red Army and in State Farms.

Pelshe became a teacher of Marxism-Leninism in 1937, and when Latvia was annexed to the Soviet Union in 1940 he returned to Latvia and worked for the consolidation of Soviet power there. He became a secretary of the Central Committee of the Latvian Communist Party, and in 1959 he became its First Secretary. In 1966

Pelshe was released from other positions and assigned to be the Chairman of the Party Control Committee (now People's Control Committee) and a member of the USSR Politburo.

Arvid Pelshe has travelled to Volgograd and to Prague on official business for the Supreme Soviet and the Politburo. But he probably had a more honorary position than an influential one. Within a short time Pelshe will probably be retired.

Viktor Grishin was born in 1914 in Serpukhov in the Moscow Oblast. His parents were railroad workers, and after graduating from a technical school Grishin worked for the railroad at a steam engine depot. Later he became the deputy chief of the railroad station in Serpukhov. He did not continue his higher education.

In 1939 he joined the Communist Party, and during the war he carried out assignments for the Party in the Soviet Army. He had previously worked as a secretary of the party committee of the railroad and later became the secretary of the Serpukhov City Committee.

After the war he worked in the Moscow Oblast Party Committee, where he became a section manager and a second secretary of the committee. He also worked as the director of the Department of Machine-Building in the Moscow City Committee. Since 1952 he has been a delegate to the Supreme Soviet and served there as a member of the Commission for Foreign Affairs in the Soviet of the Union.

In 1956 Grishin became the Chairman of the All-Union Central Council of Trade Unions, and in 1958 assigned to serve as a member of the Executive Committee for the World Council of Trade Unions. In that capacity he headed delegations to Finland, Italy, Czechoslovakia, Hungary, and North Vietnam in the early 1960's.

In the shake-up after the U-2 Affair he was named to be a Candidate Member to the Politburo and served there from 1961 to 1971. In 1967 he also became a Secretary of the Central Committee and the First Secretary of the Moscow Oblast Committee. Then in 1971 at the 24th Party Congress he was called to be a member of the Politburo, where he continued to represent the interests of the Moscow conservatives.

Dinmukhamed Kunayev was the First Secretary of the Kazakh Republic when he was selected to be a member of the Politburo in 1971. He had also been a candidate to the Politburo since 1965. His advancement to the Politburo follows the resolution of the disputes along his Kazakh Republic and the China border. It is possible that this situation influenced his selection into the Politburo. He does represent a conservative point of view.

229

Kunayev was born in 1912. He is a Kazakh. He started his career in the metallurgy industry in 1936, after completing the Moscow Institute of Nonferrous Metals and Gold. He worked as a master, a section chief, a head engineer and later as the director of miners at the Balkhash Copper Smelting Combine. He joined the Communist Party in 1939.

Later Kunayev became the director of the Leninogorsk Mine Smelter, and in 1942 he was assigned to be the deputy chairman of the Council of Ministers of the Kazakh Republic. He also became the President of the Kazakh Academy of Sciences. In 1955 he became the Chairman of the Kazakh Council of Ministers and alternatively served in that position (1955-60 and 1962-64) and also as First Secretary of the Kazakh Communist Party (1960-62 and since 1964).

As a member of the Politburo Kunayev represents Soviet Central Asia and more particularly the Kazakh Republic. Brezhnev has selected First Secretaries of various Union Republics as part of his policy to unify the top leadership of the Soviet Union. It is not probable that Kunayev's position will provide him an opportunity for further advancement.

Vladimir Shcherbitsky had also been a Candidate to the Politburo before his advancement into the Politburo in 1971. He has also continued to be the Chairman of the Council of Ministers of the Ukrainian Republic. By profession he is a chemical engineer, and he joined the Communist Party in 1941. Khrushchev selected him to be a Candidate to the Politburo in 1962.

Shcherbitsky was born in 1918 in the Ukraine. In 1934-36 he worked as an instructor in the local Dnepropetrovsk Komsomol organization. After graduating from the Chemical Technological Institute there in 1941, he became a mechanic at an experimental factory in Dnepropetrovsk, but he was called to serve in the Red Army during the war. After the war he worked in Party affairs, first in a factory Party organization and then in the Dneprodzerzhinsk City Committee. By 1952 he had ascended to the position of First Secretary of that City Committee, and in 1955 he became First Secretary to the Dnepropetrovsk Oblast Committee. From 1956 to 1961 he was a member of the Central Auditing Commission of the USSR Communist Party, after which he became the Chairman of the Ukrainian Council of Ministers. In 1962 he was named as a Candidate Member to the Politburo and became a full member in 1971.

Feodor Kulakov was born in 1918 in the Penza Oblast. His parents were farmers. He also worked on the farm and became an agronomist. In 1938 he became a manager of a department in a Sugar Combine and attended the Agricultural Institute, from which he graduated in 1941. He joined the Communist Party in 1940 and became a leader in the Komsomol regional Committee. Later he became the Chairman of the Executive Committee of the Regional Party Committee. He continued to advance in the Party in the Penza Oblast. After becoming chief of the Oblast Directorate on Agriculture, he was named Chairman of the Penza Oblast Soviet. His advancement continued to move rapidly, and he became in 1955 the Deputy Minister of Agriculture of the RSFSR and later the Minister of Grain Products of the RSFSR. In 1960 he was named the First Secretary of the Stavropol Party Committee. His next assignment was that of Manager of the Agricultural Section of the Central Committee of the Party. Since 1965 he has been a secretary of the Central Committee as well as a Section Manager. In 1971 Kulakov was called to be a member of the Politburo without having served as a Candidate Member first.

The future looks promising for Kulakov. Apparently he has greatly impressed Brezhnev because of his accomplishments in agriculture and in political work. The other three younger members of the Politburo, Polyansky, Shelepin, and Shcherbitsky are administrators and have futures in the Council of Ministers, but Kulakov's future appears to be more along lines of political and executive work. Some day he may become the General Secretary of the Party. His positions as a Politburo Member and a Secretary to the Central Committee are shared with him only by Brezhnev, Suslov, and Kirilenko.

Yuri Andropov has been a specialist in foreign affairs. He served in the diplomatic corps and became the Ambassador to Hungary. In 1967 he was assigned to be the Chairman of the Committee of State Security. He has been a hard-liner or conservative both in foreign affairs and in domestic issues. Andropov was named a Secretary of the Central Committee in 1962 and a Candidate to the Politburo in 1967. Together with Andrei Grechko, Minister of Defense, and Andrei Gromyko, Minister of Foreign Affairs, Andropov was selected to be a member of the Politburo in the spring of 1973.

Andropov was born in 1914. His parents were government workers for the railroad. He did not finish his higher education, but he did become a member of the Communist Party in 1939. As a youth he worked as a telegrapher and served in the navy. In 1936 Andropov completed his studies at a Water Transportation Tekhnikum and was assigned to work in the shipyards in the Central Committee

for the Komsomol. He was sent to the Karelian Republic in 1940 to
be the First Secretary of the Komsomol there. He continued to do
Party work in the Karelian Republic (which later became the
Karelian Autonomous Republic) as a Second Secretary to the
Petrozavodsk City Committee and in 1947 the Second Secretary
to the Central Committee of Karelia.

From 1951 to 1953 Andropov worked as an inspector and as
a manager of a sub-section of the Central Committee of the Communist Party of the USSR. This intelligence work was suspended
or possibly continued as he served as Ambassador to Hungary
from 1953 to 1957, but he resumed this work in the Central Committee after 1957 and became manager of that section.

Since 1962 Andropov has also been a deputy in the Supreme
Soviet, where he has served as a member of the Commission on
Foreign Affairs in the Soviet of the Union. He has also served on
the Committee of People's Control, but he was released from his
position as Secretary to the Central Committee in 1970.

Andropov is a relatively young man. His appointment to the
Politburo in 1973 was an indicator of Brezhnev's need for conservative support for his policies. Andropov's future depends largely on
Brezhnev's or his successor's need for this conservative support.
In this way, Andropov is a key man to watch as an indicator for
conservative trends or a move away from them. His retention in
the Politburo or an advancement in Soviet affairs could mean a
return to Stalinism.

Andrei Gromyko has had a long career in diplomatic affairs
and is probably the best known Soviet citizen in the United States.
Since 1939 he served in the Soviet Embassy in the United States,
first as an advisor and later as Ambassador. Then since 1946 he
has served as the Soviet representative in the United Nations
Security Council in New York. For a while he was the Soviet
Ambassador in Great Britain, but he returned to his work in the
United Nations. In 1953 he served also as the first deputy to the
Minister of Foreign Affairs of the Soviet Union, and in 1957 he be-
came the Minister. In the spring of 1973 he was named to be a
member of the Politburo along with Andrei Grechko, Minister of
Defense, and Yuri Andropov, Chairman of the Committee on State
Security.

Gromyko was born in 1909 in the family of a poor peasant.
He is a Russian. He joined the Communist Party in 1931 and con-
tinued his education. He received a doctor's degree in economics.
He has also been awarded a medal as a Hero of Socialist Labor.

Until 1936 he was a student in an agricultural tekhnikum, and then worked on his degree in a scientific research institute of the economics of agriculture. After 1936 he became a senior scientific worker in the Institute of Economics in the Soviet Academy of Sciences, before he started his diplomatic career.

Gromyko has been a member of the Central Committee of the Communist Party and has served as a deputy in the Supreme Soviet for many years.

Gromyko's appointment to the Politburo in 1973 appeared to be a move which was consistent with Brezhnev's policy for improving relations with the United States. His future in the Politburo depends on the success and continuation of Brezhnev's policies with the United States. Gromyko could be considered a balance in the political sense against the more conservative Andropov and Grechko. His retention or advancement in the Politburo could be an indicator for much better relations with the West.

Andrei Grechko has served as the Minister of Defense of the USSR since 1967. He is a Marshall of the Soviet Union and has a longer career in the military than Gromyko has had in the diplomatic forces. Grechko has served in the army since 1919. He was appointed as a member of the Politburo along with Gromyko and Andropov in the spring of 1973.

Grechko was born in 1903. He was 70 at the time of his appointment to the Politburo. He is a Ukrainian. He joined the Communist Party in 1928 and received his higher education at the Frunze Military Academy and at the Academy of the General Staff. He worked up the ranks in the army since 1919 as a commander of a platoon, a squadron, a regiment, and then as the chief of staff of a division. During the Second World War he was a commander of a division, an army corps, and then an army. He became the deputy commander of the troops on the First Ukrainian Front. After the war he served as the commander of the troops in the Kiev Military District. After that he served as a commander of the Soviet troops in Germany, and then served as the Chief Commander of the Infantry. In 1958 he became the First Deputy to the Minister of Defense and the Chief Commander of the United Military Forces of the Warsaw Pact. In 1967 he became Minister of the Armed Forces.

Grechko has served as a member of the Central Committee of the Communist Party and as a deputy in the Supreme Soviet for many years. His appointment to the Politburo was another attempt by Brezhnev to unify his support for improved relations with West Germany and the United States. Marshall Zhukov was used temporarily by Khrushchev for unification of his forces in 1957, and it appeared that this inclusion of the top military man of the Soviet Union in the Politburo was for the same purpose. Grechko's age and his long military career are both against him for any aspirations for retention or advancement in the Politburo.

CANDIDATES TO THE POLITBURO

There are on the average between five and ten candidates or alternates to the Politburo. These people have almost as much political power as members of the Politburo, and they function alongside them. The candidates accompany Politburo members on domestic tours and on foreign delegations. Generally, a few of them accompany the Politburo members when meeting or seeing off foreign dignitaries.

A candidate may become a member of the Politburo, may remain a candidate for a long time, or may be dropped from that position and assigned to other work. Of the 11 Politburo members of 1969 seven were candidates before becoming full members. Of the ten candidates in 1959 two had previously been Politburo members for a short time, five became and still are Politburo members, one is still a candidate, and four (including the two previous members) have been dropped.

If this pattern continues several of the present candidates will become members of the Politburo. For this reason it is important to know something about their backgrounds.

The most active candidates in the late 60's were Ustinov, Grishin, and Demichev. These three also held top government positions in Moscow and were in the public eye in both government and party functions. All three were also secretaries of the Central Committee of the CPSU, which position is also a main stepping stone into the Politburo. Ustinov, Grishin, and Demichev have had good political careers, and they are Russians rather than other nationals. These conditions are all favorable for their advancement into the Politburo. Grishin was advanced to the Politburo in 1971.

<u>Dmitrii Ustinov</u> was born in 1908 in Samara (now Kuibyshev) on the middle Volga. However, he has spent most of his life in Leningrad and Moscow. His parents were industrial workers, and he also worked in industry as a machinist. In 1927 he joined the Communist Party and enrolled in the Leningrad Military-Mechanical Institute. He graduated in 1934 as a civil engineer and worked at the "Bolshevik" industrial plant in Leningrad. He later became the plant director.

During the war Ustinov was the Peoples Commissar of Armaments, and in 1953 he became the Minister of the Defense Industry of the USSR. Since 1957 he has served in the Council of Ministers, first as its deputy chairman and later as its First Deputy Chairman. From 1963 to 1965 he was also the Chairman of the All-Union Soviet of the National Economy. In that capacity he coordinated the executive responsibilities of the Regional Economic Councils throughout the USSR.

In 1965 Ustinov was named to be a Candidate to the Politburo and a Secretary of the Central Committee. He has twice been awarded the honor of being a Hero of Socialist Labor and has received the Laureate of State Prizes. His chances for advancement looked good until he was by-passed in 1971 by the appointment of four others. Ustinov was closely associated with Khrushchev. His outlook is liberal, and he has probably been opposed by conservatives. But opportunities could easily improve for him to advance within the next few years.

Peotr Demichev was also by-passed during the 1971 expansion of the Politburo membership, and his chances for advancement also depend on the direction of future political trends. He is more conservative than Ustinov. He is also ten years younger.

Demichev was born in 1918 in Kirov in the Kaluga Oblast, which is south of Moscow. His parents were industrial workers. He joined the Communist Party in 1939, when he was serving in the Soviet Army. He graduated from the Military Academy, the Mendeleev Chemical Engineering Institute in Moscow, and the Higher Party School.

After the war Demichev worked in the Mendeleev Chemical Engineering Institute and was a leader in a regional party committee in Moscow. He worked up from being a regional committee secretary to being the Secretary of the Moscow Oblast Party Committee. In 1958 he was given administrative responsibilities in the USSR Council of Ministers and later became the First Secretary of the Moscow City Committee.

In 1962 he was named a Secretary of the Central Committee, and in 1964 he became a Candidate to the Politburo. In the 1960's he also headed Soviet delegations to Germany, Hungary, Czechoslovakia, Poland and Bulgaria.

Peotr Masherov came to the position of a Candidate to the Politburo as the First Secretary of the Belorussian Republic and retained that position. His work has been closely related to that within his Union Republic.

Masherov was born in 1918. His parents were farmers. He

graduated from the Vitbetsk Pedagogical Institute in 1939 and joined
the Communist Party in 1943. Before the war he was a teacher in
a secondary school, and during the war he was a leader of the
Partisans. Masherov advanced from a detachment commander to
that of brigade commissar. He also was a Komsomol leader and in
1947 became the First Secretary of the Belorussian Komsomol.
From that position he moved to secretary positions in the Communist Party in Minsk, Brest, and the Belorussian Central Committee.
In 1965 he became the First Secretary of the Belorussian Republic
and a Candidate Member to the Politburo.

Masherov is only four years younger than Kirill Mazurov,
his predecessor as First Secretary of Belorussia and now member
of the Politburo. It is unlikely that two Belorussians would be in
the Politburo at the same time, and Mazurov could remain there a
long time. It can be expected that Masherov's advancement into the
Politburo will not be soon.

Shafar Rashidov was born in 1917. He is the son of a poor
Uzbek farmer. His higher education was completed at the Samarkand State University and at the Higher Party School of the Central
Committee. His Party membership dates back to 1939. In his
youth he was a teacher in a secondary school and later an editor of
a Smarkand Oblast newspaper. During the war he was assigned to
political work in the Soviet Army. After the war he returned to
Samarkand, where he became the Secretary of the Smarkand Oblast
Committee. In 1947 he worked as the managing editor of the newspaper, "Red Uzbekistan." For two years afterwards he was the
Chairman of the Uzbek Writers Union. In 1950 he became the
Chairman of the Uzbek Supreme Soviet and in 1959 the First Secre-
tary of the Uzbek Republic. In 1962 he was named a Candidate
Member to the Politburo.

Rashidov is still a young man. He could have been expected
to be named a member of the Politburo before Kunayev. They are
both from Central Asia, and Rashidov was a Candidate Member
three years longer. He is also five years younger. Yet Kunayev
was named a Politburo member in 1971 by-passing Rashidov.
Rashidov does come from the more populous Republic, but it is
unlikely that both of them would be in the Politburo at the same time.
But considering that Tashkent is now the 4th largest city in the Soviet
Union, political realists have reason to expect that an Uzbek should
have a Politburo member. And Rashidov does stand better chances
than Masherov.

Milhail Solomentsev was appointed as a Candidate Member of
the Politburo in 1972. He has had extensive leadership experience

and has held major responsibilities. His outlook is fairly liberal, and his advancement is an indicator of more liberal trends in Soviet policy.

Solomentsev was born in 1913 near Leningrad. His parents were farmers, and in his youth he worked on a collective farm. But he had the opportunity to attend the Leningrad Polytechnical Institute. When he graduated from that Institute in 1940, he became a member of the Communist Party. After that he worked as an engineer and later became a director of an industrial plant. In 1954 Solomentsev was assigned to be a Secretary of the Chelyabinsk Oblast Party Committee, and in 1957 he received the position as Chairman of the Chelyabinsk Economic Region Soviet. In 1959 he was the First Secretary of the Karaganda Oblast Committee and until 1964 he served as the Second Secretary of the Kazakh Central Committee. In 1964 he was re-assigned to be the First Secretary of the Rostov Oblast Committee. This demotion probably relates to the ouster of Khrushchev, with whom Solomentsev may be identified ideologically. But in 1966 he was given a position as a manager in the Heavy Industry Section of the Central Committee of the USSR. Solomentsev continued to serve as a representative in the Supreme Soviet and has been assigned to be the Chairman of the Commission on Legislative Proposals.

His assignment as a Secretary of the Central Committee was in 1966, and in 1972 he was advanced to the position of a Candidate Member of the Politburo. Depending on the trends in Soviet policies, Solomentsev may have the opportunity soon to become a Member of the Politburo.

Boris Ponomarev was named to be a candidate to the Politburo in the fall of 1972. He retained his position as a Secretary of the Central Committee, which he received in 1961.

Ponomarev was born in 1905. His parents were government workers, and he attended the Moscow State University and the Institute of Red Professorships. He attained the rank of a professor and that of an academician. In his youth he worked in the Komsomol and in the Communist Party in the Ryazin Province during the Civil War. In 1926 he became a deputy director of a propaganda group for the Central Committee and was assigned to work in the Don Basin and in Turkmenia. In 1933 he returned to his teaching profession and became an assistant director in the Party History Institute of Red Professorships. Later he became a deputy director of the Institute on Marxism, Engelism, and Leninism.

After the war Ponomarev worked in the Central Committee of the Party and was later assigned as the Director of the Soviet on the Cominform in the Council of Ministers of the USSR. In 1954 he was named to be a Section Manager in the Central Committee. He also served as the Chairman of the Commission on Foreign Affairs in the Soviet of Nationalities in the Supreme Soviet.

His promotion to become a Candidate to the Politburo was unexpected. He was 68 years old, and he had been by-passed several times, while other Secretaries to the Central Committee had been selected. It is unlikely that he will ever become a member of the Politburo.

Grigori Romanov became a Candidate to the Politburo in the spring of 1973, when Gromyko, Grechko, and Andropov became Politburo members. There may have been some connection politically with this quest for broad support of Brezhnev's policies by the naming of Romanov to the position of a Candidate to the Politburo. It may be that Grigori Romanov had earned this recognition. He had been the First Secretary of the Leningrad Oblast Committee. But it is the first time, since the fall of tsarism, that a Romanov has been in the inner circles of the top leadership of the country.

Romanov was born in 1923. He is a Russian. He joined the Communist Party in 1944, and he received his higher education at the Leningrad Ship Building Institute. During the Second World War he served in the Soviet Army. After the war he worked in the ship building plant and became a secretary to a party committee. In 1957 he became the secretary of the Kirov Regional Committee of the Communist Party in Leningrad, and later he was named secretary of the Leningrad City Committee. In 1963 he became the Second Secretary of the Leningrad Oblast Committee, and in 1970 the First Secretary.

He has served as a member of the Commission on Construction and on Industrial Building Materials in the Soviet of the Union in the Supreme Soviet.

Romanov is a young man and may have a good future, but it may take time to see any change. It is doubtful that he will become a Politburo member soon.

SECRETARIES

The Secretaries of the Central Committee are usually Members of the Politburo, Candidate Members, or potential choices for either. They are top political leaders.

Four of the Secretaries (Brezhnev, Suslov, Kirilenko, and Kulakov) are Politburo Members, and four of them (Demichev,

Solomentsev, Ustinov, and Ponomarev) are Candidate Members.
The other three Secretaries (Kapitonov, Dolgikh and Katushev)
hold responsible positions in top government or party commissions.
It is noteworthy also that all the Secretaries are Russians rather
than other nationalities.

Ivan Kapitonov became a Secretary to the Central Committee
in 1965. Previous to that time he was active in Party activities in
the Moscow area. His most recent assignment was that of Manager
of a Party Organization Section in the Central Committee.

Kapitonov was born in 1915 near Moscow. His parents were
farmers. He received his higher education at the Moscow Institute
of Civil Engineering. Upon graduation from that Institute in 1939
he became a member of the Communist Party, and he worked as a
civil engineer. Since 1941 he has worked in party and government
work as a manager of a section, a local party organization secretary,
and the chairman of a local committee in Moscow. In 1952 he was
appointed to be the First Secretary of the Moscow City Committee
of the Party, and in 1954 he became the First Secretary of the
Moscow Oblast Committee. From 1959 to 1964 Kapitonov was re-
assigned by Khrushchev to the Ivanov Oblast Committee, and after
Khrushchev's ouster in 1964 he was assigned to be a member of the
Bureau of the Central Committee on the RSFSR and as a manager of
a Section on Party Organizations of the RSFSR Central Committee.
Later he received his assignment in the USSR Central Committee,
and in 1965 he was appointed as a Secretary to the Central Committee.

Kapitonov's association with the Moscow Party leadership,
his demotion during the time of Khrushchev's era, and the return
to a better position in the central leadership indicate that he is
conservative in his political leanings. He may soon become a
Candidate Member and may follow Kulakov's example of being
named a Politburo Member without first being a Candidate Member.
Of course, his future depends on the trends toward more conservative policies in the top leadership.

A man with a promising future is Konstantin Katushev. He
became a Secretary of the Central Committee in 1969. He was born
in 1927, which makes him much younger than any of the other top
Soviet leaders. Since his advancement coincided with a time of
indecision in the Politburo, it may be that his abilities lie in his
administrative qualifications and leadership potential rather than in
his liberal or conservative political leanings.

Katushev's home was Gorky. His higher education was at the
Gorky Polytechnical Institute, where he graduated in 1952 as a drafts-

man. In that same year he joined the Communist Party and worked
as a secretary in the Party Bureau of the Gorky Automobile Plant.
In 1959 he was assigned to be the Second Secretary of the Automobile
Plant Party Organization and later to be the First Secretary. These
positions were followed by his assignments as the First Secretary of
the Gorky City Committee and then as First Secretary of the Gorky
Oblast Committee. He was also a representative in the Supreme
Soviet and served as a member of the Commission on Construction
and Building Materials in the Soviet of the Union.

Katushev's assignments in the Central Committee also
involved him in the Moscow Party Aktiv in June, 1969, and in the
Plenum of the Central Committee. Then in 1969 he was named to
his position as Secretary of the Central Committee.

Vladimir Dolgikh was selected as a Secretary of the Central
Committee in the fall of 1972. He came to this position from that
of First Secretary of the Krasnoyarsk Krai Committee of the Communist Party.

Dolgikh was born in 1924. He is a Russian. He earned a
degree of Candidate of Sciences at the Irkutsk Mining-Metallurgical
Institute. He joined the Communist Party in 1941. He has received
the recognition as a Hero of Socialist Labor.

During the Second World War Dolgikh served in the Soviet
Army. He worked at plants in Krasnoyarsk and advanced from a
shift foreman to chief engineer. In 1962 he became the director
of the Norilsk Mining-Metallurgical Combine. In 1969 he returned
to Krasnoyarsk as the First Secretary of the Krasnoyarsk Krai.

Dolgikh has served as a member of the Commission on
Industry in the Soviet of the Union in the Supreme Soviet and as a
deputy in the Supreme Soviet. He is a young man, who has a promising future in the Communist Party.

Deputaty Verkhovnogo Soveta SSSR, Sed'moy Sozyv, Moscow:
Izdatel'stvo "Izvestiya Sovetov Deputatov Trudyashchikhsya
SSSR, 1956, 522 pp.

Deputaty Verkhovnogo Soveta SSSR, Vos'moi Sozyv, Moscow:
Izdatel'stvo "Izvestiya Sovetov Deputatov Trudyashchikhsya
SSSR, 1970, 552 pp.

Ellison, Herbert J., History of Russia, New York: Holt, Rinehart,
& Winston, 1964, 644 pp.

Fitzsimmons, Thomas et als., USSR its people its society its culture, New Haven: Hraf Press, 1960, 590 pp.

Gunther, John, Inside Russia Today, New York: Pyramid Books,
1962, 602 pp.

Izvestiya, Moscow, 1967-1975.

Lebed, A. I. et als. (eds.), Who's Who in the USSR 1965-66, New
York: The Scarecrow Press, Inc., 1966, 1189 pp.

Maxwell, Robert (ed.), Information USSR, New York: Macmillan
Co., Pergamon Press, 1962, 982 pp.

Ostrovityanov, K. V. (ed.), Istoriya Akademii Nauk, Vol. 1,
Moscow: Izdatel'stvo Akademii Nauk SSSR, 1958, 483 pp.

Pares, Bernard, A History of Russia, New Haven: Yale University
Press, 1961, 512 pp.

Vvedenskiy, B. A., Ezhegodnik Bol'shoi Sovetskoy Entsiklopedii
1959, Moscow: Izdatel'stvo "Sovetskaya Entsiklopediya",
1959, 631 pp.

_____, Ezhegodnik Bol'shoi Sovetskoy Entsiklopedii
1972, Moscow: Izdatel'stvo "Sovetskaya Entsiklopediya",
1972, 623 pp.

_____, Ezhegodnik Bol'shoi Sovetskoy Entsiklopedii
1967, Moscow: Izdatel'stvo "Sovetskaya Entsiklopediya",
1967, 622 pp.

Walsh, Warren Bartlett, Russia and the Soviet Union, Ann Arbor:
University of Michigan Press, 1958, 483 pp.

Whiting, Kenneth R., The Soviet Union Today, New York: Frederick
A. Praeger, Publishers, 1966, 423 pp.

THE PATH TO COMMUNISM

Lenin outlined the way to socialism. Stalin emphasized the concept of "socialism in one country", and in 1936 he stated that socialism had been achieved. The bases for socialism were the industrialization and electrification of the country as Lenin advocated and the collectivization of agriculture as Stalin carried out. It meant that there was no longer any private ownership of the means of production and that the whole economy of the country followed a state plan.

The path to Communism was then interrupted by the Second World War, and it was well into the 1950's before the losses could be regained. By the time that Khrushchev came to power both industrial and agricultural production were steadily increasing under the Five Year Plans, but Khrushchev did not think that the pace was fast enough. He revised the Five Year Plan and extended it to a Seven Year Plan. He then started building the conditions for strengthening and improving the society in preparation for a forward thrust toward a communist society. In the 21st Party Congress in 1959 and the 22nd Party Congress in 1961 Khrushchev outlined the steps toward Communism. He stated that the Soviet Union would soon surpass all industrialized societies, including the United States, and that a Communist society was only a short way in the future.

Even though Khrushchev's dream was somewhat unrealistic, his successors did not retreat from the path or discard the basic steps. They continued the progress toward a Communist Society.

By 1960 the world situation had changed tremendously since the 1917 Revolution both inside the Soviet Union and throughout the rest of the world. Soviet leaders looked at the changes and were strengthened in their convictions of the inevitability of communism. The Soviet Union had become second only to the United States in economic production, political power, and military strength. This was a far cry from the backward Russia of the tsars. The Soviet Union also was the first nation to launch an artificial satellite into space and around the world. It was also the Soviet Union that first launched a man into space and recovered him safely.

Outside of the Soviet Union there were also great changes that indicated to the Soviet leaders that the Capitalist system was dying. In the 1930's the Capitalist World suffered an economic depression that it could not pull out of until capitalist countries began waging war against each other and later against the Soviet Union. During this time the wealthy industrialists and government leaders of the capitalist countries became richer, but their control over their colonies grew weaker. Even with the combining of monopolies of separate states into international cartels, the capitalists may have gained more money, but they did lose political and economic control over foreign possessions. Colonies were becoming independent states both politically and economically. In addition, several of the poorer states were overthrowing capitalism and accepting socialism. The predictions of Marx and Lenin appeared to be coming true. The Phillipines, India, parts of Korea and Indo-China, and parts of Africa were gaining independence. The war to destroy the Soviet Union had failed, and in place of destruction there was an expansion of socialism. People's Democracies were set up in Poland, East Germany, Bulgaria, Rumania, Hungary, and Czechoslovakia. These events were followed by China and even Cuba, in the Western Hemisphere, becoming socialist states. Even in the stronger capitalist states, such as the United States, capitalist presidents and the candidates to the presidency, were millionaires, while poverty, discrimination, and racism still persisted in the United States.

Stalinism had adversely affected the Soviet society. Also the economic production of the United States still exceeded that of the Soviet Union. These facts were admitted by Khrushchev, but he used them to inspire Soviet citizens to reform their own society and to catch up and surpass the United States.

Three major plans were outlined to achieve Communism in the Soviet Union. The first step was to create the material-technical base for Communism by a rapid increase in the industrialization and electrification of the whole country. This step included a gigantic increase in industrial and agricultural production. The second step was the forming of Communist social relationships in society. This step included the equalizing of opportunities and broadening the base of political participation. Khrushchev announced the fulfillment of the Dictatorship of the Proletariat and the establishment of an All-Peoples Government. The third step was the creation of a new soviet man. This final step included the academic, technical, social, and moral education of the Soviet citizen. When these three steps could be accomplished, the society would achieve communism.

CREATING A MATERIAL-TECHNICAL BASE

The creation of a material-technical base included the complete electrification of the whole country, the complex mechanization and automation of production, the broad introduction of chemicals and organic compounds into economic production, and the rational use of all resources so as to attain a high cultural-technical level of society and an unprecedented increase of productive labor. It also included the realization of a classless society, in which there are no differences between life in the city and in the country, and in which there are no differences between those who do mental work and those who do physical work.

Khrushchev over-exaggerated the rapidity of the economic growth, but a scaled-down program was adopted in the 1966-1970 Five Year Plan. The first emphasis was on the electrification of the country. The plan projected an increase in the output of electrical power to go from 507 billion kilowatt-hours in 1965 to over 830 billion kilowatt-hours in 1970. The actual growth and the exaggeration of Khrushchev can be seen by comparing his figures, which projected the same growth to be from 292 billion kilowatt-hours in 1960 to 2700 billion kilowatt-hours or more in 1980. But even at Brezhnev's and Kosygin's projection the growth the production rate would be phenomenal. At the same rate of increase, compounded each five years, the output of electric kilowatt-hours may reach 2310 billion in 1980. But the actual increase of electrical output at the end of 1970 had reached only 740 billion kilowatt-hours. This figure indicates that the rate of increase between 1960 and 1965 continued on through 1970 at about 40 billion additional kilowatt-hours each year. At any rate, without compounding it, the output in 1980 would be closer to 1110 billion kilowatt-hours rather than either 2310 or 2700. Yet even that is a remarkable increase in the output of electrical power. And considering the projects for hydro-electric power dams in the Soviet Union the rate could be faster and the power output could greatly exceed that conservative projection. Only the future can tell whether the Soviet Union's projections are accurate.

The plan for increasing electrical power output in the Soviet Union has been carried out with the enthusiasm of building communism by the Soviet citizens. In 1969 seven of the twelve largest hydro-electric power dams of the world were in the Soviet Union. Additional projects are outlined for several more large ones and many more smaller dams. A tremendous project is outlined to build a power plant at the mouth of the Lena River on the Arctic Ocean for providing electric power and for contributing to the industrialization of Northern Siberia.

Hydro-electric power plants are not alone in the Soviet plans for electrifying the country. Emphasis was also placed on thermal plants, which burn coal, oil, natural gas, and other products to generate electricity. In addition, these natural resources are to be used directly for power. Oil production was outlined in 1965 to increase from 243 million tons to 345 or 355 million tons in 1970. This goal was reached, and the new projection for 1975 was 480 to 500 million tons of oil. Coal production was outlined to increase from 578 million tons in 1965 to 665 or 675 million tons in 1970. The actual coal production at that time was 624 million tons, and the new projection was 685 to 695 million tons of coal. And natural gas production was to increase from 129 billion cubic meters in 1965 to 225 or 240 billion cubic meters in 1970. Actually natural gas production was 198 billion cubic meters in 1970, and according to the plan will be 300 to 320 in 1975. According to Khrushchev, these figures for 1980 would be 690 to 710 million tons of oil, 1180 to 1200 million tons of coal, and 680 to 720 billion cubic meters of natural gas.

Neither Khrushchev's nor Brezhnev's goals have been fully attained, but Brezhnev has been much more realistic. Oil production, if the 1975 goal is reached as the 1970 goal was, would probably be about 650 million tons, not much short of Khrushchev's prediction. But at the rate of increase of coal production for the last ten years the 1980 production will be closer to 725 million tons, which falls short of both Khrushchev's and Brezhnev's plans. Natural gas will probably reach the production level of 420 billion cubic meters in 1980, rather than Khrushchev's prediction of 680 to 720.

But Brezhnev and Kosygin recognized the over-optimistic goals of Khrushchev and criticized him for being unrealistic. Even though the new plans too are somewhat visionary, they are within the range of credibility and do serve as incentives for the Soviet citizens to increase production. The result is that the people are working enthusiastically to attain these goals and to build a better society, which is the whole purpose of the campaign to build Communism. And all production is correlated to achieve this over-all objective.

Other sources of power were included in the program to create a material-technical base. They are atomic energy, solar energy, wind energy, heat energy from the interior of the earth and energy from the ocean tides. The program included the total utilization of all kinds of power for a full development of the national economy.

Building a material-technical base also involves the full utilization of all natural resources, chemical compounds, synthetic

materials, and animal and vegetable products. The production of
steel was scheduled in 1965 to increase from 91 million tons to 142
or 129 million tons in 1970. In 1970 steel production reached 116
million tons, and in 1971 it reached 132.8 million tons, which compared with 120 million tons in the United States of America.
Khrushchev's claim to catch up and surpass the United States was
realized in the production of steel. This accomplishment may be
considered even greater than reaching the goal of the Five Year
Plan. Be as it may though, the objective for 1975 was set at 142
to 150 million tons, which is well within the range of creditability.
The production of plastics and synthetic resins increased from 821
thousand tons in 1965 to 1672 tons in 1970, and the prediction for
1975 stood at 3457 tons. The production of synthetic thread
increased from 407 thousand tons in 1965 to 623 thousand tons in
1970 and was set for 1050 to 1100 in 1975. In addition, new chemical substances and the more effective use of natural resources would
greatly help in building the base. It was added during the announcement of the plan at the 23rd Party Congress in 1965 and re-affirmed
in 1971 at the 24th Party Congress that all the known resources can
be found and developed in the Soviet Union. The discovery of diamonds near Yakutsk several years before then was the completion
of the locating and developing of the known list of natural resources.

But power and raw materials are only a part of the material-
technical base. The production of industrial goods and consumer
products must also be substantially increased according to the plan.
Woven fabrics were scheduled to increase in production from $7\frac{1}{2}$
billion square meters in 1965 to more than 11 billion square meters
in 1975. During the same time the production of shoes was to increase from 486 million pairs to 800 or 830 million pairs. Other
consumer goods were to follow this rate of increased production.
Industrial goods were to be produced on a much higher scale, and
automation and remote controls would be introduced into the chemical industry, power engineering, transportation, and construction.

The program also included consideration of human problems,
displaced employees, the distribution of consumer goods and
services, and leisure time. The introduction of mechanization,
automation, and remote controls would reduce working hours and
increase the pay per hour rather than causing unemployment for
some and increased profits for others. Individual workers would
become more specialized, but at the same time they would work
together and supplement each other's work. Shortages of goods
and services both for industry and for consumer needs would be
prevented by cooperation between industrial plants and a centralized

control over the distribution of all goods and services. For example, a major power failure would be prevented by tying all power systems together so that when one system failed other systems could supply the need. This same supply arrangement would also work for all other industrial and public needs.

The programs of the 22nd, 23rd, and 24th Party Congresses have stressed the priority of developing the vast resources of Siberia and the Soviet Far East. Not only can all natural resources be found there, but they can be found in great quantities. The call for the builders of communism was to go east and develop this great land.

Agriculture also was a large part of the program. The Five Year Plans scheduled many increases, including the following: grain production averages from 130 million tons per year during 1961-1965 to 195 million tons per year from 1970 to 1975; meat production from 9.3 million tons per year during 1961-1965 to 14.3 million tons during 1970-1975; and milk production from 65 million tons per year in 1961-1965 to 92.3 million tons in 1970-1975.

Various means for increasing the production of agricultural products were scheduled to be implemented. One of them was the carousel milking platforms for dairy cows. Such a means would permit mass production of milking cows with machines in a similar manner as the assembly line in a factory. Irrigation was also stressed as a means for guaranteeing the harvest of grains and other crops during droughts.

The whole approach for creating the material-technical base of communism was directed toward the full utilization of all known means for increased production and toward the use of scientific research and engineering to develop and utilize new types of power, new materials, and new processes. The program was not only a quantitative step forward but also a qualitative development, which continues to progress toward a communist society and on within the new society.

FORMING COMMUNIST SOCIAL RELATIONSHIPS

Not only the provision of material goods and services in a highly industrialized society but also the forming of a new society are prerequisites to the realization of Communism. The concepts of a classless society, social equality, the removal of exploitation and discrimination, public ownership of property, and economic planning must all be realized during the approach to communism.

Under socialism these concepts were realized in a quantitative way in that they were guaranteed by law, but under communism they must be realized in practice. This realization is the process of forming new social relationships.

The first phase of this plan was to remove the differences between life in the country and life in the city. Part of this process is the industrialization, mechanization, and automation of agriculture, forestry, and mining. Another part is working with the relationships between people. For this process it is necessary that collective farms become industrialized state farms. All agriculture would be founded on industrial methods. Workers would have regular hours and regular pay. Working conditions would be made clean and safe. Manual labor would be decreased, and heavy labor assumed by machines. Workers would gain a balance between physical and mental tasks so that all people could exercise and develop both their minds and their bodies to attain good mental and physical health. But excess mental strain would be reduced for office workers and executives and excess physical strain would be reduced for farmers, lumbermen, and miners. All workers would have both mental and physical duties. In this way many of the differences between city life and country life and between mental workers and physical workers would be removed.

However, living conditions must be improved for both city and country dwellers. According to the program, cities will be beautified, cleansed from smoke and dirt, and renewed with trees, shrubbery, and flowers. The country villages are scheduled to have new apartment houses with plumbing and central heating. Parks, theatres, opera houses, libraries, modern schools, recreation facilities, clinics, hospitals, and all the other facilities and services found in modern cities are to be provided in rural communities. In this way the advantages of the city would be brought to the country, and the advantages of the country would be brought to the city. In addition, the disadvantages of both are to be removed. Conditions will be similar for all people, whether they live and work in a city or in the country and whether their main task is primarily mental work or physical work. These improvements would equalize working and living conditions for people.

Opportunities for all are also to be equalized under the plan. Compulsory secondary and polytechnical education, which is already free, will be made universal in the Soviet Union. The educational fund has been increased from 41.5 billion rubles in 1965 to 60 billion rubles in 1970. Schools and institutes will be available and will accept all persons. No longer will a Soviet citizen remain educated because of place of birth or conditions of his parents. Education and culture are to become as necessary and as available as air and water.

Services in the form of rapid communication with telegraph, telephone, radio, and television and rapid transportation on trains, cars, airplanes, jet aircraft, and ships are to be made available for all. These services and all other consumer needs will be provided for all citizens from the public fund. Prices are scheduled to be reduced and finally eliminated under communism.

The monetary relationship of society will be eliminated under the program to build a communist society. The principle "From each according to his abilities; to each according to his needs" will become a fact of life. No longer are wages to be paid for services or are costs to be charged for goods and services. Each person who works will have documentation to permit him to use goods and services as he needs them. Everyone will be able to do this because everyone will work. They will work not because they have to work but because they want to work.

The relationship of man to work must go through a real transformation. It is explained that work has been a drudgery during history because of the lack of goods and services. Some people exploited the labor of others to provide them with the necessities and luxuries of life. Even when industrialization made it possible for industry to produce all the goods and services for men's needs, the old relationship of exploitation remained because wealthy people learned that they could have the products of labor without work. Further increased production did not supply everyone with needed goods and services in the capitalist society, because capitalists destroyed excess products in order to keep prices high and to gain more profits for themselves. But when the means of production are controlled by the general public and the distribution of goods is available to all, people will no longer consider work a drudgery. They will work because they want to have something to do and want to express their own creative abilities. Communist doctrine teaches that man is not lazy by nature. Instead it teaches that man is basically a constructive being. He will want to work and to contribute when the society is favorable for his education, his enlightenment, and his opportunity for self-realization.

Communists counter the criticism that in the new society that some people will be drones with an attack on the concept of "original sin," which degraded man. They emphasize that man is not degraded by extra-terrestial beings or forces or by nature. They add that man has been degraded by the exploitation and oppression by other men. This degradation is removed in a socialist and in a communist society by the elimination of exploitation and discrimination through the abolishing of private property and of one man hiring another. When that degradation is removed and man becomes free physically and spiritually, he will want to work for his own health and his own happiness.

It is also pointed out that the equalization of opportunities and social relationships is not a levelling or a stereotyping process. The new society will lift people to a higher plain not lower them to a base standard. As people raise themselves to higher standards of living and goals of aspirations they will gain special skills, develop new talents, and create new inventions, processes, and artistic productions. One man will differ from another man in personality and in speciality of interest, but no man will be deprived of material necessities, educational or cultural opportunities, or the right to work and create.

Relationships between individuals and between those who provide and those who receive services are to change gradually as the society moves into communism. Also the political structure of the government is scheduled to change. Communist philosophy talks about the withering away of the state. That concept is explained by defining the state as the coercive part of the government. The administration, on the other hand, continues to exist in the communist state. The armies, the intelligence service, the police forces, and government inspectors will no longer be needed. People will not have to be coerced, because the social relationships will have done away with poverty, unemployment, and other deprivations which lead people to crime. Men will not steal, murder, or deceive others, because they will have no stimulus to do so. They can have what they need through legal processes without resorting to illegal, immoral, or unethical courses of action. When the need for state coercion disappears the state, as such, will also disappear. But the administrative functions will be handled by the people themselves.

The abolishment of the Dictatorship of the Proletariat at the 22nd Party Congress was the first step in that direction. Khrushchev announced the development of an All-Peoples Government and the reduction of state police power. This announcement included a broadening of the base of political activity and of the opportunities for the general public to participate in government administration. Not only will people be able to elect representatives to the government soviets; they will also be able to take their turns in rotation

to act as the representative. One-third of the representatives are
to be replaced each two years so that more people can have an
opportunity to serve, while retaining continuity and retaining experienced people in office. Public meetings are to be held often
and to involve more people so that the will of all the people is
heard before enacting legislation. There will no longer be politicians and government officers separate from the rest of the
society. Everyone will for a time be a politician and a government
official, but he will also be a worker in his own speciality. In this
way the Communist Party will become a mass organization for all
and will wither away as a special group in society.

However, certain conditions must be fulfilled before these
new social relationships can be fully realized. The withering away
of the state and the party is not a one-time act. It is a long process.
A high level of economic production must be attained. There must
be eliminated all traces of class divisions and class distinctions,
differences between urban and rural life, and differences between
mental and physical laborers. Another prerequisite is the attainment of a high level of educational and cultural development and the
acceptance of the communist ideology in the minds and actions of
the people. The final prerequisite is the elimination of international
hostilities and wars in a world society which accepts the concepts
of socialist brotherhood so that all peoples can live in peace and be
assured that there will be no aggressive attacks by imperialists.
Then and only then can the coercive power of the state wither away.

International social relationships are to be formed by bringing together various national and ethnic groups into one large family.
That process includes the development of national consciousness in
colonial areas, the liberation of these groups from imperialist subjugation, the development of their industry and agriculture, and the
building of cooperation between them and other socialist countries.
Nationalistic views are to be replaced by the spirit of internationalism, equality, and brotherhood of all peoples. Peace and friendship will be the basis of international relations. Each national and
ethnic group will develop its own language and culture, but all their
contributions will blend together into a common civilization. One
language and culture will become the international standard, but
local and regional differences will continue not in opposition to
the world civilization but as enrichments to it.

The social relationships of all peoples will be developed not
by coercion but by the development of the communist morality and
the communist ethic. The changes in the economic relationships
through the public ownership of highly industrialized economies and

the changes in potential of the individual through the educating and creating a new soviet man will complement the forming of the social relationships.

THE CREATION OF A NEW SOVIET MAN

Communist philosophy opposes the capitalist and pseudo-Christian belief that man due to his nature, caused by an original sin, is a degraded being, which can not be changed. The characteristics of individuals in capitalist societies are formed by the society and not by the nature of man. Man is a dignified being with potentials of unlimited development. He can be retrained and re-educated. The evils of society can be eliminated, and man can develop an outlook of equality and brotherhood with other men. Man is not the creation of "higher beings" and a slave to their will. Man is himself the creator of history. He has the potential of controlling nature and using it for his own purposes, for the social betterment of all peoples. These tenets are the bases for the concept for creating a new Soviet man.

History shows that man has been degraded, exploited, and oppressed by other men not by nature or by so-called gods. Civilization has been established by the economic relationships which men have built, and the higher development of these economic relationships has produced higher stages of society. Further development of economic relationships and education can bring all men to their highest potential— new Soviet men in a communist society.

The bases for the educating of a new soviet man lie in objective (conditions outside man himself) factors: the social ownership of the means of production, socialist democracy, and the social-political and ideological unity of all peoples.

In addition to the external and environmental changes of man are the changes in his outlook and philosophy. Everyone has some kind of an outlook or philosophy which is partially determined by his observing and imitating others in his environment. As a young person grows up in a socialistic society many of the tasks of creating the new man will automatically be solved. However, the internal changes, the attitudinal changes of man, primarily come through the acquisition of knowledge. The process of education is the key to the creation of a new man.

The communist view of learning differs somewhat from the old Russian methods and from those methods used in capitalist countries. A Russian saying was that "the mother of learning is repetition," but the communist view is "the mother of learning is application." The acquisition of facts is not sufficient. The facts must be structured in an orderly and meaningful sequence, and the learner must apply those facts in his work and in his own experience. Education can not be separated from work. Such is the basis of the scientific world outlook according to the communist program to educate a new soviet man.

The structuring of the facts, however, is a vital part of the education process. First of all the individual must learn his relationship to society. He must know his social and moral responsibility to his own people. He must recognize that political and moral maturity is based on his subordinating his own desires to his social responsibilities. He must experience friendship and comradeship in collective participation in group activity. These responsibilities include patriotism for his native land coupled with a spirit of internationalism and respect for all peoples.

Another set of structured knowledge is based on man's relationship to work. Having been freed from exploitation, the soviet man learns that work is the source of his own personal and social development. It is the source of his happiness and of his own self-realization through creating and producing products and services of all kinds. He must learn that work is the basis of all progress. He will learn to work not because he has to do so but because he wants to work and produce something. He will learn that man can not live without working and that all kinds of work are interesting, worthy of one's efforts, and stimulating to his creative abilities. His participation in work projects will help him to appreciate the achievements of others and to inspire him to equal or surpass their deeds.

Moral education is the foundation for all learning. Communist morality is based on the learning of past generations and on the new knowledge gained through new social relationships. One of the fundamental principles is the old Russian proverb "All for one and one for all." This saying has been adapted to the concepts of "collectives" in the society. It is consistent with the remark that there are no disassociated persons in the Soviet Union. A Soviet citizen is taught that he is a member of a group and that the group has activities in which he is a part. That group may be a school class, a pioneer unit, or a work crew. Each individual contributes a necessary part to the activity, but only a part. The full activity depends on each individual in the group. Social relationships are developed within the group. Conflicts must be avoided by planning the activity ahead. Individual desires should be subordinated to the planned activity but not disregarded. Violations of group discipline or mistakes of any kind should not be tolerated, glossed over, or ignored. All deficiencies should be discussed openly and corrected for the benefit of the group and the individual. Criticism and self-criticism develop honesty, genuineness, and modesty. Individual members of the group and the group as a whole should always be subject to constructive criticism for their own improvement and development. Members of a collective work together and help each other. They do not undermine each other. They aid and support each other. In this way the individual personality is strengthened and developed according to its potential.

Another fundamental principle of communist morality is the statement that "Man to man is a friend, comrade, and a brother." Enmity between people should be replaced by love and service. The dignity of the human individual should be raised to its highest level. Concern for children and for older people is a vital part of this principle. A Soviet citizen should be ready to assist and to defend other individuals at all times. He should help others overcome their deficiencies and protect them from evil influences and destructive forces. Such love is not an abstract ideal but the applied relationship among human beings.

This concept of brotherhood and service to man reinforces another basic principle, that of the struggle against the anti-social behavior of the past. The persistence of evil influences is compared to a "birth mark," which must be eradicated. Some of these influences are speculation and personal profitmaking, indifference to others' misfortunes, drunkeness, superstitions and religious prejudices, and various crimes against society. Social parasites, criminals, and hooliganism are based on human weaknesses. A person with amoral behavior is in most cases a coward. The new soviet man should become strong and build his faith on his own labor, on his creative powers, and on the unlimited potentials of human reason. He should remember that the elimination of the anti-social elements of the past directly depend on society's intolerance toward evil.

Communist morality teaches also that behavior is not a private affair. The society must work together to replace taverns and slums, discrimination and churches, card games and ignorance with clubs, theatres, cultural universities, well-built housing, books, electricity, and television. These social changes must be made so that the Soviet citizen can make proper use of his free time.

Family relationships are also a fundamental part of communist morality. It is recognized that the family is the primary cell of society and that family solidarity is necessary for social order. The changes brought about in the family after the 1917 Revolution were based on the liberation of women from subservience to their husbands. Women have been placed on an equal basis with men. They have equal rights and equal opportunities to work. Divorce is granted only in extreme cases. Man and woman should seriously consider before marriage the obligations of married life and of rearing children. The responsibilities of a Soviet citizen to his marriage partner and to his children are foremost in his social relationships. All moral principles are to be practiced first on the family level.

The educating of the new soviet man also involves the building of a higher level of physical, moral, and mental development. He should strive for perfection in these areas and maintain physical and mental health and moral purity. Physical exercises and sports are necessary for one's health. Mental health also depends on the acquisition of a scientific outlook and a high level of awareness. One should expand his knowledge of science, technology, literature, and art in addition to his own occupational speciality. Esthetic education becomes an essential part of the process of creating a new man. Moral purity includes honesty, justice, sincerity, modesty, and chastity in both one's public and private affairs. With the perfection of the individual in these respects the new man becomes capable of perfecting his relations within his local groups, within his own country, and among the peoples of the whole world.

The new Soviet man is not a dream of a far-off possibility. The process of moulding new personalities is taking place within the schools, in social activities, and in the day-to-day work projects.

As the whole society brings together the material-technical progress, the improved social relationships, and the total education process the attainment of communism becomes a reality. The question is no longer "if." It is now "when." And the answer is "soon."

SOVIET CITIZENS AND BUILDING COMMUNISM

The theory of Soviet teachings and programs must be evaluated by examining the effect on the lives of the people and the extent of their support. How well is the theory being put into practice?

A definitive answer is hardly possible, but many observations can be made. And the result of such observations provides a tentative answer. That answer is that both the Soviet government and the Soviet citizen appear to be taking the theory seriously and attempting to put it into practice.

The 23rd Party Congress in 1966 and the 24th Party Congress in 1971 reasserted Khrushchev's path to Communism. The changes in policies did not negate any of the theory. Those changes only made the theory more practical. Since 1966 the drive by economic enterprises and government institutions have continued to emphasize the practical application of the program. At a joint meeting of the Central Committee of the CPSU and of the Council of Ministers of the USSR on the 19th of June, 1969, announcements were made concerning the completion of the planning for capital construction and about the stimulation of the building industry. The announcements included the following facts:

There has been an annual increase of about 20% in the national income. In 1968 the capital investment was 61,500,000,000 rubles, which was a 5.6 times increase over 1950. During the period from 1950 through 1968 there were constructed more than 12,500 large industrial enterprises, many transportation routes, and land improvement and agricultural projects. There was also a growth of 4.6 times in the basic economic funds -- 6.4 in industry and 2.8 in housing.

The 24th Congress in 1971 and the Five Year Plan from 1971-1975 refined and extended further the programs of the 22nd and 23rd Congresses. The Council of Ministers has announced the need for a further development of the material-technical base of construction, having in mind the creation of large regional bases for the production of non-metallic materials for construction purposes. This expanded effort in capital construction is to be accompanied by added incentives for the workers through factory improvements and through increased financial benefits. There is to be an extension of credit for industry and for consumers. Consistent with the formation of new social relationships also are the plans to increase the involvement of regional and local committees for both the preparation and the execution of plans.

These facts are significant for the follow-through on the overall program. The increased capital investment has steadily increased from two to three billion rubles each year from 1961 to 1965 and from three to five billion rubles in 1966 through 1968. The plans for 1971-1975 were designed to continue and exceed that investment rate.

The changes in social relationships and those in individuals are also apparent both to the Soviet citizens themselves and to foreign tourists. One of the most popular questions to foreign tourists who have been in the Soviet Union previously is what changes have you noticed. Upon remarking about the new buildings, the new bridges, the extended subways in the major cities, and the improved transportation facilities, the foreign tourist receives another question. What about the people? How have they changed? Initially this question seems absurd, because these changes are qualitative rather than quantitative. But when the question is asked over and over, the tourist starts to take notice. The fact that the Soviet citizens ask this question is already an answer that they realize that they are changing. They are approaching the goal of becoming new Soviet citizens.

The continued and intensified drive for a better education and for better living conditions is obvious. Book stores are jammed with people, who take their books to read in busses, on trains, and on park benches. The people are constantly talking about their studies at the institutes. The program for adult education continues to amaze foreigners. So many workers are continuing their education at night.

Honesty is obvious in the Soviet Union. A girl's purse left accidentally in open view at a public place remains undisturbed, even when several groups of people mill around and pass by. Personal items left in restaurants, hotels, airports, and even on beaches somehow are returned to the owner.

Courtesy and generosity are traits of the friendly Soviet citizens. The openness and trust that exists between friends and strangers alike is almost phenomenal. Individuals will stop and talk in public places or in more secluded areas both day and night. There seems to be no fear of their being accosted, threatened, or robbed. Their response is always courteous. They answer questions, give directions, and accompany the asker to give assistance in locating something or in purchasing souveniers. They are friendly, yet they are not compromising to their teachings or to their morals. Of course, Soviet citizens are not perfect. There are those who deal in the black market. Immorality exists. Crime has not been eliminated. Yet there is an atmosphere of their dedication to high principles most of the time when one is in the presence of Soviet citizens.

Good behavior, obedience to law and ethics, service to his fellow man, and a dedication to study and to work seem to be com-

mon marks of most Soviet citizens. These principles are all a
part of the program to create a new Soviet man, and they seem to
be in practice. Are they new? When were they introduced? Have
the Russian people always been like this? These questions are
hard to answer, but there appears to have been a gradual change.
Over three-fourths of the present Soviet citizens have been born
since the 1917 Revolution. The older ones have gone through
horrors of poverty and war-time atrocities. The Russian people
have always been more "collective" in their relationships than
many other nationalities. But it is believed by the author that the
campaign to improve people has taken effect mostly during the
time since 1958 and possibly even more since 1964.

Soviet citizens believe that they are building communism.
They look forward with great anticipation to a better and happier
life. Their enthusiasm is beyond the types of excitements that
most other people have. It is not a flashing fantasy followed by
periods of despondency. Their enthusiasm continues from day to
day, week to week, month to month, and year to year. They see
the progress in their society. They reap the benefits of their work
in better housing, improved and more available consumer products,
better recreational facilities, longer vacations, shorter work
hours, and higher pay. Their continued learning brings new hori-
zons to their minds. The vigor of youth is retained among adults
because their work and their studies both bring challenges for new
opportunities for them.

Are these impressions of Soviet citizens, their relationships
with each other, and their economic growth all products of Soviet
propaganda? The test of their propaganda does continue to convey
these impressions to the Soviet citizens and to the world. The
answer might be that all of these claims are propaganda, but how
true is that propaganda? Can it be disproved by exceptions or can
it be proved by many examples? The answer to both questions is
"yes." It is both true and false or rather it is partially true and
partially false. But Soviet statements, both governmental and
individual, affirm that these claims are true. The foreign observer
has to admit also that much of it is true. The fact is that these
principles are in the process of becoming reality. Not all citizens
are progressing at the same rate, but the overwhelming majority
is progressing in these directions. Only the future can tell how
well this program will be fulfilled.

PEACEFUL CO-EXISTENCE

When Krushchev declared the slogans of "peaceful co-existence" and "peace and friendship," the basic meaning was widely misunderstood. Even though he had denounced Stalinism and advocated better international relations, he was not changing his convictions in the destiny of Communism. Neither was he preparing a mask to deceive other nations. He was really announcing a reduction of tensions both at home and abroad. His declaration was followed by a massive program of peace pledges. Long petitions were circulated to gain thousands of signatures. He initiated more trade agreements with non-socialist countries, he greatly relaxed travel regulations, he improved the scene for diplomatic negotiations, and he travelled to the United States.

Khrushchev also spoke of "burying you (capitalists)" and of "wars of national liberation." He explained that he meant that socialism and communism would outlive capitalism and that they would be around after the death and burial of the old political and economic systems of Western Europe and America. He also differentiated between aggressive wars and wars of national liberation. He spoke of just and unjust wars. The bringing of foreign troops onto the territory of other nations was considered to be aggression and to be unjust. The fighting of residents of a nation against their capitalist leaders was considered to be just acts of liberation. Aid to native liberation armies was considered humane and just, but aid to the central government to oppose Civil War was unethical and unjust. Such aid was a violation of the freedom of the people.

These slogans must be understood in the context of communist philosophy and of the programs of the Party Congresses of the Soviet Union. The premise is that Communism is the wave of the future and that capitalism was destroying itself. Efforts to help people prepare for communism are beneficial and just, but efforts to obstruct the progress of Communism are detrimental and unjust. Of course, there are qualifications on this premise. One qualification is the main difference between the USSR and China. That principle is that aggressive attacks by one nation upon another is inconsistent with Communism. The Soviet view of the transition from capitalism or colonialism to socialism and on to communism is by an internal revolution with the overthrow of capitalists both domestic and foreign.

Peaceful co-existence is the relationship between

communist or socialist countries and capitalist countries before the capitalist countries are ready for socialism. It is a period of economic competition and military preparedness. It is an attempt to prevent aggression toward socialist or colonial countries in exchange for negotiations with capitalist countries for reducing tensions. Peaceful co-existence also is a pledge for refraining from giving economic and military aid to revolutionary forces in other countries.

Peace and friendship is an extension of the same concept. It connotes increases in trade relations, tourism, cultural and scientific exchanges, and cooperation to prevent aggressive wars. Actually the emphasis of peace and friendship is a reasseration of communist internationalism, which is the attitude of an alliance of all working people of the world in opposition to imperialism, exploitation, and aggressive wars. It is an appeal to individuals to resist enmity and hostilities and to promote understanding and good will between the ordinary citizens of different countries. Friendship University in Moscow is a product of this idea. Students from all nations come and study at the expense of the Soviet Union. They learn their specialities, and they also are taught the Communist ideology. They are supposed to learn respect for different nationalities and the recognition of the dignity of man whatever his race, nationality, color, or economic condition. Peace and friendship is international humanism.

PEACE AND PROGRESS

The Soviet Union is very much concerned about preventing a military attack on her own territory. The terrible losses to life and property in the Soviet Union during World War II have left an unforgetable impact in the people and on the economy of the country. Magazine articles, books, and movies continually carry the theme of the horrors of war and the necessity for peace. A prime concern of the Soviet Union is the military defense of the homeland. Disputes with the United States and with China may be intensified to dangerous levels, but these disputes are restrained from provoking war or waging aggression. Instead negotiations are prolonged to pacify the hostilities and to agree on measures for preventing war.

The progress on the domestic scene is included in the program of building communism, which is incorporated into the Five Year Plans. Progress on the international scene is less predictable and less manageable. However, the same dedication and enthusiasm exists on this level too. Looking backward Soviet leaders can point to tremendous changes in their favor since the Communist Revolution and more specifically since World War II. Many more people are now living in socialist people's democracies. The Communist Parties in many capitalist countries are strong and loyal to Moscow. Moscow can with much assurance declare that it is the leader of a vast movement for liberating oppressed peoples throughout the world. In June, 1969, the response was very encouraging from delegations to the Moscow sponsored International Conference of Communists. This conference was followed by a call for another conference later directed against imperialism. All anti-imperialists, both communist and non-communist, were to be invited.

Yet, as in the domestic scene, the going was not easy. There have been setbacks in the communist movement. The greatest one has been the deviation of Mao Tse Tung's China, which has not only broken from the Moscow alliance but has also turned to threaten the Soviet Union with military attacks. This change of events has caused the Soviet leaders to be more concerned with the threat from China than with the threat of capitalist encircle-ment by the United States and its allies. Other problems through-out the world, and especially in the Middle East, also continue to plague the Soviet Union.

But Communist theory does not state that the international path to socialism and communism is non-violent. It stresses that aggressive wars between capitalist countries will continue in the rivalry for extending imperialism over colonial territories. The prediction is that the workers in these capitalist countries will rise up against the military-industrialist war mongers and over-throw them because the imperialist attempts to increase profits for large corporations will become tremendous financial burdens on the citizens of those countries. During the American partici-pation in the Vietnam War, Soviet leaders could point to the validity of that prediction because of the opposition in the United States to the financial drain on the economy and on the savings of the citizens and because of the popular opposition to the Vietnam War in general.

The concept of financial crises as inherent elements of the capitalist system is the basis of the communist view of the forth-coming death of that system and the continued progress of socialism and communism. It is repeated that all capital (private profits) is the result of exploitation. The whole foundation of the capitalist system is the exploitation and oppression of the working classes. The gap between the earnings of the workers and the profits of the capitalists continues to grow. The capitalists become obsessed with luxuries and extravagant tastes for the bizzare, but the workers go through periods of unemployment and poverty. The late 1920's and the depression of the 1930's in the United States are shown as evidences of the contrasts between the rich and the poor. Also pointed out are the hunger and suffering of the unemployed. The decisions of the United States Government to balance the quantities of produced goods in the society with the amount of money in circulation and the purchasing power of the workers by destroying grain and killing livestock are used as examples of the evils of the capitalist system. The continued concentration of wealth in large corporations and in international cartels reinforce in communist view of history. Communist theoreticians point out also that the United States Presidents are millionaires and so are many of the Senators. They say that the capitalist system represents only the vested interests. It is not a democracy. It is not just. Sooner or later the people will recognize that their plight is caused by the capitalists and the system, and they will overthrow it. Depression will cause civil war and a revolution, and all capitalist countries will eventually become socialist ones. This process is the course and direction of history. This process is also the progress of societies, which will follow the lead of the Soviet Union.

But international peace is essential. Aggressive wars must be prevented. Only the wars of national liberation and civil wars in capitalist countries are to occur during the transition period from capitalism to socialism and communism. The preservation of peace on the international scene thus becomes important to Soviet foreign policy. The progress of the world toward communism is considered inevitable, and the Soviet Union has the responsibility of protecting the gains and preparing for the future.

Peace and progress have also become prime concerns of the Soviet Union due to the vast industrialization and the vulnerability to attack of these industries. The economy of the Soviet Union was set back several years during the Second World War, but the gains since then, if destroyed, would mean a much greater loss now. The advance of military armaments, nuclear weapons, and missiles extends the Soviet effort from measures to defend the homeland to a great effort to prevent hostilities which might erupt into a world war.

The position of the Soviet Union as one of the two major powers in the world has given its leaders a broad outlook toward world responsibilities. The exploration of space by both the Soviet Union and the United States also provides new insights into the relationsips between the two countries. The concepts of peace and progress of these two great countries may come in line with each other and help them achieve the initial goals of Khrushchev for peaceful co-existence and peace and friendship -- economic competition and relaxed diplomatic relations.

The invitation of President Nixon to come to Moscow in 1972 and the agreements on strategic arms limitations, increased trade, and cooperation in space are evidences of the continued policy of peace and friendship and of co-existence. Brezhnev's visits to West Germany and to the United States in 1973 also were renewed efforts to promote peace and cooperation on the international level. These visits were followed by substantial increases in trade between the Soviet Union and the United States, and this fact further demonstrates the qualitative changes in the Soviet society.

SOURCES FOR CHAPTER VIII -- The Path to Communism

Izvestia, Moscow, 1967-1973
Pravda, Moscow, 1967-1973
St. Louis Post Dispatch, St. Louis, Missouri, 1967-1973
Shakhnazarov, G. Kh. et als., Obshchestvovedeniye, (4th ed.)
    Moscow: Izdatelstvo Politicheskoy Literatury, 1966,
    384 pp.
Shakhnazarov, G. Kh. et als., Obshchestvovedeniye, (9th ed.)
    Moscow: Izdatelstvo Politicheskoy Literatury, 1971,
    366 pp.
Shakhnazarov, G. Kh. et als., Obshchestvovedeniye, (10th ed.)
    Moscow: Izdatelstvo Politicheskoy Literatury, 1972,
    366 pp.
Shakhnazarov, G. Kh. et als., Social Science: A Textbook for
    Soviet Secondary Schools, Washington, D. C.: U. S.
    Department of Commerce, 1964, 330 pp.
SSSR v Tsifrakh v 1967 godu, Moscow: Izdatelstvo "Statistika",
    1968, 159 pp.
SSSR v Tsifrakh v 1971 godu, Moscow: Izdatelstvo "Statistika",
    1972, 240 pp.

CHAPTER IX

SOVIET AGRICULTURE

Russia was primarily an agricultural country before the 1917 Communist Revolution. The Soviet Union has continued to rely heavily on agricultural production, and most of the people were living on farms for more than forty years after the Revolution. It was not until 1961 that the Soviet Union could announce that 50% of the people were classified as urban and the other 50% rural. Even in 1972, those percentages were still 58% urban and 42% rural.

Historically, Russian farmers lived in small communities and worked on the surrounding lands. For safety from marauders they built fortress walls around their villages and ventured outside the walls to work the fields only in groups. With the institution of serfdom, noble lords replaced patriarchial leaders or princes as the owners and managers of one or more communities. The serfs continued to live in the villages and work in the fields. The practice of American farmers living in isolated homes several miles from other farmers was never a part of Russian history. The introduction of the New Economic Plan in 1921-24 did not significantly alter that arrangement. With the coming of collectivization these communities with their outlying lands were established as Collective Farms. The larger ones became State Farms. Initially there was little difference in the appearance of the farming community, except for a gate at the entrance with a sign bearing the name of the Collective Farm.

Of course, the collectivization process was much more difficult than putting up a sign. Since the emancipation of the serfs in 1861, the farmers had been allotted plots of land, which they were buying from the Tsarist Government on long term notes. After the 1917 Revolution, these farmers were told that the land now belonged to them and that no more redemption payments were necessary. The introduction of the New Economic Policy had enabled them to buy and sell land, and this opportunity caused the combining of smaller holdings into larger private farms. However, the homes usually stayed in the community villages, and the changing of land holdings mostly effected the fields. Private holdings increased substantially for some farmers during that period, and it was these farmers who were later called kulaks and who became the opposition to the collectivization process. But when the collectivization was completed, most of the villagers remained in their former homes and farmed the outlying fields.

Since agricultural machinery and tools were in short supply and since the farmers were rather independent people, the Soviet Government established Machine Tractor Stations to rent the machinery and tools to the collective farms on a rotation basis and to regulate the work on the farms. Not until 1958 were these Machine Tractor Stations abolished. By that time, the problems of opposition were fairly well solved and the supply of machinery and tools was adequate to distribute to the farms that were previously being served.

Agricultural production in the Soviet Union has been inadequate for several reasons. The production of farm products did not increase at the same rate that people moved to the cities. The supply could not keep up with the growing demand.

One of the major problems has been caused by the northerly location of the Soviet Union. The cold climate and the short growing season have always restricted the production of agricultural products. In the area around Moscow and north toward Leningrad, the principle efforts of the farmers have been directed toward frost resistent crops and livestock. A typical farm in this general area would have fields of cabbages, beets, turnips, and potatoes. It may also have pear and apple orchards with mustard grass planted between the trees. The livestock would consist primarily of pigs and geese. More sensitive plants and animals have difficulty facing the early frosts and cold winters with temperatures down to 40 degrees below zero. North of this area there is very little agricultural production.

South of Moscow toward Kiev is the Black Earth Belt which is the best farm land in Europe. The soil is rich and fertile, or at least it was before it was farmed so extensively. The growing season is longer and the winters are not quite as cold, but the climate is still a major problem. The rainfall is usually adequate for grain, which has become the major crop. This area has been referred to as the "Bread Basket of Europe." The main grains have been wheat, rye, oats, and millet. Sunflowers, peas, and beans are also major crops here. Khrushchev tried to introduce corn on a large scale, but the acreage has not equaled that of the other crops mentioned.

South of the Black Earth Belt in the Ukraine and east toward the Volga River is an extension of the grain-growing area. The Ukrainian Republic and the Rostov and Volgograd Oblasts of the Russian Republic are also responsible for most of the livestock --

cows, pigs, sheep, goats, and horses.

Another good grain-producing area is the Kuban, which is located in the North Caucasus Region. The mountain regions of the Caucasus and the Pamirs, in Central Asia, are also important for their production of livestock, particularly sheep and goats.

Khrushchev tried to develop his Virgin Lands Project in North Kazakhistan, but the lack of rain prevented the full realization of his dreams. Even irrigation met insurmountable difficulties. The dry land would absorb the water before it reached the fields, or at least before it reached the end of the rows in the fields. The use of water pipes and sprinklers helped to overcome the problems, but this operation was an enormous undertaking for such a large area. This area did not increase production for Khrushchev, but by 1971 the grain production almost matched that of the Ukraine or about 20% of the total grain production in the USSR for that year. The production of potatoes also increased, but both potatoes and sugar beets had not become major crops for the Kazakh Republic by 1971.

Other agricultural areas in the Soviet Union are the Belorussian Republic, the Baltic Republics, the Moldavian Republic, the region between the Volga River and the Ural Mountains, the coastal regions of the Soviet Far East, and the Fergana Valley in the Uzbek Republic. Most of these areas face the problems of cold weather, short growing seasons, lack of rainfall, and poor soil, but collectively they make a good contribution to Soviet agricultural production.

The Fergana Valley near Tashkent is exempt from many of those problems, however. The climate is warm, and this valley has become a major producer of cotton. The nearby rivers supply adequate water for irrigation, and this area is rapidly becoming a major producer of vegetables, berries, fruits, and melons.

The rest of the Soviet Union which includes the Permafrost and Taiga zones of the North, most of Siberia and the Far East, and the desert areas of Central Asia, contributes very little to agricultural production. In addition to the limited available area, the Soviet Union also faces the problem of fertilizers. Only since 1960 has any major effort been made to produce chemical fertilizers. The chemical products of the country have been given priority in industrial enterprises. Khrushchev started a program to divert chemicals for fertilizer production, and in 1960 he announced threefold increase in the use of chemical fertilizers. However, there is still a shortage.

There are basically three types of farming in the Soviet Union. The largest type of enterprise is the State Farm, which operates like an industry. It concentrates on the extensive production of a few varieties of crops or livestock. It may be a grain farm, a beef cattle farm, or a horse-breeding farm. The operation is mechanized, and the workers live in apartment houses and work in shifts, as a rule. Of course, the type of farming, the development of the operation, and the emphasis by the management allows for deviation from that pattern.

The most common type of operation is the Collective Farm. It has a greater variety of crops and livestock, but it concentrates on extensive farming of grains, cultivated row crops, poultry, livestock, and fruit. The workers usually live in individual homes and work according to the need on the farm. During planting and harvesting seasons they work extra long hours, and during slack seasons they have free time. They are not paid as the State Farm workers are in the form of wages per hour. They receive a portion of the production which comes both in the form of goods and in the form of cash derived from the sale of the products to the government. The amount of income varies from year to year in relation to the production on the farm.

The third type of farming is the individual plots of collective farmers or other workers who have access to land, which they can work during their free time. A collective farmer is permitted to have an acre or two of land for his own use. He raises garden vegetables, a few chickens, a cow or two, and possibly a pig or a goat. His operation is intensive farming. The work is done primarily by hand and with small tools. He concentrates on the type of produce which requires a lot of special care, e.g., thinning, weeding, and hand-picking. He uses not only his garden plot but also spaces along roads and streams. The practice is to grow as much as he can wherever he can find a place. The production from these plots can be used by the family, and the excess may be sold for a profit at the farmers' markets in the cities.

The difference between the extensive and intensive farming in the Soviet Union is poorly understood by people in capitalist countries. The statement is made that most of the fresh vegetables are produced by individuals on private plots, which may be true, but this fact is not evidence of a failure of collectivized farming. The reason for this fact is that there is a planned division of labor

268

between the extensive farming on the State Farms and the Collective Farms and the intensive farming done by individuals. Some types of farming are done best in large fields with mechanized equipment. Other types of farming must be done in small plots with hand labor. This latter type of farming is reserved in the Soviet Union for those who work small plots, and they are given the incentive of keeping the profits from their work. This production fulfills a great need in the economy.

The living conditions on a farm, even on an industrialized State Farm, are still not comparable with those in a city. The individual homes are small, have no plumbing, and are not centrally heated. In most cases, these homes are old, have been repaired by the occupants, and are still in poor condition. Some people have been able to build new homes, but in most cases these new homes are small and lack modern conveniences. The program to build apartment houses with plumbing and central heating had effected the cities much more than the farms. Some farms have this type of housing, but much more needs to be done to eradicate the differences in the living conditions between the cities and the country.

Efforts have been made on the farms to provide community services, however. Generally there is a community dining hall, a school, a small park, and a playground. Some farms have a store and a house of culture for group activities. Most farmers have to go to an industrial town in order to sell their extra produce, buy clothes and a few staple foods, and have their recreation. The local school usually includes only an elementary education, i.e., through the first four grades. Since the introduction of boarding schools during the time of Khrushchev, the children may attend school in a nearby town and have the opportunity of a secondary education.

Work on the State Farm and on the Collective Farm is done by work crews. They go into the fields or to the barns in groups and do the work collectively. In this way they go from task to task and do what is necessary under the supervision of the farm manager or a brigade leader. In cases of rain or wind storm they may be dismissed from work for a day or more. Other days they work longer hours to make up the difference. The principle of the collective working arrangement is to finish tasks more rapidly and in this way remove the drudgery of the work. The talking, singing, and laughing also contribute to making the atmosphere more pleasant. At noon they have lunch in a common dining hall, relax for a while, and then return to work. Women work alongside men,

269

and they are relieved from preparing the noon meal. Ordinarily
they do prepare the breakfast and the evening meal and keep the
home straight and clean. Some of their chores, e.g., laundry,
may be done for them by other workers.

Work assignments are divided among individual workers in
some cases. One person may be responsible for a certain number
of chickens, cows, or pigs. Another person may be a cook, a
waiter or waitress, a laundry man or maid, or repairman. Individuals are also given responsibilities in the work crews. One person is the crew leader, and other people may have particular
assignments due to their abilities and training. But everyone is
responsible to the farm manager or director, who is elected to
supervise the activity on the farm and to conduct the administrative
work. He usually has one or more assistants, who have administrative responsibilities.

Small Collective Farms have been considered inefficient, and
many of them have been combined into larger Collective Farms,
State Farms, or Agrogorods. The Agrogorod or agricultural city
was a dream of Khrushchev's, and this concept has enlarged several
State Farms. In the more densely populated areas there has been
a major transformation in the size of Collective Farms as a result
of consolidation. There was a decrease from 44,900 Collective
Farms in 1960 to 32,256 in 1972. But there was an increase of
State Farms from 7,375 in 1960 to 15,505 in 1971. These figures
reflect the consolidation of Collective Farms and the forming of
State Farms. This fact is particularly significant for this trend
when one considers the vast expansion of agricultural lands brought
about by the Virgin Lands Project in Kazakhistan during that time.

Life on the Soviet farm has undoubtedly improved during
this consolidation process. The larger farms are more capable of
providing community services in the way of education, hospitalization, and recreation for its workers and their families.

For the 1965-1970 and 1971-1975 Five Year Plans, there has
been substantial increases in the investment in agriculture,
increases in the pay for farm products, and greater incentive for
overfulfillment of quotas. This additional support of agriculture
should continue to improve the living conditions on the Soviet Farms.

AGRICULTURAL PRODUCTION

The total tilled land in the Soviet Union increased from 203
million hectares (one hectare equals 2.47 acres) in 1960 to more

than 209 million hectares in 1965, mostly due to the Virgin Land Project. By 1971, that figure had reduced to more than 207 million hectares. More than half (118 million hectares) of this land was planted in grain crops, and half of the grain fields (64 million hectares) were wheat. The planted area for other grains was ranked in the following order: barley (21.6 million hectares), rye (9.5 million hectares), oats (9.6 million hectares), peas and beans (5.2 million hectares), millet (2.4 million hectares), corn (3.3 million hectares), buckwheat (1.8 million hectares), and rice (0.4 million hectares).

Technical crops in 1971 were planted on 14.8 million hectares of land in the Soviet Union. About one-third of this area was planted in sun flowers, about one-quarter was sugar beets, and the rest was cotton and flax. Vegetables accounted for slightly less than 10 million hectares, and potatoes were more than three-fourths of those vegetables. Hay and fodder were planted on about 65 million hectares, and there were about another 18 million hectares lying fallow.

The amount of production in tonnage is probably more meaningful than the land area. Also the production of animal products can only be reflected in weight or units. In order to do that and to show the distribution of production throughout the Soviet Union, the production figures are listed here by product and by Union Republic.

Grain production totalled 181,000,000 tons in 1971. This amount reflected an increase over the last several years. In 1940, that figure was 95 million tons, in 1950 81 million tons, in 1960 125 million tons, in 1965 121 million tons, and 169 million tons in 1968. Of the total tonnage in the Soviet Union in 1968 more than 89 million tons were produced in the Russian Republic, almost 32 million tons in the Ukrainian Republic, over 14 million tons in the Kazakh Republic, over three million tons in the Belorussian Republic, and about two million tons each in the Moldavian and Lithuanian Republics. Other Union Republics with grain production between a half a million tons and one million tons ranked in order were: Latvia, Kirghizia, Azerbaidshan, Georgia, Estonia, and Uzbekistan.

In the summer of 1972 there was a very serious drought in the Western part of the Soviet Union. In many places there was no rain from the first of May until the first of September. Grain production fell to 168 million tons that year, and large imports of grain were required to feed the people. Similar declines in production also were in other agricultural products, particularly potatoes.

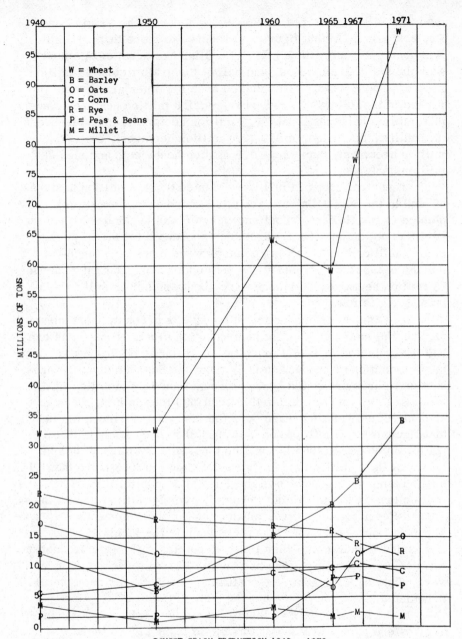

SOVIET GRAIN PRODUCTION 1940 - 1972

Sugar beet production totalled 93,600,000 tons in the Soviet Union in 1968, but it was only 75,700,000 tons in 1972. In 1940 that figure was 18 million tons, in 1950 it was 20 million tons, in 1960 it was almost 58 million tons, and in 1965 it was over 72 million tons. Of the total tonnage almost one-third was produced in the Russian Republic. The Ukraine actually was the greatest producer of sugar beets with a total tonnage of 46,010,000 in 1971. The Kazakh and Moldavian Republics each produced over two million tons, and the Kirghiz Republic almost matched them. The Belorussian Republic produced 778,000 tons of sugar beets, and the Lithuanian Republic produced 549,000 tons in 1971.

Most of the sunflowers were grown in the Russian and Ukrainian Republics. The total tonnage of sunflower seeds for the Soviet Union in 1971 was 5,658,000. The Russian Republic produced 2,599,000 tons, and the Ukrainian Republic 2,641,000 tons, leaving only the Moldavian Republic with 331,000 tons and the Kazakh Republic with 90,000 tons as the only other significant producers of sunflower seeds. Sunflower seed production in the Soviet Union doubled between 1950 and 1960, but it has held fairly constant since that time, except for a decline in 1972 to 5,030,000 tons due to the drought.

Potato production in the Soviet Union has increased gradually since 1950, but the increase has not been constant. The tonnage has fluctuated from 88,600,000 tons in 1950 down to 71,800,000 in 1963 and back up to 93,600,000 tons in 1964. The 1968 figure for potato production was more than 101 million tons, and in 1970 it fell back to 96,600,000 tons. But with the drought in 1972 potato production fell even further to only 77,800,000 tons. More than half of the potatoes are grown in the Russian Republic. The Ukraine and Belorussia rank next with about 21 percent and 13 percent, respectively. The only other major producers of potatoes are Lithuania, Latvia, Kazakhistan, and Estonia in that order. Each of these areas produces between one and three percent of the Soviet potato production.

Other vegetables totalled 20,300,000 tons of production in 1970. This figure was an increase from approximately 9 million tons in 1950 to over 16 million tons in 1960, and to over 17 million tons in 1965. But the steady increase in that production also suffered a decline in 1972 due to the drought. That year the vegetable production in the Soviet Union was only 19,100,000 tons. The Russian Republic produces about 50% of the vegetables, the Ukrainian Republic about 40%, and the other significant vegetable production is in the Uzbek, Kazakh, Moldavian, and Belorussian Republics, in that

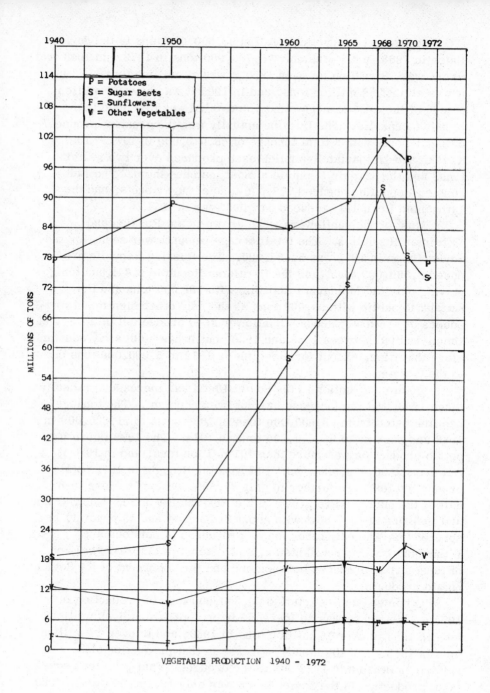

VEGETABLE PRODUCTION 1940 - 1972

order.

The number of cattle in the Soviet Union in January, 1973, was 104,000,000 head, which included 41,700,000 milk cows. This figure was an increase from 87,000,000 head of cattle, including almost 39 million milk cows in 1965, and from 75 million head of cattle, including 34 million milk cows in 1960. Slightly more than half of all the cattle produced in the Soviet Union are raised in the Russian Republic. The Ukraine raises about 25%, Kazakistan about 6%, Belorussia about 5%, Uzbekistan about 2%, and all other Union Republics raise less than 1% of the cattle each. The milk cows in each Union Republic average between one-third and one-half of the total cattle there.

The livestock census in 1971 stated that there were 139,900,000 sheep, 71,400,000 pigs, and 5,400,000 goats. In 1973 the sheep and goats were listed together at 144,500,000 (a decline of 100,000 head). These figures indicate a good increase in the production of sheep and pigs, except for the drought year of 1972.

In 1966 there were 125 million sheep, almost 53 million pigs, and almost 6 million goats. In 1961 there were 129 million sheep, 58 million pigs, and over 16 million goats. In 1951 there were 83 million sheep, 24 million pigs, and over 16 million goats. About half of the sheep and pigs are raised in the Russian Republic. Approximately one-quarter of the sheep are raised in the Kazakh Republic, and approximately one-quarter of the pigs are raised in the Belorussian Republic. The other main producers of sheep are the Belorussian, the Kirghiz, and the Uzbek Republics (about 6% each). Azerbaidzhan, Turkmenistan, Tadzhikistan, Armenia, Georgia, and Moldavia each produced between one and four thousand sheep in 1968. The main producers of pigs are the Russian Republic (50%), the Ukraine (30%), Belorussia (6%), Kazakhistan (4%), Lithuania (3%), and Moldavia (2%). Goats are raised primarily in the Caucasus and Pamir Mountain ranges.

About half of the meat, milk, and eggs are produced in the Russian Republic. The Ukraine produces about 25% of these products, and Belorussia, Kazakhistan, Lithuania, Latvia, and Moldavia each produce sizable amounts. Of course, each Union Republic produces several thousand tons of meat and milk and several million eggs. The total production of these products for the Soviet Union in 1972 was 13,600,000 tons of meat (dead weight), 83,200,000 tons of milk, and 48,200,000,000 eggs. The tonnage of meat went from about five million tons in 1950, to eight and one half tons in 1960, to 10 million tons in 1965, and to 11,6 million tons in 1968. The tonnage of milk went from 35 million tons in 1950, to

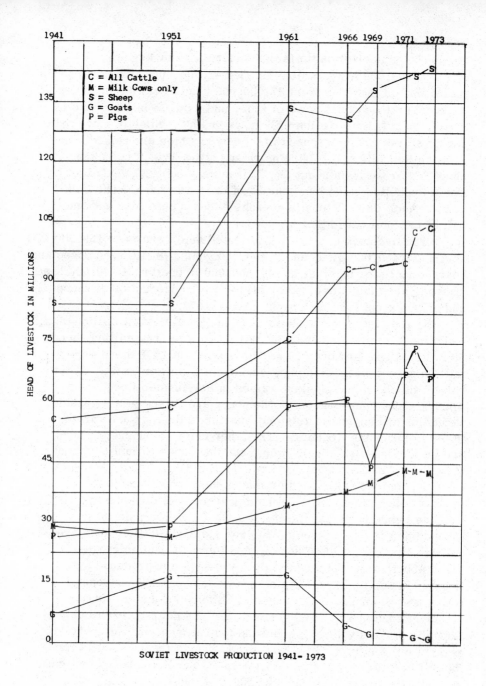

SOVIET LIVESTOCK PRODUCTION 1941- 1973

Legend:
C = All Cattle
M = Milk Cows only
S = Sheep
G = Goats
P = Pigs

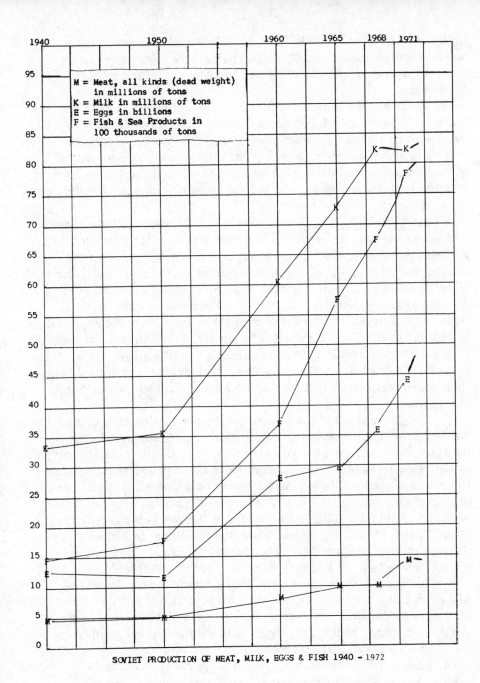

1940   1950   1960   1965   1968   1971

M = Meat, all kinds (dead weight)
      in millions of tons
K = Milk in millions of tons
E = Eggs in billions
F = Fish & Sea Products in
      100 thousands of tons

SOVIET PRODUCTION OF MEAT, MILK, EGGS & FISH 1940 - 1972

277

to almost 62 million tons in 1960, to 72 1/2 million tons in 1965, and to 82 million tons in 1968. The number of eggs increased from 11 billion in 1950 to 27 billion in 1960, 29 billion in 1965, and 35.5 billion in 1968.

Fish can hardly be considered an agricultural product, but since fish makes up a large portion of the Russian diet, the production of fish should be mentioned here. The Soviet figures on fish include sea animals, whales, and other sea products, not all of which are food products, but some indication of the effort devoted to this activity and of the relation to other food products may be seen.

In 1971, the Soviet Union produced 7,811,000,000 tons of fish and sea products. This was an increase from 1,755,000,000 tons in 1950, 3,541,000,000 tons in 1960, and 5,774,100,000 in 1965. During these years the Russian Republic produced about 80%, the Ukraine about 10% and Lithuania and Latvia about 4% each. Estonia produced about 1 1/2% of the sea products. Each of the inland Union Republics also produced large quantities of fish, even though the percentage of the total is small. For example, in 1965 Kazakhistan produced 91,200 tons of fish, but of course, Kazakhistan is on the Caspian Sea. But Belorussia and Moldavia produced from their lakes and rivers in 1965, 4,800 tons and 2,200 tons of fish, respectively.

The value of all these figures on the production of agricultural and sea products beyond the statistical record is in the relationships between times and areas. The significance of the time relationships is the rapid increase in the production of these products. The significance in the area relationships lies not only in the comparision of one area with another but also in the wide distribution and expansion of areas. The total significance of these figures is the consistency of the theory of building communism and the actual practice. Even though practice in agriculture lags behind the theory and the programs, there is a real effort to try to conform to them.

The graphs show substantial increases in the production of wheat, barley, sugar beets, sheep, cattle, and fish. There have also been moderate increases in the production of peas and beans, vegetables, pigs, milk cows, eggs, and meat. Agricultural products which showed little increase or a decrease were rye, oats, corn, millet, sunflowers, and goats. But grain production in general has not kept up with the needs of the country, and lower yields since 1969 have caused the Soviet Union to import large quantities.

There has been a shortage of cattle for many years. The collectivization process, when kulaks killed cattle instead of turning them over to the Collective Farms, reduced the number of livestock. It took several years to recover this loss. The Second World War also caused the death of many livestock, mostly cattle, and only small gains could be made in replacing them until the middle 1950's. This shortage has caused not only the scarcity of meat and milk products but also of leather. Even in the late 1960's there was still a shortage of leather.

The great increases in agricultural production took place after Khrushchev became influential in making policy decisions. Brezhnev and Kosygin have continued an emphasis on agriculture. The priority that they have placed on agriculture is reflected in the graphs, but Brezhnev and Kosygin have not been able to attain their goals in agricultural production.

The increased emphasis on consumer products in the Soviet Union reflects on the need for increased agricultural production. The products which have had the greatest increase indicate the consumer demand, which has become a more important factor in planning production since the early 1960's.

In comparing consumer needs against actual production one must look at the figures of population increase. In 1940 there were 194 million people in the Soviet Union. Due to the terrific losses during the war the population had decreased to 181 million in 1951. Since that time the population has steadily increased. In 1961 there were 216 million, and in 1972 there were 246 million citizens. From 1951 to 1968 there was more than a thirty percent increase in the population. This figure compares with about a 100% increase in the production of meat and milk, about 200% increase in the production of eggs and fish, and more than 100% increase in the production of wheat and vegetables. It is seen that the production of basic food items has increased much more rapidly than the population since 1951.

Yet, there was a food shortage in 1951. Food rationing lasted for several years after the Second World War. Agricultural products are also diverted to industrial needs and to foreign aid programs. There continues to be a greater demand for agricultural products than there is a supply. The problem of surpluses has not come to the Soviet Union, and it probably will not come for a long time considering the need in the Soviet Union and the hunger problems throughout the world and the involvement of the Soviet Union as a world leader and its responsibilities in extending foreign aid.

The Program of the 24th Party Congress and of the 1971-1975 Five Year Plan included plans to increase agricultural production even more than the previous plans. The demand is for better farming methods, more use of chemical fertilizers, and the production of more agricultural machinery and tools. The industry will continue to bring a larger percentage of the farmers to the cities, and the small number of people will have to supply larger amounts of food for the increased urban population.

The problems of inefficient farm labor, a cold climate with a short growing season, the need for more fertilizers, droughts, the scarcity of good farm land, and the lack of equipment continue to hold back agricultural production. As the programs and follow-through work attack these problems there can be a blending of the theory and practice so that this phase of building communism can meet its objectives. But agriculture is a problem which can not be managed as easily as industry, and the Soviet Union needs to keep striving to meet the demand for agricultural products. Khrushchev's ouster was partially due to his failure to solve the agricultural problem, and Brezhnev and Kosygin are criticized for the same deficiencies, even though there is increased production in many farm products.

Baransky, N. N., Economic Georgraphy of the USSR, Moscow: Foreign Languages Publishing House, 1956, 413 pp.

Dewdney, John C., A Geography of the Soviet Union, New York: Pergamon Press, 1965, 154 pp.

Jorre, George, The Soviet Union--The Land and Its People, New York: John Wiley & Sons, Inc., 1967, 379 pp.

Lyalikov, N. I., Ekonomicheskaya Geografiya SSR, Moscow: Gosudarstvennoye Uchebnoye Pedigogicheskoye Izdatel'stvo, 1959, 343 pp.

Narodnoye Khozyaystvo SSSR v 1965 g. - Statisticheskii Ezhegodnik, Moscow: Tsentral'noye Statisticheskoye Upravleniye pri Sovete Ministrov SSSR, 1966, 910 pp.

Narodnoye Khozyaystvo SSSR v 1967 g. - Statisticheskii Ezhegodnik, Moscow: Statistika, 1968, 1008 pp.

Pravda, Moscow, 1969-1973.

Razgildeyev, Gennady (Soviet Exchange Scholar), Lecture at the University of Missouri-Rolla, Rolla, Missouri, September 12, 1968.

SSSR v Tsifrakh v 1971 godu, Moscow: Izdatelstvo "Statistika", 1972, 240 pp.

SSSR v Tsifrakh v 1967 godu, Moscow: Izdatelstvo "Statistika", 1968, 159 pp.

Vvedenskii, B. A., et als., Ezhegodnik Bol'shoi Sovetskoi Entsikolpedii 1968, Moscow: Izdatel'stvo "Sovetskaya Entskilopediya," 1968, 621 pp.

Whiting, Kenneth, The Soviet Union Today, New York: Frederick A. Praeger, Publishers, 1966, 423 pp.

CHAPTER X

INDUSTRY AND TRANSPORTATION

Since the 1917 Communist Revolution, the emphasis of the Soviet economy has been on heavy industry. Light industry and consumer goods have only recently received an increased share of the budget. Transportation facilities have lagged behind the rest of the economy. Spare parts and repair work have also been sacrificed to the drive to build new industrial plants and equipment. Electrification and industrialization of the country have taken priority since the First Five Year Plan.

The light industry and the transportation facilities, which were inherited from the tsarist regime, have continued to serve the economy. Shortages and inconveniences have been tolerated in order to accomplish greater tasks. The Second World War was a further setback to industry and transportation. Many installations and facilities were completely destroyed and reconstruction lasted well into the early 1950's.

Before the war about 50% of the industry was located within 25 miles of Moscow. Leningrad and Kiev also were major locations of industry. Leningrad was blockaded for almost three years during the war and much of the industry was destroyed or crippled by enemy shelling. Kiev was captured by the enemy, and industry there was greatly damaged. Moscow was threatened by attack for several months. The enemy came very close to the city, and it became necessary to start moving industry to the east to prevent its capture or destruction. Many industrial plants were disassembled and moved to the Urals or on to Siberia. Where transportation was lacking, people carried machine parts on their backs in order to restore industry in a new location. During this time there was an industrial boom in the Urals. After the war the boom continued farther east in an attempt to diversify the location of industry for defense purposes.

The electrification of the Soviet Union was planned before the war, but the industry relied heavily on coal rather than on hydro-electric power stations. In fact, more than 2/3 of all power as late as 1950 came from coal. The hydro-electric power plant at Dniepropetrovsk was built in the 1930's, but it was destroyed during the war. Other smaller plants were also destroyed, and it was about 1950 that they were restored and put back into operation.

The locations for fuel for power came primarily from the Donetsk Coal Basin in the Ukraine, the Kuznetsk Coal Basin in Siberia, the Karaganda Coal Fields in Kazakhistan, and the oil fields in Baku. Before the war the production of oil had increased only 3.5 times since 1913. The great increase in oil production came after the war. In 1955 it had increased 8 times over the 1913 production.

Mining and metallurgy before the war were developed at Magnitogorsk. The most talked-about achievement was the Donetsk and Kuznetsk link-up with Magnitogorsk. These two coal producing areas shipped coal to Magnitogorsk for the metallurgical plant there. Instead of the train returning with empty railroad cars, the iron ore at Magnitogorsk was transported to Donetsk and Kuznetsk for supporting metallurgical plants at these locations. Coal and ore were also shipped from these areas to Moscow for a metallurgical plant there. The nonferrous mining, mostly copper, had been developed in the Ural Mountains, Kazakhistan, and Armenia. The production of nickel did not develop until 1934, when a nickel plant was put into operation in the Ural Mountains. The Ural Mountains had also become important for the production of zinc, lead, and aluminum.

Most of the machine-building enterprises were in Moscow, Leningrad, and Kiev. Rostov-on-the-Don, Gorky on the Volga, and Sverdlovsk and Chelyabinsk in the Ural Mountains had also established important machine-building plants.

The chemical industry was very small before the 1917 Revolution. Moscow and Leningrad developed the largest chemical plants before the Second World War, and new chemical industries were being developed at Kiev, Sverdlovsk, and Gorky.

Lumber had been the primary building material before the 1917 Revolution. The large forest region makes lumber plentiful, and there were many locations for producing lumber. Arkhangelsk had become the main producer. The Volga and Kama River systems provided transportation for logs, and sawmills were established along their banks. Stalingrad (now Volgograd) became the second largest producer of lumber and wood products.

Other building materials were primarily stone and cement. Granite and marble came from the Karelian region (north of Leningrad), and marble and other stones were produced in the Urals. Cement was produced at Donetsk, in the Urals, and at Kuznetsk. The production of these building materials was fairly well limited to these areas before the Second World War.

Before the 1917 Revolution, the textile industry was centered near Moscow and St. Petersburg (now Leningrad). At that time about half of the cotton, which was the principle textile, came from abroad. The domestic cotton was grown mostly in the area near Tashkent. By 1950 there was enough cotton grown near Tashkent and in the Caucasus Mountain area to meet the needs of the country. Flax and wool had by this time also become major textile products in Soviet industry. Before the 1917 Revolution, these products were made into linen and clothing primarily in the homes. But by 1950 linen mills were located at Kostroma, Smolensk, and Ivanovo, and there were woolen mills at Moscow, Ivanovo, Kharkov, Klinsky, and several other places, including Omsk in Siberia. Cotton mills were located primarily near Moscow and Leningrad, in the Caucasus, and in Central Asia, but the number of them had increased by 1950 to over 25 separate mills.

Food processing plants shortly after the Second World War were still located primarily near Moscow, Leningrad, and Kiev and along the Volga River valley and in the North Caucasus Mountain region. Of course, smaller meat packing plants, flour mills, and fish processing plants were scattered fairly well throughout the populated areas.

Large manufacturing plants were practically all located near Moscow, Leningrad, Kiev, and in the Urals before the Second World War. They had developed in the areas of heavy population and near the mining regions. The recognition for diversifying the locations of this industry did not become so apparent to Soviet leaders until during the Second World War, when Moscow and Leningrad were so heavily shelled.

Transportation had not changed substantially between the First and Second World Wars in the Soviet Union. Rather than building new equipment and facilities, the Soviet government repaired the old railroad tracks and relied on them for most transportation needs. The rivers served as the second principal transportation routes. Most of the roads remained unsurfaced, except for main highways between Moscow and Leningrad and between Moscow and Kiev. A greater emphasis was placed on building streets in the major cities. In Moscow there was also constructed the famous Moscow Subway, which became the pride of all Soviet citizens.

By 1950 about 85% of the freight and passengers for long distance transportation still were going by way of the railroad. Short distance freight was transported by truck or wagon, and people often had to walk or ride in trucks or wagons.

Communist theory advocates the public ownership of all means of production. This concept includes all industry, the plants, the factories, installations, equipment and tools. It also includes all equipment and facilities for transportation. The ownership and operation of industrial and transportation facilities also require centralized planning and coordination with the Five Year Plans. Rather than relying on the principle of supply and demand, the Soviet Government places priorities on all phases of the economy. Production and maintenance must have top priorities in the plan before they receive any emphasis in the work projects of the country. This arrangement has caused great advances in some lines of production and almost no activity in others. The production of automobiles, for instance, has lagged way behind that of other highly industrialized societies. To compensate for this difference, the Soviet Government heavily subsidizes transportation on trains, river boats, and airplanes. A Soviet citizen finds it less expensive to travel by these than to buy and operate a car, even if cars were more readily available.

The financing of the industrialization program in the Soviet Union does not come from direct taxes on the citizens. The money actually comes from the profits or the mark-up on goods sold to the citizens or to foreign markets. By increasing prices the government increases its revenue. This profit is actually the same money that is called "surplus value" and one of the basic evils of the capitalist system. But there is a profound difference according to Communist theory. This money is "surplus value," when it goes to a private person or a private corporation. It is the "turnover tax" when it goes to the public treasury. In other words, the "surplus value" is a form of exploitation of man by man, but the "turnover tax" comes from the economy to serve the needs of society. Rather than private citizens benefiting as they do with "surplus value," all citizens benefit by having free education, free medical care, and other services paid from the "turnover tax." It then becomes public money for public purposes and does not exploit or discriminate against anyone.

According to the Five Year Plans the rate of the "turnover tax" is regulated. This rate is not a straight percentage as in a sales tax. It is closer in concept to the mark-up price on goods. Some goods are marked up 5%, others 25%, and still others 100% or more. The difference is based not on the cost of production or by competition, because there is no competition in the Soviet Union, but by the determined needs of the society. All prices become parts of the economic plans, and these prices are the same everywhere in the country for the same items. Costs for transportation, storage, or damaged units are not necessarily reflected in the prices of the goods. Some goods may be sold at prices under costs. This policy is true for many services, such as education, medical care, and transportation. Other goods are sold at high prices, even though the cost of production is low and the availability of the goods is high. Ready-made clothing fits into this group. For this reason many people buy the cloth and patterns in order to make their own clothing.

The price system and the distribution of goods started to change in the early 1960's though. It was discovered that planned production and the fulfillment of quotas caused large stocks of unsold merchandise in some products and continued shortages in others. Previous to 1960 these problems were attacked by attempting to correct mistakes in the next Five Year Plan.

Gosplan (the State Planning Committee) coordinates reports which channel up through local Soviets from individual enterprises to the Oblast Soviets to the Union Republic Supreme Soviet and Council of Ministers and on to the USSR Supreme Soviet and Council of Ministers. These reports contain lists of the available resources, potential manpower, and estimated production capabilities for the five year period. Gosplan analyzes the reports, prepares statistics, compares previous production with the planned needs of the society, and prepares a new budget and a new plan. The new plan is then discussed at the various levels of the soviets and suggested revisions are made. Finally, Gosplan prepares a revised plan, which must be approved by the USSR Supreme Soviet and the Central Committee of the Communist Party. The new Five Year Plan, at least according to current practice, is then announced at a Party Congress. Once announced, the new Five Year Plan becomes the law of the land and is strictly enforced both by category of production and by period of time. Time blocks are broken down by year, then by quarter, then by month, and finally by day so that quotas of production can be established and that the plan can move ahead according to the schedule or faster. This whole process is Democratic Centralism in action. Democratic Centralism is the means for forming and enforcing policies both in the political and economic sectors of the Soviet Government.

But the planning did not take into consideration all the problems. The needs and the desires of the consumers were sometimes neglected. Industries found not only shortages of certain items but also items with the wrong specifications. The individual customer also met this same problem. Industry found that it could better or at least faster meet the quota requirements by producing only one style, one size, one color, or one other similar specification. This specialization helped work crews to increase their quantity output and surpass the quota requirements. When bonuses and other incentives were introduced to encourage workers to surpass the quota, this problem of disregarding actual needs multiplied. For example, a customer may have found only one size of shoes available in the store. There were plenty of shoes but none to fit him.

Professor Yevsei Liberman of Kharkov University assessed the problem and made suggestions for improving the situation. His plan was first introduced on a small scale in the early 1960's and now his suggested reforms have been accepted throughout the whole country. He suggested that the quota should not be considered to be fulfilled until the produced item was sold. By doing this the producer would have to relate his production to the needs of the customer. He also suggested that the producing enterprise should receive a bonus or a percentage of the profit from the sale of goods. This profit would accrue to the enterprise for bonuses to the workers and for the improvement of the enterprise facilities, including the services to the employees and their families.

These suggestions were gradually adopted and were found to be both practical and consistent with the concept of centralized planning and public ownership. Contrary to the thinking of some people these reforms were not an abandonment of any socialist principle or the acceptance of any capitalist concept. All property remained in public ownership and control. Profits were not going to individuals except through wages and public services. There was no exploitation of man by man but rather increased public service by society.

The adoption of Liberman's suggestions also caused the introduction of better merchandising techniques in the stores. Producing enterprises wanted their products sold. This desire lead to advertising, promotion plans, and salesmanship. These techniques have helped industries obtain their needed supplies, and the general public has become more satisfied with the purchase of consumer goods.

The changes introduced by Khrushchev and Brezhnev have also helped the economy. The high priority on heavy industry has been relaxed so that light industry and consumer goods could set higher production goals. This shift in the economy has increased the supply of many needed products and helped raise the standard of living of the Soviet citizens.

INDUSTRIAL PRODUCTION

The great increase in the production of electric power at hydro-electric power plants and in the production of oil and natural gas has shifted the reliance from coal to these other sources of power. As of 1967 coal accounted for less than 40% of the fuel consumption in the Soviet Union, but the increased needs for power have caused an increase in the production of coal. In 1940 the Soviet Union produced 166 million tons of coal. That figure increased to 261 million tons in 1950 and 510 million tons in 1960. However, since 1960 the increase in the rate of coal production has not been as rapid. In 1968 the Soviet Union produced 594 million tons of coal, and in 1970 coal production was 625 million tons. In 1972 coal production reached 655 tons.

The campaign to electrify the country really got under way after 1950. There was a seven times increase in the output of electrical power between 1950 and 1970. This great difference is largely attributable to the construction of a number of very large hydro-electric power dams and the construction of atomic reactors for generating electricity. Four very large hydro-electric power dams, each with a potential of over one million kilowatts, were constructed one right after the other. The one at Kuibyshev on the Volga was completed in 1955, the Volgograd dam was completed in 1958, the Bratsk dam was completed in 1961, and the Krasnoyarsk dam was completed in 1967. Each of these power plants was larger than the preceding one, and a new one larger than all of them was placed under construction In 1969 at Sayansk in the Krasnoyarsk Krai. Other hydro-electric power plants have been constructed at numerous locations north of Moscow to Murmansk, along the Volga River, in the Caucasus Mountains, in the Urals, and in Central Asia. For each hydro-electric power dam, there are also several thermal power plants which operate on coal, oil, or natural gas. In addition, an atomic electric power station has been constructed at Novo-Voronezh, and another one is planned for construction at the mouth of the Lena River in Siberia.

In 1940 the output of electrical power totalled 48.3 billion kilowatt hours. By 1950 it had increased to 91.2 billion kilowatt hours, and by 1960 it was 292 billion kilowatt hours. In 1965, that figure was 507 billion kilowatt hours, and in 1968 it reached 638

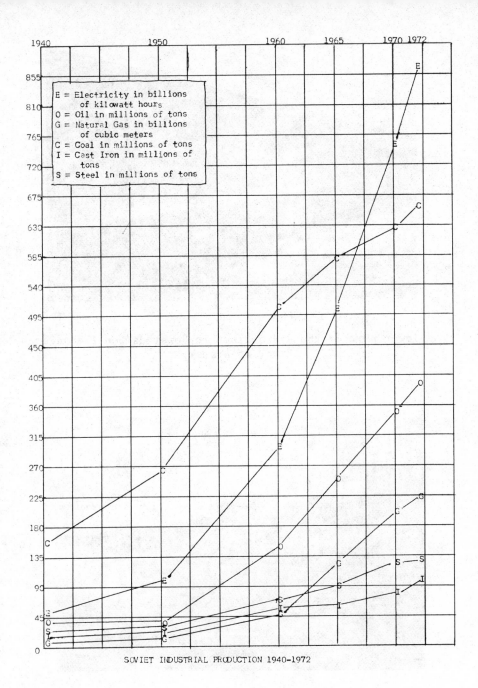

SOVIET INDUSTRIAL PRODUCTION 1940-1972

289

The lower part of the Hydro-Electric Power dam on the Angara
River at Bratsk.

The upper part of the Hydro-electric Power dam on the Volga
River near Volgograd.

billion kilowatt hours. In 1970 that figure was 740 billion kilowatt hours, and in 1972 it was 858 kilowatt hours.

The production of oil and natural gas also increased many times over from 1950 to 1970. The discovery and development of oil and gas fields in new areas have made this increase possible. The richest area lies between the Volga River and the Ural Mountains. Pipe lines for oil and for gas have been constructed from this area east to Omsk and Novosibirsk and west to Moscow and other cities. Oil and gas fields have also been developed along the lower Don River, near Lvov in the Ukraine, along the Pechora River in the north, and in Central Asia near Bukhara and Tashkent. Oil production has increased from 31.1 million tons in 1940 to 37.9 million tons in 1950 and on to 148 million tons in 1960. In 1965 that figure was 243 million tons, and in 1970 it was 353 million tons. In 1972 oil production increased to 394 million tons. Natural gas production increased from 3.4 billion cubic meters in 1940 to only 6.2 billion cubic meters in 1950. But in 1960 that figure reached 47.2 billion cubic meters, and in 1965 and 1970 it reached 129 billion and 200 billion cubic meters, respectively. By 1972 natural gas production was 221 billion cubic meters.

Iron and steel production, which came second after the electrification of the country for the industrialization of the Soviet Union, has also increased very rapidly, particularly since 1950. The main iron ore and manganese mines are in the Ural Mountains and the Caucasus Mountains, but the Krivoy Rog Basin in the Ukraine, the Karaganda Basin in East Kazakhistan, the Kuznetsk Basin in Siberia, the Angara-Ilim Basin near Bratsk, and Kursk in the Ukraine and locations on the Murmansk Peninsula have all become production areas for iron and steel. The production of cast iron has increased as follows: 14.9 million tons in 1940, 19.2 million tons in 1950, 46.8 million tons in 1960, 66.2 million tons in 1965, and 85.9 million tons in 1970, and 92.3 million tons in 1972. Steel production has increased at about the same rate. In 1940 steel production reached 18.3 million tons, and in 1950 27.3 million tons of steel were produced. In 1960, 1965, and 1970 the production of steel was 65.3 million tons, 91 million tons, and 116 million tons, respectively. Steel production in 1971 was 121 million tons, and for the first time the Soviet Union surpassed the United States. In that year U.S. production of steel was 120 million tons. Soviet steel production continued to increase and reached 126 million tons in 1972.

The production of electrical power and of iron and steel is

the basis of most industrial production. The figures on the production of these resources can be used as an index for showing industrial growth. Electrical power increased seven times over between 1950 and 1970, and cast iron and steel increased more than four times and more than five times, respectively.

Industrial products are so numerous and so diversified that it is difficult here to give an overview of economic growth in the Soviet Union. For this reason, examples of several products and their increase in production are shown in chart form.

Product	1940	1950	1960	1965	1968	1970	1972
Metal cutting instruments in thousands of units	58.4	70.6	156	186	200	202	210
Synthetic resins and plastics in thousands of tons	10.9	67.1	312	803	1293	1672	2035
Automobiles in thousands	145	363	524	616	800.9	916	1379
Tractors in thousands	31.6	117	239	355	423	459	478
Grain combines in thousands	12.8	46.3	59	85.8	101	99.2	95.7
Paper in thousands of tons	812	1180	2234	3231	4000	4200	4600
Cement in millions of tons	5.7	10.2	45.5	72.4	87.5	95.2	104
Cloth (all kinds) in millions of square meters	3300	3374	6636	7498	8242	8647	9145
Leather shoes in millions of pairs	211	203	419	486	597	676	645

Product	1940	1950	1960	1965	1968	1970	1972
Radio receivers in thousands of units	160	1072	4165	5160	7000	7800	8800
Television sets in thousands of units	.3	11.9	1726	3655	5700	6700	6000
Refrigerators in thousands of units	3.5	1.2	529	1675	3200	4100	5000

Another significant fact concerning the industrialization of the Soviet Union in regard to building a material-technical base for achieving communism is the improvement of the production capability of the individual worker through education and by providing equipment and tools. An average for all Soviet industry shows the production capability of one worker based on 100 in 1940 had reached 372 or was almost four times greater in 1965. Based on 100 in 1958 the 1965 figures was 142 or almost one-and-one-half times greater.

ADVANCES IN SOVIET TRANSPORTATION

Local transporation in the larger cities in the Soviet Union has kept in pace with that of other modern cities, except for automobiles. Moscow, Leningrad, Kiev, and Tashkent also have two advantages in transportation over most cities of the world. One advantage is the wide streets, which were built straight and which are kept very clean. The other advantage is the subways. These cities can boast of not only rapid service but also cleanliness, comfort, and beauty.

The Moscow Subway was first built in the 1930's as the beginning of building communism from the bottom up. It has marble walls, crystal chandeliers, statues, and stained-glass windows in the subway stations, and each station has its own special type of beauty. Particularly since 1950 the subway lines have been extended to reach all parts of the city. In 1972 they had just opened a new section and other sections were under construction.

The subways in Leningrad, Kiev, and Tashkent were built later. Kiev had just a small section open in 1964. But these new subways are following the same pattern as Moscow's. The service is good; trains run every few minutes during the day often up until midnight. The cost is only 5 kopecks (about 6¢).

Most cities also have streetcars or trolley buses which are also inexpensive to ride. There are also taxis, but they are not always available when one wants one. People line up at taxi stands and wait turns. But the price is low; short rides usually cost only 25 to 40 kopecks and a long ride across Moscow costs about one ruble.

The major difficulties with transportation in the Soviet Union are met when one travels from city to city by car or truck. Only the major roads are asphalted. Most highways are narrow, and only near big cities are there divided highways. However, traffic is light, and there is no need for super highways.

The construction and maintenance of roads are major problems in the Soviet Union. The wide expanse of the land makes long distances between populated centers. The initial construction is very expensive, but the maintenance is even more difficult. The cold winters destroy large parts of the asphalt and cement roads. And in the Far North road construction is next to impossible because of the permafrost which causes shifts in the surface of the land between warmer and colder days. For these reasons highway transportation has received a lower priority than that of trains, riverboats, and airplanes.

Historically the rivers were the main transportation routes in Russia. The Volga boatman is legendary for the great feats of towing the barges upstream, but the Don, the Dnieper, and other rivers also were used for both passengers and freight. Stalin expanded the use of rivers by constructing canals. The White Sea Canal which connected Arkhangelsk with Leningrad was started in 1928 and completed in 1937. It still is a major transportation route for lumber, fish, and furs from the north. In 1937 the canal between the Moscow and Volga Rivers was completed. This canal enables the transportation of freight and passengers from Moscow to cities along the Volga River and vice versa. Another major canal is the Volga-Don Canal which was completed in 1952. This canal permits riverboats and barges to travel all over the western part of the country. They can go from the Caspian Sea or from Moscow across the canal to the Don River, go north along the Don or go south to Rostov or on into the Black Sea, and go from the Black Sea along the Dnieper River to Kiev. The construction of this canal was a major advance in Soviet transportation.

Railroads were an important means of transportation during the tsarist regime. Most of western Russia was well supplied with

railroads, and the transcontinental railroad to Vladivostok in the
Far East had been built. This Siberian railway track was expanded
during the Soviet era. There are now two tracks all the way, and
there are spurs through the Urals to Novosibirsk and through
Central Asia. The old tracks have been maintained throughout the
whole country, and new engines and railway cars have been
supplied. Most long distance transportation for both passengers
and for freight is still by rail. Transportation costs are low, and
most Soviet citizens have these costs paid by their employer or by
the trade union for official business or for vacations. Trains are
always well filled with passengers and well loaded with freight.

Air transportation has become more popular since the
Second World War. The facilities have been greatly expanded,
and the costs for passenger service have remained low. There is
little difference in the cost of riding the airplane and the train.
The tendency has been to use air transportation for long distances
and rail transportation for shorter ones. Particularly since 1960
there has been a substantial jump in the number of passengers and
the tonnage of freight carried on Soviet airlines. The cost of
construction and maintenance of airports is high. The same problems apply here as for highway construction and maintenance
except for the distance of roads. The priority has been to improve
airports rather than highways for that reason.

Actual figures for the advancement of Soviet transportation
are shown in the following chart. The freight is shown in billions
of ton-kilometers and the passenger traffic is shown in the number
of passengers times kilometers in billions.

Type of Transportation	1940	1950	1960	1965	1970	1971
Freight						
All types	487.6	713.3	1885.7	2764.0	3829.2	4084
Railroad	415.0	602.3	1504.3	1950.2	2494.7	2762
Sea	23.8	39.7	131.5	388.8	656.1	695.1
River	36.1	46.2	99.6	133.9	174	180
Oil Pipeline	3.8	4.9	51.2	146.7	282	376

Type of Transportation	1940	1950	1960	1965	1970	1971
Automobile & Truck	8.9	20.1	98.5	143.1	220.8	238
Air	.02	.14	.65	1.34	1.88	1.99
Passenger						
All Types	106.3	98.3	249.5	366.6	549	581.8
Railroad	98.0	88.0	170.8	201.6	265.4	274.6
Sea	.9	1.2	1.3	1.5	1.6	1.7
River	3.8	2.7	4.3	4.9	5.4	5.6
Automobile & Bus	3.4	5.2	61.0	120.5	198.3	211.1
Air	.02	1.2	12.1	38.1	78.2	88.8

Recent policy decisions have made changes in Soviet transportation which are not readily noticeable in the figures. One decision was the agreement with Italy to construct an automobile plant at Tol'yatti on the Volga River near Kuibyshev. Previously Gorky has been the main center for automobile production. The Gorky plant boasted of its five millionth car in March, 1967. Now Gorky will have a competitor in automobile production. This decision reflects the strong demand for cars in the Soviet Union, and it is probable that there will be a substantial increase in the production of cars.

Another decision has greatly affected river transportation. The introduction of hydro-foils has caught the interest of the Soviet people. Hydro-foils are seen on the Moscow River, the Don River, the Volga River, the Finnish Gulf, the Black Sea, and many other places. These boats are streamlined, and they go at very high speeds. Regular routes have been established on the Black Sea from Odessa to Constansa, Rumania and Varna, Bulgaria. This means of transportation is surely to expand.

The use of supersonic jet airlines has become a part of
Soviet aviation. Not only have transoceanic flights been established
between Moscow and Montreal and between Moscow and New York
City, but transcontinental flights from Moscow to Tokyo have been
established not only for the Soviet citizens but also for all Europeans. Soviet advertising claims the shortest airline route between
Europe and Japan. In 1969 the Soviet Union tested the large TU 144
supersonic airliner which seats 120 people and cruises at 1500 miles
per hour. It is reported to have a range of 4000 miles. The entry
into the international airline competition also advances the Soviet
standards of transportation. The TU 144 was scheduled to be
operational in the middle 1970's which puts the Soviet Union ahead
of France and England in the production of this type of large supersonic airplane.

The decision to open the Northern Sea Route to vessels of
all nations is another great advance in Soviet transportation and
industry. This Northern Sea Route has been operational since the
1930's for a few months a year. In the 1950's nuclear powered ice
breakers were introduced to increase the time during the year that
the sea route could be used. This route runs east from Murmansk
across the northern shore of the Soviet Union to the Bering Strait
and south to Soviet ports on the Pacific Ocean and beyond. Increased use of this sea route could mean a greater effort to keep
the area ice free by nuclear powered ice breakers so that this much
shorter sea route to Japan could be used by all European merchant
fleets. This decision could help develop the whole Arctic region.
And the construction of a nuclear power station at the mouth of the
Lena River would contribute much more to the project of harnessing
nature in the Far North.

PROSPECTS

Planning and operation of Soviet industry and transportation
meet problems and revisions of policies. The attempt to tie production and services closer to the needs of the people both in the Soviet
Union and abroad has caused many adjustments in the original plans.
Waste of products and man hours of work is constantly being eliminated. Cutbacks in the production of some goods have been ordered
due to waste. Increased production of steel caused some workers
to consider steel to be plentiful, and they did not maintain work discipline in protecting and conserving steel from misuse. Cuts in
delivery and in actual production resulted from the recognition of

this waste.

The harsh winter of 1968-69 had a damaging effect on the Soviet economy. The flu epidemic greatly reduced the total man-hours of work. Difficulty in fighting the deep snows and cold weather caused further delays in both industrial production and transportation achievements. But the economic plans were adjusted to compensate for these temporary losses. Spring and summer, 1969, were accompanied by a greater effort to meet these deficiencies.

Recognition of the need to increase international trade as a means to stimulate the Soviet economy was accepted by Brezhnev and Kosygin in 1971 and 1972. Substantial increases have been made, and even greater possibilities are expected to develop through the 1972 trade agreements with the United States. Consistent with the agreements with President Nixon in Moscow in May, 1972, the Occidental Petroleum Company of Los Angeles, California signed an agreement in July in Moscow to supply the Soviet government with a wide range of scientific and technical services. This agreement involved $3,000,000,000.00 to cover the 5-year contract.

Khrushchev may not have been realistic in his dreams to catch up and surpass United States production, but his goal to multiply Soviet production has become the program of the Brezhnev and Kosygin administration. The achievements, particularly in steel production, have been phenomenal, but there are still many problems. Brezhnev and Kosygin have had to adjust their schedules and at the same time strive to meet more realistic goals. They have set new plans for production to be more closely related to industrial and consumer demands and have opened new sectors for the production and distribution of goods. The great effort to expand foreign trade in 1973 by Brezhnev's visits to West Germany and to the United States are sure to increase Soviet industrial production to meet the needs for exchange. Chancellor Willy Brandt of West Germany stated that these agreements brought about a stage of "productive co-existence" rather than merely "peaceful co-existence." This trend definitely effects the production and living standards of the Soviet Union. Prospects for increased industrial production in the Soviet Union appeared to be greater than ever.

Baransky, N. N., Economic Geography of the USSR, Moscow:
    Foreign Languages Publishing House, 1956, 413 pp.
Cronkite, Walter, CBS News, New York, January 27, 1972
Dewdney, John C., A Geography of the Soviet Union, New York:
    Pergamon Press, 1965, 154 pp.
Jorre, Georges, The Soviet Union - The Land and Its People,
    New York: John Wiley & Sons, Inc., 1967, 379 pp.
Kovalev, S. M., et als, Ezhegodnik Bol'shoi Sovetskoi Entsiklopedii
    1972, 624 pp.
Lyalikov, N. I., Ekonomicheskaya Geografiya SSSR, Moscow:
    Gosudarstvennoye Uchebnoye Pedigogicheskoye Izdatelstvo,
    1959, 343 pp.
Maxwell, Robert (ed.), Information USSR, New York: Pergamon
    Press, 1962, 982 pp.
Narodnoye Khozyaystvo SSSR v 1965 g. - Statisticheskii Ezhegodnik,
    Moscow: Tsentral'noye Statisticheskoye Upravleniye pri
    Sovete Ministrov SSSR, 1966, 910 pp.
Narodnoye Khozyaystvo SSSR v 1967 g. - Statisticheskii Ezhegodnik,
    Moscow: Statistika, 1968, 1008 pp.
Pravda, Moscow, 1967-1973.
Razgildeyev, Gennady (Soviet Exchange Scholar), Lecture at the
    University of Missouri-Rolla, Rolla, Missouri: September,
    1968.
SSSR v Tsifrakh v 1971 godu - kratkii statisticheskii sbornik,
    Moscow: Izdatel'stvo "Statistiki", 1972, 240 pp.
SSSR v Tsifrakh v 1967 godu - kratkii statisticheskii sbornik,
    Moscow: Izdatel'stvo "Statistiki", 1968, 159 pp.
St. Louis Globe Democrat, St. Louis, Missouri, January 1, 1969.
St. Louis Post Dispatch, St. Louis, Missouri, 1967-1973.
Vvedenskii, B. A., et als, Ezhegodnik Bol'shoi Sovetskoi
    Entsiklopedii 1968, Moscow: Izdatel'stvo "Sovetskaya
    Entsiklopediya", 1968, 621 pp.
Whiting, Kenneth, The Soviet Union Today, New York: Frederick
    A. Praeger, Publishers, 1966, 423 pp.

CHAPTER XI

SOVIET EDUCATION

Education in Russia before the 1917 Revolution was not provided for the majority of the population. The sons and daughters of the nobility had tutors and were prepared for higher education at home. Many of these youths went on to study in universities at Moscow, St. Petersburg, Kazan, and other cities. In addition, there were some schools, mostly college-preparatory, in the more heavily populated places. Some of the landed estates also provided education for at least part of the children. Leo Tolstoy spent several years at Yasnaya Polyana as a school teacher. But education was primarily a private affair, and there were no compulsory education laws. Estimates at the time of the 1917 Revolution were that from 75% to 85% of the people in Tsarist Russia were illiterate.

Anatoly Lunacharsky was named the first Commissar of Education after Lenin came to power. He continued and expanded the education process both in numbers of students and in the scope of the curriculum. His work was aided by Nadezhda Krupskaya, the wife of Lenin. Together they experimented and greatly improved the quality of education for the youth.

But their work was interrupted by the policy to eliminate illiteracy completely. The priority of education was placed on providing a fourth grade education for everyone, including adults. It was decided that when everyone learned the basic skills of reading, writing, and doing arithmetic problems, the priority would shift to provide secondary and later higher education for the youth. This new policy lasted through the 1930's. Anyone who could read and write was recruited as a teacher. The quality of education for a while was sacrificed to the quantity. Fourth grade education became universal and compulsory. It was also provided by the government at no cost to the student. Stalin could announce by the 1940's that illiteracy had been completely eliminated in the Soviet Union.

After the Second World War the expansion of education opportunities continued. Secondary schools had been established in the cities. Adult education was made available for scientists and engineers in the universities, and the institute system was established for providing continuing education for working people. The institute system grew very rapidly, and the education there became very closely related to occupational needs. However, the institutes were much more diversified than Western technical schools. They prepared musicians, artists, teachers, and many other professionals as well as skilled technicians.

After the elementary education program had achieved its basic goals, the next step was to provide education through the seventh grade for all students. This step was followed by extending that education through the tenth grade. During this time new universities were founded, many institutes were established, and research academies were expanded. Education advanced more rapidly in the larger cities and in the western part of the country. In the 1960's practically all children everywhere in the Soviet Union had the opportunity to complete the seventh grade. In all cities they could continue through the tenth grade, if they were capable. Only in the remote areas did the opportunity end with the seventh grade.

Khrushchev tried to improve education by making it available to more youth and by relating it closer to the needs of the society. He added the eleventh grade, which the students would return to after they had worked one year. He said that he was relating school with life. He also created boarding schools, which were means of consolidating small schools and making education available where it had been lacking. These boarding schools brought children from outlying areas into the towns and cities to attend school. The children stayed at the school six days a week and could see their parents only on Sundays, but they did have the opportunity to attend school for the first time or at least they could continue beyond the lower grades.

As educational opportunities were expanded the policy of free compulsory universal education continued. Even university education was free, and the students also received stipends for additional living expenses. Workers who attended institutes were given two hours off their work schedule in order to take four hours of instruction without any fees and without any loss of pay.

The drive for more and better education has inspired the Soviet citizens. The concept of creating the New Soviet Man depends on quality education, and the effects of these programs are evident in public places in the Soviet Union as well as in the achievements in industry, science, and space exploration. It is common to see Russian citizens reading technical books and journals on subway trains, or busses, in airplanes, on park benches or just about any place a person has the occasion to sit and wait. Books are inexpensive in the Soviet Union, and there are always crowds in the book stores. The desire to learn has become a part of their way of life.

SOVIET SCHOOL ORGANIZATION

Soviet education is a life-time process. The mother takes her baby to the nursery at her place of employment as soon as she returns to work after giving birth. This time is usually between three and six months. The nursery is supervised by doctors and/or nurses under the administration of the Ministry of Health. The child stays in the nursery during working hours of his parents until he is three years old. The parents take turns taking the child to the nursery and bringing him home after work. This three years is a period of some training, group activities, and health care, but it is really not a part of education. However, the children do learn how to behave in a group situation, and this learning is important later on. The nursery, like the other phases of care, training, and education, is free to the parents, but it is not compulsory. Grandmothers and other retired relatives often take care of the younger children.

The next phase for children is the kindergarten. It too is not compulsory and is supervised by the Ministry of Health. The kindergarten also is located near the place of employment of the parents. But its orientation is directed toward learning processes rather than local health care, at least the emphasis is in that direction. Supervision is usually done by young people who are preparing to become elementary school teachers. Three or four months of supervision of kindergarten children is a part of their teacher training. The young children learn to dance and sing. They also have projects for growing flowers and vegetables or for making handicraft items. The children are taken on excursions to parks, to the woods, to public buildings, and many other places in order to increase their awareness of the community. It is common to see a group of these children walking double file, holding hands, and following their supervisor quietly along the sidewalk. In their garden area they also play games, have sports, and prepare for reading and arithmetic. The time in kindergarten is made very pleasant for them, and they learn group discipline well so that when they enter school there are few adjustment problems.

A boarding school in the outskirts of Leningrad.

Signs showing the various career possibilities
for youth at a kindergarten in Moscow.

At the age of seven the Soviet children leave the kindergarten and enroll in the first grade. This event is a big occasion. On the first day the children dress well, carry a bouquet of flowers, and walk with their parents to school. There is a ceremony, and the children are accepted into school. They start the first of September and continue until the last week of May.

The first four years make up the elementary school program. The children study their native language (which depends on the Union Republic where they live), arithmetic, music, arts, penmanship and sports. In the first two years they learn to read and write, and the next two years they increase their proficiency. Arithmetic becomes more complex each year. In the first year they learn to add, subtract, and multiply with numbers up to 100. In the second grade their numbers range up to 10,000. For the third and fourth grades they work with numbers up to 100,000 and 100,000,000, respectively, and they learn about division, distances, money, squares, cubes, and fractions. In the third grade geography of the Soviet Union is added to their courses, and in the fourth grade they start ancient history and nature studies.

Soviet children attend school six days a week. The first quarter runs from September 1st to November 4th. A few days of vacation are given them to celebrate the anniversary of the 1917 Revolution on November 7th. The second quarter runs to the 30th of December. Again they have a few days off to celebrate. New Year's Day is a major holiday in the Soviet Union and is observed much the same way as Christmas is other places. Fir trees are decorated, and people exchange gifts. There are bright lights and even a Santa Claus (who is called Grandfather Frost). After the New Year's vacation the school resumes, and the third quarter runs from January 12th to the 21st of March. There is a short spring vacation at this time, and then the fourth quarter begins. The fourth quarter is interrupted on May 1st, which is International Labor Day. On that day no one works, and school is closed. But the classes resume and continue until the last of May.

The last week of May and the first two weeks of June are examination times. Special examinations are given to students who are finishing the 7th and 10th grades. The successful completion of these tests are necessary for the student to be accepted on the higher level.

The 5th through 7th grades are called the incomplete secondary school. It is comparable to junior high school in the United States, and the children are twelve to fourteen years old. In the

304

5th grade all children must start a foreign language, which is usually Russian for the non-Russians and English, German, or French for those students who already know Russian. The study of the same foreign language continues, as do most other subjects, from the time it starts until the student graduates from the 10th grade.

Classes of each subject are not held every day of the week. They could meet only once or twice a week or any number of times up to the six days. In this way a student has an opportunity to study more subjects and to continue subjects which he started previously by meeting that class on a one or two day schedule. Most courses do continue, and this is the method for keeping the students in touch with the subject material until they take the comprehensive examinations upon their completion of secondary school.

The other subjects in the 5th grade are literature, sports and shop. Arithmetic advances to decimals, roman numerals, common denominators, and the metric system. History and geography take a world-wide scope, and a course in botany is started.

In the 6th and 7th grades the students continue an expanded study of the same subjects. Mathematics becomes algebra and geometry in the 6th grade, and botany is replaced by zoology. Also physics is added. In the 7th grade the physics continues, and chemistry and mechanical drawing are added.

Not all students enroll in the 8th grade. Those who do not pass the comprehensive exams in June do have a second chance to take the tests, but if they fail twice, they are directed toward occupational training in a teknikum or toward a distributive education program in an uchilishche. This system is somewhat similar to the British and other European systems, where 11 or 12 year old students take tests to determine their continuation in school. But the Soviet student is about 14 years old when he takes these tests.

Students who live in remote places may not have the opportunity to go beyond the 7th grade. However, much of this deficiency was corrected by the establishment of boarding schools.

The 8th, 9th, and 10th grades are called the complete secondary school. The courses are continuations of the earlier ones. But new emphases are made, and new courses are added. Literature now includes foreign (Western) literature. Biology has moved into the study of anatomy, physiology, and hygiene. The same foreign language is continued, and history concerns the modern era. In the 9th grade mathematics courses include algebraic functions, geometry, and trigonometry. Literature, history, physics, chemistry, economic geography, and the foreign language remain the regular course, but practical courses are also offered. These practical courses include metal working, civil defense, sewing, electricity, electronics, agro-chemistry, auto mechanics, animal husbandry, sheep raising, and others. Male students also start their military training in the 9th grade. These practical courses and military training continue into the 10th grade. The emphasis in the 10th grade is also on the Soviet contributions to learning - literature, history, and social studies.

Every student graduating from the 10th grade must take the social studies course. It is not history, sociology, or psychology. It is a course on the theory and practice of communism. It is a detailed study of the program for building communism through the three steps of: building a material technical base, formulating new social relationships, and creating a new Soviet man.

For a few years after 1958 Khrushchev advocated an 11th grade program. Actually, it was a postponement of the 10th year program so that students could have one year of practical work before graduating. He said that school was divorced from life. Physical labor had become distasteful to some students, and he wanted to correct their attitudes. But Brezhnev reversed this decision. The present 9th and 10th grade series of practical courses replaces this need. In addition, the young people are given work projects during the summer months through their Pioneer and Komsomol organizations, which are also the providers of most of their recreation and extra-curricular programs while they are in school. There are also other work assignments for secondary school students during planting and harvest times. The school collective pitches in to help the collective farmers during these peak seasons. School is suspended at these times.

Book List for the 1971-1972 School Year

First grade

Primer for reading   Reader "Little Star"
Penmanship   Reader "Native Word"
Russian language   Mathematics

Second grade

Russian language   Reader "Native Word"

306

Mathematics
Reader "Little Flag"

Diary for observations

Third grade

Russian language
Reader "Our Native Land"
Reader "Native Word"

Mathematics
Dictionary for spelling
Nature studies

Fourth grade

Russian language
Native literature
Mathematics

Tales of history
Nature studies

Fifth grade

Native Literature - reader
Russian language - textbook
Mathematics
Dictionary for spelling
Botany
Physical geography

History of the ancient world
English language - textbook
French language - textbook
Spanish language - textbook
German language - textbook

Sixth grade

Native Literature - reader
Algebra
Algebra workbook
Geometry
Geometry workbook
Physics
Zoology

Geography of the continents
History of the Middle Ages
English language - textbook
French language - textbook
Spanish language - textbook
German language - textbook

Seventh grade

Native Literature - reader
Russian language - textbook
Four-place Math tables
Mechanical drawing
Physics
Inorganic chemistry

Geography of the USSR
History of the USSR
English language - textbook
French language - textbook
Spanish language - textbook
German language - textbook

Eighth grade

Russian literature
Russian literature - reader
Foreign literature - reader
Geometry - supplement
Mechanical drawing
Physics
Man (anatomy, physiology,
   and hygiene)

Economic geography of the
   USSR
Modern history
History of the USSR
English language - textbook
French language - textbook
Spanish language - textbook
German language - textbooк

Ninth grade

Russian literature
Russian literature of the
   19th century - reader
Russian language - supplement
Algebra and elementary functions
Geometry
Geometry - workbook
Trigonometry - supplement
Physics
Inorganic chemistry
General biology
Economic geography of foreign
   countries
Modern history
Current History
History of the USSR -
   imperialist period

History of the USSR - Soviet
   period
English language - textbook
French language - textbook
Spanish language - textbook
German language - textbook
Metal working - work
Civil defense
Animal husbandry - work
Clothing - work
Electrical technology - work
Radio electronics - work
Agro-chemistry - work
Auto mechanics - work
Tractors - work
Sheep raising - work
Military training - textbook

Tenth grade

Soviet literature
Soviet literature - reader
Algebra and elementary
   functions
Physics
Astronomy
Social sciences
Social sciences - reader

Organic chemistry
Recent history
History of the USSR - Soviet
   period
English language - textbook
French language - textbook
Spanish language - textbook
German language - textbook

308

Students who complete the 10th grade are subjected to another battery of tests to qualify them for higher education. These examinations are very competitive, and most of the secondary school graduates do not qualify, but not passing does not mean an end to their education. In addition to universities and institutes there are also other educational programs, the tekhnikum and the uchilishche.

Students who do not pass the regular examinations after the 7th and 10th grades are given other examinations for acceptance into the tekhnikum. They can complete their secondary education here and continue their preparation as a technician in one of several lines of work.

The uchilishche is also a work-related program. Graduates from the 10th grade may enter the uchilishche without a special examination. The course for this program lasts for one or two years, depending on one's speciality. It trains people to be store clerks, bookkeepers, economists, and specialists in other commercial lines of work. Not only do 18 year olds take these courses, but also adults attend the program in the evenings after work. The young people also receive work experience. There are sections, which alternate with each other to work for two days at a time in stores or offices. In addition to having no school fees, these students are paid for their work.

There are also many types of specialized institutes, evening schools, and national schools, which cater primarily to adults. The evening schools and national schools are designed primarily to provide secondary education. They emphasize reading, writing, arithmetic, and some science so that these adults can continue their education in a specialized institute and prepare themselves for advancement in their work. The national schools teach the non-Russians to use the Russian language. Separate schools are used for different language groups, but the students are soon prepared to continue their studies with Russian language materials. The specialized institutes accept workers who have completed the equivalent of secondary education and have Russian language proficiency. These workers then are able to improve their abilities as technicians, mechanics, machine operators, or almost any type of industrial or farm work. Later on they can take more courses in advanced institutes to work for academic degrees.

Soviet citizens attend these schools and institutes on released time from their places of employment and continue to work part time. They are paid for their work, and they do not have to lose any wages or pay any fees for attending school part time.

HIGHER EDUCATION

The most common types of higher education in the Soviet Union are the polytechnical, pedagogical, agricultural, medical, and engineering institutes. They resemble community colleges and are located in most large cities. However, they are much more specialized than American colleges. They have set curricula for the students and are designed to prepare students for their vocations. In this sense they do not resemble liberal arts colleges.

Most of the students in these institutes come directly from secondary schools. They apply and take entrance examinations in the summer, but only about 20% to 50% of those tested are actually admitted. However, these entrance examinations can be taken again in subsequent years. Those who are admitted are organized into collectives, and each member in a collective has the identical class schedule. But before classes start in September, these students go with the collective to a work project, usually a farm to help harvest tomatoes or some other crop.

Many of these institutes operate on a shift basis. Students may start at 8:30 a.m. and have classes until 1:30 p.m. or start at 2:30 p.m. and have classes until 7:30 p.m. During this time they have three double periods. One class, in the afternoon shift for example, starts at 2:30, has a five minute break at 3:15, and lasts until 4:00. The next class goes from 4:15 until 6:00, and the last class from 6:10 until 7:30. The student is in class all the time, except for breaks. With him are the same students in every class. This group of students is his collective with whom he studies, works, and has recreational activities.

These classes for the most part are held six days a week without the student having any free time during his shift. There are some exceptions to this, particularly for the upper classmen, who may have two or three free periods off during the week or may have Saturday off. But they also have other activities, such as meetings of the Komsomol, DOSAAF, nurses, or some other organization. (Some of the organizations are discussed in the following section.) Often these extra activities are in the evening, and students do not get home before 9:00 or 10:00 p.m. Their study time is in the morning or afternoon, depending on the shift they are in. They study in the institute library or at home. Those students at a dormitory are provided a study hall, which they may use until midnight.

The program for a regular day-time student lasts for four or five years, depending on his curriculum. A prospective teacher at a pedagogical institute may have a four year program, if she is preparing to teach one subject, or a five year program, if she is preparing to teach two subjects. Upon completion of the program the student receives a certificate rather than a bachelor's degree. The only degrees are the candidate's degree, which is roughly equivalent to a master's degree in the United States, and a doctor's degree, which is considered to be a higher degree than the American doctorate. Post-doctoral research work could lead to yet a higher degree or research rank, that of an academician, but this title is given only to outstanding research scientists. But not all institutes are certified to give these higher degrees. Some of the advanced study may be done by correspondence, but the student also has to attend a university or degree-granting institute in Moscow or other large educational center.

There are 40 universities in the Soviet Union. They have both undergraduate and graduate programs, and their main emphasis is on science and engineering. But the Soviet Union considers most scholarly work to be science, and university students may study economics, literature, history, law, or foreign language rather than physical sciences, natural sciences, or engineering. As in the various institutes the curriculum for each student is set. He can not design his own program or take elective courses. However, since many university students are seeking graduate degrees, they are not all organized into collectives in the same way as in secondary schools and institutes.

Higher education in the Soviet Union is also free of tuitions and fees. Students usually receive stipends based on their achievements. The scale of the stipend increases as the student progresses, and this is an incentive for the student to get good marks and to continue his education.

Class work in both the institutes and in universities is primarily done by the lecture method. The teacher may ask questions and require some written work, but this course work does not constitute an important part of the grade. The students work together, and one student may answer the question for another. They sit two at a desk and look at each other's work. There is a definite lack of individual accountability during the course. The grade, however, is determined by the final examinations, at which time the student is usually tested orally. He goes by himself into a room with three teachers, and these teachers ask him questions, which he must answer to their satisfaction. This program causes some students

The Pedagogical Institute (teachers college) in Volgograd.

to be slack during the term and to cram for the final examination. Make-up course work is usually done during the week preceding the final, and in this way the students review and prepare for the final.

University students generally live in dormitories at the campus, but otherwise a university campus in the Soviet Union does not resemble an American campus. There are no fraternities or sororities. Competitive sports are not a part of the university life. Sports more closely resemble professional sports in the United States, and students do not have the time to participate. The students do belong to the Komsomol and academic groups usually, but these support rather than detract from his studies. Of course, there is social life, but that is within the activities of the Komsomol or on a personal basis.

There are also many other institutions of higher learning in the Soviet Union. The broad system of these institutes covers most types of higher education in the United States from the state colleges to professional colleges. They include both the applied courses and the art courses, but each institute is specialized for the particular purpose. Adults take courses at these institutes to improve their proficiencies at the job. Sometimes they must take these courses to be qualified for promotion or for a transfer to another position. Young adults also enroll in these institutions rather than pursuing the more academic courses in the other programs. But these institutes are definitely colleges, and they do grant undergraduate certificates rather than degrees.

In addition to the university system there are several academies, which are both educational and research institutions. The most important one is the Academy of Sciences, but there are also an Academy of Medical Science, an Academy of Agricultural Sciences, a Military Academy, an Academy of Architecture, an Academy of Arts, an Academy of Pedogogical Sciences, and others. These academies grant doctor degrees and also the rank of academician, which is yet a higher research achievement.

YOUTH ORGANIZATIONS

The role of the youth organizations is much broader than that of similar organizations in other countries. They include both boys and girls, and their activities are much more diversified. Actually the youth organizations supplement the school system, because they provide most of the recreation and extracurricular activities.

The Pioneers is an organization of young people between the ages of 9 or 10 and 14 or 16. Most students belong to the Pioneers. The standards are high enough to provide incentives for behavior and performance but also low enough to include most young people. The Pioneer has the privilege of wearing the uniform and neckerchief. They wear the red neckerchief even when they don't wear the rest of the uniform. The uniform consists of a cap, a white shirt or blouse, and dark (usually green or brown) trousers or skirts. A Pioneer also wears a pin, which bears the words "Always Prepared."

The red neckerchief and sometimes the uniform are worn in school. Both are worn for most of the activities. Pioneers are seen going on excursions, working at projects, and participating in sports. They have special tasks similar to that of merit badges for American Boy Scouts. They make handicraft items and learn many different skills. They also work together picking berries and fruit and helping with other agricultural or industrial tasks.

Pioneers also have group singing and dancing. They put on skits, plays and other programs for the public. Usually they have a Pioneer Palace or Clubhouse, where they conduct their various activities and put on variety shows. The Pioneer Organization is the center of life for the Soviet Young People. They work hard, but they also have a lot of fun.

The Pioneers are supervised by older youth, who are members of the Komsomol (Young Communist League). But the Pioneers also have leadership positions and learn responsibility.

Upon finishing the 7th grade or reaching the age of 14, the Pioneer can qualify to become a member of the Komsomol. It is a preparatory organization for potential members of the Communist Party. A student can be a Komsomol member from the age of 14 to his early 20's. At the age of 28 a person loses his membership, unless he or she has become an active leader of the Komsomol. These adult leaders are usually members of the Communist Party or persons who would qualify for membership.

Adults can look back and say that their time in the Komsomol was the best time of their lives. Komsomol members work hard on all sorts of projects, but they also go on hunting trips, fishing trips, excursions to the beach or mountain resorts, holiday demonstrations, and sport competitions. They help build bridges, hydroelectric power dams, new cities, and new factories. They also plant trees and harvest crops. Komsomols work with the Pioneers providing recreational facilities and equipment and guiding their activities at school and at camp.

The Komsomol organization is set up like the Communist Party organization. There are committees and sectors: the sports sector, the education sector, the cultural-public sector, the political sector, the organization sector, and the general sector. Each sector has the responsibility of providing leadership and directing activities.

A special assignment of Komsomol members is to work in shock brigades among adult workers. They are to set examples for increasing production. The vigor and vitality of the young people are used to inspire adults to be more adaptable and more creative.

Another project of the Komsomols is to construct and maintain Youth Cafes. These cafes are used for the entertainment of Soviet youth and for foreign guests. Like all other activity of the Komsomol organization, the Youth Cafes have a political responsibility to promote peace, friendship, and enthusiasm for Communist ideals. There is a mixture of hard work, good times, and politics. The main purpose of the Komsomol is an auxiliary service for the Communist Party. It is the Komsomol that provides the candidates for Communist Party membership.

There are also other organizations for the youth. Many of them also include adults. There are hunting and fishing societies, mountain-climbing groups, and groups for many different hobbies. However, these other organizations are subordinate to or supervised by the Komsomol or the Communit Party. In fact, all organizations in the Soviet Union are responsible to the Communist Party.

DOSAAF (The Voluntary Organization for Assistance to the Army, Aviation, and the Navy) is another important organization at institutions of higher learning in the Soviet Union. Meetings are held in the evenings at the institutes, and both male and female students participate. A large number and possibly the majority of the students belong. The actual activities are directed mostly to civil defense and to military preparedness. DOSAAF reflects a greater military orientation in the Soviet Union than is present in the United States. The Soviet students learn to accept the inevitability of military conflict and their duty in defending their country. DOSAAF in this way complements the Soviet education.

All organizations, including the Communist Party, are also educational institutions. The members have council meetings and discussion groups. They read books and journals in order to discuss and learn from each other. Their joint experiences also supply materials for discussion on methods for improving themselves and their work. Their education is devoted to the whole man. They emphasize the physical, mental, social, and moral perfection of man. They are helping to create the New Soviet Man.

EDUCATION ADMINISTRATION

Educational institutions on all levels have a similar pattern of administrative organization. At the top of all institutions is a director or a rector, who supervises the administrative and executive authority. He has assistants in charge of the different aspects of work: one for educational work, another for administrative-business office work, and in institutions of higher learning an assistant for scientific-research work.

Under the assistant rector for education are the various facul'tety (colleges or schools). Under the facul'tety are the otdeleniya (departments), and under the otdeleniya are the kafedry (chairs over sections). An example of this organization is the Volgograd Pedagogical Institute, which has the following organizaion for preparing teachers. There are five facul'tety: mathematics, physics, foreign languages, history and philology, and natural sciences and geography. The facul'tet of foreign languages has three otdeleniya: English, German, and French. The otdeleniye of the English language has several kafedry: grammar, pronounciation and intonation, lexicology and phonetics, literature, etc. The facul'tet is supervised by a dekan (dean), and the otdeleniya are supervised by senior teachers. A kafedra is a specialist who may be the only one of that type in the institute or who may have a few junior teachers working (teaching and doing research) with him.

The main legislative or policy-making authority lies in an Educational Council, which is made up of the director and his assistants, the department chairmen or all faculty members in smaller schools, and representatives from various youth and social organizations, including members of the Communist Party. This council meets about twice a month to discuss problems related to education, to schedules or the calendar of events, and to faculty research or work projects. This education council also supervises research at institutes of higher learning and hears candidates for degrees defend their dissertations. It also oversees the teaching and research responsibilities of all faculty members.

316

Once a year there is conducted a conference for all the faculty and teaching assistants, each of whom has the opportunity to present a report on his scholarly work. This conference is conducted to promote research and to contribute knowledge from the work to other faculty members.

There are also several committees and other organizations. At each school there is a student organization, either a Pioneer Organization or a Komsomol Organization, depending on the age of the students. This organization provides the extra-curricular activities and the necessary equipment and materials.

At larger institutions, particularly higher education, there is also a student-professional union, made up of a dozen or more students and faculty members. This union, where it exists, assumes the responsibility of supervising evening events, obtaining sport uniforms or show costumes, and providing musical instruments or other equipment. It also oversees student problems, e.g. health, accident, etc., and makes arrangements for group or individual therapy or recreation. The union is really a student club, which sets up choral groups, dance groups, sport competitions, and excursions to camps. The students participate in these activities free of charge or for a small cost for major undertakings.

The expanded responsibilities for students and for faculty regarding research are at institutions of higher learning. The elementary and secondary schools do have some of these responsibilities in coordinating with the Pioneers and with teacher improvement, but their work is mostly done by the school director and a faculty council, which meets twice a month or when necessary.

PROGRESS IN EDUCATION

One of the best ways to measure progress in education is by counting the number of students at each level for different years. The increase in enrollment is a good index to the society's effort toward education.

In the school year 1914-15 there were only 9,656,000 students enrolled in school, and 9,031,000 of these students were in the first four grades. At that time there were only 625,000 students in the upper grades. By 1940-41 the total figures had increased to 35,552,000 enrolled; 21,731,000 in the first four grades, and 13,821,000 in the upper grades. In 1950-51 the total figure was 34,752,000 enrolled; 20,120,000 in the first four grades, and 14,632,000 in the upper grades. By 1960-61 these figures had increased to 36,187,000 total, 18,747,000 in the lower grades, and

17,440,000 in the upper grades. The most recent figures available, those for 1971-72, were 49,220,000 total, 19,770,000 in the lower grades, and 29,450,000 in the upper grades. These figures not only reflect a substantial increase in the total number of students, but they also show a much larger percentage of them who continue their education. The total figures for 1971-72 represented about 20% of the total population enrolled in school and about 59% of those enrolled were on the secondary level. Comparing percentages with 1914-15 one sees that only about 6% of the total population was enrolled in school and about 6 1/2% of those enrolled were in secondary education. By 1940-41 these percentages had increased to about 18% of the total population enrolled and about 31% of those enrolled were on the secondary level. These figures show the priority given to compulsory elementary education before the Second World War and the stress given to secondary education since then.

The increase in the number of those who graduate from institutions of higher learning also shows substantial progress. In 1914 there were only 12,100 students who graduated that year. In 1940 that number was 126,100, in 1960 it was 343,300, in 1967 it was 479,400, and in 1971 it was 672,800. These figures multiplied about ten times between 1914 and 1940 and another five times between 1940 and 1971.

The quality of education is more difficult to measure. The achievements in science, engineering, social science, and art reflect on the quality of education, but these achievements can not be accurate measures. However, the great accomplishments of the Soviet Union in industry and in space exploration indicate that education is preparing the Soviet citizens well to carry out the programs of the country.

Another index to the quality of education is the dedication of Soviet citizens to learn. The moulding of attitudes and motivating students to want to learn are major educational accomplishments. The Soviet education system apparently has been successful in doing these tasks. The reading habits of Soviet citizens give a good indication of success in that area. The techniques used in Soviet education to motivate students also can be studied and found reliable. One of these techniques is the ceremonies for students on their first days and for graduating students. At these times the student is dressed in his finest clothes, given praise from school officials and community leaders, and presented with a holiday atmosphere. Graduating secondary students are also taken in a

group to Moscow or another large city to spend a few days to celebrate their graduation. These students are permitted to stay up
all night for the first time. It is a recognition that they have now
grown up, and shortly, at their 18th birthday, they gain the full
rights of citizenship--the right to vote and to be elected to local
offices, the right to marry, and the right to work.

School children also receive a daily motivation not only
through their collective activities but also by their individual school
diaries. Assignments are listed daily in these diaries, and parents
must initial the entries to show that the student has completed his
assignment. This procedure supplements the quarterly report
card, which also motivates the students to achieve. The grades
run from numbers 1 through 5 with 5 being excellent. When a
student receives a 5 or when he receives all 5's, he is praised highly
by teachers, parents, and other students. The Pioneers and
Komsomols are also very interested in the student's diary and his
report card. Poor school performance can restrict or even sus-
pend his sport and social activities.

Accusations of indoctrination are often directed toward educational processes. The fact that Soviet education relies highly on
the lecture and demonstration methods causes some people to
direct this criticism against the quality of Soviet education. But
lectures and demonstrations are only a part of the process. The
emphasis not only on Soviet education but also on all learning
experiences and research activities in the Soviet Union is practice.
The theory must be tested by the learner. Much of this practice is
obtained in group activities, but each student must be a participant.
The excursions and field trips provide one such method. Discussions
and debates help to provide another test. These activities are done
in the school and coordinated with related activities in the youth
organizations. Learning facts is one step, but the organizing of
those facts into a practical experience reinforces that step. The
Soviet student learns to receive and to perform, which are objectives of quality education.

Another accusation has been directed toward the emphasis on
science and engineering and toward the lack of emphasis on social
sciences and humanities. This accusation has been true to a certain
degree. The building of communism has as its first step the industrialization of the country, and Soviet education has been preparing
the youth to fulfill these roles in science and industry. But every
student must also learn geography, history, foreign language, art,
music, and political theory. The viewpoint on the presentation of

these subjects is heavily influenced by the communist philosophy and Soviet patriotism, but other countries also teach their own cultures through the presentation of these subjects.

The lack of an emphasis on social sciences was corrected after the announcement of the second step of building communism, that of establishing new social relationships. Starting with 1963 students graduated from secondary schools have been required to complete the study of a new course entitled social science. This course outlines the whole program for building communism and for creating the New Soviet Man.

In 1968-69 there was initiated another campaign to improve the teaching of history in Soviet schools. More use was to be made of new research in history and archeology. There has been recognized a need for continual improvement of education in social sciences and humanities as well as in science and engineering.

The diversity and comprehensiveness of Soviet education can be better understood by looking at a breakdown in the number of students who graduate in different specialities in higher education. The following chart provides that breakdown.

Graduates from Institutions of High Learning (in thousands)

Speciality	1940	1950	1960	1965	1970	1971
All specialities	126	177	343	404	631	673
Industry and Construction	24	30	95	140	214	244
Transporation and Communications	6	6	16	19	28	30
Agriculture	10	13	35	36	69	63
Economics and Law	6	11	25	32	51	52
Health, Physical Culture, and Sports	17	20	31	31	43	47
Education	62	94	139	142	219	230
Art and Cinematography	1	3	2	4	7	7

As has been previously stated, the students in higher education in the Soviet Union specialize to a much greater extent than do American students. The graduates from these institutions do know their specialty very well, but they must rely on their secondary education for their knowledge of other disciplines. In this sense they do lack the broad education that American students gain in a liberal arts college.

But the quality of their education is also reflected in the scholarly research that is done in the Soviet Union. The amount and kinds of research contribute to the educational level of the society both in schools and in occupational life. The most noteworthy research organization in the Soviet Union is the Academy of Scienes, which publishes several hundred thousand books, journals, and reports each year.

THE SOVIET ACADEMY OF SCIENCES

The organization and activities of the Soviet Academy of Sciences are so complex that a detailed discussion is impossible here. The importance of the Academy of Sciences to education is the scope of the organization and activities, which can best be presented in outline form. The Soviet Academy of Sciences is the world's largest scientific research organization and publishes works on all kinds of scientific and scholarly subjects. On January 1, 1972 there were 240 academicians and 435 corresponding members of the USSR Academy of Sciences and more than one million research scientists who worked with them in 2648 scientific research institutues, branches and departments. These numbers do not include the 506 academicians, 592 corresponding members, and 62 acting members of the academies of sciences of the Union Republics.

The USSR Academy of Sciences is an All-Union organization, a Russian Union Republic Organization, and a coordinator of the other 14 Union Republic academies of sciences. Its main center is in Moscow, but near Novosibirsk is Academy City, which is a second center and acts as a depository of duplicate records and reports and as a separate major scientific research institution. There are also branches of the USSR Academy of Sciences in the Urals, in the Soviet Far East, at Yakutsk, on the Kola Peninsula, in Dagestan (in the North Caucasus Region), at Komi, and at other locations.

The central organization of the Soviet Academy of Sciences

is divided into four sections: The Section of Physical-Technical and Mathematical Sciences, the Section of Chemical-Technological and Biological Sciences, the Section of Social Sciences, and the Section of Earth Sciences. Each section is further broken down into departments, departments are divided into institutes, and institutes are subdivided into divisions. Each phase of scientific and scholarly research has groups of scientists at several locations. These scientists meet in conferences and publish articles in journals to coordinate their work and advance knowledge in their special areas. The structure of this massive organization in 1970 was as follows:

I Section of Physical-Technical and Mathematical Sciences
   Department of Mathematics

   a) The Institute of Mathematics
   b) The Institute of Applied Mathematics
   c) The Computer Center

Department of General Physics and Astronomy

   a) The Institute of Earth Magnetism, Ionosphere, and
       Dispersion of Radio Waves
   b) The Institute of Kinetics and Combustion
   c) The Institute of Cosmo-Physical Research and Aeronautics
   d) The Institute of Crystallography
   e) The Institute of Semi-Conductors
   f) The Institute of Radio Technology and Electronics
   g) The Institute of Theoretical Astronomy
   h) The Institute of Theoretical and Experimental Physics
   i) The Institute of Thermo-Physics
   j) The Institute of Precise Mechanics and Computer Techno-
       logy
   k) The Institute of Physics
   l) The Institute of the Physics of High Pressures
   m) The Institute of the Physics of Metals
   n) The Institute of the Physics of Solid Bodies
   o) The Institute of Physical Problems
   p) The Institute of Civil Engineering
   q) The Main Astronomical Observatory
   r) The Crimean Astronomical Observatory
   s) The Scientific Council on Radio-Physics and Radio Tech-
       nology

t) The Scientific Council on the Physics of Solid Bodies
u) The Scientific Council on the Physics of Low Temperatures

Department of Nuclear Physics

a) The Institute of Nuclear Physics
b) The Moscow Energetics Institute
c) The Siberian Energetics Institute
d) The Scientific Council on the Complex Problem of "Cosmic Rays"

Department of Physical-Technical Problems of Energetics

a) The Institute of Electro-Mechanics
b) The Kazan Physical-Technical Institute

Department of Mechanics and Control Processes

a) The Institute of Automation and Telemechanics
b) The Institute of Automation and Electronomy
c) The Institute of Hydrodynamics
d) The Institute of Material Studies
e) The Institute of Machine Studies
f) The Institute of Mechanical Cybernetics
g) The Institute of the Problems of Mechanics
h) The Institute of the Problems of Information Transmission
i) The Institute of Theoretical and Applied Mechanics
j) The Institute of Theoretical Problems of Chemical Technology
k) The Institute of Electrodynamics
l) The Scientific Council "Scientific Bases of Durability and Plasticity"
m) The Scientific Council on the Theory of Machines and Work Processes
n) The Scientific Council on Friction and Lubricants
o) The National Committee of the USSR on Remote Control
p) The National Committee of the USSR on Theoretical and Applied Mechanics

II The Section on Chemical-Technological and Biological Sciences

Department of General and Technical Chemistry

a) The Institute of High Molecular Compounds
b) The Institute of Catalysis
c) The Institute of Oil-Chemical Synthesis
d) The Institute of New Chemical Problems
e) The Institute of Organic Chemistry
f) The Institute of Physical Chemistry
g) The Institute of Chemistry and the Technology of Rare
    Elements and Mineral Resources
h) The Institute of the Chemistry of Plants
i) The Institute of Chemical Kinetics and Combustion
j) The Institute of Chemical Physics
k) The Institute of Electro-Chemistry
l) The Institute of Element Organic Compounds
m) The Scientific Council on Synthesis, the Study, and
    the Application of Absorbents
n) The Scientific Council on the Theory of Chemical
    Structure, Kinetics, Reactive Properties, and Cata-
    lysis
o) The Scientific Council on Chromatography

Department of Physical Chemistry and the Technology of Inorganic
Materials

a) The Institute of Inorganic Kinetics and Combustion
b) The Institute of Inorganic Chemistry
c) The Institute of Metallurgy
d) The Institute of Organic and Physical Chemistry
e) The Institute of General and Inorganic Chemistry
f) The Institute of the Chemistry of Silicates
g) The Scientific Council on the Problems of "Physics and
    Chemistry of Semi-Conductors"
h) The Scientific Council on Physical Chemical Mechanics,
    Surface-Active Substances and Surface Phenomena
i) The Scientific Council on Pure Substances and Physical-
    Chemical Methods of Analysis

Department of Biochemistry, Biophysics, and Chemistry of Physio-
logically Active Compounds

a) The Institute of Biologically Active Substances
b) The Institute of Biological Physics
c) The Institute of Biochemistry

324

d) The Institute of Biochemistry and the Physiology of Micro-Organisms
e) The Institute of Biophysics
f) The Institute of Microbiology
g) The Institute of Molecular Biology
h) The Institute of Radioactive and Physical-Chemical Biology
i) The Institute of the Physiology of Plants
j) The Institute of the Chemistry of Natural Compounds
k) The Institute of Cytology
l) The All-Union Biochemical Society
m) The All-Union Microbiological Society
n) The Scientific Council on Biological Physics
o) The Scientifc Council on Radio Biology
p) The Scientific Council on Cytology
q) The United Scientific Council on "The Chemistry and Biochemistry of the Exchange of Properties and Control by the Exchange of Properties"
r) The Scientific Council on the Biochemistry of Animals and Man
s) The Scientific Council on Molecular Biology
t) The Scientific Council on the Physiology and Biochemistry of Plants
u) The Scientific Council on Photosynthesis

Department of Physiology

a) The Institute of Higher Nervous Activity and Neuro-Physiology
b) The Institute of Physiology
c) The Institute of Evolutionary Physiology and Biochemistry
d) The All-Union Physiological Society
e) The Laboratory for the Study of Nerve and Humoral Regulation
f) The United Scientific Council on "Physiology of Man and Animals"
g) The Scientific Council on the Problem of "Physiological, Biochemical and Structural Bases of Evolution of Animals and Man
h) The Scientific Council on the Problem of "Ecological Physiology"

Department of General Biology

a)   Biology-Soil Institute
b)   The Biological Institute
c)   The Botanical Institute
d)   The Institute of the Biology of Internal Waters
e)   The Institute of the Biology of Development
f)   The Institute of Botany
g)   The Institute of Microbiology and Virusology
h)   The Institute of the Morphology of Animals
i)   The Institute of General Genetics
j)   The Institute of Photosynthesis
k)   The Institute of Cytology and Genetics
l)   The Institute of Evolutionary Morphology and the Ecology
      of Animals
m)   The Institute of the Ecology of Plants and Animals
n)   The Zoological Institute
o)   The Limnological Institute
p)   The Murmansk Maritime Biological Institute
q)   The Paleontological Institute
r)   The All-Union Botanical Society
s)   The All-Union Hydro-Biological Society
t)   The All-Union Society of Helminthologists
u)   The All-Union Society of Soil Scientists
v)   The All-Union Entomological Society
w)   The Helminthology Laboratory
x)   The Forest Studies Laboratory
y)   The Scientific Council on "Biological Bases of the
      Rational Use, Reformation, and Preservation of the
      Plants of the World"
z)   The Scientific Council on the Problem of "Biological
      Bases of Mastering, Reconstructing and Preserving
      the Animals of the World"
aa) The Scientific Council on the Problem of "Hydro-Biology,
      Ichthyology, And the Use of the Biological Resources
      of Reservoirs"

III The Section of Social Sciences

Department of History

a)   The Institute of Archeology

b) The Institute of Oriental Studies
c) The Institute of History
d) The Institute of History, Philology and Philosophy
e) The Institute of History, Language, and Literature
f) The Institute of the Peoples of Asia
g) The Institute of Slavic Studies
h) The Institute of Ethnography
i) The Archeological Commission
j) The Archives of the Academy of Sciences of the USSR
k) The Laboratory for the Conservation and Restoration of Documents
l) The Scientific Council on the Complex Problem of "The History of the Great October Socialist Revolution"
m) The Scientific Council on the "History of Historical Sciences"

Department of Economics

a) The Institute of Africa
b) The Institute of Latin America
c) The Institute of World Economics and International Relations
d) The Institute of Economics
e) The Institute of Economics and the Organization of Industrial Production
f) The Institute of Economics of the World Socialist System
g) The Central Economics-Mathematics Institute
h) The Scientific Council on the Complex Problem of "The Scientific Bases of Planning and Organizing Social Production"
i) The Scientific Council on the Complex Problem of "Economics, Planning, and Organizing Industrial Enterprises"
j) The Scientific Council on the Complex Problem of "Economic Competition of the Two Systems and Under-Developed Nations"
k) The Scientific Council on the Problem of "Scientific Bases for Setting Prices"
l) The Scientific Council on the Problem of "The Application of Mathematics and Computer Techniques in Economic Research and Planning"
m) The Scientific Council on the Problem of "Business Accounting and the Material Stimulation of Production"

327

n)   The Scientific Council on the Problem of "Economic Effectiveness of the Basic Funds, the Capital Inlay, and New Techniques"

Department of Philosophy and Law

    a)   The Institute of Government and Law
    b)   The Institute of the History of Natural Sciences and Engineering
    c)   The Institute of Philosophy
    d)   The Soviet Association of International Law

Department of Literature and Language

    a)   The Institute of World Literature
    b)   The Institute of Russian Literature (Pushkin's House)
    c)   The Institute of the Russian Language
    d)   The Institute of Linguistics
    e)   The Scientific Council on the Complex Problem of "The Uniformity of the Development of National Languages in Relation with the Development of Socialist Nations"
    f)   The Scientific Council on "The Theory of Soviet Linguistics"

IV The Section of Earth Sciences

Department of Geology, Geophysics, and Geochemistry

    a)   The All-Union Mineralogical Society
    b)   The Geological Institute
    c)   The Geo-Morphilogical Commission
    d)   The Institute of Geology and Geo-Chronology of the Pre-Cambrian Age
    e)   The Institute of Geology and Geophysics
    f)   The Institute of Geology and the Development of Combustible Fuelds
    g)   The Institute of Geology of Ore Deposits, Petrography, Mineralogy, Geochemistry
    h)   The Institute of Geophysics
    i)   The Institute of Geochemistry and Analytical Chemistry
    j)   The Institute of Mining
    k)   The Institute of Natural Sciences
    l)   The Institute of the Earth's Core

m) The Institute of Perma-Frost Studies
n) The Institute of Mineralogy, Geochemistry, and Crystal-Chemistry of Rare Elements
o) The Institute of Earth Physics
p) The Commission of Determining the Absolute Age of Geological Formations
q) The Commission of the Study of the Fourth Period
r) The Commission on International Tectonic Maps
s) The Mineralogical Museum
t) The Scientific Council on Geothermal Research
u) The Scientific Council on the Physical-Technical Problems of Developing Useful Minerals
v) The Scientific Council on the Physical-Technical Problems of Concentration of Useful Minerals
w) The National Committee of Geologists of the Soviet Union
x) The Polar Geophysical Institute
y) The Council on Seismology

Department of Oceanology, Geography, and Physics of the Atmosphere

a) The Geographical Society of the USSR
b) The Institute on Volcanology
c) The Institute of Geography
d) The Institute of Geography of Siberia and the Far East
e) The Institute of Oceanology
f) The Institute of Physics of the Atmosphere
g) The Committee on Meteorites
h) The Oceanographic Commission
i) The Council on the Problems of Water Resources

The fore-going list of scientific institutions in the Soviet Academy of Sciences is fairly complete as far down as the institute level. But there are sub-divisions of practically all of these institutions. The Academy is a living and changing organization, and the structure of institutes and scientific councils differ somewhat from year to year. Yet the major sections and departments have maintained the same for several years, except for the recent reorganization of the Department of Earth Sciences into a Section of Earth Sciences. This statement is also true for most of the institutes.

The main point of the presentation of this list of scientific institutions is to relate the scope of research to education. The benefits of discovery of scientific truths are transmitted through journals, reference books, textbooks, and lectures to students both in the Academy of Sciences and in other institutions of higher learning. The Academy of Sciences grants advanced degrees to students and research workers, and many of the scientists at the Academy teach both there and at other educational institutions and universities. There is very close cooperation between science and education in the Soviet Union.

OTHER ACADEMIES

The Academy of Pedagogical Sciences, although not nearly as large as the Academy of Sciences, is directly concerned with improving education in the Soviet Union. It had 52 active members and 77 corresponding members in 12 scientific research institutes, 15 experimental schools, 285 support schools, the State Scientific Library on Public Education, and the Scientific Research Pedagogical Archives. It serves as the national organization for school teachers and also works very closely with the Ministries of education.

On the All-Union level there are also the Academy of Medical Sciences, the All-Union Academy of Agricultural Sciences, and the Academy of Arts. They too conduct scholarly research work and disseminate the results through conferences and journals. Practically every phase of knowledge is pursued in some academy or research institution in the Soviet Union. It all adds up to what the Soviet citizens call a cultural revolution in their society.

Alekseyev, S. P. & Kartsov, V. G., Istoriya SSSR, Moscow: Gosudarstvennoye Uchebnoye Pedigogicheskoye Izdatel'stvo, 1960, 159 pp.

Belyavskaya, O. P. et als., Bibliografiya Izdanii Akademii Nauk SSSR - Ezhegodnik 1964, Moscow: Izdatel'stvo "Nauka", 1966, 1005 pp.

Bereday, George Z. F. et als., The Changing Soviet School, Boston: Houghton Miflin Co., 1960, 154 pp.

Bol'shaya Sovetskaya Entsiklopediya (3rd ed.), Vol. 1, Moscow: 1970.

Counts, George S., The Challenge of Soviet Education, New York: McGraw-Hill, 1957, 330 pp.

Education in the U.S.S.R., Bulletin #14, Washington, D. C.: Office of Education, Dept. of H. E. W., U. S. Gov' t Printing Office, 1957, 226.

Kashin, M., "The School and the Young Pioneer Organization", Soviet Education, Vol. 6, No. 4, pp. 35-46, February, 1964.

Kovalev, S. M. et als., Ezhegodnik Bol'shoi Sovetskoi Entsiklopedii 1972, Moscow: Izdatel'stvo "Sovetskaya Entsiklopediya", 1972, 624 pp.

Levin, Deana, Soviet Education Today, New York: Monthly Review Press, 1963, 179 pp.

Narodnoye Khozyaystvo SSSR v 1965 g. - Statisticheskii Ezhegodnik, Moscow: Tsentral'noye Statisticheskoye Upravleniye pri Sovete Ministrov SSSR, 1966, 910 pp.

Narodnoye Khozyaystvo SSSR v 1967 g. - Statisticheskii Ezhigodnik, Moscow: Statistika, 1968, 1008 pp.

Pares, Bernard, A History of Russia, New York: Alfred A. Knopf, 1966, 611 pp.

Razgildeyev, Gennady (Soviet Exchange Scholar), lecture at the University of Missouri-Rolla, Rolla, Missouri: September 12, 1968.

Soviet Commitment to Education, Bulletin #16, Washington, D.C.: Office of Education, Dept. of H. E. W., U.S. Gov't. Printing Office, 1959, 135 pp.

SSSR v Tsifrakh v 1971 godu - kratkii statisticheskii sbornik, Moscow: Izdatel'stvo "Statistika", 1972, 240 pp.

SSSR v Tsifrakh v 1967 godu - kratkii statisticheskii sbornik, Moscow: Izdatel'stvo "Statistika", 1968, 159 pp.

Utah Educational Review, Vol. 53, No. 3, January, 1960.

Whiting, Kenneth, The Soviet Union Today, New York:
    Frederick A. Praeger, Publishers, 1966, 423 pp.

CHAPTER XII

SOVIET LITERATURE

The Golden Age of Russian Literature had ended with Tolstoy and Chekhov. The whole society experienced a profound transformation. Serfdom had been abolished in 1861, and the position of the nobility in Russia changed rapidly. Industry attracted workers from every level of society, and the leisure class fused into the rest of the society. The thinkers and writers became involved in social and political movements. No longer could a person stand aside and depict society only in literature and art. The times called for active participation.

The reign of Nicholas II was marked with social, political, and military upheaval. The Russo-Japanese War ended in defeat in 1904-05. Bloody Sunday in 1905 was the beginning of the end of tsarist autocracy. The new Duma was seeking a stronger political voice. Illegal labor unions grew stronger and caused strikes in industry. Political parties became organized on an effective basis, and not all political leaders were exiled. Even though opposition voices were not welcomed, they were expressed openly without immediate reprisals. Those persons who were arrested, sentenced to prison, or exiled wrote political essays, social treatises, and slogans.

The First World War proceeded drastically for the Russians. Military defeats weakened further the desire of the people to support the old society or to rebuild it. Revolution was the mood of the people. Great changes were immanent. The time was not to reflect but to act.

When the 1917 Revolution took place the people had lost the political and religious leadership of an endowed Tsar. The new leaders inspired many, but others could not immediately identify with them. Internal conflicts in the minds of men and civil war throughout the country drove people to think either about self-preservation or about self-aggrandizement, both of which required active participation in the daily events.

Those who adhered to the Soviet leadership worked hard to establish the new order. They demanded that society discard the old and accept the new. All work was to have a direct meaning to the new life in the country. All writings were to be practical and instructive. They were also to be progressive, i.e. to support the new communist society.

Many members of the former upper classes, including authors, resisted the social and political changes. Some of them fled abroad, and others were killed during the Civil War. What was left of the old literary tradition disappeared. Even the refugees were not able to recapture it.

GORKY

The only well-known, pre-revolutionary Russian author to accept Communism was Maxim Gorky. But he too lived for several years in Western Europe after the 1917 Revolution. His writings were primarily reflections of his early life and the conditions of that time, but he did write about the revolutionary struggle and was recognized by Lenin as the foremost Soviet author.

Alexei Maximovich Peshkov (Gorky) was born in Nizhny Novgogod (now Gorky) in 1868. His childhood was difficult and sad. His father died when Gorky was only four years old. His mother then took him to live with his cruel grandfather. After having only three years of elementary school, Gorky lost his mother and was forced by his grandfather to leave and earn his own keep at the age of ten. For a while he worked in a shoe shop and later as a dish-washer on a Volga River steamboat. As a young man he travelled throughout European Russia and worked in shops, on farms, on steamboats, at markets, and several other places. He was refused admittance to Kazan University, but he advanced his learning by reading books. In the early 1900's he was living in the Caucasus Mountains, where he began to write.

Gorky's first published work was a story, Makar Chudra, which was printed in the Tiflis (Tbilisi) newspaper in 1892. He continued to write stories for newspapers, and in 1895 he wrote The Song About a Falcon, which is praised highly in the Soviet Union today. It is a lyric about a falcon striving for freedom in the tradition of Pushkin's eagle in Uznik (A Prisoner) and Lermontov's Tuchi (Clouds) and Parus (A Sail). But Gorky's falcon is not seeking just his own freedom. It calls others to struggle for a brighter future and for greater achievements. This falcon does not fear death, and it criticizes the snake, as Gorky does cowardly people, for not accepting the challenge.

Six years later the same spirit was presented in another short lyric, Pesnya O Burevestnike (A Song About a Storm Petrel), but this bird forecasts a storm (a revolution) and welcomes it. This lyric is also a call for meeting the challenges of the times.

One of Gorky's better productions, recognized both in the Soviet Union and abroad, is The Lower Depths, which was produced in the Moscow Art Theatre for the first time in 1902. It was declared a success at that time and still plays there and at many theatres throughout the world. This play is a comedy about the very poorest people in the city. They are not only poor economically, but also culturally and socially. But Gorky presented them as having dignity and resourcefulness in spite of their depravity, cruelty, ignorance, and animal instincts. He showed the talent and initiative of these poor individuals to improve their lives. This work is realistic, yet humorous. Its greatness lies in Gorky's profound understanding of people in his ability to enable people to see the faults and weaknesses of themselves and their own acquaintances in the characters of the play.

Probably the most provocative writing of Gorky's was his novel, Mat' (Mother), which he wrote in 1906. It was considered as the first literature in the world that depicted the broad picture of the proletarian revolutionary struggle and the characterizations of the revolutionary workers. The Mother's son, Pavel Vlasov, is a socialist, who calls for the elimination of private property and for granting all the means of production to the working people. Gorky also points out heroic activities of the "collective" of the party organization in its inseverable relationship with the life of the working people. The Mother in the story accepts the concepts of revolution and socialism because of her religious beliefs.

After writing Mother, Gorky lived for several years in Italy, and his novel was not widely accepted in Russia until after 1917. While in Italy, Gorky wrote Tales About Italy in 1912, and in 1913 he started writing a trilogy about his life experiences. This first part, Childhood, was written in 1913-14 while he was still in Italy. The other two parts, To the People and My Universities, were written in 1916 and 1923, respectively, after he returned to his homeland.

In this trilogy Gorky described the suffering of people, their hungry lives, and their poverty, but he also praised the common man by pointing out strength of character, courage, and willingness to work and help others. These stories are realistic expressions of Russian life before the 1917 Revolution. It was from these stories particularly that it was said that Gorky went to the people and then came from the people. Soviet leaders have continued to praise Gorky for being so close to the working people and for identifying with them.

Shortly after Lenin's death in 1924, Gorky wrote his memories of him in an essay, which he entitled V. I. Lenin. He reminisced the events around his contacts with Lenin and praised Lenin as a man and as the leader of the new Soviet State.

In 1925 Gorky wrote another novel, Delo Artamonovykh (The Affairs of the Artamonov Family), which is the story of a Russian family through three generations from 1861 to 1925. This novel reflects the social changes and the path of the family members from serfdom and slavery to that of masters of their fate. Gorky intended this novel to be a history of a great epoch in the lives of ordinary people. It showed how the revolutionary struggle and its victory affected the people of Russia.

From 1925 until his death in 1936 Gorky wrote short plays and magazine articles. His writings became examples or patterns for other Soviet writers, and he was considered the authority on Soviet literature. The names of some of his articles were About Literature (1930), About Socialist Realism (1933), About Plays (1933), About Language (1934), The Report on the First All-Union Conference of Soviet Writers (1934), About Culture (1935), and others. After his death in 1936 he was eulogized and ranked alongside Pushkin and Tolstoy. The place of his birth, Nizhny Novgorod, was renamed Gorky in his honor.

MAYAKOVSKY

Vladimir Mayakovsky set a new pace for literature in Russia. He was dynamic, daring, and provocative. His poetry struck out against the evils of the old society and bolstered support for revolutionaries. At the time of the 1917 Revolution he was still a young man, and his verses captured the enthusiasm of the new era. Mayakovsky was a product of a changing and violent society, and he expressed the verses, slogans, and chants of the agitators. He called out "at the top of his voice" (which became the name of one of his poems). His verses were short with loud bursts followed by quiet pauses and other loud bursts. But Mayakovsky was much more than the ordinary rabble-rouser. His expressions were packed with emotion and vigor. He had rhythm, style, and purpose. He had acquired the realism of the new society. His writings were practical and instructive. They were progressive and challenging.

He not only wrote and recited poetry, but he also prepared placards with provocative drawings and slogans. He participated in the 1917 Revolution and in the Civil War. He contributed his talents to inspire others to action.

Mayakovsky was born in the Caucasus in 1893. He attended school in Kutaisi, and after the death of his father in 1906, he moved with his mother and sisters to Moscow. He continued his education there and participated in political discussion groups. His association with revolutionaries caused him to be arrested and sent to jail, but since there were no serious charges against him he was soon released. But he did have time to read and learn, and later he attended the Moscow Art School, where he learned both art and poetry.

His first writings were published in 1912, and in 1913 he presented on stage in St. Petersburg his poem, Tragedy, which was shocking to the public for his critical remarks toward social relationships, hypocrisy, God, and love. He also portrayed people with physical handicaps and expressed their suffering and pain. Rather than presenting something for amusement, Mayokovsky depicted life as he saw it in the slums and jails of that time.

In 1915 Mayakovsky wrote the poem, A Cloud in Pants, which is an expression of great frustrations. He had at first called the poem "The Thirteenth Apostle," but the censor considered the title blasphemous and the first six pages too revolutionary. It was only after the 1917 Revolution that the poem was printed in full. The message of the poem was denunciations of love, art, society, and religion. Mayakovsky believed that these concepts in his country before the 1917 Revolution were as empty and meaningless as a "cloud in pants." He stressed that they were removed from the people and void of sense or feeling.

A similar theme was presented in 1918 in a short drama entitled Mystery Farce or Mystery Bouffe (Misteriya-buff). It was presented on the first anniversary of the 1917 Revolution and carried the message of wiping the earth off with a flood (a revolution), which destroyed the so-called "clean" people and left only the workers and peasants to create a new world, a communist society, free from persecution and slavery. In this work Mayakovsky throws out the farce of the old society and accepts the new life with genuine values.

Mayakovsky's next poem was 150,000,000 which put the whole citizenry of the Soviet Union in 1920 against the world forces of capitalism. The poem was intended to point to the victory of communism, but it is recognized more for its artistic form than for its content.

But Mayakovsky regained recognition with his poem, Left March, which he also published in 1918. This poem was written like a marching song, which beat to cadence. It was a call to arms, which he delivered to revolutionary sailors during the Civil War. It was a patriotic appeal to struggle against slavery and violence and to work for the future. Mayakovsky used the slogans and calls of the Civil War, thus arousing enthusiasm and vitality into the hearts of those fighting against intervention and imperialism. Each verse of the poem ended with the steady cadence, "left march, left", which inspired movement and pointed toward the proper direction—to the left.

In the fall of 1919 Mayakovsky started to work for the Russian Telegraph and News Agency. During this time he placed placards with drawings and slogans in the windows of the agency, and later he compiled these slogans in a book.

His better poems after that time were Vladimir Il'ich Lenin, which he wrote to eulogize Lenin as the leader of the revolutionary proletariat. This poem was written shortly after Lenin's death and was widely accepted in the Soviet Union. In 1927 Mayakovsky wrote Khorosho (Very Well), which was recognized as an expression of the real course of revolutionary events and of the concrete-historical path of the Soviet people toward socialism. This poem traces three stages of the revolutionary struggle--between March and November, 1917; the years of the Civil War; and the time of socialist construction. As in his other poems, Mayakovsky utters loud bursts of passion followed by silence, but his message is directed more toward the positive aspects of patriotism and the construction of a socialist society. Soviet critics say that these two poems are some of the best expressions of socialist realism, because they reflect the Soviet reality in its movement toward communism.

But Mayakovsky did not continue to express positive views. He was more accustomed to attack evils than to promote the new life. In 1927 and 1928 he wrote Klop (The Bedbug), in which he attacked the remnants of bourgeois attitudes in the minds of the Soviet workers, and Banya (The Bathhouse), in which he attacked Soviet bureaucracy. Two years later Mayakovsky committed suicide, at which time he left a note not blaming anyone and asking others not to blame him or to gossip about him.

Mayakovsky was recognized for his contributions to socialist realism, and his mistakes have been almost forgotten and forgiven.

Today in Moscow at the intersection of Gorky Street and Sadovoye Koltso (Garden Ring) is Mayakovsky Square and an enormous statue dedicated to him. He has been given a prime location in Moscow and a prime place in Soviet literature.

OSTROVSKY

In 1932 a novel by Nikolai Ostrovsky entitled Kak Zakalyalas' Stal' (How Steel was Tempered) appeared in the journal Molodaya Gvardiya (Young Guard) in serial form. In 1934 it was published as a book, and very quickly six million copies were sold. Ostrovsky became famous throughout the Soviet Union.

The man was an unusual person. He had been blind since 1928 due to serious wounds which he had received during the Civil War eight years earlier. Ostrovsky was weak physically after that, and he died in 1936. But he was acclaimed as a literary genius in the Soviet Union. Unfortunately, however, his career was cut short before he could publish his second book.

Nikolai Ostrovsky was born in 1904 in a village in the Western Ukraine. He received only three years of formal schooling, after which he worked in a cafe as an apprentice to a furnace stoker and an electrician. But he read profusely. In 1919 he joined the Komsomol and volunteered to serve in the Red Army. He fought with the First Cavalry Army of Budeonny until he was seriously wounded and discharged in 1920. After the war he became a member of the Communist Party and continued to work as a leader of the youth in the Komsomol. His health became worse as time went on, and he had to rely on others to help him. After the setback he had in 1928 he lost his eyesight and had to remain in bed. But Ostrovksy did not give up. He had people read to him so that he could increase his knowledge, and in 1928 and 1929 he began to compose short stories. But his one outstanding work, How Steel was Tempered, did not appear in print until 1932, just four years before his death.

How Steel was Tempered is considered to be one of the best examples of socialist realism. Ostrovsky depicted living examples of Soviet youth who were building a new socialist society. He stated that the youth had been tempered like steel. Young people had been subjected to the high heat of revolution and war and then to the cold discipline of collective organization, of intelligent awareness, and of purposeful action for building socialism. The basis of the story is the life of a young revolutionary, Pavel

Kochargin, who becomes involved in the conflict between the proletarian youth, the workers, the Red Army soldiers, and communist leaders on one side and the industrialists, the speculators, the White Guards, and the Trotskyites and careerists who had infilitrated into the Communist Party on the other. The Soviet youth grows up in the story as the new masters of society, who have a true socialist approach to labor. These young people are dedicated to the revolutionary deeds of their fathers and to the challenge of building socialism through their own labor. The novel is full of faith in man and his enthusiasm and romantic dedication for building the future. The novel denies the concept of "a generation gap" and shows the ability for the older and younger people working together in the struggle for liberating mankind. It stresses the moral and political unity of all the Soviet people.

Ostrovsky's novel was a new type of literature, which differed dramatically from that of the Golden Age of Russian Literature. It was written for a purpose, and it achieved that purpose. The novel was instructive and progressive. It was a practical means of inspiring the soviet youth to build socialism and to help defend the Soviet Union during the Second World War. This approach and purpose were criticized in non-socialist countries, but the novel was widely accepted in the Soviet Union for following the guidelines of Gorky and Mayakovsky and for setting further guidelines to be followed by Fadeyev and others.

SHOLOKHOV

Mikhail Sholokhov is the greatest author in the Soviet Union today. He started his writings in the 1930's and was still writing in the 1970's. His work is well diversified. It achieves the purposes of socialist realism, and it also achieves the humanism of the great literary productions of previous generations. His works have been read widely within the Soviet Union and around the world.

Sholokhov was born in 1905 on a farm in the valley of the lower Don River. The Don River had influenced his whole life, and it is the major subject of his writings. He still makes his home in Rostov-on-the-Don.

He started school in a church-related elementary school, and after 1918 he continued in a Soviet secondary school. In 1920 he participated in the Civil War in a quartermaster regiment and helped set up a Komsomol cell at one of the stations. After the Civil War he continued to work as a brick layer and as an unskilled laborer. Later he moved to Moscow and worked as a bookkeeper, but he soon returned to the Don River valley.

Sholokhov first published Stories of the Don in 1925. From then through 1940 and later he continued to write about life along the Don River. His great masterpiece was Tikhii Don (The Quiet Don), which he published in four volumes (1928, 1929, 1933, and 1940). For this work he did research in libraries and archives of Moscow and Rostov as well as among the descendants of the Don Cossacks, who still lived along the Don River. The Quiet Don is rich in historical facts and in the popular sayings and songs of the Cossacks. Rather than emphasizing the political aspects of socialist realism, Sholokhov emphasized the human and social aspects. This work is an historical novel, an epic, and a panorama of social and personal events. It covers the period of time from 1912 to 1922 during the most violent years of the formation of the new society, but the length of time is not as important as the depth of perception Sholokhov had in the significance of events and in the emotional conflicts of human beings. Historical events and personal incidents intertwine and affect each other. Human relationships are drawn together and broken asunder by military events and personal tragedies. Full emotions of tender love and of despicable hatred are expressed in unconventional and raw passages. Life events are bared so that the reader feels the full impact of war, tragedies, horrow, rape and murder. Yet the Don River and life flow steadily on and on. But Sholokhov was not content in expressing the evils of life. He also depicted positive heroes, who had the purpose of creating and building a new life, a new society. Like the Don River, which must go on to the sea, human events also must go on to a greater and fuller life. Life too has a purpose beyond the present.

Sholokhov's next major writing was Podnyataya Tselina (Virgin Soil Upturned), which is a continuation of history during the years of collectivization of agriculture. This work was begun before the completion of the third volume of The Quiet Don, and it too lasted several years. The first volume was completed in 1932, but the second volume was not published until 1959.

Virgin Soil Upturned is also a struggle of the people along the Don during great changes in the society. There are those who represent the progressive people and who work for collectivization of agriculture and those who represent the kulaks and landowners and fight against the building of socialism on the farms. The hero, Davydov, is a communist who has a group of loyal supporters, and against him is the "villain," Polotsev, who also has a number of followers. The action of the story is based on the contacts and conflicts between these peoples, and the struggle of these individuals represents the struggle of the whole society at that time. This book is another example of socialist realism tinged with raw humanism.

Sholokhov wrote other works of less significance during the 1940's and early 1950's, but in 1957 he published a short story, Sud'ba Cheloveka (The Fate of Man), in 1959 he finished the second volume of Virgin Soil Upturned, and in 1959 Collected Works.

The Fate of Man is an interesting, heart-warming story about a man and his family during the Second World War. When the war breaks out the man is called to the front and leaves his family at home. Both he and his wife are concerned about his safety, and even though he is wounded and becomes a prisoner of war, he does return home safely. However, the air raids on a nearby factory destroyed his home and killed his wife and children. He suffers the loss of his family and the thoughts of a lonely life. But he finds an orphan boy, who is also lonely and destitute. Both the man and the boy start a new life together as father and son, and a new happiness comes to them. This story is typical of the experiences of many Soviet citizens after the war, and the plot is an instructive message for people to forge ahead in spite of their misfortunes and catastrophies.

In March, 1969, excerpts of Sholokhov's new novel, Oni Srazhalis' za Rodinu (They Fought for Their Native Land), appeared in Pravda. This novel deals with two problems, that of family relations and that of peoples who suffered during the purges of the 1930's. The main character, Nikolai Strel'tsov, begins wondering about his wife's friendship with another man, and his questioning continues to other men and their loyalty. The problems of crime and punishment, both just and unjust, are aired in the novel. Nikolai's brother was freed from prison camp after having served there for nine years. This situation causes more questions.

Answers to his questions are obtained in talks with the Director of a Machine-Tractor Station and later in talks with his brother on a fishing trip. The Director tells him that for five years after 1937 Stalin ruled the country with his eyes closed. Blame is put on Yezhov and Beria, and Stalin finally begins to correct some of the injustices. Nikolai's brother is one of those who is freed as a result of Stalin's awakening. After the brother returns, Nikolai goes fishing with him. On this trip questions are raised about the

Crimean Tatars, the Kalmyks, and the Ossetians, who were exiled during the Second World War. Their punishment is considered unjust. But corrections are made. Mistakes of individuals and of national leaders can be temporary. As in the case of the brother, the mistake was corrected not only by freeing him from prison but also by an assignment for him to work in the Military General Staff with General Zhukov in Moscow.

The novel criticizes the "cult of the personality" and gives praise to the Communist Party and the native land. Nikolai and his brother both vow to serve faithfully and justly to the end. This novel is another example of Sholokhov's ability to relate individuals to the society and to provide instruction for their personal life and their social obligations.

Sholokhov has maintained a balance in his writings between socialist realism and humanism. In the long range he has had a much greater influence on the course of Soviet literary development than did Gorky, Mayakovsky, or Ostrovsky. But the trend toward humanism did not mean a trend away from socialist realism in an attempt to attain greater freedom of expression. He has denounced those writers who have published their works abroad under pseudonyms and has supported the Communist Party both in his official position as a representative in the Supreme Soviet and in his unofficial relations with his literary associates.

FADEYEV

Aleksander Fadeyev also humanized socialist realism. He tried to incorporate into his writings the panoramic approach of Leo Tolstoy. Fadeyev was critical of writers who wrote mechanically and also those who wrote romantically. He tried to personalize his writings and make his heroes real people. He showed both their strengths and their weaknesses.

Fadeyev's greatest literary work was his novel Molodaya Gvardiya (The Young Guard). It is a novel about the young partisans during the Second World War. Not only has the novel been required reading for Soviet youth, but it has also been made into a two-part Soviet film. It depicts young people who become heroic symbols for setting examples of patriotism and dedication for all Soviet youth. But it is much more than a patriotic appeal. It describes real people and real events during the war. The novel brings the reader into the midst of the battles and of the scenes behind the enemy lines. Examples of ingenuity and bravery are shown in real circumstances.

Aleksander Fadeyev was born in Kirmy on the Volga River north of Moscow, in 1901, but he spent his childhood and youth in the Soviet Far East. In 1918 he joined the Communist Party and took an active part in the underground revolutionary work in Vladivostok, which was occupied by the Japanese interventionaries. He continued to fight against the counter-revolutionaries and was seriously wounded in 1921.

His experience in the military underground then gave him the basis for most of his writings. His first short story, Razliv (The Flood), was published in 1923. Shortly after that he published another story, Protiv Techeniya (Against the Current), but his fame did not come until he published the novel Razgrom (Destruction) in 1926. These writings were all about the Civil War period (1918-21), and the novel was considered to be exceptionally good because of its realism and patriotic enthusiasm. He also wrote Posledniy iz Udege (The Last of the Udegs), Molodaya Gvardiya (The Young Guard), Leningrad v Dni Blokady (Leningrad in the Days of the Blockade), and part of a book entitled Cheornaya Metallurgiya (Ferrous Metallurgy) before his death in 1956. Fadeyev was an organizer and administrator in the Union of Soviet Writers.

The Young Guard was first written in 1945, and it received a first class Stalin Prize. Later, 1951, Fadeyev revised and enlarged the novel in order to present a broader picture of the resistance to the Nazi occupation during the Second World War.

The story of The Young Guard takes place among the members of a Komsomol organization at the town of Krasnodon in the Eastern Ukraine. Their group starts with five teenagers, who take upon themselves an oath to death to defend each other, the Soviet people, and their native land against the Nazi occupationary forces. These young people recruit others to help them conduct acts of sabotage and espionage against the Germans and to coordinate their efforts with the Communist Party and with the Red Army. There are many tense times when two or three teenagers are sneaking through the night in pitch darkness to meet others or to carry out an assignment against the Germans. Their exploits involve cold, hunger, injuries, and death. They sacrifice their lives to the fulfillment of their oaths, but their work caused havoc among the Germans and rendered great aid to the Red Army.

The activities of the young people in the story, The Young Guards, parallels reality. Many deeds of the Soviet teenagers during the period of Nazi Occupation were told throughout the Soviet Union after the war, and the praise for the unselfish efforts of these young people is directed toward the heroes of The Young Guard in honor to all those who served in the para-military underground against the Nazis.

Fadeyev is responsible for making these heroic deeds known to the Soviet citizens and to people throughout the world. The greatness of his work lies in his perception in depth of the contribution of the Komsomol members and in his portrayal of life-like personal experiences. It is his personal touch to humanize socialist realism.

TVARDOVSKY

Aleksander Tvardovsky is a popular Soviet poet, who has written verses about the main events of his time. His best-loved poems are: Strana Muraviya (The Country of Muravia), in which he relates the legendary country of happiness with his own native land at a collective farm; Vasilii Terkin, in which he expresses the struggles and successes of the ordinary soldier while driving the Nazi soldiers back to Berlin; and Za Dal'yu-Dal' (Far Far Away), in which he describes the mastering of nature by those who are building communism in the 1960's. For this latter poem he received a Lenin Prize.

Tvardovsky was born near Smolensk in 1910. He lived on a farm, but his parents were great readers and spent many winter nights reading aloud in their home. At the age of 14 Aleksander began to write poems and notes which were published in the Smolensk newspaper. He was only 25 years old when he published his poem, The Country of Muravia.

During the Second World War he worked on front-line newspapers and wrote poems, songs, and sayings, which he based on conversations with the ordinary soldiers. His poem, Vasilii Terkin, appeared a few verses at a time in the military newspapers in 1942. He also accompanied the soldiers first as they retreated to the Volga and later as they advanced back toward Berlin, all the while writing, reciting, and printing verses, which he compiled into a book, Kniga Pro Boytsa (A Book About A Warrior).

It took ten years (from 1950 to 1960) to write the poem Far Far Away, which is an account of continuing time along a road into the future, a trip both in space and time. It differs from his other

poems in that there is neither a subject nor a main character.
The poem is an attempt to obtain a wider perspective of the events
since the 1917 Revolution. It is a communication between the
author and the reader for expanding the awareness of both. In a
sense Tvardovsky's poem is an attempt to ask questions and understand the meaning of life. This poem contains criticism of "The
Cult of the Personality" (Stalinism) and praise for Leninism. He
ends his poem with the following verse:*

> Dear to me is the world, large and difficult,
> I am in it--the son of my native land.
> I am full with it as a wonderful dream -
> To go up to selected mountain peaks,
> I am on the way with it to the very end,
> And to me all the burdens are light.
> I am stronger than all its enemies:
> Its enemies are my enemies.
> Yes, I am blessed with a proud strength
> And in this world I am--The strong man
> I am with you, Moscow
> I am with you, Russia,
> I am with you, starry Siberia.
> *a free translation by the author.

Continuing the same approach Tvardovsky wrote another
poem, Terkin Na Tom Svete (Terkin in Another World), which also
took him about ten years (from 1954 to 1963) to write. This poem
is a sequel to Vasilii Terkin, but it is a fairy-tale poem of this
warrior in the modern world. The fight is against traces of the
cult of the personality, bureaucratism, and dogmatism in the
society. Actually the poem is a satire against some of the problems
which the Soviet Government was trying to overcome. The poem
reasserts the theme of socialist realism and denies the existence
of a paradise or heaven, which was believed long ago. Tvardovsky
attacks those who think about death and the past and directs his
thoughts to the living and their future.

PASTERNAK

Boris Pasternak was a poet, who was not a politically motivated as the other leading writers of his time. He subordinated

the concept of socialist realism to humanism, and his master-piece, Dr. Zhivago, is recognized worldwide as a portrayal of human love in the midst of terror. Pasternak was aware of world and national issues, but human values to him were the substance of life.

Pasternak was born in Moscow in 1890. Both of his parents were educated. His father was a painter, and his mother was a musician. At an early age Pasternak became interested in art and music, and he started to study music at the University of Moscow. But he became interested in religion and philosophy and stressed these subjects in his further study. He continued to look for a meaning in life and in the violent events during his time.

He began writing in the early 1920's. His first published work was Vozdushniye Puti (Aerial Journeys), a collection of short stories, which appeared in 1925. In 1931 he wrote Okhrannaya Gramota (Safe Conduct), which consisted of some of his personal memoirs. But poems became his most popular and also his most controversial works. One of his better poems at that time was Vtoraya Zhizn' (A Second Life), which he wrote in 1932 about life in the Caucasus Mountains.

Most of his poems remained unpublished rather than meeting the criticism of the publishers. During the 1940's he began to translate English masterpieces into Russian. His best work in this area was his translation of Shakespeare's Hamlet.

After the death of Stalin, Pasternak again began publishing his poems. Ten of them appeared in the literary journal Znamya (Banner) in 1954. Also that year he announced that he was preparing for publication of a new book, Dr. Zhivago.

Dr. Zhivago was not appreciated by Soviet publishers for a long time. But Pasternak, after not being able to publish this novel in the Soviet Union, made arrangements to have it published in Italy. In 1957 it was published in Italian, and within a very short time it appeared in English and other languages. In 1958 Dr. Zhivago and its author, Boris Pasternak, were awarded the Nobel Prize for literature. But the unorthodox and illegal publication of Soviet literature abroad caused Soviet authorities to criticize Pasternak and to have him refuse the award. Acclaimed abroad for a great masterpiece and criticized at home for mistakes, Boris Pasternak died in 1960.

Dr. Zhivago went on to be considered to many to be the best literature to come out of the Soviet Union since the 1917 Revolution. The novel was made into an American film, which also became very popular in the United States and in many foreign countries.

The problem of the novel was not so much that it was critical of the Soviet Union as it did not overly praise the heroes of the Communist Revolution. Pasternak attempted to be objective. He also depicted individuals in their personal relations with other human beings rather than showing them either for or against the new society. Zhivago was more neutral toward the two sides of the conflict. Zhivago in many ways resembled Pierre in Tolstoy's novel, War and Peace. His love for people was greater than his love for social orders and customs.

In the novel, Doctor Yuri Zhivago is a member of the nobility class. His family arranges his marriage to a beautiful and lovely girl of the same class. Their married life is happy, and Zhivago accepts his role as a medical doctor and as a devoted husband to a wonderful person. However, the war (World War I) changes their lives. His wife lives with her parents while Zhivago serves as a medical doctor at a field hospital near the front lines. During their separation Zhivago works very closely with a nurse, a beautiful girl of a lower class. He falls in love with her without really knowing it himself.

After the war Zhivago returns to live with his family, but the Communist Revolution has changed their pattern of living. Their large home is made into an apartment house, and they have to sacrifice necessities as well as luxuries for the benefit of others. He does not really complain, but he can not stand to see his wife lack for food, clothing, and fuel during the cold winters. In desparation he steals wood from a public fence and takes it home for fuel. He is caught, and only with the intervention of his half-brother, who became a Communist, is he able to avoid punishment. However, he has to take his family from Moscow. His brother helps him travel by train to Siberia to live on a country estate. During the travel and his residency in Siberia Zhivago experiences the horrors of the Civil War and encounters Reds, Whites, and armed bandits.

But Zhivago attempts to practice medicine and to write poetry. Their new life in Siberia is a happy one. They brought their son with them, and soon his wife becomes pregnant again. During the long winter Zhivago becomes bored and lonely, even though he is happy with his wife and his son. As spring comes Zhivago sees the beauty of nature in Siberia and enjoys it, but his life is not as happy as it ought to have been.

His life is changed when he learns that his nurse friend is now working as the librarian in the local village. He goes to the library to do research for his writing, but he begins to recognize his love for Lara. At this time he experiences a greater happiness than he had ever known.

Lara had had a sad life. As a young girl she had been abducted by an older friend of her family, and she had become his lover. She left him for a younger man, but her marriage to him was also unhappy. This man became the leader of armed bandits who ravaged and plundered towns for their own gain. He had deserted her, and she had been forced to relocate her residence and to work as a librarian.

Both Zhivago and Lara lived happily together but not for long. Zhivago's former wife leaves and he doesn't see her again. Lara also has to leave for her safety because of her former relationship to the armed bandit. Lara is taken to the Far East by her former lover, but he breaks his promise to protect her and abandons her there.

Zhivago is alone. He hates all the violence and has to run away for his personal safety. Finally he returns to Moscow through the help of his half-brother and tries to find a new life. But he is never really happy again. Years later he sees on the street a woman, who could have been Lara, but while chasing her to find out for sure, he falls and dies.

His half-brother had helped him on many occasions, and now he wanted to help his family. He finds a young girl, who had a life story much like that of Lara's daughter, but she is more interested in her future life than the past. She represented the new generation of Soviet youth.

Pasternak may have tried to portray an objective witness of the Revolution and Civil War period, but he did not portray a neutral observer. All through the novel Dr. Zhivago expressed his thoughts, his feelings, and his reactions to events. But his expressions are non-political in the overall sense. He criticizes the actions of individuals and abhors the destruction of life and property. He does refer to Christian teachings and to his belief in religious principles, but he does not attack Communism.

In 1968 and 1969 Soviet citizens were saying that Dr. Zhivago would be published in the Soviet Union. Soviet exchange scholars in the United States saw the American film and praised it. They have also read the Russian version of Dr. Zhivago, which was printed by the University of Michigan Press. If their remarks are true, Dr. Zhivago may yet become recognized as a masterpiece of Soviet literature in the U.S.S.R.

Several of Pasternak's unpublished poems were finally published in the appendix of Dr. Zhivago. This poetry also gives
Pasternak the claim of a great poet.

YEVTUSHENKO

Yevgenny Yevtushenko has become a popular poet not only
for his writing but also for his reciting of poetry. At public places
he has drawn crowds of over 15,000 people. His poetry appeals to
young and old alike, but he has received some criticism for the
subject matter being too controversial.

Yevtushenko was born at Zima in the Irkutsk Oblast in 1933.
He is a descendant of Ukrainian exiles who were sent to Siberia
during the time of the tsars. The independent spirit of these people
became a part of his life, and he has been a non-conformist both in
his behavior and in his poetry. His parents were both well educated,
but they were divorced and left their son on his own. Yevtushenko
lived in Siberia from his birth to 1944, when his mother moved him
to Moscow when she was singing for the troops. But after the war
he returned to Irkutsk Oblast to work with his father on geological
expeditions for a while.

His education was interrupted by the war. He was deprived
of paper and textbooks, and he related times when he wrote between
lines of newspapers and library books. But he was able to continue
his education and did graduate from the Gorky Literary Institute in
Moscow.

Yevtushenko started to write poems when he was still a young
boy, but he was not able to publish any of them until he was 19. In
1952 he was befriended by an editor of the journal, Soviet Sport,
and was able to have poems published in that journal. One of his
first poems was Razvedchiki Gryadushchego (Scouts of the Future),
which was published in 1952. In 1955 he published a book of verses,
entitled Tretii Sneg (The Third Snow), and following that time his
poems have been very numerous each year. In 1961 he published
Babi Yar in the Literary Gazette. This poem was about the persecution and killing of Jews in a small town near Kiev during the
Second World War. It rapidly became very popular and also controversial, because of the reference to anti-Semitism among Soviet
citizens. But the emphasis was against the atrocities of the Germans,
and the poem was consistent with anti-German feelings in the USSR
since the war.

In 1962 Yevtushenko published a poem Nasledniki Stalina
(The Followers of Stalin), which also bordered on criticism during
Stalin's time and criticism of present leaders. Yevtushenko was
critical of negative conditions no matter where or when they
existed. His satire could be interpreted by the reader and the
hearer, and for this, Yevtushenko became popular in both the Soviet
Union and abroad. He travelled widely in the early 1960's to France,
East Germany, England, Finland, and Cuba.

When Yevtushenko was criticized for one poem, he quickly
wrote another one which was more acceptable. In 1962 he wrote
Khotyat Li Russkie Voynu? (Do the Russians Want War?), which
went right along with Khrushchev's peace program. In 1965 he also
praised the Soviet efforts in constructing hydro-electric power dams
in his poem Bratskaya GES (The Bratsk Hydro-Electric Power
Station).

In 1963 Yevtushenko wrote two stores; one about his own life,
A Precocious Autobiography, and another entitled Kiriny Bog
(Chicken God).

Even though Yevtushenko has been a controversial writer, he
has also been very popular, particularly with the youth. For
several years he worked on the editorial board of the youth magazine, Yunost' (Youth), but in May, 1969, he was dropped from that
position. But Yevtushenko had not been affiliated with the dissident
youth, who have been criticized and punished for subversive writings.
He remained a positive critic and a loyal citizen of the Soviet Union.

DUDINTSEV

Vladimir Dudintsev became well known in the Soviet Union
and abroad in 1956 when his novel Ne Khlebom Edinym (Not by Bread
Alone) was published in the journal Novy Mir (New World). Later
this novel appeared in book form in the Soviet Union and was translated into many foreign languages. The book was at first widely
accepted for portraying current living conditions in the Soviet Union,
but after being considered as a critical attack against the Soviet
system by the foreign press, it was also criticized by Soviet authorities. But it is not only the controversial nature of the book but also
its study of human values in the Soviet society that makes the novel
popular.

Dudintsev was born in 1918 in Kupyansk in the Khar'kov
Oblast of the Ukraine. He attended Moscow State University and

graduated from there with a law degree in 1940. During the war he commanded an infantry unit, and later he was assigned to serve on a military tribunal in Siberia. After the war he worked on the editorial staff of the newspaper, Komsomolskaya Pravda (the official newspaper of the Young Communist League).

His best known writing is Not By Bread Alone, but he wrote and published several other stories. In 1948 he published the story Stroitel' (A Builder), and in 1952 he published a short story entitled U Semi Bogatyrev (At Seven Warriors). Then in 1953 he published Na Svoyom Meste (In His Own Place). These stories were considered to be good literature, but Dudintsev was still not well known until 1956 when he published Not By Bread Alone.

Since then he has published Besheniy Mal'chishka (The Furious Rascal) in 1958, Sborniki Rasskazov dlya Yunoshestva (Collections of Stories for Young People) in 1958, and Novogodnaya Skazka (A New Year Tale) in 1960. The 1958 writings were interesting stories, but they were politically neutral. In 1960 he returned to the theme of his 1956 novel.

Both Not By Bread Alone and A New Year Tale relate the conditions of an individual worker in the midst of a highly organized and industrialized society. The individual is an inventor, who tries to work by himself outside of the collective for providing inventions for the collective. His work is superior, but he is not accepted. He is criticized and even punished for not cooperating with the industrial bureaucracy, but he later enjoys a measure of success when his ideas are incorporated by another work crew and found to be beneficial. Various characters are presented in the novel in a way that portrays the problems of massive organizations. Dudintsev stated that he was not criticizing the labor and social problems to condemn them but to improve them. However, Soviet citizens could see their own frustrations and anxieties in Dudintsev's characters and their activities. The value of these writings are in their departure from socialist realism and praise for the Soviet system far enough to take a more objective look at human problems.

SOLZHENITSYN

In 1962 the Soviet Union and the whole world was surprised by the publication of a book, One Day in the Life of Ivan Denisovich, by Alexander Solzhenitsyn. Even though Stalin had been strongly criticized by Khrushchev, there had not been such an exposure of the cruel guards and horrible conditions in the correctional labor camps during the time of Stalin. Khrushchev apparently aided Solzhenitsyn to publish this work, but it was the first strike against the human misery that existed for a time in the Soviet Union.

Alexander Solzhenitsyn was born in 1918, and he graduated from Rostov University. In 1945 he was arrested and sent to a correctional labor camp for eight years. These eight years provided him with the experiences, on which he has since written several stories. After his release from the camp he taught school first in a village near Vladimir and later at Ryazin. During this time he started to write. But he did not become well-known until 1962, when he published One Day in the Life of Ivan Denisovich. For his merit he was recognized and given a position on the editorial board of the Soviet Writer's Union.

This book may be called an exposure or a sensational writing. It is full of vulgar expressions and animalistic behavior of the prisoners. This type of writing probably does describe well the lives of the people in these camps, but it does not achieve the level of good literature. The greatest achievement of this book is that it was written and put in print, thereby substantiating the rumors concerning the bad conditions which have existed in Soviet correctional labor camps.

In 1963 Solzhenitsyn published two more short stories in the Soviet literary magazine, Novy Mir (New World). One of these was Sluchai na Stantsii Krechetovka (An Incident at the Krechetovka Station) about an army lieutenant who was assigned to work at a railroad station during the war. The lieutenant tried to live an exemplary life. He resists temptations to go against official policies and against moral codes. Yet he is faced with inequities among soldiers on troop trains who have been forced to go without food for days and who have been separated from their units. The main incident involves an apparently educated and refined soldier who has been separated from his unit. The lieutenant tries to help him, but later he suspects the man of being a spy because of his ignorance concerning well-known places and dates. The lieutenant then has the man arrested, but he never finds out whether or not the man is guilty. The doubt remains in his mind about the justice of this incident.

The second story is Matrenin Dvor' (Matryona's House), which is about an elderly woman and her house. The poor peasant woman lived alone for many years after having been abandoned by a collective farm. She has no income, except for a boarder's rent money, and she has to pilfer peat and fuel wood. Matryona is called to help other people, but she is not paid for her labor. People consider her to be gullible, and they take advantage of her. They even lay claim to an addition onto her home. But when they remove that addition, it is struck by a train while crossing the tracks. Matryona and others are killed, but the story shows that it was Matryona rather than the others who was wise, frugal, and good. The story is a satire on the selfishness of people as well as a portrayal of poor living conditions in the remote areas of the Soviet Union.

Both of these stories are critical of the living conditions of these people, but they do bring out in simple language the hopes, fears and loves of the individuals. They are a definite break from socialist realism, and they stress the gap between reality and human values.

Since 1966 Solzhenitsyn has fallen from favor in the Soviet Union. He has continued to publish his writings outside of the Soviet Union, and he has become more critical of institutions in his country.

Two books which were published abroad were The Cancer Ward and The First Circle. These books are a continuation of the story in his book, One Day in the Life of Ivan Denisovich. But Solzhenitsyn is more critical of the Soviet police and security forces, not only during the time of Stalin but also since then. Solzhenitsyn allied himself with the young dissidents, and in 1967 he distributed a protest letter at the Conference of the Soviet Writers' Union, which he boycotted.

TRENDS IN SOVIET LITERATURE

The role of socialist realism in Soviet literature is changing. The approach to literature of Mayakovsky, Ostrovsky, and Fadeyev has become a thing of the past. A blending of humanism into socialist realism, as done by Sholokhov, is the current fashion for Soviet literature. Sholokhov has helped to maintain the standard for other Soviet writers.

However, there are those writers, who deviate to a greater degree from the main stream of Soviet literary thought. Yevtushenko, Solzhenitsyn, and Dudintsev tread on the frontier of newer trends. In addition, there are those who have been seriously criticized by the Soviet Government and even punished for their "subversive" writings and activities. Andrei Sinyavsky published stories abroad under his pseudonym, Abram Tertz. His writings were openly critical of the Soviet way of life. Both Sinyavsky and his associate, Yuli Daniel (who published abroad under the pseudonym of Nikolai Arzhak) were arrested and sent to a correctional labor camp in 1965. In 1968 two more young dissidents, Yuri Galanskov and Alexander Ginzburg, were also strongly criticized, arrested, and sent to a correctional labor camp. These arrests have been protested by other young intellectuals, but Soviet policy has remained firm in opposing "subversive" writings and in continuing to emphasize socialist realism as the Soviet literary standard.

At the 1967 Conference of the Soviet Writers' Union it was apparent that a gulf was developing between the older and the younger writers in the Soviet Union. Mikhail Sholokhov commented on this problem at the conference. His remarks were published in Izvestia. Part of them were:

> At the first conference of writers 71% of the delegates were under 40, at the second conference this percentage was only 20.6%, at the third it was 13.9%, and at the present conference it is only 12.2%. We are getting old, brother-writers! And isn't it time to think about attracting the young people into the conference and into the directing organs of the departments and of the Writers' Union. . . .

Sholokhov criticized those who were seeking greater freedom in literature and those who were boycotting the conference. He also differentiated between "freedom" and "anarchy" and emphasized the responsibility of Soviet authors. But he also encouraged them to be daring in their research and in their creative works.

Sholokhov's novel, They Fought for the Native Land, extracts of which were published in Pravda in March, 1969, provided an example of that philosophy. He did explore human problems, criticize the mistakes of Stalin and the related results in people's lives, but at the same time praised the overcoming of those problems and mistakes. This novel also treaded near the frontier of Soviet literary thought, but it helped to establish the bounds between "freedom" and "anarchy."

The publishing of literary works abroad continues to be a violation of Soviet policies. Also the guidelines of socialist realism continue to emphasize positive portrayals of Soviet life rather than negative and "subversive" ones. Criticism of both the past and the present must be constructive rather than destructive. Criticism and satire are acceptable tools in literature, and both are very prevalent in all Soviet writings. But they must be used to build up the society rather than to undermine it. Literature, as industry and agriculture, has the responsibility of helping to build communism and to create new Soviet men.

These guidelines, as asserted by Sholokhov, do not limit the scope of Soviet literature. Actually they support the broad areas of Soviet reality and the creative potential of those who follow the path for building a communist society.

As new writings appear there will probably be a refinement of these re-established guidelines. New types of Mayakovskys, Ostrovskys, and Fadeyevs will appear, and a new leader will soon take over the role of Sholokhov. But Soviet literature will remain as an integral part of political theory.

Bocharov, G. K. & Belen'ky, G. I., Rodnaya Literatura, Moscow:
    Izdatel'stvo "Prosveshcheniye", 1964, 352 pp.
Brown, Edward J., Russian Literature Since the Revolution,
    London: Collier-Macmillan, Ltd., 1969, 367 pp.
The Christian Science Monitor, Boston, March 6, 1968.
Crowley, Edward L., et als (eds), Prominent Personalities in
    the USSR, Metuchen, New Jersey: The Scarecrow Press,
    1968, 792 pp.
Dement'ev, A., Naumov, Ye, & Plotkin, L., Russkaya Sovetskaya
    Literatura, Moscow: Izdatel'stvo "Prosveshcheniye", 1965,
    359 pp.
Dudinstev, Vladimir, Not By Bread Alone, New York: E. P.
    Dutton & Co., Inc., 512 pp.
Izvestia, Moscow, May 27, 1967.
Lebed, Andrew I. et als., Who's Who in the USSR 1965-66, New
    York: The Scarecrow Press, 1966, 1189 pp.
Mal'tseva, K. V. & Zhdanov, N. S., Literaturnoye Chteniye na
    Russkom Yazyke, Moscow: Gosudarstvennoye Uchebnoye
    Pedagogicheskoye Izdatel'stvo, 1958, 288 pp.
Pasternak, Boris, Doctor Zhivago, New York: Pantheon Books Inc.,
    1958, 559 pp.
"Boris Pasternak" Encyclopedia Britannica, Vol. 17, Chicago:
    Encyclopedia Britannica, Inc., 1966, 1239 pp.
Pravda, Moscow, March 12-15, 1969.
Shevchenko, P. A. & Florinsky, S. M., Rodnaya Literatura,
    Moscow: Gosudarstvennoye Uchebnoye Pedagogicheskoye
    Izdatel'stvo, 1961, 430 pp.
Slonim, Marc, An Outline of Russian Literature, New York: The
    New American Library, 1958, 175 pp.
Solzhenitsyn, Alexander, One Day in the Life of Ivan Denisovitch,
    New York: Frederick A. Praeger, 1963, 211 pp.
_____, We Never Make Mistakes, Columbia,
    South Carolina: University of South Carolina Press, 1963,
    100 pp.
Vasys, Anthony et als., Russian Area Reader, New York: Pitman
    Publishing Co., 1962, 484 pp.
Yevtushenko, Yevgeny, A Precocious Autobiography, New York:
    E. P. Dutton & Co., Inc., 1963, 124 pp.

CHAPTER XIII

ART AND MUSIC

The history of the peoples of the Soviet Union is rich in various forms of artistic expression. Folk art in the form of brightly painted plates, bowls, dolls, and toys carved from wood and decorated rugs and baskets woven from wool and fibers have long been a part of the respective cultures. Minature paintings of legendary and historical events adorn plaques, jewel cases, plates and bowls. Folk songs and dances have since ancient times been accompanied by the balalaika and accordian.

Painting was developed early through the Christian and Moslem religions. Artists of the Russian Orthodox Church produced icons, which depict deity, angels, and saints for use in religious services, and these icons have become great art treasures. Painters of Central Asia have produced minature paintings which illustrate the events in the lives of statesmen and religious leaders. Byzantine architecture came to Russia with the Christian religion. Now the western part of the Soviet Union has many spires, cupolas, and towers as epitomized by St. Basil's Cathedral on Red Square. The mosque with its blue dome and the minaret decorated with geometric designs in blue and white reflects a different culture in Central Asia which came with the Moslem religion. Today paintings and architecture have drawn from the past and borrowed from many other cultures to form a great variety of artistic works.

The ancient ballads and the traditional folk music also have blended with the learning of the masters to produce symphonies, ballet, opera music, and popular music which are all loved by the Soviet citizens. A great contribution in this respect has come from the Gypsies who are widely scattered throughout the Soviet Union. Now folk choirs and folk dance troupes travel widely to preserve the music and to entertain the people. World wide recognition of achievement has been gained by the Russian Ballet, which has become a hallmark of the Russian people.

Epic stories have been incorporated into great literary works and later produced on the stage. Much of the theater is devoted to these works not just in the Russian Republic but also among the other national groups. Fables, legends, and historical events are the subjects of opera and ballet which are performed in cities throughout the Soviet Union. The quantity and quality of these productions have constantly increased and improved. Now the Soviet

Union claims to be the most theatrical country in the world.

PAINTINGS

One of the largest collections of original paintings in the world is at the Hermitage in Leningrad. The Hermitage was formerly the Winter Palace of the Tsars, who collected art treasures through gifts and purchases from foreign royalty. Their holdings were increased after the 1917 Revolution by the acquisition of the private collections of the Russian nobility. Now there are more than two million separate pieces of art, including gold and silver figurines and ornamentation, crystal chandeliers, malachite urns and furniture, elegant wood carvings, massive sculptures, and thousands of paintings. Many of the great paintings of all times from various cultures are now on exhibit in the Hermitage. Among them are Leonardi da Vinci's "Madonna Lita", Rembrandt's "The Return of the Prodigal Son", Nocolas Lancret's "Camargo the Dancer", Van Gogh's "The Hovels", and Picasso's "Boy with a Dog." The Russian collection includes Ivan Shishkin's "A Forest", Ivan Aivazovsky's "Ninth Wave", Karl Bryullov's "The Last Day of Pompei", and Ilya Repin's "Volga Boatmen."

The largest collection of Russian and Soviet art, however, is at the Tretyakov Art Gallery in Moscow. It was founded by Pavel Tretyakov in 1856 and given to Moscow in 1892. Now it has more than 40,000 art objects, which represent art from the eleventh century to the present. A few of the famous paintings there are Vasnetsov's "Bogatyrs", Karl Bryullov's "Horsewomen", Ivan Shishkin's "Morning in a Pine Forest", Levitan's "Golden Autumn", Vasiliev's "In the Crimean Mountains", Deineka's "Defense of Petrograd", and Nissky's "Upper Volga."

Icons and religious works of art are housed in the Hermitage, Tretyakov Gallery, and in many other galleries, museums, and cathedrals. Probably the most famous icon is "The Vladimir Mother of God", which was painted on wood in the early 12th century and is now located in the Tretyakov Gallery. This Icon is a representation of the Mother of God holding the Christ Child to her face. The facial expressions depict love and agony. All attention is centered on the faces, which command respect, love, and sympathy.

A Russian icon is a special form of art. It may depict God, the Mother of God, the Savior, saints, or angels. The faces are light, almost shining. The rest of the painting is usually dominated

"Vladimir Mother of God"

by black and red on a golden background or tones of green and blue. The face of the icon is an object of worship, which is displayed in churches and holy places. Even in museums icons command reverence and respect. The Soviet Government today is attempting to restore and preserve icons and other religious art as a part of the cultural heritage of the Russian people.

Minature paintings are also a special form of art. They depict events, both historical and legendary. In Central Asia these paintings illustrate a whole chain of events within a broad scene. Typical of these Central Asian minatures are hunting expeditions, receptions of foreign royalty, military expeditions, or a marriage. A hunting expedition may show people on horseback chasing and shooting arrows at leopards, antelope, bears, rabbits, foxes, and deer. Standing by are some people playing harps and tambourines and others holding vessels of oil. Another minature illustrating a home scene (marriage or birth celebration) may depict various events in different rooms, in the front yard, and in the backyard. Many people are in this scene - the master of the house, guests, servants, musicians, dancers, and other entertainers. Characteristic of these paintings are the great detail, the bright colors, and the variety of activity in the one minature painting. Looking at these minatures is comparable to reading a story, and the lives of these people, their clothing, customs, and activities, are presented vividly to the spectator. Some of the better known minature paintings in the Soviet Union are the minature paintings which illustrate the poems of Alisher Navoi and Babur-Namah in Central Asia during the 15th and 16th centuries. But Russian legends of the "fire bird" and the "little hunch-backed horse" are also subjects for minature paintings.

The nineteenth century brought to Russia the paintings of Western Europe. Following the trends of the West came several outstanding painters, whose works are recognized as invaluable holdings of the Hermitage and Tretyakov Gallery. One of those painters was Karl Bryullov (1799-1852). He painted women of the aristocracy, both Russian and foreign. He also painted portraits and historical events. One of his best-known paintings was "The Horsewoman", which he painted in 1832. She is riding a black stallion, which appears wild and anxious to run. Yet the horsewoman appears dainty and is dressed in a flowing white skirt, a blue blouse with long sleeves, and a black hat with a trailing green scarf of transparent material. On one side of the lady on a horse is a small dog, which is ready to run with the horse, but on the other side is a small girl, dressed in a pink dress and a white petticoat. The small girl grasps a golden

KARL BRYULLOV
"THE HORSEWOMAN"

rail at the edge of the porch of the mansion, and she is accompanied by a high-bred house dog, which looks at her and shares her awe and fear of the horse. Other famous paintings by Bryullov are "An Italian at Noon" of a lady picking grapes; "The Bakhchirsaria Fountain" showing lavishly dressed ladies and their servants around an outside gold fish pond; "Bathsheba" depicting a nude lady fixing her hair and a black servant at her feet. All of these paintings show the influence of French and Italian art. His experiences in those countries introduced him to subjects of many other paintings, one of which was his "Last Day of Pompei".

Ivan Aivazovsky (1817-1900) also travelled abroad to Western Europe, Africa, and America, but he spent most of his life near the Black Sea and painted mostly seascapes. He painted over a span of sixty years, and his art form changed from the Romantic style of Bryullov to the Realist style of the last part of the century. Many of his paintings illustrated only the sea and the sky. His best Romantic painting was "The Ninth Wave", which he displayed in 1850. It shows five men on a raft in a stormy sea. The foreboding sea is being somewhat tempered by the rays of the morning sun, and the mixed emotions of fear and hope are expressed in the various shades of green, blue, and violet in the water and the shades of yellow, orange, and pink in the sky. Aivazovsky expressed Realism in one of his very last paintings, "Among the Waves", which depicts a struggle between the sea and the sky during a storm of dark clouds and high waves. No living being is seen in the picture, but the scene is full of the action of natural forces. The greenish-blue sea clashes with the brownish-grey sky, and the colors of one merge into the colors of the other.

A contemporary of Aivazovsky was Ivan Shishkin (1832-1898), who was as dedicated to the forest as Aivazovsky was to the sea. He studied in an art school in Moscow and travelled later to many places in Western Europe, but he returned to his home in the Kama River valley to paint landscapes. Shishkin's paintings are so realistic that the viewer feels that he is standing at a window overlooking the forest. One of his great paintings was "Wind-fallen Wood", which he painted in 1888. This painting depicts giant trees, newly sprouted mushrooms, dry twigs, and all the detail of an undisturbed place in an old forest. But Shishkin's best-known painting was "Morning in a Pine Forest", which depicts animal life in the forest. A mother bear and three cubs are playing on a broken, up-rooted tree in the midst of a dense forest. The sunshine is mistily shining through the

IVAN AIVAZOVSKY
"THE NINTH WAVE"

IVAN SHISHKIN
"MORNING IN A PINE FOREST"

ILYA REPIN
"ZAPOROZHTSY"

trees, and one of the cubs is looking off into the rays of the sun.
One can feel an excitment for life as he sees these young bears
encountering the break of a new day.

One of the first Russian painters to produce art masterpieces
depicting the common people was Ilya Repin (1844-1930). He also
painted portraits. "The Volga Boatmen", first displayed in 1873,
brought Repin fame. This painting revealed the hard life of the
Volga River barge haulers who were being used as beasts of burden.
Artisticly speaking, a greater work though was "The Religious
Procession", which he painted in 1880-1883. It is rich in detail
both as to the characteristics of the people portrayed and the relationships between them. There were monks, a choir, military
officers, peasants, and cripples. These people crowded together
in a long line on a pilgrimage, but the peasants and cripples were
restrained by the military officers from joining the main lines of
the procession. The class structure of the state and the church was
vividly portrayed in this painting. Another famous painting by
Repin was his "Boyarina Morozova", which depicts the nobelwoman
Morozova being conveyed away on a sleigh from her people. An
historical event is presented in which Morozova was being taken
to prison because of her defiance to Patriarch Nikon's religious
innovations. Morozova's determination and the allegiance of the
people are clearly depicted in the facial expressions. Even more
famous is Repin's painting "Zaporozhtsy", which is a painting of
Cossacks composing a letter to the Turkish Sultan. The Cossacks
have only a few strands of hair on their scalps and long bushy
moustaches on their faces. They are all acting boisterously and
laughing. The painting conveys the crudeness and vulgarity of
this band of warriors. In these paintings and many more Repin
expressed scenes of events vividly and almost shockingly to the
people of Russia. He made a major contribution to the acceptance
of naturalism and realism in art. He also painted portraits of
Tolstoy, Tretyakov, Stasov, and himself. These paintings are
now housed in the Hermitage and in the Tretyakov Gallery, and
reproductions of them are found all over the world.

Another famous paintings is "Bogatyrs", which was painted
by Viktor Vasnetsov (1848-1926). Bogatyrs were epic heroes, who
fought to control and expand their land holdings. In this painting
three Bogatyrs have ridden their horses to a hill to scout for enemies.
Dominating the picture are huge men and huge horses, both bushy
with hair and wild-looking. The men are wearing armor and have
for weapons a bow and arrow, a sword, and a mace. The background

ILYA REPIN
    "THE RELIGIOUS PROCESSION"

ILYA REPIN
"BOYARINA MOROZOVA" Detail

portrays wild and remote, rolling hills. In the foreground are trees, short and dwarfed by the size of the men and horses. The viewer is impressed by powerful warriors who would stop at nothing for what they want.

Another aspect of Russian life was presented by Vassily Polenov (1844-1927) in his paintings of familiar scenes. "Grandmother's Yard", painted in 1878, shows grandmother, dressed in black and using a cane, and a grown granddaughter, dressed in pink and helping her grandmother, walking along a path away from an old, somewhat dilapidated wooden home with pillars and steps badly in need of repair. The yard is overgrown with flowers (holly hocks) and weeds. Polenov painted a similar painting in the same year, which he called "Moscow Backyard", which shows a wider view of possibly the same house from the rear. Children are playing in the yard, and a baby is crying. The mother is carrying a pail of water from the house - possibly to a horse which is hitched to a cart on the other side of the yard. More detail, such as chickens, broken-down out-buildings, a clothesline, and a covered well are in the foreground, and in the background are the spires, cupolas, and bell towers of churches and cathedrals. Over all is a partially cloudy, blue sky. In these paintings and others Polenov showed the lives of the people in their daily pursuits rather than the activities of the nobility or peasantry.

The lives of the people were also expressed by Konstantin Savitsky (1844-1905) in his paintings "Repair Work on the Railroad" and "Off to War". Both paintings show many people in small groups. The people are concerned only with those near them, but a broad scene is shown of various activities of ordinary people whose composite makes up the activity of the picture. A story is told like that of a mural or a minature painting, but the story is about people conforming to tasks of the society. Savitsky's work is outstanding for his realistic portrayal of events and the detail and accuracy presented.

Isaac Levitan (1861-1900) painted mostly rural landscapes, some of which showed houses and other buildings, but the scenes are all quiet, still, and peaceful. His "Golden Autumn" is a scene along a small stream lined with yellow birch trees. The grass is still green, and a few shrubs are changing from red to brown. The sky is a deep blue with a few misty clouds. Another painting by Levitan is "Above Eternal Peace", which illustrates s small church and a graveyard on a promontory point on a river bank. The land and the river are quiet and still, and the clouds in the sky are heavy with a greenish-blue cast and with yellowish-green sunlight shining over the clouds. His other paintings emphasize trees, houses, or ponds, but they all carry a theme of silence, which is the name of yet another one of his paintings.

A striking painting which is hanging in the Tretyakov Gallery is "In the Crimean Mountains", which was painted by Feodor Vasiliev (1850-1873). He died in his youth the same year he painted this outstanding scene. In the center of the painting is a cart pulled by two oxen. A woman and a boy are riding in the cart, and an old man is walking alongside. On the path are broken limbs of trees, and across the path on a knoll are four tall evergreen trees, which are bare of needles, except for the very tops. Beyond the knoll are more trees, which appear smaller, either due to distance or their actual size. The ground and the trees have various shades of green and brown, but the sky has shades of blue, purple, grey, and white. Apparently it is twilight, and it is difficult to determine whether the expanse beyond the tall trees is a large hill overlooking a purple valley or clouds, which form a pathway into the sky. One can not help from being awed by the impact of this beautiful painting.

During the First World War, the Russian Revolution, and the Civil War there was a period of decline in the arts. Not only were the quantity and quality of new paintings interrupted, but also the preservation of earlier masterpieces was endangered. Fortunately, much of the art was retained in private collections and later acquired by the Hermitage, Tretyakov Gallery, and other galleries and museums. Much credit goes to Anatoly Lunacharsky, the People's Commissar of Education, for his efforts in preserving art and advocating the maintenance of high standards for new artistic productions.

Events of the times also brought new trends in art forms. Paintings reflected events in the lives of the people - war, industry, agriculture, and at home. But the concept of art also changed. Lenin said that "Art belongs to the people", and the themes of artistic productions began to inspire people and to motivate them toward the needs of the society. The style of painting was no longer that of naturalism or realism in the old sense. The new trend became known as "Socialist Realism", which means that art should reflect the contemporary scene and be optimistic. This trend adheres to the belief that art should educate and ennoble man and teach him to feel joy, beauty, and happiness. Art changed also in other countries, but the Soviet Union rejected those trends of abstractionism, cubism, and formalism. Soviet art accepted instead paintings with a meaning of the event depicted. The event should be real, easily understandable, and applicable to social needs.

Alexander Deineka (1899-1969) has been a leader in contemporary Soviet art. His "Defense of Petrograd", painted in 1919, portrays

Feodor Vasiliev
"In the Crimean Mountains"

soldiers, both men and women, marching toward battle and above them on an overhead bridge are wounded soldiers returning. The background is a bleak and dark image of the city as seen in a distance. The expressions on the faces of the soldiers are stern and dedicated. Another war painting was his "Outskirts of Moscow, 1941", which depicts bombed-out buildings, a damaged truck, and broken boards all partially covered with a dirty snow. The sky is stormy and foreboding. Neither of these pictures show determination in the expressions of people but desolation in the aftermath of war. The horrors of war are also shown in his "Defense of Sevastopol", which illustrates the actual fighting between soliders and sailors both armed with rifles and bayonets. The city is on fire, and both the sky and the ground are red.

Deineka has produced many paintings. In 1956 he painted "A Tractor Driver" and "By the Sea". The tractor driver stands tall and straight in the foreground of the painting. The trees, barns, cattle, and fields are dwarfed by his size. He looks forward with cap in hand ready to face the future. "By the Sea", on the other hand, depicts women working. They are hanging fish on a rod above their heads. The viewer's eyes focus on the hands of the women as they tie the fish to the rods. In the background near the sea are other women in or near boats. They too are busy working. The work theme was also the subject of his painting, "Friends", which he displayed in 1962. This picture shows a man and his grown son standing in front of a plowed field. They appear strong, contented, and proud of their work. The man folds his arms, and the lad has his hands on his hips. The people in Deineka's paintings look afar off. Even in a recent painting "Free Run", Deineka shows girls in gym suits running up a hill away from a stream, but they, even though active, appear cast in an impersonal role. The event appears more important than the individuals. There is a lack of warmth in the feeling for the people, and the lesson ' do you likewise' seems to dominate the sensations perceived from his paintings.

Mitrofan Grekov (1882-1934) produced paintings resembling those of Repin. Apparently they were not as greatly influenced by socialist realism as those of Deineka. In 1923 Grekov produced "To the Budeonny Detachment", which shows a man riding his horse and leading another one across the steppe. He is going on slowly and steadily. The picture is very realistic, and the man commands a certain empathy. Grekov's best-known painting is "Tachanka",

Alexander Deineka
"A Tractor Driver"

ALEXANDER DEINEKA
"THE OUTSKIRTS OF MOSCOW, 1941"

Icons and the Lord's Supper on the walls
in St. Basil's Cathedral in Moscow.

Mitrofan Grekov
"Tachanka"

which he painted in 1925. It depicts a team of horses racing across the steppe and pulling a cannon to the front lines. In the distance are other teams doing the same thing. Attention is focused on the action and energy of the horses and men. Grekov's other paintings also depict men and horses. They are colorful and full of life.

Arkady Plastov (1893-1972) has painted people pursuing their daily tasks. His style is somewhere between that of Deineka and Grekov. But he has not attained the vivid expressions of Repin. Yet he has been one of the foremost contemporary Soviet artists. His "Tractor Driver's Supper" gained him recognition as a good example of 'socialist realism'. It pictures a girl pouring milk into a bowl for her father and brother. They are in a field, which is partially plowed. The tractor idles near by. The supper appears to be only a short refreshment for the men who are working a long day. The color and shadows indicate that the sun is setting, but that seems to cause no interference in the daily schedule. This picture is typical of Plastov's success in painting a quick view into the lives of people. In 1954 he painted "Spring", which is a picture of a nude lady dressing her small daughter as they both emerge from a bath house. The mother is caring for her daughter before she cares for herself. The bath house and the enclosed dressing area are built of logs. There is no roof, and in the distance one can see a house and some trees, between which are patches of snow. The people in "Spring" and in "Gathering Potatoes", which he painted in 1956, have kind and gentle faces. Plastov reaches into the inner feelings of his subjects. In "Gathering Potatoes" he shows two women with head scarfs and full dresses kneeling and bending over to pick potatoes and put them into baskets. Their hands appear strong and sinewy, but their faces are soft and full of feeling. A similar touch of human emotions was captured in his "August of a Collective Farmer", in 1957, which depicts a group of men and women unloading grain from a truck. A man is signing the work order in the background, and in the foreground are a child playing in the wheat, an old man with a cane standing near his dog, and several geese looking and pecking at the grain. In this painting Plastov expressed the roles of various people and animals in a real life situation. In 1960 he maintained this skill in "Summer", which accomplishes the same effect in a more leisurely situation. A man is resting by a tree where he is having a snack. One woman is pouring milk into his cup, and another woman is walking by carrying a bucket covered with a cloth. A small girl, who wears a scarf as does her mother, clings to her

ARKADY PLASTOV
"TRACTOR-DRIVERS' SUPPER"

Arkady Plastov
"Spring"

mother's dress. Nearby is a cow, and in the background are milk cans and a dog. Plastov has incorporated 'humanism' with 'socialist realism' and has attained a high recognition in Soviet art. His paintings are numerous, but two more should be mentioned. He attempted a panorama scene in "Holiday", in which he illustrated a sulky race with a large crowd of people and a river in the background. The horses and the men on the sulkies are exerting great effort, but the people in the background lack the detail that makes them an integral part of the scene. They are only background. This picture further exemplifies Plastov's concentration on one thought, that of the people actively engaged in the real life situation. He does not attempt to portray the panoramic scenes that Grekov and Repin achieved so well. But he does accomplish the portrayal of human emotions of the main subjects of his paintings. This is very true in a recent painting, which he called "Sunshine". It depicts a young mother lying on her back in a garden surrounded by flowers, shrubs, and trees and guarded by a big dog. In the foreground are baskets, pitchers, and buckets of vegetables and berries, and near her is a large sunflower. But she is lying there shielding her eyes from the sun as her baby is feeding on her breast.

Quite a variety of paintings is seen in Soviet galleries and museums. Probably the paintings of Deineka and Plastov are regarded as the best examples of 'socialist realism', but other painters have produced several outstanding paintings and some have painted only one which is recognized as a great painting.

Tair Salakhov comes from Azerbaidzhan and paints a different type of art, which resembles murals rather than pictures. He is young. He was born in 1928. His concept of 'socialist realism' lacks the 'humanism' of Plastov's art. Even his portraits are cool and impersonal. In 1957 he painted "From Shift Work", which shows men and women workers walking home from work along a pier. They carry coats, lunch boxes or tool kits, and other personal possessions. They face the wind, which blows their clothes, and waves are splashing against the pier. Behind them is an elevated road, along which trucks are going to the work site. In 1959 he painted a similar painting, but this time without people, which he called "The Morning Train", which shows oil cars crossing on a railroad overpass and trucks on the road below speeding to work. The plainness of the picture emphasizes the drive to meet the demands of industry. The same conviction and dedication are expressed in Salakhov's portrait of "Kara Karaev" (a reknowned

TAIR SALAKHOV
"FROM SHIFT WORK"

TAIR SALAKHOV
"THE MORNING TRAIN"

Azerbaidzhan composer). In this portrait, which Salakhov painted in 1960, Karaev appears plain yet stern. He is sitting with his elbows on his knees and his hands folded under his chin. Near him is his grand piano, but the room is bare except for this and a partially seen picture on the wall. Apparently Karaev is presented not so much as an individual but as a symbol of greatness. Similar facial expressions are found in Salakhov's "Repairmen", which he painted in 1961. Six men are back to back on the forecastle of a motor launch. They are sitting and looking off into space while waiting for the launch to arrive at the distant shore. Their hands are crossed in ways to hold their coats tight and to protect them from the wind. But there is no interaction between the men, and their facial expressions are neutral. Again in 1967 Salakhov painted his "Women of Apsheron", which depicts several Azerbaidzhan women with impersonal facial expressions. They are standing and looking in different directions. One holds a baby, which is only partially seen. A young boy sits on a lower level in the foreground, and a girl sits on a higher level in the background. An imagery of curved lines forms the ground, which appears to be pocked with holes. This picture particularly lacks human feeling and leans toward an abstractness, which is not typical of other Soviet art.

Many patriotic paintings are seen in Soviet galleries and museums. Boris Ioganson (1893-) represented a scene of the early period of Soviet power in his "Interrogation of Communists", which he painted in 1933. Two communists are standing before a military tribunal in a room with a woven rug and elegant furniture. Military officers are seen from the rear and the side, and the two communists are in the focal point of the picture. Their faces are full with conviction and loyalty to the communist cause. Ioganson's painting "Victory Holiday" portrays the celebration on Red Square at the end of World War II. In the background are St. Basil's Cathedral, Spassky Tower of the Kremlin, Lenin Mausoleum, and the Kremlin wall. The red star is seen brightly atop Spassky Tower. In the sky are yellow and red fireworks and bluish beams of search lights scanning across the way from all angles. In the foreground is a great crowd of peoples, mostly women and children, carrying flags, bouquets, scarfs, and musical instruments. The people wear the costumes of several nationalities to represent the international character of the Soviet Union, and everyone is smiling, laughing, or singing.

War has had an impact on the Soviet Union beyond the comprehension of anyone who has not experienced military invasion and

BORIS IOGANSON
"INTERROGATION OF COMMUNISTS"

occupation. These events are also portrayed in art by many painters and sculptors. One such painting is Feodor Bogorodsky's (1895-1959) "Glory to Fallen Heroes", which depicts a mother and Soviet officers kneeling near the bier of a dead soldier. Dry leaves have fallen across the floor. In the background to the right are two soldiers on guard fully dressed in uniforms and medals and well armed. To their left is a large red star. Alexander Laktionov (1910-) painted a happier scene in his "Letter from the Front" in 1947. In the doorway of a home are a mother, a young daughter, and a young son. Just outside the door are a soldier and a young lady. They are all focusing their attention on the boy who is reading a letter. The mother holds the first page, and the boy continues to read the second page. They are all smiling. The soldier holds a crutch, and one arm is in a sling. The young lady has a red arm band, which indicates her service to the country. The mother and children are dressed plainly, but their clothes are typically Russian. The girl, for example, has a brocade blouse and in her pig tails are red bows. Across the yard are other apartment buildings, a man walking along a path, and in the distance an old church spire. Yet another famous wartime painting is Sergei Grigoriev's (1910-) "At Home with the Family", which portrays a soldier who has returned home. The soldier is sitting in a chair and playing an accordian. Around him are his mother, wife, and children. They are all smiling. The mother sits behind the table, which is set for dinner. His wife leans over his shoulder, and his children are in the foreground facing him. One child is on a tricycle, and the other is sitting on a suitcase. The home is simple, but the family love appears rich and sincere.

Recent paintings of different types include mural-type paintings and other creative productions by artists from several Union Republics. A painting by K. Makaradze, from Soviet Georgia, is called "Georgian Land", which was displayed for the 50th anniversary of the Communist Revolution. It shows a barefoot woman with her arms extended in an indication of gratitude for a bountiful harvest. This indication is further supported by a man standing near her holding some grapes and by a cornfield in the background. On both sides of the couple are other men and a woman holding bowls, carrying a pouch, or having a knife to indicate their contribution to the harvest. For the exhibition for the 24th Party Congress in 1971 the painting "Friendship of Peoples" by N. Fedosov was displayed. This painting shows a group of young ladies of various nationalities holding hands and standing in a large circle. The native costumes of the girls and the wide expanse of fields and a winding river in the background add to the theme fo worldwide peace and friendship. At the same exhibition V. Sidorov presented a painting with a more home-like theme in his "Time of a Cloudless Sky", in which he depicts two boys lying on the grass and reading a book. They are in a large country yard. In the background are houses, farm buildings and two large leafy trees. Not far away is a calf looking at the boys. The message in this painting appears to be the leisurely reading in a peaceful atmosphere rather than an identity of the boys or the place. Other recognized paintings from different Union Republics are those of Salakhov from Azerbaidzhan, Makaradze from Georgia, already mentioned, and Z. Khabibullaev from Tadzhikistan. Khabibullaev painted a picture in 1967 called "Bakhor", in which he depicts two Tadzhik men sitting on a rug spread for a meal. One man is playing a stringed musical instrument, and the other listens. The background of this picture and the place they are sitting are abstract. The colors he uses in his paintings are also unrealistic. In another painting by Khabibullaev which he calls "The Kara-Kul' Meteorological Station" is primarily rolling and swerving lines of purple, blue, yellow, and green with various shades and mixtures of each which represent the high mountains beyond the station. The station itself is in the foreground and is dwarfed by the high mountains both in its size and in its simplicity. This painting and another one called "Shugnanka", apparently the name of the woman in the picture, painted by V. Boborykin, were displayed at the Tadzhik Art Exhibit in 1971. "Shugnanka" is also a display of vivid colors. The woman is dressed in a Tadzhik multi-colored dress of jagged lines of blue, red, green, yellow, and black on a white background and has over her head and shoulders a shawl with large flowers of red, lavender, orange, and pink and leaves of green and yellow on a black background. Under her dress she wears pantaloons with dark blue and red stripes. She is sitting on a rock near a fast-flowing stream. By her side is a large woven basket of reddish fruit, probably tomatoes. The rocks are purplish with blue, white, and green casts streaked along them. The water is whitish with swirls of blue, green, gray, and light purple. The women's face is a golden brown. Her large eyes are neatly made-up, and her lips are a bright red. The multi-colored dress of the peoples of Central Asia come forth in the paintings and dominate the whole scene.

There is really no end in describing the paintings in the Soviet Union. The range of types, themes, and styles is as broad

V. Boborykin "Shugnanka"

as the varieties of peoples themselves. Each Union Republic has its
own artists, both professional and amateur. Their paintings are on
exhibit throughout the country. But Soviet art is for the people and
not for the sake of art itself. Painters are encouraged to produce
creative works which express the positive scenes, which are inspira-
tional and promote the cultural heritage and the contemporary
values of the people. Away from the cultural centers of Moscow
and Leningrad there appears to be a greater variety of paintings.
Various nationalities are encouraged to develop their own art, but
the guidelines of 'socialist realism' extend to even the most remote
areas. It is constantly repeated that "Art is for the People", i.e.
for the enjoyment, proper growth, and inspiration for moral and
social values.

SCULPTURE AND MONUMENTS

The statues, busts, and many works of sculpture throughout
the Soviet Union require a special account on Soviet sculpture. A
tourist was noted to ask when seeing the tourist sights, "Where is
the Lenin monument factory?" The monument work in the Soviet
Union rea ches proportions which compare with any country.
The most striking monument in the Soviet Union and probably
the largest in the world is Mamaev Kurgan (Mamaev Hill burial
grounds) near Volgograd at the site of the worst fighting of the
Battle of Stalingrad in 1942-1943. The tall "Mother-Homeland",
which is a statue of a woman holding a raised sword and turning
back to motion others to follow, stands 170 feet into the air. It
faces stair steps which lead down to a peaceful reflection pool. On
both sides of the steps are rock walls with sculpture work of events
which happened during the Battle of Stalingrad. Other enormous
monuments, small only in comparison with the "Mother-Homeland",
stand in the monument complex. One is a statue of a Soviet soldier
armed with a machine gun. At his feet is the caption "Stand Firm
Unto Death". Another statue is a mother holding her dead son, and
it is captioned "Place of Grief". This whole monument complex
was built in seven years, from 1960 to 1967, and was under the
supervision of one of the Soviet Union's great sculptors, Yevgeni
Vuchetich, and his assistants.
Another leading Soviet sculptor is Nokolai Tomsky, who is
Chairman of the Soviet Academy of Arts。 His work includes the

statue of Mikhail Lomonosov, which has stood at the Moscow State University since 1953. He also has made marble busts of Karl Marx, Sergei Kirov, Nikolai Gogol, and many others.

Sculpture work is also included in the art treasures of the Hermitage, the Tretyakov Gallery, and other galleries and museums throughout the country. Probably the most famous of these are "The Crouching Boy" by Michaelangelo in marble in 1530 and a figure of "Voltaire" by Jean Antoine Houdon in 1871. Both of these sculpture works are at the Hermitage.

Most monuments and sculpture work in the Soviet Union commemorates an event in the history or an outstanding leader. Monuments to Lenin are the most numerous. There is at least one in practically every city. A statue to Bogdan Khmelnitsky, the Ukrainian leader who united the Ukraine with Russia, is at a prominent street corner in Kiev. This statute shows Khmelnitsky charging on a horse. Similar statues are in other cities honoring their heroes. Few are in marble. Other stones are used, and much work is done in bronze.

Monuments to the tsars and those to Stalin have mostly been removed. There is still one of Tsar Nikolai I on a horse near St. Isaac's Cathedral in Leningrad. Not far from there near the Neva River stands a statue of Peter the Great riding his horse on a wave to commemorate his founding of the city with a seaport. For a long time there was only a marble slab over the grave of Joseph Stalin, but now there is a marble bust of him over his grave near the Lenin Mausoleum on Red Square in Moscow. Not far from his grave is the grave of Mikhail Kalinin, the first President of the Soviet Union, and a bust of him has stood there since shortly after his burial. Other busts of Soviet leaders are at their grave sites along the Kremlin wall.

Most of the older statues and monuments which have been retained or built anew are those of the great artists - writers, musicians, and painters of the past. Statues to Pushkin and to Gorky are on Gorky Street in Moscow. Also on Gorky Street is a tall statue to Mayakovsky, revolutionary poet and author.

BALLET AND OPERA

As Vienna is known for the waltz, Russia has been known for its ballet and opera. Russian ballet and opera are acclaimed for their emotional and psychological impact. People from the world

over are attracted to "Swan Lake" and "Sleeping Beauty", two great
ballets by Tchaikovsky, and "Romeo and Juliet" and "Cinderella",
two great operas by Prokofiev. These performances are a part of
the billing every season, and they are always attended by large
crowds of people, many of whom have seen these classics many
times.

Attending a ballet or an opera is a moving and memorable
experience. The plots are usually based on well-known stories
from history, legends, or literature and focused on the struggles
between opposing forces. The story, however, is only a part of
the excellence. The accompanying music attains the highest quality
of symphonic art, and the opera singing or ballet dancing in perfect harmony with the orchestra and the story sends emotional
stimuli throughout the audience. The spectators shudder, weep,
rejoice, and gasp with awe as the performances progress. Every
sense of one's being is touched, and this is what makes the Russian
ballet and opera the great successes of artistic expression.

Mikhail Glinka (1804-1857) is considered to be the father of
Russian composers. Having studied music in Western Europe he
returned to his native Russia to compose an opera based on folk
songs and Russian nationalism. He took for his theme the Times
of Troubles and the beginning of the Romanov Dynasty and named
his production "Life for the Tsar". This opera is now called "Ivan
Susanin" after the name of the man who was credited for saving
the life of Tsar Mikhail Romanov. This opera continued to be
popular in Russia before the Communist Revolution of 1917 and has
resumed this popularity since then under its new name. Glinka's
second opera "Ruslan and Ludmila" has equalled if not surpassed
the first. It is based on a fairy story of young lovers in early Kiev.
Ludmila is taken away from her beloved Ruslan by the wicked
Chernomor. Ruslan and other suitors struggle to rescue Ludmila
against Chernomor and his evil cohorts and against each other.
With magic, choral singing, dancing girls, storms of lightening
and thunder, and intrigue the opera takes the audience through all
the struggles to the final victory of Ruslan and his marriage with
Ludmila. From this children's poem Glinka composed the music
with a courageous Russian spirit and an emotionally rich lyric. By
this means Glinka set the bases and marked the paths for the development of Russian classical opera. From his style and standards
emerged the following, which became known as the "Moguchaya
Kuchka" (variously translated as the "Mighty Mound", "Mighty

Five", and "Mighty Circle"). This group, which included Borodin, Rimsky-Korsakov, Mussorgsky, Tchaikovsky, and others, carried on the creative principles of classical opera and ballet, which were established by Mikhail Glinka.

Alexander Borodin (1833-1887) composed one outstanding opera, "Prince Igor," but he died before it was premiered. The finishing work was done by his associates, Nikolai Rimsky-Korsakov and Alexander Glazunov. Special attention has been given to "Prince Igor" because of its blending together of the history, legends, and folk music of the Russian people. Borodin was a Russian nationalist, and he wanted to preserve the heritage in this opera. The story was taken from "The Lay of Igor's Campaign", as recorded in the ancient chronicles of early Novgorod. To it was added the legends of the Bogatyr spirit and the sense of unity of the Russian people. Much of the music was arrangements and adaptations from the folk ballad "Sparrow Hills" and other folk songs. In this artistic blending and arranging lay the genius of Alexander Borodin.

"Prince Igor" is a tale about a battle between the Russians and the nomadic Polovtsian tribes in the 12th century. In preparing to battle against the Polovtsi, Prince Igor and his men are stunned by an eclipse of the sun, which they take as a bad omen. Prince Igor is taken captive, and the honor or Russia appears to be lost. His wife, Princess Yaroslavna mourns the defeat of her husband, but she sends Ovular (who is half Russian and half Polovtsian) to rescue him. Meanwhile Prince Igor's son is attracted to the daughter of the Polovtsian leader, Konchak, who requests Igor and his son to join the Polovtsy and take their choices of Polovtsian girls as wives. They are tempted by the Polovtsian dancers, but Prince Igor declines the offer to the anger of Konchak. In the evening Ovular comes to the Polovtsian camp and rescues Prince Igor and his men. Once again Prince Igor has the chance to restore honor and glory to the Russian people. He returns to Princess Yaroslavna, rejoices with her and their people before setting out again to fight the Polovtsy. Finally there is the victory for the Russians, and this time Konchak's daughter comes to the Russian camp to marry Igor's son Vladimir. As the opera ends there is a wedding feast and much rejoicing among the Russians. In spite of the temporary setback, the Russians have maintained their honor and have gained victory over the nomadic Polovtsy.

The events of the opera are developed by the musical score. Highlights of the opera are "The Song of the Army of Igor" and

"The Polovtsian Dances." The music for the dances starts with slow, rhythmic movements and proceeds to faster whirling strains. The cheerful melody of "Sparrow Hills" is followed by excerpts from Tatar, Hungarian, and Arabic songs to portray the culture of the Polovtsy. Rushing sounds and loud rumblings climax in a turbulence of slow and peaceful movements and of clashing, dissonant sounds and loud bursts. These different musical patterns were used to identify the conflicts between good and evil, between the Russians and the Polovtsy. Such contrasts have been used by the other composers and have become typical of Russian opera and ballet.

Modest Mussorgsky (1834-1881) worked closely with Borodin to help establish the nationalist tradition of Russian music. His best known opera is "Boris Godunov", based on the drama by Alexander Pushkin concerning the popular leader during the Time of Troubles. Unlike Borodin, Mussorgsky used few folk songs, but his music was based on the folk song idiom. It is said that Mussorgsky's musical work was influenced by every day Russian speech patterns. But he did have a somewhat peculiar approach which involved combinations of modal and tonal elements, which pass from modal to tonal and from one mode to another, much like those of the human voice.

Mussorgsky also composed music for the piano and orchestra, a collection of which he called "St. John's Eve." Later he used this music for a folk opera, "The Fair at Sorochintsy", but he died before this opera was completed. However, this work was revised by Nikolai Rimsky-Korsakov and became the classic production "Night on Bald Mountain" which was premiered in St. Petersburg with Rimsky-Korsakov conducting.

Nikolai Rimsky-Koraskov (1844-1908) helped finish the great works of Borodin and Mussorgsky and composed several of his own operas. These works include "May Night", "Snow Maiden", "Sheherazad", "Mlada", "Night Before Christmas", "Sadko", "Mozart and Saliera", "Boryanina Vera Sheloga", "Servilia", "Golden Cockrell", "The Maid of Pskov", and many orchestral pieces, including the acclaimed "Spanish Caprice." The music of Rimsky-Korsakov was also based on the Russian folk songs, but he added gentle tenderness and poetic charm in his lyrics which were almost pictorial in their expressions. His music is sincere and warm and is appreciated by peoples throughout the world.

His first two operas were "May Night", based on a story by Nikolai Gogol, and "The Snow Maiden", taken from a fairy tale by

Nikolai Ostrovsky. But probably his most outstanding opera was "Sadko", taken from a legend of an ancient minstrel of Novgorod who travels around the world in the search for the bird of happiness. Sadko fights against the Vikings, and he is even opposed by the city fathers of his own Novgorod. From there he goes to the pyramids of Egypt and finally seeks happiness in India. But his search is in vain, and on his return home he enters the fantasy world of the Kingdom of the Deep in the depths of the ocean. Here the music portrays the hostility, bewilderment, and confusion of the mystical world, but it later proceeds to depict the love for the homeland, in line with the nationalism of the Moguchaya Kuchka, as its final theme. In this vein Sadko returns home to Novgorod to find true happiness. The music for the fantasy world is complex, including extensive use of instrumentalism with searching melodies and harmonics. But the music for the real world is simple, with vocal harmony and original recitative. In "Sadko" and his many other works Rimsky-Korsakov greatly influenced the development of Russian and world musical culture. His opera "Sheherazad" was based on the Arabian tale and included lyrics of Arabian music. The tunes of the orchestral piece "Spanish Caprice", likewise, were taken from Spanish dance themes. But the opera "The Maid of Pskov" is a social-historical musical drama which reflects the popular liberation aims of the inhabitants of the free cities of Novgorod and Pskov during the ascension to power of Ivan the Terrible. The music is courageous and rigorous and has a great appeal to the people in the Soviet Union today. The broad spectrum of Rimsky-Korsakov's musical works appeals to peoples of many cultures and persuasions. Rimsky-Koraskov was truly one of the world's greatest musicians and a source of great pride for the peoples of the Soviet Union.

Peter Tchaikovsky (1840-1893) added yet another dimension to the music of the 19th century. He was probably the world's foremost composer, and it was his creative genius that helped identify the ballet with Russia. His outstanding ballets "Swan Lake" and "Sleeping Beauty" have all the characteristics of the opera, but the ballet dancing personifies the emotions expressed in the music. The conflicts between the good and evil in these productions are accompanied by music and dancing which fully depict these forces. The good forces are portrayed by soft, flowing movements in rhythm with peaceful, harmonious orchestrations and song. The evil forces, on the other hand, are portrayed by jerky movements with quick plunges and dissonant music with loud percussion. The synchronization of the dance movements, the music, the lights, and the stage settings takes the audience through all the emotions of the story, not in a melodramatic way but in a truly artistic performance. No words can really express the beauty of these ballets. One has to experience these classics for himself.

"Swan Lake" is a story of Prince Siegfried who goes hunting for swans, but he meets the Swan Queen who appears to him in human form and pleads to him to save her from a curse of an evil magician. This scene is at a peaceful lake. The Swan Queen is white and beautiful. She dances together with the other white swans in harmony with soft melodies. Everything good, beautiful, and true is portrayed in this scene. But the opposing forces of the evil magician introduce a double for the Swan Queen, who for a long time confuses Prince Siegfried, but who appears as a black swan. Her dances are accompanied by dissonant music, and the stage settings are dark and dismal. She represents everything bad, ugly, and false. The deception caused conflict between the opposing forces. Upon the discovery by the Swan Queen that Prince Siegfried has been beguiled by the black swan, she bids farewell to him and plunges into the lake. Prince Siegfried recognizing his mistake also takes his own life by following his lover into the lake. Their deaths somehow break the curse of the evil magician, and Odette is no longer a Swan Queen but a beautiful lady, and Prince Siegfried again lives to join his lover.

"Sleeping Beauty" also uses these contrasts between Sleeping Beauty and the Witch. In the final destruction of the Witch, Sleeping Beauty arises in glory at the kiss of her prince, and the Witch disappears in a puff of fire and smoke as she falls through a hole in the stage. But the music is not taken from folk songs or from his previous compositions. Tchaikovsky's music was original with each work. It was tailored to the story, which he developed into a melody, which is simple and spontaneous. The audience enjoys the music along with the story rather than by recalling familiar tunes. This ability to create melodies was the special gift of Tchaikovsky.

Tchaikovsky's greatness lies not only in the quality of his work but also in the quantity of his compositions. His six symphonies are probably as well known as his operas and ballets. He also wrote orchestral music, popular songs, a cantata, and music for plays. His operas include "Eugene Onegin", "Queen of Spades",

Iolanta", "The Sorceress", and "The Water Nymph". His ballet "Nutcracker" is also performed often in the Soviet Union and abroad. Various musical selections from his works are favorites of many people, and these selections usually include "The March of the Slavs", a marching song based on a Serbian folk song and on the Tsarist national anthem 'God Save the Emporer', "The Italian Caprice", orchestral music based on a Roman carnival, "Romeo and Juliet", an overture-fantasy based on the work of William Shakespeare, and "The Great Sonata" written for the piano.

By the time Tchaikovsky died in 1893 and after the death of Rimsky-Korsakov in 1908 the era of the Moguchaya Kuchka was over. It was several years before there was a rebirth of the musical greatness of Russia. Of course, the great works of the masters were preserved and served as patterns for the next generation of composers. But at the same time the new influences of the Soviet society affected all composers. The first noteworthy ballet after the 1917 Revolution was "Red Poppy" by Reinhold Gliere in 1927.

Reinhold Gliere (1875-1956) is considered to be the founder of the Soviet opera and ballet. His ballet "Red Poppy", now called "Red Flower", is based on a romantic story of friendship between the Soviet sailors and the Chinese which develops when a Soviet ship comes into a Chinese port. Gliere's contribution consisted of mass scenes and popular music, which became the trend of Soviet ballet and opera in the 1930's. Gliere also composed opera music. He worked with Talib Sadykov of the Uzbek Conservatory as his co-composer in the Uzbek opera "Leili and Medshnum" and later wrote the opera "Rashel", in 1942, basing it on the work of de Maupassant, 'Mademoiselle Fifi'. But his great contributions were the ballets, which included the "Bronze Horseman" in commemoration with Pushkin's 150th birthday in 1949, "Taras Tulba", in 1952 after the story by Nikolai Gogol, and "The Daughter of Castille" in 1955, after his earlier ballet "The Comedians", which he revised in closer conformity to the literary source, Lope de Vega's 'Fuenteovejuna'. With these works Gliere bridged the gap between the preceding generation and that of his own.

Closely associated with Gliere was another founder of Soviet ballet, Boris Asafiev (1884-1949). His first noteworthy ballet was "The Flame of Paris", which was based on the French Revolution and its aftermath. He followed Gliere's example in the use of masses of people and popular songs of the times. He used as a motif the singing of the French anthem 'The Marseillaise' and drew heavily

from 'Carmagnole' and 'Ca ira'. "The Flame of Paris" has become
to be considered in the Soviet Union as a model of Soviet heroic
ballet. But probably a better ballet, artistically speaking, was his
"Fountain of Bakhchisarai", which was based on the poem by Pushkin.
In this ballet he followed the style of Borodin by using soft, rhythmic
melodies for the Gurilyov and Maria romance and the harsh, dissonant music for the Tatar Khan Girei. The dancing of Zarema, the
khan's wife, was accompanied by Oriental music, and the Polish
scenes were accompanied by the polanaise, mazurka, and waltz.
In all Boris Asafiev composed 27 ballets and many other types of
music. He became an academician in the Soviet Academy of Arts.
His other most often mentioned ballets are "The Prisoner of the
Caucasus" and "The Heart of the Mountains" for which he drew many
songs and dances from the Caucasus Mountains and hymns of heroism
and courage. Asafiev became known for his cross-cultural music,
which is consistent with Soviet internationalism, and for his tying
in the popular songs of Moscow and Leningrad to show the unity of
the peoples.

Popular songs became a part of Soviet operas and ballet in
the 1930's. Probably the peak of this trend was accomplished by
Ivan Dzerzhinsky (1909 -   ) in his opera "The Quiet Don", which
was based on Mikhail Sholokhov's book by the same name. The
leading song from this opera was "From Border Unto Border",
which was a patriotic, revolutionary song which was the most popular song in the Soviet Union for some time. The literary appeal
of Sholokhov's book and the catchy tune of this song contributed
much to the success of the opera. In addition, this opera was one
of the few attended by Stalin, who gave his official approval and
remarked that this was the first time that the concept of 'socialist
realism' had been put to music. In this sense "The Quiet Don" became a symbol and a pattern for the future development of opera
in the Soviet Union. Dzerzhinsky continued to write operas based
on Soviet reality and the revolutionary past. None really matched
"The Quiet Don", but those worthy of mention are "Mother", taken
from Gorky's work, "Battleship Potemkin", based on the revolutionary activity on this ship during the Communist Revolution, and
"Virgin Soil Upturned", again from the book by Sholokhov by that
name. These operas were very repetitious of "The Quiet Don",
and the marching songs became monotonous.

Dmitri Shostakovich (1906 -   ) is one of the greatest Soviet
composers and winner of several prizes for his symphonies, choral
music, and music for films, but his operas and ballets have not

been so regarded. His first opera "The Nose" was considered to be too abstract and naturalistic. The orchestra produced sounds of trotting horses, the noise of a razor, and nasal sounds by singers holding their noses. Shostakovich's second opera "Lady McBeth of Mtsensk" was more successful, but it was one of the operas attended by Stalin, who was quite critical of both the music and the story. Stalin said the music was dissonant and that the story was animal-istic. In addition, Shostakovich did not abide by the precepts of 'socialist realism' in these operas. He also composed the music for ballets - "The Golden Age", "Bolt", and "Shining Brook" - but these too did not receive the praise of his symphonies. By 1972 Shostakovich had composed 15 symphonies and many musical scores for films. It has been the symphonies which have brought him fame around the world. His 5th, 7th, and possibly the 15th have gained the greatest acclaim. His style is traditional and leans toward the Russian classics of the 19th century. The music is generally simple with much harmony, some dissonance, and many poetic melodies. Most of his music is designed for orches-tras and is not as adaptable to the human voice, but it is appreciated both in the Soviet Union and internationally. He is considered to be a master composer and has somewhat a father image for the younger composers in the Soviet Union.

It was Sergei Prokofiev (1891-1953) who has gained the greatest reputation as a composer of Soviet opera and ballet. He had left his homeland before the Communist Revolution, but he returned to stay in the 1930's. His operas include "Semyon Kotko", "Betrothal in a Nunnery", "War and Peace", and "The Story of a Real Man." Prokofiev wrote several ballets, the most important of which are "Romeo and Juliet", "The Stone Flower", and "Cinderella". It has been said that Prokofiev carried on where Tchaikovsky left off.

"Semyon Kotko", taken from Katayev's story 'I Am the Son of the Working People' was completed in 1939. This story is about a young man who returns home after the First World War. Semyon Kotko is driven from his town by a German detachment, and the town is destroyed. Semyon and his friends, except for his girlfriend who was forced to marry a landlord, leave to join the Partisans. In this opera Prokofiev fulfilled a dream which he had about developing a plot with real human beings experiencing the passions of love, hatred, joy and sorrow. For this he created new music and captured the melodies which expressed these passions. Even though his music was not immediately appreciated, it later became understood and accepted after the decline of the 'popular song' era of opera.

Prokofiev's "War and Peace", after Tolstoy's novel, has been considered his greatest success. He painstakenly interpreted the whole novel in thirteen scenes in his musical composition which took eleven years to write. The main episodes of the novel were presented in the thirteen scenes, each one with melodies peculiar to the scene. He maintained basic chords, often returning to C major, and then combining transitional chords to distant tonalities and deliberate dissonances, including weird, non-harmonic sound effects. In such a way he described the numerous emotions of love, fear, aspirations, longings, and hopes, which are all so prevalent in Tolstoy's writings.

In his ballet "Romeo and Juliet" Prokofiev interpreted with music the great work of Shakespeare in much the same style as he did for "War and Peace." He also used the techniques of Tchaikovsky and Borodin for expressing the conflicts between good and evil and between love and hate. By leit-motifs Prokofiev also identifies each of the characters and their good or evil personalities. "Romeo and Juliet" has received world-wide acclaim. It has been performed at the London Royal Opera House and at the New York Metropolitan Opera House, where it was praised as much as it is in the Soviet Union. The pantomime of the ballet dancers brought fame to Galina Ulanova as Juliet and Alexei Ermolaev as Tybalt. It was brought out clearly that the success of a ballet is a composite work of many artists - the composer, the director, the choreographers, the orchestra, the ballet dancers, the stage crew, and many others. All of these artists working together with the musical compositions of Prokofiev contributed to this great masterpiece.

Prokofiev did not attain the vivid contrasts and characterizations of his first two ballets in "Cinderella", yet it also has obtained regular billings in the Soviet opera and ballet theatres. It was based on the fairy tale by Perrault, which everyone knows, and therefore it has had wide appeal. "The Stone Flower", however, did approach the artistic level of "Romeo and Juliet", even though it was slow to gain its recognition. Prokofiev died before "The Stone Flower" was premiered, and it was several years after his death that a young choreographer, Yuri Grigorovich, gave it the right to be considered a classic, when he produced it with an all-youth cast. "The Stone Flower" was taken from an old Russian legend about a young man seeking permanent beauty. He leaves the real world to carve a flower of stone inside a mountain. The fairy-queen of the mountain tries to captivate him as her servant, but he escapes to find true beauty in the love of his real sweetheart, the girlfriend of his youth. Prokofiev did identify the personalities of the people, both real and fantastic, and Grigorovich brought these personalities to life in his 1957 production of "The Stone Flower".

The reputation of Sergei Prokofiev is known equally well for his piano and violin concertos, his symphonies, and his music for film sound tracks. Possibly his most appealing works were his symphonic fairy-tale "Peter and the Wolf" and his Fifth Symphony. It was the Fifth Symphony, which recalls the music of the opera "War and Peace", the films "Alexander Nevsky" and "Ivan the Terrible", and even scenes from the opera "Semyon Kotko". These works typify the creative genius of Prokofiev as well as the music of his great ballets.

Aram Khachaturian (1903 -   ) is one of the more prominent Soviet ballet composers, particularly since his revision of the opera "Spartacus" in the late 1960's. It was based on the story of a Greek slave revolt against Roman guards in the first century B.C. The ballet is concerned with the conflict between the slaves and the guards, and not only the music and the ballet dancing depict this conflict between light and darkness, good and evil, and true and false, but bright colors of red, blue, and yellow accompanied by loud sounds of drums and cymbals provided an emphasis to this conflict. This ballet was also under the direction of Yuri Grigorovich. Playing the role of Spartacus, Vladimir Vassiliev moves across the stage as a soaring falcon, and even though Spartacus is killed, he is depicted as a courageous and romantic hero who conquers his enemies by his death. He ascends above the guards on their pointed swords in glory. Then in the final scene he lies dead among his friends as his wife, Phrygia, danced by Ekaterina Maximova, leans over his body and raises her arms high in respect and devotion. "Spartacus" was considered one of the leading Soviet ballets in the early 1970's.

Khachaturian composed a ballet "Happiness" in 1939 about an Armenian farm festival and a love affair between two young collective farmers. In 1942 he selected the parts which he liked best and revised and renamed the ballet, calling it "Gayaneh". Again in 1952 and 1957 he revised the ballet, but he kept the new name. The later revisions changed the time to the post-war era and introduced a Russian hero, who leaves the collective farm upon learning that he has caused the death of a friend. But he returns to confess and is accepted by the people.

Actually Khachaturian gained his fame by his symphonies and concertos. His Violin Concerto, 1940, and his Second Symphony, 1943, are considered to be outstanding musical productions. As in his ballet, his concertos and symphonies are greatly influenced by his nationalism and strong patriotic zeal. The Second Symphony was dedicated to those who fought, suffered, and died in the war.

Tikhon Khrennikov (1913 -) has served as the First Secretary of the Board of the Composers Union of the USSR. He has long been an advocate of 'socialist realism' and was one of the few composers who was not criticized severely at the First All-Union Congress of Soviet Composers in 1948. Khrennikov has consistently followed the precepts of nationalism, praise and service to the Communist Party, criticism of the influences of the Tsarist regime and the West, and dedication to simplicity and realism. Likewise he has opposed formalism, cosmopolitanism, and anti-revolutionary revisionism.

Khrennikov began writing operas in the 1930's and followed the 'popular song' trend of the times. "In Storm", based on the Russian Civil War and on the kulak rebellion, was considered to be the better one of the time. But it has the weaknesses of the 'popular song' operas of monotonous marching and unimaginative recitatives. In 1957 he composed another opera "Mother", after Gorky's work, but it too followed the 'popular song' tradition. He used many songs, including 'The Marseillaise', 'Comrades', and his own song 'We've had Enough Sorrow'. He also wrote several popular songs, including those used in the Soviet production of Shakespeare's play 'Much Ado About Nothing'. These songs remained popular for several years.

A promising young composer is Rodion Shchredin, born in 1932, who has gained fame as a pianist and as a composer of ballet and opera. His first ballet "The Hunchbacked Horse", based on a Russian legend, was first performed in 1956 and revised in 1960. His music shows some evidence of a trend away from the traditional. He is considered an eclectic. Part of his style is to use energetic, percussive beats, but he also uses a repetitive lyric with dissonant harmonic combinations. Another typical lyric for him is the chastushka (a two or four line folk verse, usually humorous or topical, sung in a lively manner). This last style was background music for his 1961 opera "Not Just Love." This opera was based on a love triangle between two young people and an older woman, who falls for an innocent kiss by the young man. Each of the three typify Soviet characteristics

- the young man, one who is energetic, but contemptuous of farm life; the young girl, a symbol of beauty and innocence; and the older woman, a manager of the collective farm and thereby a symbol of the establishment. Rather than identifying these personalities by his music, Shchredin uses harmony, dissonance, and the chashtushka to portray their relationships and their interactions. Shchredin has also made a name for himself as a pianist not only in the Soviet Union but also in the West, including his Piano Concerto No. 2 at New York.

Another pianist who has made a name for himself also as a composer is Kara Karayev (1918 -   ) from Baku. He uses Azerbaidzhan music, instruments, and stories. One of his early works was as co-composer of an opera "Motherland", which concerns a soldier on leave during the Second World War at his home on an Azerbaidzhan collective farm. The hero, Aslan, is accompanied by Major Sergeev, and together they portray the harmony between the Azerbaidzhan and Russian people. For this opera Karayev received a Stalin prize. But his more important work was his ballet "Seven Beauties", which is a story that draws a comparison between seven exotic dancers in a fantasy and seven workers in real life and shows the triumph of the real people over the Shah, his evil Vizier, and their false values and fantasy.

Karayev is equally well-known for his symphonies. "Leili and Mejnum" (1947), taken from Azerbaidzhan poetry, was very popular in that republic. He also composed various symphonies, such as "Albanian Rhapsody" in 1954 and "Vietnamese Suite" in 1955. But in 1956 he composed another ballet, which he dedicated to Prokofiev. This ballet was "Path of Thunder" based on South African folk lore and a love story between a black youth and a white girl. Karayev has soft, melodic music, which becomes lyrical and full of passion for the love scene, but their conflict with the girl's father and the other whites is accompanied by harsh, dissonant music. In the conflict the young lovers are killed, but the people rise up against the injustices to them and direct themselves toward the Path of Thunder, the way to liberation. Karayev's music advances the theme of the story, and the theme is fully consistent with the precepts of socialist realism.

A discussion of Soviet composers must include Vasily Solovyov-Sedoi, (1907 -   ) even though he composed only one ballet "Taras Bulba", taken from Gogol's literary work. Solovyov-Sedoi's recognition has come primarily from his composition of popular songs, among which are "Beloved City", "The Komsomol Song",

"Play My Accordian", "Nightingales", and "Midnight in Moscow". The song "Midnight in Moscow" (sometimes translated as "Moscow Evenings") has been popular for more than ten years and has become the theme-song of Radio Moscow. But the ballet "Taras Bulba" also has great merits. It includes flowing melodies of the Ukrainian Cossacks and rhythmic dancing. This ballet may not have the depth and the range of emotional lyrics of the classics, but it has been enjoyed for its melodious music and excellent dancing.

The newer or less well-known composers have written several works which are worthy of mention here. One of these is the opera "Jalil" in 1957 by Nazib Zhiganov (1911 -). This opera is based on a story of a Tatar poet who fought the enemy in the Second World War, was captured, and died in their prison. The introduction of Tatar music and the skill of Zhiganov to inspire sympathy for the poet and respect for Tatar and Soviet nationalism brought awards for Zhiganov and an opportunity to have "Jalil" staged at the Bolshoi Theatre in Moscow, where it was warmly received. Another composer, an Azerbaidzhanian, wrote the opera "Sevil", which was first performed in Baku in 1953. This composer is Fikret Amirov (1922 -), who has received the rank of a People's Artist of the Azerbaidzhan Republic. His opera "Sevil" is taken from a 1928 novel about the attempts of an Azerbaidzhan woman to improve her status in life, but she meets with resistance. Her struggle is represented by the music with leit-motifs and timbres. The climax is a chorus scene in which the heroine is joined by the people. A third composer with potential is Andrei Petrov (1930 -), who has already composed a symphonic poem "Radda and Loiko" after Gorky's poem, and two ballets "Cherished Little Apple" and "Stationmaster". The first ballet was for children and concerned the life of the Russian horticulturist, Ivan Michurin, and his successful experiments with fruits, vegetables, and grains. The second one was taken from Pushkin's work, and it enjoyed a long run in Leningrad.

The success of the opera and ballet also depends so much on the performers, choreographers, directors, and many other people. Any attempt to name them would become a lengthy list or neglect many equally as praiseworthy, but the following ballet dancers have attained such reputations that it is impossible to discuss Soviet ballet without at least mentioning them. They are Anna Pavlova, Vlasav Nijinsky, Galina Ulanova, Alexei Ermolayev, Maya Plisetskaya, Vladimir Vasiliev, Ekaterina Maximova and Mikhail Lavrovsky. These names and several others are among the greatest ballet dancers of all times.

Concert programs, music ensembles, folk choirs, and cho-
ruses are all a part of the Soviet culture. Along with the ballets and
operas these programs are performed every season in the Bolshoi
Theatre and in the Palace of Congresses in Moscow and in opera
houses and concert halls throughout the Soviet Union, e.g. Leningrad,
Kiev, Odessa, Novosibirsk, Tashkent, and practically every Soviet
city. Travelling troupes provide a wide range of productions to
the Soviet citizens by spending short engagements in many cities
and returning to them for repeat performances. The performers are
not only those who are trained in Moscow and Leningrad, but each
Union Republic and some Autonomous Republics have their own
ballet, opera or other musical program which is taken to the cities
along with the classics and most popular ones. Not only do the
Soviet people have the opportunities to enjoy good music and artistic dance, they also have many chances to participate in their local
groups and even travel to many places. National artists and republic artists are titles which are given to those people who excel,
and these titles are greatly coveted. But even more important is
the fact that these musical productions do give the people an exposure to culture in a country in which it is a disgrace to be considered "uncultured."

Abraham, Gerald (ed.), The Music of Tchaikovsky, New York:
   W. W. Norton & Co., 1946.
Barsamova, N. S., Ivan Konstantinovich Aivazovskii; Moscow:
   Izdatel'stvo Akademii Khudozhestv SSSR, 1963, 58 pp.
Calvocoressi, M. D., Modest Mussorgsky - His Life and Works,
   Fair Lawn, N. J.: Essential Books, 1956.
Deineka, A., "Okraina Moskvy 1941 god"; A. Laktionov, "Pis'mo s
   Fronta", Ioganson, B., "Prazdnik Pobedy", Bogorodskii,
   "Slava Pavshim Geroyam", & Grigor'ev, S., "V Rodnoi
   Sem'ye", Ogonyok, No. 19, May, 1970, pp. 16ff.
Deineka, A., "Druz'ya", Ogonyok, No. 16, April 1971, pp. 16f.
Dianin, Serge, Borodin (trans. from Russian by Robert Lord),
   London: Oxford University Press, 1963.
Dolgopolov, Igor', "Bryullov", Ogonyok, No. 52, December, 1969,
   pp. 16-18.
Fitzsimmons, Thomas et als., USSR - its People, its Society, its
   Culture, New Haven, Conn.: Hraf Press, 1960, 590 pp.
Gofman, I., "For a Master Artist - Tair Salakhov", Kul'tura i
   Zhizn', Nov. 1968, p. 32.
Gorin, I. P., Obraz Sovremennika v Sovetskoi Zhanrovoi
   Zhivopisi, Moscow: Sovetskii Khudozhnik, 1969, 251 pp.
Ioganson, B., "Dopros Kommunistov", Ogonyok, No. 5, Jan.
   1971, p. 8f.
Kolosova, Nadezhda, "Tchaikovsky The Spell-Binder", Sputnik,
   #8, August, 1970, pp. 53-65.
Krebs, Stanley D., Soviet Composers and the Development of
   Soviet Music, New York: W. W. Norton & Co., 1970.
Lebedev, P. I. "Dostoyaniye Naroda", Ogonyok, No. 30, July,
   1968, pp. 16-17.
Lebedev, Polikarp, "The Tretyakov Gallery: Treasury of Russian
   Art", Sputnik, January, 1971, pp. 97-114.
Lepeshinskaya, Olga, "Neobyknovennyi balet", Ogonyok, No. 24,
   June, 1968, pp. 16-17.
Likhachova, Irina, "New Shostakovich Symphony", Sputnik, #4,
   April, 1972, pp. 17-21.
Martynov, Ivan, Shostakovich - The Man and His Works, (Trans.
   by T. Guralsky), New York: Philosophical Library, 1947.
Maxwell, Robert (ed.), Information U. S. S. R., New York:
   Pergamon Press, Macmillan Co., 1962, 980 pp.

Nestyev, Israel V., Sergei Prokofiev - His Musical Life. (Trans.
by Rose Prokofieva) New York: Alfred A. Knopf, 1946.
Nisskii, G., "Pokloneniye Prirody", Ogonyok, No. 28, July, 1968,
pp. 8-9.
Obolensky, Dimitri, Art Treasures in Russia, New York: McGraw-
Hill Book Co., 1970, 174 pp.
. . . . . "Our Great Artist - On the 125th Year from the Birthday of
Ilya Efimovich Repin", Kul'tura i Zhizn, Aug. 1969, p. 17.
Paramonov, A., Gosudarstvennaya Tret'yakovskaya Galereya -
Sovetskoye Iskusstvo, Moscow: Izobrazitel'noye Iskusstvo,
1970, 244 pp.
Pekelisa, M. S. (ed.), Sovetskaya Muzykal'naya Literatura, Moscow:
Izdatel'stvo "Muzyka", 1972, 580 pp.
Plotnov, Andrei, "Pravda Nashikh Dnei", Ogonyok, No. 22, May,
1971, pp. 16ff.
Polyakova, Lyudmila, Soviet Music, Moscow: Foreign Languages
Publishing House, @ 1958, 184 pp.
Popova, El'vira, "Talant, Dobrota, Sluzheniye", Ogonyok, No. 27,
July, 1969, pp. 16-17.
Prokofieva, Maria, "Sergei Prokofiev", Sputnik, #4, April, 1971,
pp. 104-111.
. . . . . . "Russian Ballet", Sputnik, Feb. 1969, pp. 52-65.
. . . . . . "Russian Bass - Ivan Petrov", Sputnik, #10, October,
1969, pp. 58-62.
Salisbury, Harrison E. (ed.), The Soviet Union: The Fifty Years,
New York: Harcourt, Brace & World, 1967, 484 pp.
Seroff, Victor I., The Mighty Five - the Cradle of Russian National
Music, New York: Allen, Towne & Heath, Inc., 1948.
Shanina, N. F., Ivan Ivanovich Shishkin, Moscow: Izdatel'stvo
Akademii Khudostv SSSR, 1964, 47 pp.
Suleiman, Khamid, Minatures of Babur-Namah-32 reproductions,
Tashkent: "Fan" Publishing House, 1970.
Suleiman, Khamid, Minatures to the Poems of Alisher Navoi - 32
reproductions, Tashkent, "Fan" Publishing House, 1970.
. . . . "The Arts in the Soviet Union - Special Issue", The Atlantic,
June, 1960.
. . . . "The Hermitage", Sputnik, April, 1971, pp. 78-102.
Tikhomirov, Roman, "Opere - Dolgaya i Schastlivaya Zhizn",
Kul'tura i Zhizn', No. 8, August, 1971, pp. 6-8.
Vasil'ev, F., "V Krymskikh Gorakh", Ogonyok, No. 30, July,
1969, p. 24f.

Vasin, V., "Stadion 'Dinamo'. Futbol"; Fedosov. N., "Druzhba
Naradov"; & Sidorov, V., Pora Bezoblachnogo Neba", Ogonyok,
No. 18, May, 1971, p. 16ff.
Volodarsky, V., "Tretyakovskaya Galereya", Kul'tura i Zhizn',
July, 1968, pp. 40-41.
Zakharov, Rostislav, "Proslavlennyi v Mire", Kul'tura i Zhizn',
No. 8, August, 1971, pp. 8-11.

CHAPTER XIV

SOVIET FOREIGN POLICY

Starting from the 1917 Revolution and extending to the present time the major emphasis of the Soviet Foreign policy has been defense. Aggressive military campaigns were rejected at the time of the ouster of Trotsky in the 1920's. The cessation of hostilities with Germany in 1917 was one of the first tasks of the new government. This action was followed by organizing the army to defend Soviet territory from internal strife and foreign intervention during the Civil War of 1918-1921. After the death of Lenin, Stalin advocated "Socialism in one country" and began consolidating Soviet power. His Five Year Plans were the means of building an industrialized base for this consolidation and for increasing the defensive forces of the country.

Diplomatic agreements were made with Germany in 1922 and with Great Britain in 1924. In 1923 agreements had been made with China. These agreements brought to light another facet of Soviet foreign policy, which is ideological expansionism. The Communist International or Comintern, as it was called, advocated through diplomatic channels, both overtly and covertly, the extension of communism. As differences arose, the diplomatic relations with other countries were strained, but in the early 1930's ideological expansionism was temporarily reduced in scope.

In 1933 diplomatic relations were established between the Soviet Union and the United States of America. In the following year the Soviet Union entered the League of Nations. The theme of the League of Nations, collective security, was accepted by the Soviet Government, and the Soviet delegate to the League of Nations, Maxim Litvinov, became popular in that body by his advocating disarmament.

The pre-war power politics in the middle and late 1930's caused the Soviet Union to act and to react in order to defend its own territory. First there was the non-aggression pact with Germany, but it was accompanied by annexation of territory as a buffer between Germany and the Soviet Union. The annexation of parts of Rumania and Poland and the former Tsarist holdings of Estonia, Latvia, and Lithuania might be classified as aggression or as protective reaction against the threats of Nazi Germany. Attacks against Finland were of a similar nature. This annexation also was accompanied by the Soviet policy of ideological expansionism. After the war these territories became integral parts of the Soviet Union.

The attack of Nazi Germany against the Soviet Union brought into focus all the military aspects of Soviet foreign policy. The former policy of the tsars to obtain warm water ports was re-emphasized. The difficulties in obtaining foreign military aid due to the lack of sea ports became very apparent. Of course, the most basic needs were those of defending the territory and consolidating the ideological tenets within the society. The scorched earth policy was used to slow down the German attacks, and partisan bands were organized to fight against selected units of the invading army. Liberation of occupied territory became a major responsibility of these partisans. But defense of the industry, major cities, and transportation routes was the prime objective for which millions of Russians died during the war. Kiev fell to the Germans, Leningrad was surrounded and blockaded but never fell completely, Moscow repelled the Germans, and Stalingrad, even though utterly destroyed, became the turning point of the war. After Stalingrad the Russian people and the army rose to drive the Germans back to Berlin. Retaliation against the Nazis and liberation of occupied areas, even territories of other countries, became other aspects of Soviet policy.

Liberation meant not only the liberation from military occupation but also from economic control by capitalists. The agreements with the United States and other allies to liberate occupied areas and to establish democratic governments became the means of resuming the policy of ideological expansionism. In this way Eastern Europe, including Poland, Hungary, Bulgaria, East Germany, Rumania, and later Czechoslovakia became socialist democracies and a part of the Soviet bloc of nations.

ADMINISTRATION OF FOREIGN AFFAIRS

Another aspect of Soviet defense policy, primarily a domestic issue, is the relation between the Soviet Government and the Communist Party, on one hand, and the army and police forces on the other. The Soviet Government has always maintained that the armed forces and the police forces are instruments of the government and never masters of it. Officers of the tsar's army were included into the Red Army initially until young communists could be raised and trained to replace them. The purges of the 1930's by Stalin and his officials made this replacement complete. The popularity of military leaders during the war was curtailed after the war so that such men as General Zhukov of the army or Lavrenti Beria of the police never ascended to top government or party positions. The state power has been constantly held by the General Secretary (First Secretary) of the Communist Party and the Chairman of the Council of Ministers of the Soviet Government. Recently the Chairman of the Presidium of the Supreme Soviet has shared this power to a greater degree. But the army and the police have been held subordinate to the Council of Ministers as has the Minister of Foreign Affairs.

Subordinate to the Council of Ministers are the Ministry of Defense, the Ministry of Foreign Affairs, the Ministry of Internal Affairs, the Ministry of the Defense Industry, and the Committee of State Security, as well as the other economic and political ministries. Not only do these ministries and committees answer to the Chairman and the whole Council of Ministers, but the Chairman is responsible to the Politburo of the Communist Party. Decisions of political power are made collectively in the Politburo and strengthened by the Central Committee of the Communist Party. The separate ministries, even the Ministry of Foreign Affairs and the Ministry of Armed Forces, have no autonomy.

The responsibility of the Armed forces and of the diplomatic staffs to the Communist Party is evident further in the structure of these organizations on each level of the organizational chart. Political sections and political officers exert their influence and their control throughout the administrative and functional units of these ministries.

Political activists are attached to units of these ministries to serve as instructors in the policies of the Communist Party and the Soviet Government. These activists also coordinate with the line officers of the diplomatic, military, and police organizations and review their decisions. They act as direct lines of communication to the Central Committee of the Communist Party so that the decisions of functional units can be supported or even countermanded by the Central Committee in order to maintain consistent policies and political control. In effect, this is the concept of "collectivism" and "democratic centralism" in practice.

The Ministry of Foreign Affairs has been delegated the responsibility of maintaining Soviet embassies, consulates, and missions throughout the world. The Minister of Foreign Affairs also works closely with the United Nations and acts as head of the

Soviet delegation to that organization. The various ambassadors and diplomatic officials report to the Ministry in Moscow, which collects, collates, and files data on all areas of the world. The organization of the Ministry is broken down on a geographical basis so that area specialists within the respective sections keep current on the diplomatic, economic, and military activities of assigned countries. Periodic reports and depth studies are prepared by these specialists so that the Council of Ministers and the Central Committee have intelligence reports on which to evaluate policies and make decisions.

The Ministry of Defense has been delegated the authority over the various branches of military service - the army, the navy, the air force, strategic missiles, etc. The organization of the Ministry is further broken down into directorates on a functional basis, such as operations, intelligence, signals and communication, topography and mapping, etc. There are also general directorates on administrative matters, such as general affairs (recruitment, research, and general administration), personnel, military training, equipment, and military justice. Within the Ministry are also the units of the Political Directorate and the Counter-espionage Directorate.

MILITARY AND PARA-MILITARY PRACTICES

It has not been the practice of the Soviet Government to assign large numbers of troops on foreign territory. The major exception to this are the troops in East Germany. Rather than assigning large numbers of Soviet troops in Eastern Europe, the Soviet Government has helped support the local military units within the Warsaw Pact in Poland, Hungary, and other countries. Along with these local military units are Soviet military advisers. Most of the Soviet troops are assigned to military districts within the Soviet Union, and they have been trained primarily to defend their country from foreign aggression.

Professional soldiers are trained in the military academies, but the larger part of the military units are formed from draftees, who are enlisted for two years in the army or three years in the navy. Training is directed not only to the physical development of the soldier or sailor, but it also prepares him to operate mechanized equipment. This training includes the operation of tanks, rocket launchers, artillery, aircraft, missiles as well as trucks, radios, radar, and all the support equipment. The activities of the present-day Soviet soldier or sailor differ drastically from those of twenty five years ago. The industrialization and mechanization have permeated the Soviet military to the same extent as they have the whole Soviet economy.

The military equipment is supplied by the Ministry of the Defense Industry. Rather than military contracts to private companies, as is done in the United States, the military equipment needs are met by the Ministry of the Defense Industry and its plants, factories, mills, and various enterprises. There is close coordination with the other economic ministries under the operation of the Five Year Plans to produce the needs of the military. But the production of military goods is decided by the political party officials so that the emphasis has been on defensive weapons rather than offensive ones.

For land warfare the tank serves as the main military equipment. For the air it is fighter planes armed with missiles, short range and medium range missiles, and anti-aircraft artillery armed with surface to air missiles. For naval operations it is the submarine armed with missiles and the new helio-copter carriers. In addition, the Soviet military relies on medium range and long range missiles for interception of foreign missiles and for retaliation against foreign military attacks.

A study of Soviet military operations seems to leave the impression of a defense posture lacking the ability for a mass aggressive attack on another country. Missiles are sufficient for the initial attack, but there appears to be a lack of the means to transport troops on land, in the air, or on the sea. Trucks and trains are the main means of transporting troops. These methods are best suited for defense rather than offense.

This posture is a reflection of the Soviet policy to denounce military aggression but to favor wars of national liberation. The extension of Communist ideology is considered to be attained better during times of internal strife in other countries rather than as a result of Soviet military aggression. This role, in turn, is not the responsibility of the armed forces, except in an advisory capacity. It is the role of the diplomatic forces and of the intelligence services. The Ministry of Foreign Affairs, as has been mentioned, is responsible for the covert intelligence activities. In this time of a prolonged Cold War and the division of the world into blocs by the Super Powers of the Soviet Union and the United States, the activities of the covert intelligence agencies greatly affect foreign policy.

The covert intelligence activities, both espionage and operations, were conducted within the Communist International (1919-1939) and the Communist Information Bureau (1948-1956) as well as within and outside the diplomatic channels. These activities are also conducted in the military, foreign trade, and news-gathering centers. Coordination with local Communist Party organizations and with defectors within the target country has provided the opportunity for conducting these activities. The Committee on State Security of the Soviet Union is now the major organization for conducting and coordinating these covert intelligence operations.

The Committee of State Security, however, is also subordinate to the Council of Ministers and has not attained a Ministry-level position. It is supervised closely by the Politburo through its own network of political officers within the KGB (Committee of State Security). It is probably even more accountable to political authority than its American counterpart, the CIA.

The Committee of State Security has both geographic and functional directorates. The geographic directorates and their subordinate sections collect, collate, file, and report data derived from both overt research and covert espionage activities. In turn, these data and intelligence estimates are used for operations, which are supervised by the functional directorates. The functional directorates are concerned with training and assigning espionage agents, conducting counter-espionage activities, intercepting communications, encoding and deciphering official messages, and when necessary sabotage, kidnapping of officials, and assassinations. The activities of the Committee of State Security range from the normal research functions of a university or industrial enterprise on one hand, to para-military activities and actual military strikes, on the other.

The hit-and-run strikes of the Soviet Partisans during the Second World War and of the Viet Cong in Vietnam are one of the tactics of underground or covert intelligence operations. Specially-trained military personnel effectively work with the Soviet advisors, who may be KGB agents, to further the policy of the Communist Party both in occupied territories and in war zones. It is in this sense that the Soviet Government can denounce aggression but support wars of national liberation to further communist ideological expansion.

Another aspect of Soviet foreign policy is that of influencing world public opinion. Summit conferences, Soviet bloc conferences, disarmament conferences, and the proposed conference against imperialism are various ways of influencing world opinion. The United Nations also serves as a place for Soviet delegates to expound on Soviet policy. Of course, this aspect of foreign policy is one of the major assignments of the diplomatic officials. A great effort is also spent by the various publishing houses, the film industry, Radio Moscow, and other communications media for influencing world public opinion. The number and variety of Soviet publications in many languages distributed throughout the world is probably greater than that of any other country, including the United States.

The Ministry of Foreign Affairs, the Ministry of Defense, the Ministry of the Defense Industry, the Committee of State Security, the Ministry of Culture, and the various communications media all work together in their own way to defend Soviet territory and to further Communist ideology, which are the main aspects of Soviet Foreign Policy.

The Soviet Government and the Communist Party with their policies have antagonized most countries of the world. Breaking with their allies in 1918 by signing a separate peace with Germany, repudiating all foreign debts of the Tsarist Government, nationalizing foreign property on Soviet territory, and the ideological attacks against religion and capitalism were all affronts to national policies and the personal convictions of their leaders. The advocation of the overthrow of capitalism and the building of communist societies throughout the whole world further conflicted with the interests of other countries. It has seemed to many people that the policies of the Soviet Government were in direct conflict with those of other governments and that all "hot spots" were the result of communist activities.

According to the view espoused by Soviet officials the world has been colonized and exploited by capitalist imperialists and that it is the policy of the Soviet government to liberate people from colonialism and imperialism - not by military aggression but by aiding those who are fighting wars of national liberation. In addition, the Soviet Government's main foreign policy is the defense of its own territory and people from foreign attack. In these two views are contained the various aspects of Soviet foreign policy and the activities within the organizations responsible for furthering that policy.

SOVIET - EAST EUROPEAN RELATIONS

As the Soviet Union liberated Eastern European countries
from Nazi occupation these countries established socialist democratic governments. Poland, Rumania, Bulgaria, Albania, East
Germany, and Hungary were assisted by Soviet advisors to recon-
struct the economy and the society. Austria, Czechoslovakia, and
Yugoslavia followed different courses. Austria was under joint control by the Soviet Union and its Western Allies. Czechoslovakia,
which had developed a high standard of living between the two World
Wars, attempted to re-institute a capitalist democracy. However,
Czechoslovak Communists with the help of Soviet aid changed that
course so that Czechoslovakia also adopted a socialist democratic
government and joined the Soviet-sponsored Cominform in February,
1948. The Cominform was organized in Belgrade, Yugoslavia in
October, 1947 to promote unity among the Eastern European Democracies and the Soviet Union. It was a part of the Soviet policy of
ideological expansion. Yugoslavia soon rejected the concept of the
Cominform and asked the Soviet Union to recall its advisors so that
Yugoslavia could develop an independent course of socialism. This
brought about a rift between the Soviet Union and Yugoslavia which
lasted for twenty years. From 1948 to 1956 the Cominform provided an alliance between the Soviet Union, Eastern Germany,
Poland, Hungary, Rumania, Bulgaria, and Albania.

Soviet ideological expansionism had been countered by Western
Powers in Iran, Turkey, Greece, and other nations as well as in
Eastern Europe. Iran, Turkey, and Greece remained out of the
Soviet orbit, but the organization of the Cominform and Soviet influence in Eastern Europe established a de facto recognition of
Soviet influence in Eastern Europe. But this de facto recognition
did in no way mean de jure recognition by the Western Powers,
which joined the chorus of Winston Churchill with his terms of an
"Iron Curtain" and a "Cold War." This Cold War reached its peak
when the Soviet Union established a blockade of Berlin, which had
been under joint occupation of Soviet and Western Powers. This
blockade of 1948 and the Western Airlift to break that blockade
lasted until April, 1949. The Western Powers, under the leadership of the United States of America, then established the North
Atlantic Treaty Organization to help contain Communist Expansion-

ism in Europe.

The death of Stalin in 1953 and the ascension to power of Nikita Khrushchev caused changes in Soviet-Eastern European relations. During this transition there were attempts to promote peaceful coexistence and friendship. These attempts were countered by some Soviet leaders. Reaction to the North Atlantic Treaty Organization caused the establishment by the Soviet Union of the Warsaw Pact in 1955 to provide for mutual assistance and a unified command among the Eastern European socialist democracies. But this action was followed by Khrushchev's "secret speech" in February, 1956, in which he denounced Stalinism and by the abolishment of the Cominform in April of that year. The year before, Khrushchev had gone to Yugoslavia to help improve relations with that country.

Khrushchev's reforms were interpreted in Eastern Europe as a relaxation of Soviet influence and as a recognition of Yugoslavia's right to maintain its own national policies. This interpretation was strengthened by the re-establishment of Gomulka as the First Secretary of the Communist Party of Poland and the acceptance of some reforms demanded by the Polish people in October of 1956. Hungary too tried to reform its government at that time. But there were those in Hungary who followed the propaganda of Radio Free Europe in Munich to change completely the government. The crisis in Hungary was further complicated by the confrontations of foreign policy of the Soviet Union and the Western Powers in the conflicts between Israel and the United Arab Republic. The introduction of British and French troops into the Mid East conflict provided a justification to the Soviet Union to use troops of the Warsaw Pact in Hungary. The prevention of a coup in Hungary and the maintenance of a socialist democracy there, albeit under different leadership, helped to establish limits on the reforms for socialist democracies under the leadership of Nikita Khrushchev. This action was opposed by Yugoslavia, and the Soviet-Yugoslav rift continued for another ten years. Soviet influence in the socialist democracies of Eastern Europe also continued without much change for the next ten years. Even the change of leadership from Khrushchev to Brezhnev and Kosygin in 1964 did not significantly alter Soviet policy there.

But in 1968 the influence of Soviet Foreign Policy was again re-affirmed in Eastern Europe. Peaceful co-existence and normalization of international relations still did not mean that socialist democracies could run independent courses. Reforms in Czechoslovakia were unacceptable to Soviet policy. The Soviet Government announced that these reforms were actually an attempt for Western Germany to undermine Czechoslovakia and take over its government. To meet this change the Soviet Union lead the Warsaw Pact nations in a military occupation of Czechoslovakia to "normalize" relations there. It was demonstrated to the world that the Socialist democracies of Eastern Europe were being defended both from territorial changes and from ideological changes, the two main tenets of Soviet Foreign Policy.

In January, 1969, the Soviet Government resumed diplomatic talks with Western Germany to improve relations. Other attempts were used to establish a policy in Eastern Europe which was acceptable to European powers and to socialist countries throughout the world. In March, 1969, a Warsaw Pact summit conference was held in Budapest, Hungary to discuss many international events including the problem of European security. The major decision of this conference was to have a World Meeting in Moscow in June, but the June meeting was not united on anything except to plan another meeting to condemn imperialism. However, the major Soviet purpose as far as Europe was concerned was to diminish the threat of West Germany in Eastern Europe. In December, 1969, the Warsaw Pact nations met again in Moscow and issued a declaration that authorized Warsaw Pact nations to have contacts with any European nation, including West Germany. This declaration was followed immediately by diplomatic talks between the Soviet Union and West Germany on a non-aggression pact and the recognition of diplomatic relations. In 1970 these talks continued with many substantive agreements, which prepared the way for the actual agreement on disarmament and diplomatic recognition in 1972.

By 1972 the Soviet-Eastern European Relations had greatly improved. The diplomatic recognition agreements between the Soviet Union and Western Germany were a major achievement. It had helped to give de jure recognition to the Soviet and Warsaw Pact action in Czechoslovakia in 1968 by the government of Western Germany, which had been accused of infiltrating and undermining the Czech government. These agreements also helped to bridge the differences between the Soviet Union and the Western Powers.

Other events, however, weakened Soviet influence in some countries of Eastern Europe. Albania rejected Soviet policies in regard to the Chinese People's Republic, and Albania has become an ally of the Chinese in the Sino-Soviet disputes. Rumania has maintained a somewhat independent position and has approached the position of Yugoslavia in relation to the Soviet Union. But Yugoslavia has improved its relations with the Soviet Union. Tito visited Moscow, and the 20-year rift has been substantially mended, but Yugoslavia still has not affiliated with the Warsaw Pact.

Eastern Europe remains the primary sphere of influence of the Soviet Government. The policies of defense of its territory and of its ideology remain. But the threats against Soviet leadership have diminished both from the possibilities of foreign intervention by the West Germans or the NATO forces and of internal revolts in the socialist democracies. The Soviet Government has attained a desired level of security in Western Europe.

SOVIET-CHINESE RELATIONS

The success of the Chinese Communists in 1949 in establishing the People's Republic of China was also a success for the policies of the Soviet Union in expanding Communist ideology. Economic and military aid continued to be given to the Chinese Communists by the Soviet Government. Territorial differences were openly discussed and mutually resolved as late as 1958. But by 1960 there appeared a beginning of conflicting interests both in territorial disputes along their common border in the Far East and on ideology, when Khrushchev advocated peaceful coexistence with the United States and toured there in 1959. A border dispute between India and the People's Republic of China found the Soviet Union supporting India.

The May, 1960, Summit Conference and its failure due to the U-2 spy plane incident were criticized by the Chinese as being evidence that Khrushchev's coexistence policies toward the United States were a deviation from the principles of Communism. The verbal attacks against the Soviet Union by China increased from that time and really became hostile after the Cuban Crisis in 1962, at which time the Soviet Union withdrew its missiles from Cuba in response to American protests and the agreements between Nikita Khrushchev and President Kennedy of the United States. In the summer of 1963 Mikhail Suslov of the Soviet Poliburo travelled to Peking to attempt to reconcile the differences between the Soviet Union and the Chinese People's Republic. But this conference was not successful. Even the removal of Khrushchev in October, 1964, did not bring about a reconciliation. The Chinese Premier, Chou En-Lai, visited Moscow in November of that year, but his efforts too ended in failure. With the return of Chou En-Lai to China the verbal attacks between China and the Soviet Union became more and more hostile.

        By the time of the 50th Anniversary of the Russian Revolution,
in November, 1967, the ideological rift between the Chinese People's
Republic and the Soviet Union reached a peak. The official New China
News Agency attacked personally Khrushchev, Brezhnev, and Kosygin
and called them traitors to the road of the October Revolution and to
Marxism-Leninism. Previous to this the attacks were against unnamed
revisionists. The Soviet Union, in turn, directed its attacks of dogmatism directly to Mao Tse-tung of China. But the rift was not just
an ideological one. Border disputes were arising, and troops were
amassed on both sides of the border of China and the Soviet Union.
The Soviet Government charged that the Chinese People's Republic
had embarked on an expansionist policy and accused the Chinese of
repeated border encroachments. The Chinese, in turn, claimed that
Soviet territory in the Far East had been taken by unfair treaties
imposed by the Russians on Chinese emporers.
        In 1968 the territorial differences between China and the Soviet
Union resulted in many border skirmishes. In March, 1969, a
battle, admitted by both sides and claiming many deaths, took place
on an island in the Ussuri River not far from Vladivostok. Each
side accused the other of aggression and of plans to occupy its territory. Official protest notes were exchanged, and the fighting continued the whole month of March. Soviet requests for talks did not
receive a response from the Chinese.
        The Warsaw Pact summit conference in Budapest, Hungary in
March, 1969, and the Communist Summit Meeting in Moscow in June
of that year both were concerned with the Chinese-Soviet rift and
fighting. The Soviet Union tried to obtain support of its position at
these conferences, but there was division among the delegates on
both the Chinese and Czechoslovak questions. But the Soviet Union
did obtain in the June meeting a resoltuion to have yet another
meeting of world leaders, both communist and non-communist to
condemn all imperialism, which was understood to include that of
the People's Republic of China. At this June meeting Brezhnev
denounced China and warned that China is preparing for a war against
the Soviet Union. In July the Chinese responded that the Soviet Union
was forming an alliance with the United States to prepare for a war
against China.
        On through the summer of 1969 several hundred border inci-
dents took place along the border of the Soviet Union and the Chinese
People's Republic, not only on the Ussuri River but also at many
other points including the Sinkiang border with Soviet Central Asia.
Finally in October a Soviet delegation flew to Peking to start talks
on the border disputes. The Soviet Union proposed a resumption of

normal trade and diplomatic relations, a cessation on the insulting polemics, and a joint regulation of the common border. But the Chinese continued to demand their claims on Soviet territory.

In April, 1970, it was announced that the Soviet-Chinese talks had reached an agreement on the withdrawal of border troops and the creation of a joint commission to survey and define the 4000-mile border. Following this agreement the difference between the Soviet Union and China turned toward policies in the Vietnam War. The tension between the two countries was greatly reduced, but the ideological differences persisted. Apparently the Soviet proposal was accepted because there have been better relations, the insulting polemics have all but ceased, and the border clashes were discontinued.

The basic question concerning the primacy of Soviet or Chinese leadership of the Communist World Movement has not been resolved. The visits of President Nixon to China and the Soviet Union in 1972 and of Comrade Brezhnev to West Germany and the United States in 1973 have strained the uneasy understanding between the Soviet Union and the Chinese People's Republic. But these visits and the establishment of a United States Diplomatic Mission in Peking have assured both countries that the United States was not conspiring with either for the overthrow or attack on the other. The problem of supremacy still exists, but the hostility has been replaced by a resumption of diplomatic relations and trade. The end of the Vietnam War has also reduced the rivalry for aiding the North Vietnamese, and there has developed a more stable relationship between the Soviet Union and China.

SOVIET-ARAB RELATIONS

Interest in the Arabic peoples on the part of the Soviet Union has probably been enhanced by the large number of Soviet citizens who have professed the Moslem faith and the economic needs for the oil resources found in Arabic countries. But the actual opportunity for better Soviet-Arab relations came with the construction of the Aswan Dam in Egypt in 1956 and with the Arab-Israeli Conflict of the same year. When the United States, Great Britain, and the International Bank withdrew financial support for the Aswan Dam, the Soviet Union stepped in to provide the necessary financial assistance. The Soviet Union also provided military equipment and advisors to President Nasser for the Arab-Israeli Conflict. Since 1956 there has been a great improvement of Soviet-Arab relations, even though the United Arab Republic has continued to outlaw the Communist Party in its country.

Soviet statements have accused Israel of being a capitalist base, supported by the United States, in Arab territory. The victory of Israel in 1956 and again in 1967 has been termed by the Soviet Union as aggression against the Arabs. The problem of the Jews in the Soviet Union and their dissension has also become a part of the issue of Soviet support of the Arabs against Israel.

The Soviet policy of aid to the Middle East has been much broader than that to the United Arab Republic. President Nasser was generally recognized as the leader of the Arab world and did receive well over $2 billion in military aid from the Soviet Union by 1967. However, Soviet aid has also gone to Syria, (both before its unification in 1958 with the UAR and after its secession in 1961), Iraq, Algeria, and Yemen. Attempts to improve relations with Iran, Turkey, Saudi Arabia, and Pakistan have also been met with various measures of success.

In 1955 the Soviet Union recognized Syrian independence, and this action was soon followed with arms deliveries and trade and aid agreements. The Soviet advisors also helped train military officers. After the unification of Syria with the United Arab Republic in 1958, the Soviet economic aid continued for oil development, railroad building, and construction of a dam on the Euphrates River. During the 1967 War and immediately afterwards Syria received arms, industrial equipment for railroads, pipelines and electronic equipment from the Soviet Union.

Iraq started to receive Soviet aid in 1958 after a revolt in that country. The Soviet Union agreed to help train military officers and to give military aid. By 1962 Iraq was dependent on the Soviet Union for military supplies and was receiving much economic assistance for the construction of industrial installations, including a ferro-concrete plant, a clothing factory, and a radio center. Iraq, in turn, fought in Jordan against Israel in the 1967 war and cut oil shipments to the West.

Algeria did not receive Soviet aid in its struggle for independence from France. But the Soviet Union was quick to grant diplomatic recognition to the new government in 1962. This recognition was followed by massive military aid, Soviet advisors, and military equipment. The new president of Algeria, ben Bella came to Moscow in 1964 and received great honors as well as promises for even more Soviet aid. His successor, Col. Houari Boumedienne, although not the favorite of Moscow, did reap the benefits of the Soviet promises for aid. In the 1967 War the Algerian Army joined the UAR against Israel and refused to recognize the cease fire. Afterwards Col. Houari Boumedienne went to Moscow and criticized Soviet neutrality during the war. But Algeria was moving along the socialist path and continued to receive large amounts of economic aid from the Soviet Union. The Soviet Union has helped with a metallurgical complex, a fertilizer factory, oil refining equipment, and mining equipment. By 1967 Soviet aid to Algeria was in excess of $230 million.

Saudi Arabia has not supported the role of the United Arab Republic as the world leader of the Arabs. It has also not established any significant relations with the Soviet Union. The only part of the Arabian peninsula to make an alliance with the Soviet Union has been Yemen.

Yemen was aided by Egyptian troops in its civil war in 1962 and in the establishment of Yemen as a republic. Soviet aid to Yemen had come through the United Arab Republic until the 1967 War, but after that time Soviet planes and ships came directly to Yemen. But economic aid to Yemen has not been substantial. The Soviet Union is interested in Yemen primarily for its strategic location on the southern tip of the Arabian Peninsula on the Red Sea and the Arabian Sea.

Iran plays an important role in the Middle East, but it is outside the Arab community and Soviet influence. Its citizens, even though Moslems, are a different people, more related to the Europeans than the Arabs. Iran has had a long history of hostility toward the Russians and the Soviet Union. Russian troops had occupied parts of Iran during both World Wars, but the Soviet Union did agree to withdraw its troops in 1946. But relations between the Soviet Union and Iran did not improve substantially even with the payment of $8 million and 11 tons of gold to Iran in war debts in 1954. Differences were again made clear when Iran joined the Baghdad Pact (CENTO) in 1955, and the Soviet Union sent several notes to Iran protesting this action. Several Iranian actions, including nationalizing of a Soviet oil concession in Northeastern Iran, signing a treaty of defense assistance with the United States in the case of a Soviet attack, recognizing Israel, and severing relations with the United Arab Republic - all antagonized the Soviet Union. But in the early 1960's an improvement of relations began between Iran and the Soviet Union. In 1965 Iran signed an agreement with the USSR to reconstruct a steel mill complex in Iran in exchange for Iranian gas to be piped into the Soviet Union.

Another strong power in the Middle East is Turkey, which is non-Arabic but Moslem. The history of opposition of Turkey and Russia is very long. Many wars were fought by Tsarist Russia against Turkey for access to the Black Sea. Attempts of the Soviet Union to influence Turkish policies after the Second World War were met with American aid to Turkey, and Turkey has maintained a close alliance with the United States against the Soviet Union during the Cold War. In 1952 Turkey became a member of the North Atlantic Treaty Organization, and in 1955 Turkey joined the Baghdad Pact (CENTO). In 1955 and 1957 the Soviet Union warned Turkey against military alliances with the United States. But in 1955 the Soviet Union and Turkey did begin agreements for economic assistance to Turkey to construct a sheet-glass factory and a caustic soda and calcium plant in Turkey. Even with this economic aid from the Soviet Union, Turkey continued its military alliance with the United States and in 1960 allowed the building of American nuclear and rocket bases in Turkey under strong Soviet protests. In 1961 and 1962 the Soviet Union repeatedly sent protest notes to Turkey denouncing Turkey's participation in NATO and American military maneuvers there. In the fall of 1962 an agreement was made by President Kennedy of the USA and Chairman Khrushchev of the USSR to remove Soviet missiles from Cuba and American missiles from Turkey as a result of a crisis in Russo-American relations. But Turkey continued its economic relations with the USSR and concluded an agreement in 1963 for more trade and for a six-man Soviet delegation to come to Turkey regarding a new hydroelectric plant on the Soviet-Turkish border. The economic and diplomatic relations between the Soviet Union and Turkey continued to improve in 1966 and 1967 in spite of the NATO and American military presence in Turkey. In 1967 the Turkish Premier Suleyman Demirel visited the Soviet Union.

On the Eastern edges of the Moslem, non-Arabic world are Afghanistan and Pakistan. These countries do have largely Moslem peoples, but there is no strong alliance with other Moslem countries. Afghanistan has remained neutral and friendly to its large neighbors, the Soviet Union and the Chinese People's Republic. Afghanistan is an agricultural country with little industry and minimal military or diplomatic significance. Pakistan, on the other hand, is a new state, having gained its independence from India in 1947. Pakistan has opposed India, a Hindu state, on religious and territorial grounds. After the war over Kashmir with India in 1966, Pakistan met with its enemy in Tashkent of the Soviet Union, which acted as mediator for the peace settlement. Since then the Soviet Union has been closer to India than to Pakistan. Pakistan, in turn, has supported the Chinese People's Republic in its border dispute with India. In the war in East Pakistan, which ended in the establishment of the Republic of Bangledesh, the Soviet Union supported India over Pakistan. In 1971 the Soviet Union and India signed a 20-year friendship pact, which further alienated the Soviet Union from Pakistan policies.

The center of Soviet-Arab relations is in Cairo. After the 1967 War the Soviet Union was quick to help the United Arab Republic restore its defense capabilities. By January, 1968, the Soviet Union had spent more than $250 million more on aid to the UAR in arms, jet aircraft, tanks, missile-firing patrol boats, and other military equipment. The Soviet Union also increased its military missions in the United Arab Republic, Algeria, Iraq, and Yemen. In addition, the Soviet Union substantially increased the number of ships it had in the Mediterranean Sea. These ships included three or four heavy cruisers, six missile-firing destroyers, approximately 12 submarines, several LST-type vessels, and various supply and auxiliary vessels. This build-up in the Mediterranean Sea was continued all through 1968 and 1969. In October, 1968, President Nasser flew to Moscow and concluded a new Russian-Egyptian Arms Pact for the delivery in 1969 of 100 to 150 supersonic jet fighters and 500 tanks equipped with an infra-red guidance system.

But by 1969 there were some indications that the Soviet Union was seeking a balance of power in the Mediterranean Sea and was not trying to provoke the United Arab Republic to attack Israel. Soviet Foreign Minister Andrei Gromyko arrived in Cairo in December, 1968, to discourage President Nasser from launching an amphibious invasion on the Sinai Peninsula. Gromyko was advocating a political, rather than a military, settlement of the Arab-Israel conflict. In January, 1969, the Soviet Union asked Great Britain to join in an effort to prevent a resumption of the Mideast war. In this proposal the Soviet Union was advocating a withdrawal by Israel of the territory taken from the UAR in the 1967 War. The Soviet Union also attempted to stop the delivery of British and American jet aircraft to Israel and reaffirmed its position that it had no intention of supporting the Arab drive to push Israel into the sea. But at the same time the Soviet build-up of ships in the Mediterranean Sea continued. In 1970 helicopter carriers added to the Soviet fleet there.

In January, 1970, Nasser flew secretly to Moscow to discuss the military raids that Israel and the Arab states were exchanging. This event was followed by reports of over 5000 Russian troops in Egypt. Also in April, 1970, there were reports that more supersonic jet planes and surface-to-air missiles were supplied the United Arab Republic by the Soviet Union. But the Soviet Union was at the same time striving for a political settlement, which was being discussed in the United Nations and resulted in a 90-day cease-fire, starting in August, 1970. At the end of the 90 days there was another three-month, even though unofficial, extension of the cease-fire in the Arab-Israeli conflict. These positions were fully supported by the Soviet Union.

With the death of President Nasser in September, 1970, there was a re-evaluation of Soviet-Arab relations. The new President, Anwar Sadat, resisted pressure from his advisors and military officials to attack Israel. This action was accompanied by police action against local communists and a decrease in the UAR's dependence on Soviet assistance. In February, 1971, Sadat signed a peace proposal sponsored by the United Nations which included the withdrawal of Israeli forces from Arab territory and the Arab pledge to end hostilities with Israel. Even though Israel rejected this proposal, the United Arab Republic continued the truce. In May, 1971, Sadat re-affirmed his policy by ousting some of his opponents, and reducing the Soviet influence there. But he signed a 15-year friendship and cooperation treaty with the Soviet Union. Then in August, 1970, Sadat further strenghtened his independence from the strong Soviet influence by the establishment of a unified Arab Federation including Eqypt, Syria, and Libya.

Skirmishes have continued along the common borders of Israel and the new Arab Federation, but a renewal of the war has been averted. If it was the policy of the Soviet Union to attain a balance of power as a means of averting this war, then the Soviet policy succeeded. But if the policy has been ideological expansionism, the Soviet Union has failed. In July, 1972, President Anwar Sadat announced that Soviet advisers and military personnel were being told to return home. The Soviet Union confirmed this fact by stating that these advisers had completed their functions. Both countries tried to tide over the apparent break in foreign relations by re-asserting the principles of the 1971 15-year friendship treaty. Rather than being an open break such as Tito and Stalin had 24 years earlier, the United Arab Republic was reducing the reliance on the

Soviet Union by rejecting ideological expansionism but by still
accepting Soviet military aid.

SOVIET-AMERICAN RELATIONS

The foreign policies of the Soviet Union and of the United
Stated of America have been primarily concerned with each other
since the Second World War. Since these two countries have become the two largest military and industrial powers in the world,
many of the international affairs of all countries are influenced by
their foreign policies. They are the contenders for world supremacy
with the extension of republican democracy and capitalism as the
American goal or with the extension of socialist democracy and
communism as the Soviet goal. These two ideologies met face to
face in most international affairs and in the foreign policies of
many nations.

Winston Churchill announced in 1946 that the world was
divided into two camps separated by an Iron Curtain. He was also one
of the first to use the words, "Cold War" to describe the relationship
between those camps - the United States of America and the Soviet
Union. The post-World War II era was overshadowed by the rift
between these powers. The center of attention was first in Europe
with the joint occupation of Germany. But the Soviet liberation of
Eastern Europe and the ensuing establishment of socialist democracies in that area became a major controversy between the USA
and the USSR. The attempted extension of this Soviet policy to Greece
and Turkey was resisted by the United States in the form of the 1947
Truman Doctrine, which became a policy of containment of Soviet
expansionism. Differences in Europe resulted in the formation of
the North Atlantic Treaty Organization in 1949 under the sponsorship
of the United States and of the Warsaw Pact in 1955. This pattern of
collective security was followed by the United States in forming such
organizations as CENTO, and SEATO throughout Asia. The Soviet
Union protested this encirclement of its territory by US military
bases.

This rift further resulted in an arms race with both nations
stretching their national budgets to outdo each other in defensive
and offensive military capabilities. In addition, there was a great
increase in the number of people employed by each country to engage
in intelligence activities. Espionage agents and counter-espionage
agents were dispatched by both powers to practically every country

in the world to gather intelligence data and to check on the activities of their counterparts. Soviet agents in the United States and American agents in the Soviet Union were detected, arrested, and imprisoned or exchanged.

The Korean War (1950-1953) became a test between the Soviet Union and the United States and also set a pattern for indirect activity against each other. The Soviet Union helped arm and train the North Koreans and encouraged them to unify Korea under their leadership. When North Korea invaded the South, the United States reacted by leading a United Nations Army against the North Koreans. This war ended in a re-affirmation of the division of Korea into two zones - the North to be a socialist democracy allied with the Soviet Union and the South to be a capitalist republic allied with and occupied by American forces.

With the death of Stalin in 1953 and the ascension to power of Nikita Khrushchev in 1957, the relations between the USSR and the USA gradually began to change. Khrushchev's program for 'peaceful coexistence' brought about a decrease in tensions, but the animosity between the countries continued.

Soviet leaders respected President Dwight Eisenhower as the World War II American General who lead American forces to meet Soviet troops in Berlin. His pledge to end the Korean War, if elected, was kept, and he had not advocated the occupation of North Korea or a final victory as the solution. Nikita Khrushchev wanted to reduce further the tensions with President Eisenhower and requested an invitation to visit the United States.

This visit was realized in 1959. Nikita Khrushchev came to the United States, talked long with President Eisenhower, toured the country, and agreed with Dwight Eisenhower at Camp David in Maryland to have a Summit Conference of World Leaders in Paris the following year. Khrushchev returned to the Soviet Union with a new spirit of cooperation in some things and of competition in others with the United States. It appeared that his policy of 'peaceful coexistence' was being accepted by both the Soviet Union and the United States. But at that time there was no reduction of military build-up or of intelligence activities.

The May, 1960, Summit Conference failed. Aerial espionage by the USA had been conducted for several years. The Soviet Union had protested the intrusion of American so-called weather planes over the Soviet territory for years. The United States had developed new high-flying U-2 planes, which were being used for aerial espionage in the late 1950's, but the Soviet Union had not been able to intercept them. Until the Soviet Union developed such capabilities there was no discussion of this activity. But in 1957 the Soviet Union developed and launched its first artificial satellite, which had the capability of aerial espionage far beyond that of the U-2 plane. At about the same time the Soviet Union developed a means for intercepting the U-2 planes and succeeded in so doing in the spring of 1960. The bringing down of the American U-2 plane in Soviet territory and the admission by President Eisenhower of its espionage mission was enough to destroy the Summit Conference in Paris. This was the end of the 'Spirit of Camp David' and the postponement for the improvement of American-Soviet relations.

But the improvement of relations did proceed on lower levels. The so-called Iron Curtain began to disappear. Official delegations from both countries started to visit the other country. American tourists were accepted in the Soviet Union, and gradually this tourism became a big business for the Soviet Union. Negotiations were started on trade agreements and on some political issues.

On the military level, however, conditions grew worse. The American installation of missiles in Turkey was countered with the installation of Soviet missiles in Cuba. Khrushchev had announced his support for the liberation of Cuba by Castro. At the 22nd Party Congress in 1961 Khrushchev repeated his condemnation of aggression but continued to advocate wars of national liberation. The Soviet build-up in Cuba was untenable to the United States. President Kennedy protested the Soviet installation of missiles and ordered a blockade of the Havana Harbor. Soviet policy and American policy met a direct confrontation on the high seas near Cuba in October, 1962, as the Soviet ships bearing more missiles approached Cuba. United States and the Soviet Union had installed a direct telephone line, known as the Hot Line, between the respective heads of state to help prevent an accidental beginning of a third world war. By the use of this direct Hot Line the confrontation ended peaceably with the return of the Soviet missiles, the removal of American missiles from Turkish territory, and a general reduction in hostilities between the two countries.

The first major diplomatic agreement between the United States of American and the Soviet Union for limiting the arms race and reducing tensions was the treaty for banning atomic tests in the atmosphere, which was signed by representatives of these two countries and of Great Britain in 1963. This action was followed by another treaty in 1968 to bar the spread of nuclear weapons, and this treaty was signed by the United States, the Soviet Union, and 59 other states. Negotiations continued on related issues, including prohibition of atomic tests under the sea, the limitation of strategic arms, and the establishment of consulates in both countries.

The major foreign policy issue in regard to Soviet-American relations during the 1960's and early 1970's has been the Vietnam War. Vietnam, like Korea, was divided during the Second World War with the northern part an ally of the Soviet Union and the southern part becoming an ally of the United States. The civil war between the National Liberation Front and the Saigon Government in South Vietnam evolved into another confrontation between the United States on one side and the Soviet Union and the Chinese People's Republic on the other. The Soviet Union supplied training of military personnel, arms, and equipment to the National Liberation Front and to the Army of North Vietnam in accordance with the Soviet policy of aiding wars of national liberation. The United States followed its policy of containing communism and gave aid to the Saigon Government. The fighting escalated to include a massive troop buildup of American forces in South Vietnam and air strikes against North Vietnam. The Soviet Union and China responded by increasing their aid and assistance to North Vietnam. In spite of the widespread death and destruction, the war continued without being resolved. American policy changed to bring about a reduction of ground troops and an increase in the air and naval forces. Both the United States and the Soviet Union were committed to policies of limited war. The Soviet Union provided equipment and arms and military advisors but not troops. The United States provided troops in South Vietnam but engaged only in air and naval warfare in the North. Supply routes of North Vietnamese forces turned to Laos and Cambodia, and South Vietnamese forces armed and advised by the American army fought in those countries also. In addition, American intelligence activities, including para-military activity, substantially increased in Laos. With the reduction of American ground forces in South Vietnam there were increased attacks from the North threatening the defeat of South Vietnam. In 1972 President Nixon renewed the bombing of North Vietnam, including the previously out-of-bounds Port of Haiphong. He also ordered a naval blockade of that harbor. Even though the Port of Haiphong was the major route of Soviet aid for the North Vietnamese, the Soviet Union did not retaliate. But it became even clearer that the resolution of this conflict was not to be attained by military means but rather by a political agreement.

The Soviet Union had continually condemned the United States for military aggression in Vietnam, but it has held to its policy of granting support in arms and equipment rather than sending in troops. Both the United States and the Soviet Union were intent on keeping this war from becoming a third world war.

In January, 1969, peace talks commenced in Paris for resolving the differences of the Vietnamese War. These talks continued, were interrupted, resumed, and again interrupted for several years, and little political progress was achieved. The four parties at the peace table, the United States, the Saigon Government, the National Liberation Front of South Vietnam, and North Vietnam did not demonstrate the ability to end the fighting.

In 1971 and 1972, personal diplomacy became a major tool of both the United States and the Soviet Union. The Soviet Union invited West German Chancellor Willy Brandt to Moscow in October, 1971, and negotiations between these two countries brought about diplomatic recognition of each country by the other. Soviet leader Kosygin visited Canada also in October and made new trade agreements with the Canadian Government. This visit by Kosygin was a return invitation by the Canadian Premier Trudeau who travelled to the Soviet Union during the summer of 1971. Communist Party Leader Brezhnev left the Soviet Union for Yugoslavia in late October and substantially improved relations between those two governments. The Soviet President Podgorny travelled to North Vietnam the same month and returned there again in June, 1972, to discuss the Soviet-North Vietnamese relations in regard to the war. Other Soviet visits included those to France, Norway, and Denmark.

The United States also made major state visits. Presidential aid Kissinger prepared the ground-work for President Nixon to visit Peking in February, 1972, and Moscow in May, 1972. The February visit to Peking was mostly a courtesy call without much substantial agreement with the Chinese. But the May visit to Moscow was the time for the announcement of several American-Soviet agreements, including a nuclear arms limitation agreement, a bilaterial trade accord, an agreement on the "rules of the road" for military ships and planes, and plans for joint ventures in scientific research and space exploration. Discussions on the war in Vietnam did not bring about such dramatic results, but agreements were made for further attempts on both sides to end the war. This last agreement was demonstrated by Podgorny's visit to Hanoi in June, 1972.

The Cease-Fire in Vietnam in January, 1973, marked a beginning of better relations between the Soviet Union and the United States. President Nixon then announced that 1973 was the "Year of Europe," which implied an improvement of relations with the Soviet Union. In May of that year Brezhnev visited West Germany, and Chancellor Willy Brandt announced that "peaceful co-existence" had become "productive co-existence" as a result of the trade agreements he made with the Soviet Union. Then in June, 1973, Brezhnev came to the United States for an official visit. Further trade agreements were made, including the sale of Pepsi-Cola in the Soviet Union. "Productive co-existence" also became the new relationship between the Soviet Union and the United States.

Soviet and American foreign relations had substantially improved since 1956, but there had been no major change in the basic positions of the two governments. The Soviet Union still was dedicated to the defense of its own territory and that of its allies and to the concept of ideological expansionism, including that of wars of national liberation. But there was much evidence on both sides that an all-out war must be averted and that foreign policies should rely heavily on diplomatic and economic means rather than on military ones. But the Soviet Union, as the United States, relied on the concept of a balance of military power, supported by propaganda to gain world opinion, as the guarantee of its national security.

Christian Science Monitor, Boston: 1967-1968.

Dallin, David I., Soviet Espionage, New Haven: Yale University Press, 1955, 558 pp.

Ellison, Herbert J., History of Russia, New York: Holt, Rinehart and Winston, 1964, 586 pp.

Furtsev, V. K. (ed.), Noveishaya Istoriya (1939-1971), (2nd ed.), Moscow: Izdatel'stvo "Prosveshcheniye", 1971, 254 pp.

Garder, Michel, A History of the Soviet Army, New York, Frederick A. Praeger, 1966, 210 pp.

Izvestia, Moscow: 1967-1973.

Kolkowicz, Roman, The Soviet Military and the Communist Party, Princeton, New Jersey: Princeton University Press, 1967, 385 pp.

"Moscow Summit", Newsweek, May 29, 1972, pp. 34-55.

"Moscow Globetrotters," Newsweek, Sept. 20, 1971, pp. 43-45.

Mosely, Philip E. (ed.), The Soviet Union, 1922-1962 - A Foreign Affairs Reader, New York: Frederick A Praeger, 1963, 488 pp.

Pares, Bernard, A History of Russia, New York: Alfred A. Knopf, 1966, 611 pp.

Penkovsky, Oleg, The Penkovsky Papers, Garden City, New York: Doubleday and Co., 1965, 411 pp.

Pravda, Moscow: 1967-1973.

Razgildeyev, Gennady, (Soviet Exchange Scholar), Lecture at the University of Missouri-Rolla, Rolla, Missouri: September 12, 1968.

St. Louis Post Dispatch, St. Louis, Missouri: 1967-1973.

Salisbury, Harrison E. (ed.), The Soviet Union: The Fifty Years, New York: Harcourt, Brace & World, Inc., 1967, 450 pp.

Schneierson, Vic (Trans.), Soviet Foreign Policy - A Brief Review, Moscow: Progress Publishers, 1967, 285 pp.

Seth, Ronald, Unmasked! The Story of Soviet Espionage, New York: Hawthorne Books, 1965, 306 pp.

Walsh, Warren Bartlett, Russia and the Soviet Union, Ann Arbor: University of Michigan Press, 1958, 640 pp.

Whiting, Kenneth R., The Soviet Union Today, (revised ed.), New York: Frederick A. Praeger, 1966, 381 pp.

Wolfe, Thomas W., Soviet Power and Europe - 1945-1970, Baltimore: The John Hopkins Press, 1970, 516 pp.

CHAPTER XV

THE SOVIET CITIZEN

A few characteristics of the Soviet citizens prevail whether
the people are Russian, Uzbek, Ukrainian, Georgian, Tadzhik,
Buryat, or any one of the many national groups in the Soviet Union.
They seem to be friendly, energetic, and enthusiastic. They have
positive outlooks, drives for self-improvement, and willingness to
help others. People in public places push in crowds in the stores
and one the busses, but they take their turns standing in line to
make purchases. They hurry walking from place to place, but they
slow down while making purchases or while working on the job.
Of course, it is difficult to generalize about the characteristics of
249,000,000 people, but these things seem to be common throughout
the country. Yet many of these characteristics may fit people anywhere. The Soviet citizens are ordinary people, not too much
different from Americans. It may be as a Moslem monk said in
Tashkent, "We are all the same. Only our languages are different."
Khrushchev advocated the "creation of a New Soviet Man,"
which was to be accomplished through education and work. The
effect of this program, which is still in operation, may alter the
behavior of the people. There are signs in the schools, in industrial
plants, and at collective farms listing the moral codes, the obligations and responsibilities of the students/workers, and the incentives for increased achievement or production. The drives for self-
improvement may be stimulated by these signs, the competition
among groups, and the incentives promised. Other attitudes may be
formed through education and by social custom. It is difficult to
say how far the program for creating a New Soviet Man has gone.
The hospitality of a brigade leader on a collective farm in
Samarkand was attributed by him to his Moslem religion. His statement was that his religion was to invite the stranger in, feed him,
and give him a place to sleep, if needed. He and other Moslems
maintain this type of hospitality, but so do Russian people in
Volgograd and Pyatigorsk. Friendliness and hospitality seem to be
a widwspread virtue of Soviet citizens rather than of any particular
national or ethnic group.
Morality is both taught and practiced in the Soviet Union. The
moral codes are taught in schools and are listed on bulletin boards
in many public places. Morality is also enhanced by the position of

432

the government on anti-social behavior and by the absence of porno-graphic literatures, sex films, night clubs, and other commerciali-zation of sex. Night life in public places usually stops at 11 p.m. Dance orchestras stop at that time, restaurants close, and motion pictures end. Except for people going to work on night shifts, there are very few people on the streets after midnight.

Anti-social behavior is rarely published in the newspapers and then only in general terms in short notices. Soviet citizens claim that there is little crime, almost no political dissent, and few social problems. Drunkenness is recognized as a problem. Many people drink wine, cognac, vodka, and other drinks, but there is little drunkenness in public places. People lose their jobs after coming to work drunk repeatedly. This does occur, but it is impossible to know the frequency of this problem and other anti-social problems.

But the paternalistic nature of the Soviet society has encouraged its citizens to be friendly, courteous, and helpful but also to be re-served and guarded against close relationships with new acquaintances, particularly with foreigners. The organized collectives have also re-enforced these relationships and caused the members of the col-lective to be very close to each other, but it is difficult to develop lasting friendships with people outside the collective. Young adults are immature for their ages for the same reasons. The paternal relationship with their teachers or work supervisors and the close relationships in educational, work, and social activities with those in their collective tend to shelter young adults from individual com-petition and strife.

The absence of real discussions on controversial issues also shelters the Soviet citizen. Not only is there the absence of propo-nents of capitalism, religion, or individualism in their discussions, but there is also the strong belief that everything printed by the Soviet Government is true. They are taught that Communist teachings are synonomous with objective science. Their scholarly publications first discuss the fallacies of the Western scientific approach and then praise the Communist scientific approach as the true course to knowledge. The Soviet citizen learns to accept what he reads and what he is told as being accurate and is sheltered from making any decisions concerning the accuracy of ideas new to him.

The paternalism is particularly evident in the Soviet news-papers. Articles and pictures of Western life are portrayed in nega-tive terms, and articles and pictures of life in the Soviet Union are portrayed in positive terms. Having their thinking directed in this way the Soviet citizens develop the positive outlook on life and become convinced in the theory and practice of the Soviet society.

Soviet citizens believe that they have a one-class society with no rich and with no poor. They also believe that their society is moving ahead faster than any other society. Consistent with this thinking is the belief that any deficiencies in their society were caused either by the backwardness during the time of the tsars or by the destruction during the time of the war. They also believe that these deficiencies are being overcome in a systematic order according to the popularly accepted five year plans.

The positive attitudes of the Soviet citizens become a part of their ego. In turn, they become very defensive against any criticism and are alienated as much by criticism of the society or the philosophy as by criticism of their personal attributes. Soviet citizens are proud of their knowledge of their own life and of world conditions. They cannot accept the fact that they are being trained to follow superimposed teachings rather than to become active leaders in discovering a new and better life. Introspection is not an acceptable type of analysis, and attributing their behavior to anything other than the stated objectives is completely foreign to their concepts of self. In fact, they are very much offended by persons who explain their behavior by their personal attributes and individual desires.

There is another side to the social behavior of Soviet citizens though. In groups they react quite differently. They do assume roles naturally as any other people do. The de facto leader is not always the de jure leader. There are respective roles assigned to each member of the collective, but personality differences do cause the people to accept different roles. As in Western groups, there are social leaders, intellectual leaders, and even scape goats. The scape goat is blamed for lack of achievement by the group. And both natural leaders and designated leaders do gain a role of superiority over people in the group and those outside of the group. This feeling of superiority is particularly evident by people in large crowds in stores, on buses, and even on busy streets when these people dominate themselves over other members of the crowd. Tour guides are the most obnoxious this way.

Yet another aspect of a Soviet citizen is the private view of himself. This view is seldom shared with other people and is a spark of individualism. They may resist participation in a demonstration or a work project for other than the stated reasons. Some people say privately that they believe in God. It may also be admitted that they really know very little even about life in their own country. Some recognize racial differences and ask themselves about their being a

Jew, a Gypsy, or a Tatar. But with others they will not discuss these feelings and resent others who do. When a Soviet citizen does confide with another person about such things, he demands that the other person tell no one about their conversation. This type of privacy is guarded very closely, and even the Soviet Government professes to guarantee the privacy of one's own home. This reason is the one stated for not having public telephone directories in the Soviet Union.

The personal prejudices of Soviet citizens are also seen in their public behavior. Consumers do not prefer Soviet literature, music, and art. The demanded items of this sort are the classical (pre-revolutionary) works and the foreign imports. Rather than relying on one newspaper for the news, many Soviet citizens buy five or six papers, e.g. the national, the regional, the youth, the vocational, the sport, and the literary newspapers. One man was seen to glance at his newspaper, which on that day contained only a speech by Brezhnev, and throw it down in disgust. But other people sublimate their personal feelings with too much drinking, too much eating, and other types of indulgences.

But the side of the behavior most often seen of a Soviet citizen is the joyful, carefree, and sincere interaction with other human beings. He may be walking down the street eating an ice-cream sandwich during a snow storm. He may be pointing out the pictures of his friends who are listed on the honor board, or he might be giving a stranger directions to his destination and accompanying him part way there. Or he may be sitting on a bench in a train station eating a hard-boiled egg from the lunch he just bought from the food stand. There are so many aspects of life in the Soviet Union. But sincerity in human relations is evidenced in the common usage of the adjective "prostoi" (genuine, simple) in speaking of other people. A "prostoi" person will not accept a gift without giving one in return, but he is usually first to offer his gift when seeing off or welcoming people. He will want you to take his picture and to have you send him a copy. But he will not want you to take pictures of places he considers restricted or to do anything else which may be harmful to his homeland. When another person falls or injures himself, he reprimands him and advises him to be more careful next time. He is self-reliant and also expects other people to be so.

FAMILY RELATIONS

Family life in the Soviet Union is based on love and concern for each of the members of the family. The concepts of "free love" and those of "taking children away from partents" are not a part of Soviet life. Husband and wife are married in official ceremonies after having had a blood test and having received a license. Children live with their parents. Parents are instructed to care for their children and to feed and clothe them. Out of love for their children and from social pressure, parents provide a good family life for their children and teach them to adjust to family beliefs and social teachings. Parents are responsible for their children until they attain the legal age of 18.

When a couple wants to get married they go to ZAGS (the registry bureau) to obtain a license. They must present a medical certificate and their passports. Then there is a waiting period before they are married. This waiting period is prescribed by law, and it may also depend on the availability of housing for them. When they are ready to marry, they make an appointment at a wedding palace. Even if there is a church or private ceremony, there must also be a civil ceremony so that the wedding can be officially recognized.

The marriage ceremony and the dinner are festive events. Relatives and friends go with the couple to the marriage palace and wait for their appointed time. The bride has a wedding dress, usually white, and the groom wears a suit. They are well dressed for the occasion. Usually other couples are there to be married, and they take their turns. Attendants direct the couple to the room where the marriage is to be performed. The couple enters the room and is followed by their group. As the bride and groom approach the table, where sit three people, a judge and two lay judges, the others in the group stand back to witness the marriage. On both sides of the table are flags, flowers, and decorations. The atmosphere of the room is pleasant and gay.

The actual ceremony is simple. A few questions are asked by the judge. The couple pledges loyalty to the government and to each other. Promises are made to each other, and the groom gives his bride a ring. They kiss each other, and they are pronounced married. The information from the license is recorded, and the couple is congratulated by the three people performing the ceremony and by their relatives and friends. Then an attendant directs the group into an adjoining room where they have a dinner prepared for them.

The dinner at the marriage palace may be the big celebration, or the couple may have this dinner at home, in a restaurant, or at another place. It has been traditional in the Soviet Union to have big feasts, group singing, and dancing at the dinner celebrating the marriage. Tradition also holds that this event should be at the home of the bride, but there are variations of this.

Some people rent taxis to take the couple and their group from the wedding palace to the bride's home. These cars are decorated with strings of flowers. The whole process - the wedding, the entourage, the dinner, and the seculsion of the married couple - is a happy and memorable event.

Some married couples may still have to live with relatives until they obtain housing for themselves. The housing shortage has been greatly alleviated though, and the husband and wife now generally move into an apartment or an individual house.

One or two children per family is common in the Soviet Union, particularly in the cities and among the Russian people. Rural people and the people in Central Asia, particularly the Gypsies, tend to have more children.

The mother has some time off before and after the baby is born. When she returns to work, she may take the baby to the nursery at her place of employment or leave him with a relative or friend to care for him. The nursery has one or more doctors and some nurses to take care of the babies. The mother is permitted to have time off work to breast-feed the baby.

After work the mother brings the baby home. This way children spend much of the time during the first three years with their mother or with a family member at home. When the child is three he is eligible to go to kindergarten. His mother or father, whoever leaves last for work, takes the child to the kindergarten, which may be in the apartment house area or at the place of employment. However, the kindergarten also is not obligatory, and many children continue to be cared for by their grandmother or elderly aunt. When the parents arrive home they bring their children from the kindergarten or the baby tender to their own home. The children then stay in the house or the neighborhood to be with the family or neighborhood friends. They can play in the apartment house yard and ride the swings or merry-go-round or be in the house with their parents.

On the days-off of one or both parents, the children spend the time with their parents. They may go to the park, to the zoo, or to other places of recreation. Of course, many children stay home during this time and help their mothers in the apartment. Rural children have a cat or a dog and can play with them. Pets are rare in the cities. But city children do have good playgrounds.

Special attention is directed toward children by the society. Other children are instructed to help take care of younger ones. Parents are reminded to carry out their obligations to their children. Child neglect is a serious offense in the Soviet Union. In extreme cases the children become welfare cases and are placed in institutions with orphans.

Parents buy toys, games, and dolls for their children. In large cities there are special stores, "Children's World," which sell clothing and toys for children. Department stores also have large sections with dolls, toys, books, games, etc. for children. Children are given things to play with. Christmas is not celebrated as such by most Soviet citizens, but New Year's Day is celebrated in almost the same fashion. Grandfather Frost is the Russian Santa Claus. He wears a red and white costume, and he brings gifts for the children. Large fir trees on New Year's Eve are decorated much in the same way as a Christmas tree. Family members and friends exchange gifts at this time too.

In the Parks of Culture and Rest and in other locations there are street stands, which rent bicycles, tricycles, peddle cars, and similar vehicles for children. Parents pay only a few kopects for their children to have one of these for an hour or two.

The relationship between brothers and sisters is lacking in many Soviet homes, because there is only one or two children in a family. When there is more than one child, usually there is an age span between them. Children do not have the opportunity to be close to brothers or sisters in most Soviet homes, particularly among those who live in apartment houses. Even in the small wooden homes in the cities there are few children. Only in rural homes or among non-Russian families are there more than two or three children in a family. For these reasons the close friends of children are outside the home, and at home a child may be lonely for companionship. Of course, he can invite his friend to play with him, but this is done for short periods of time. Most of a child's recreation comes from the organized group outside the home rather than from his own arrangements. Small apartments, heavy school assignments, housework, and busy out-of-home activity schedules, and the lack of brother or sister at home deprive a Soviet child of close friendships with people his own age in his home environment. The home then becomes an environment of parent-child relationships, which may be closer for these reasons. But this relationship could be either child-centered or parent-centered rather than provide child-child companionship. The effect is that Soviet children receive great attention from their parents both in the form of discipline and in the form of love.

The Soviet family eats quite well. They do not have prepared cereals or many of the other prepared or frozen foods which are available to Americans. They prepare their own soups, breads, casseroles, and drinks. For breakfast they may have porridge, which is similar to Cream of Wheat or cracked wheat, or boiled rice. Fried eggs, scrambled eggs, or omelets are also common breakfast foods. Sour milk, which is about half way between buttermilk and yogurt, is also served for breakfast. Cider takes the place of orange juice as a breakfast drink, and tea replaces coffee.

There are a variety of breads in the Soviet Union. Dark bread (whole wheat and rye flour) is probably the most common. A light bread, which resembles French bread, is also very common. In the Georgian Republic there is a special type of sour bread, which is baked in a round loaf. All the breads are tasty, and they are eaten at every meal usually without butter or jam. Sometimes marmalade is served with the bread.

For lunch and for dinner soups are usually served. The lunch may be eaten at the place of employment and is usually the biggest meal of the day. Borsch is a cabbage and red beet soup, which also contains strips of beef, pork, and fish and vegetables, including onions. Borsch and other soups are usually served with a scoop of sour cream. Solyanka is another popular soup. It consists of cabbage, bits of meat (bologna, beef, pork, and fish), onion, dill pickles, and sour cream.

Along with the soups people usually eat a salad, which may be a cole slaw or a sliced cucumber and chopped green onion salad. They are garnished with sour cream. Sardines and other fish also are used to make salads.

A common meat dish is boiled rice with bits of pork. This dish is spiced and served with a meat patty, usually pork. A fancier meat dish is two beef chops served with creamed carrots, red cabbage slaw, and French fried potatoes. Another one is beefsteak, which is a piece of fried meat with a fried egg served on top and garnished with red cabbage slaw. It is also served with French fried potatoes.

Sturgeon, carp, and many other fish are eaten regularly in the Soviet Union. Fish are usually boiled rather than fried.

Pirozhki (turn-over pies) are also a part of the regular diet. Usually these turn-overs contain chopped meat and onion. They can

439

be bought from street vendors, in cafes, in restaurants, or almost any place where food is served. It is usually served at home too. Pastries are served with the ice cream. There may be cinnamon rolls, custard filled rolls, or frosted rolls covered with chopped nuts.

Tea is served at almost every meal. When coffee is available, it is usually the Turkish variety, i. e. it is thick and strong and served in a small demitasse cup. Water is almost never served with meals. In its place may be mineral water (carbonated water) or compote (the sugar water from canned fruit with a few pieces of the fruit).

Of course, the broad spectrum of foods in the Soviet Union is impossible to be discussed in a page or two. But the foregoing does give a picture of common food of the Russian people. Russian food is not as spicy, and the desserts are not as sweet as in some other countries. The other nationalities, particularly the Georgians and the Tatars, like spicy foods and use lots of onions in their food preparation. All through the Soviet Union one can buy different varieties of shashlik (shish-ka-bob). In the east it is made from lamb, and in the west from beef. Shashlik is usually spiced and may have a lot of green onion.

The other living patterns of the family are similar to peoples in other societies. At home the children study, while the parents read the newspaper or watch the television, until bed time.

YOUNG PEOPLE AND RECREATION

Young people in the Soviet Union enjoy themselves much like young people everywhere. They watch soccer and ice hockey games, go swimming and sunbathing, and camp in the woods, attend movies and the theatre, dance, sing, and eat and drink. They also enjoy walking, hunting for mushrooms, or just strolling along a river bank. But to a greater degree they sunbathe, go for long walks, and attend the theatre more than their non-Soviet counterparts.

Physical exercise and good health are highly regarded values. Recreation is as much for health as it is for enjoyment. A good tan is also a sign of good health. Physical endurance is another mark of achievement. A Soviet citizen gains much enjoyment by being tan, strong, and physically active. The acquiring and having these traits have become a form of recreation in itself.

The center of city recreation, however, is at the Park of Culture and Rest. Each city has one or more such parks, which differ from the other parks with trees, flowers, and fountains. A Park of Culture and Rest is the community recreational area. It has theatres, movies, dance halls, rides (ferris wheels, etc.), open-air lectures, group singing, places to buy eats and drinks, and many other attractions. There are always large groups of people walking in the park, particularly in the evenings. They sit and listen to a lecturer talk about world events or sit and participate in the group singing. Trouble-makers are asked to leave, because these events are taken seriously by the audience and participants. People may come and go leisurely, but all the activities close at 11 p.m. The crowds start to dwindle by 10:30, and only a few people are still wandering through the park after 11:15.

Many Soviet citizens just go walking along the streets, by a river or lake, or through the parks. The walking itself is their recreation. Of course, the association with their family and friends while on these walks add to the enjoyment of the exercise and the views of the river, the fountains, the flower gardens, and statues.

Motion picture theatres are well attended. The admission fee is only 50 kopecks. These theatres usually have a snack bar or even a restaurant, where people waiting for the next show eat and drink and at some places dance. The buildings are often quite elaborate. In some theatres there are paintings, figurines, and stained glass windows. However, not all motion picture theatres are this highly decorated. Some places have plain halls with movable, wooden chairs. Even so, there is usually a good crowd at the movies.

Motion picture films may be Soviet-made or they may come from India, Europe, or the United States. Foreign films are dubbed in with Russian dialogues. These films are often stories of crime episodes or musicals. The Soviet-made films are generally historical stores, based either on the Second World War or on the novels of the authors of the last century. Recently there have also been produced some light comedies, based on family quarrels or misunderstandings between friends.

The stage theatres also play a significant role in the Soviet Union. Ballet, opera, and rama are a part of the Russian heritage, and these performances are made available in cities throughout the Soviet Union. The Bolshoi Theatre and the Palace of Congresses in Moscow, and the Kirov Theatre in Leningrad are probably as widely known internationally for their ballet and opera as any theatres in the world. But these performances are not limited to the large cities.

The Palace of Congresses (in the background), churches, and spires in the Moscow Kremlin.

The Palace of Culture in Volgograd. (The banner reads "The present generation of Soviet people will live under communism.")

Each city, town, or collective farm has a stage theatre. For a nominal fee - ranging from one ruble to three rubles - a person can see these performances. The admission cost varies with the performance and with the seat in the theatre. These theatres also range from the modern Palace of Congresses in the Kremlin to a plain hall with a stage on a collective farm. There are also large theatres with artwork in the halls, restaurants in the ante rooms, stained glass, and pillars. Palaces of Culture are of this type and are quite elaborate.

There are both local theatre groups and the nationally-known travelling troupes from Moscow, Leningrad, Kiev, and the other large cities. Ballet and opera are usually the works of the great composers of the last century, but there are also operettas and amateur performances. Variety theatres present such performances and also drama and comedies.

The stage theatre plays a greater role in the lives of the Soviet citizens than it does in the American society. The major difference is the extent of these performances throughout the country. In addition, people of all ages and from all walks of life attend the theatre quite regularly. The theatre is a source of great pride for Soviet society as well as a popular form of recreation for its citizens.

Other types of performances, such as the circus, puppet shows, choirs, and dance groups are also presented throughout the country. Exhibits and museums for art, economic achievements, folk lore, famous persons, minerals, flowers, and handicrafts are in each Union Republic. Admission to these performances and exhibits is free or may cost a few kopecks. Soviet citizens go to these attractions, stop off at these places while taking their long walks, or are conducted there in groups of tourists, pioneers, or some organization.

Sports stadiums and swimming pools also attract many people. Soccer is by far the most popular sport, but Soviet citizens also play hockey, basketball, and tennis. Golf and bowling are practically unknown in the Soviet Union. Swimming is very popular both at the public pools and at the beach. Pools are marked off for competitive swimming, but at the beach there is more sunbathing or leisurely swimming.

Fishing and hunting are also very popular. Fish constitutes a large part of the diet, and people go fishing both for food and for recreation. The vast river systems provide this opportunity for people throughout the whole country. Hunting, however, is not quite as freely available. People have their own fishing equipment, but the use of guns is more restricted. Guns are usually the property of the trade union or a society of hunters, and a person uses a gun when he participates in a hunting trip with other members of the union or society.

Young people participate in most of these activities. It is more common for them to go in groups rather than just two persons. This is true for both single persons and married persons. The groups may be small, three to five persons, but seldom are there just two persons and almost never just one person going alone.

Dating couples often go with a group to cafes or restaurants, where they eat, drink, and dance. Of course, they go to performances and exhibits, but for an evening event at the restaurant, the ballet, the opera, and a drama they dress up. Day time activities are less formal. Also evenings at the Park of Culture and Rest, at a movie, or on a walk are casual.

Affection is rarely displayed in public places. Kissing is generally restricted to persons in love with each other and then usually in privacy. During the time of Stalin, kissing was not permitted on the movie screen, but even though that restriction has been relaxed, promiscuous kissing is condemned by the society. Occasionally signs of affection, including kissing, are seen in public places, but usually young people do not walk arm in arm or even hold hands. Holding hands is considered childish. Walking with arms around each other is crude.

Public facilities and natural resources provide the opportunities for recreation for all ages. Wholesome recreation is advocated for good health and enjoyment. It is part of the government policy regarding the "right to rest." Behavior which detracts from good health and wholesome enjoyment is socially unacceptable. There are no night clubs, no burlesque shows, and no houses of prostitution. Instead, there are clubs of the trade unions and professional societies and public restaurants, where people eat, drink, and dance. In these places there is a good atmosphere, and people have the music of a live orchestra. Sometimes a person may drink a little too much and have to be restrained by his friends, but rarely is there any public disturbance. Then too, the evening ends at 11:00 p.m. so that people can return home before midnight.

Most of the activities of the Soviet young people though are organized by their educational institutions, the Komsomol, or the trade union. This is true both for social activities and work projects. One sees this paternalistic nature of the society in all phases of life in the Soviet Union.

Educational institutions supervise both the academic programs and the social activities. The academic programs are rigid, and the teachers and students cannot deviate from the teaching plans. The students also have little opportunity to change the programs or to improve the conditions. They get along with few blackboards, chalk rock to write with, and no duplicating equipment, no waste baskets, or no water fountains. The social programs also lack the input of the young people for improving them. Generally student dances are supervised by the teachers to the dissatisfaction of the students. Rest periods between every third or fourth dance are used for games supervised by the teacher in charge. These games are lotteries or guessing games with small prizes for those who win. Of course, this time allows a rest period for those who are tired from dancing, but it also causes many students to leave the dance. Students don't care much for the music, unless they can get their own combo to play jazz or foreign music.

The Komsomol has many meetings and work projects for the young people. These activities are also supervised by adult leaders. Even when a student is selected as a delegate to a regional or national meeting, he has no opportunity for input. At these national meetings there is no input requested and no social activity provided. The participants only listen to the talks of the leaders and follow their instructions. These meetings are more like pep assemblies which are to enthuse and motivate the participants.

The directed activities of the youth in academic, social, and political programs take most of the time of the young people. In addition, young men are involved in some military training and girls in training for military nurses through the DOSAAF (so-called Voluntary Association for Assisting the Army, Aviation, and the Navy).

The rigidity of these programs apparently is a part of the overall program to create a New Soviet Man. If so, this man becomes an occupationally-oriented worker with a good knowledge of his own specialty but with little practice to exercise his own initiative. He also has little understanding of other disciplines and points of view. He becomes a follower rather than a leader.

For example, a student who is becoming a history teacher studies little besides history. Every class is a history class, except for a class in Marxism-Leninism and possibly another class for a reading knowledge of a foreign language. His language class is not taught by teachers in the language department but by special teachers in the history department who teach the language only for history students in a way designed for them specifically, i.e. reading history.

The lack of emphasis on creative work for the young people stifles their initiative. Reading, listening, and speaking are the main requirements for participation, and few people learn to write well. Written work is seldom required at the institutes, and mediocre work is accepted. Even the teachers resist written work. Only the specially talented people are encouraged to write, draw, or create artistic works. Of course, this trend extends even to professionals, who are guided by the Writers Union or the Union of Artists and restricted by the precepts of "socialist realism."

Young people do not really have much free time. Their studies, their political and social club meetings, and their work assignments take most of their time. When the people do have free time though, they do get together with their friends for an evening. They invite a few friends to their apartment, where they eat, drink, and dance. Eating and drinking are favorite pastimes. These events are not comparable to Western cocktail parties. There are fewer people. They eat more. And they sit and talk rather than stand. However, the event serves the same recreational purpose.

Quite a few students live in institute dormitories. Life there has a special character. Young men and girls live in separate rooms, but their rooms are on the same floor, and they spend lots of time together. Of course, the dormitory is supervised by a house mother (komendant), a duty lady or guard who checks on people going and coming, and a student chairman of the dormitory collective. Regulations prohibit loud noises or radios late at night and prohibit drinking alcoholic beverages. But the students do play table tennis, play cards, dance, and do have good times. They prepare food for themselves and their friends and have little parties in their rooms. There are dining halls and buffets provided, but these little parties are something extra for their enjoyment.

There are dispensaries in the dormitories, and other students, who usually live at home, come to the dormitory for two weeks or a month to receive treatment or have rest in the dispensary section of the dormitory. Many of these students come for the recreation at the dormitory rather than for medical treatment.

Students do receive stipends for spending money. Of course, the education is free, but they need extra money for food and clothing and for recreation. Their parents provide them an extra 20 or 30 rubles a month for this purpose. This help is enough to care for their needs, and students do not have part-time jobs to help them with their schooling.

Educational and social opportunities are below standard for those living in smaller towns and in agricultural communities. Higher education, of course, is only available in the larger cities. But the secondary schools and the kindergartens are maintained largely by the enterprises, where the parents of the students work. Also the cultural facilities and parks are financed the same way. Uncertified teachers are hired to teach in these areas, and the quality of other social services likewise suffers due to the lack of qualified leadership.

In the summer and at other assigned times students are organized into work brigades to help pick berries, harvest tomatoes, or do other work. At these times they also have recreational activities, such as soccer, swimming, hiking, picnicking, etc. They are supervised during these times by a teacher, who is responsible for their work and their safety. When the young people break the regulations, the teacher is reprimanded or punished. Of course, the teacher, in turn, corrects the young people involved.

Young people are also punished for minor crimes in a variety of ways. The deprivation of privileges may be used for the least serious offenses, but for more serious offenses they are separated from their collective and assigned to other work. Some of them are assigned to work under the supervision of an adult at an industry or at a collective farm. The term of this work may be several months or a year. The most serious offenses and repeated offenses cause the person to be sent to a youth colony or detention camp.

But most of the behavior problems of the students are solved through the counseling by the other students in the collective and by the supervising teacher. Students, either formally or informally, are paired off and do watch each other's behavior. Much of this big brother or big sister relationship comes automatically after the continued indoctrination for acceptable behavior in educational, social, political, and cultural affairs. The result is that there are really few behavior problems among the Soviet youth.

Movies and television shows receive a lot of attention by young people. Soviet films are produced to entertain and to teach people at the same time. All films carry messages of proper behavior and proper attitudes. Patriotism and defense of the motherland and of public property are the most common messages. But people are also advised not to become drunk. Short features show the dangers of being drunk. One film depicted a young couple who drank and later killed a man by running over him with their car. Detective stories never praise the criminal. The spectator always knows who are the "good guys" and who are the "bad guys" in Soviet films. There are no sex films. There may be a scene of a naked girl in swimming, but there are no pornographic or suggestive scenes. On the contrary, the spectator is instructed to honor and respect other people and to defend them. He is taught that evil, hate, war, and death are parts of life, but he is also taught to endure and to overcome these things even to the loss of his own life.

RELIGION

Few Soviet citizens attend church regularly. Social pressure is very strong against active participation in churches. The law prohibits the teaching of religion to children, and those who do attend church lose privileges and opportunities in employment situations and in social activities.

But there are those who do attend church. Since the Russian Orthodox Church was the state church before the 1917 Revolution, most Russians who attend church go there. The Soviet Government also recognizes the Russian Orthodox faith as a religion and considers other faiths to be only religious sects. This attitude of the people and of the government does give some strength to the Russian Orthodox Church. In most cities there is at least one Russian Orthodox Church, which is active and has services on Sunday and possibly on other days for those who have to work on Sundays. These churches are usually packed with people, most of whom are retired. But there are also some young people and a few middle-aged people.

Since the teaching of religion to children is prohibited by law, there are no Sunday School classes. The church service is limited to a vesper-like service, in which the priest chants a few passages and the people respond with a chant. There may be a choir, which sings a few songs, but there is no communion or sacrament passed among the congregation. The priest may deliver a short sermon, but it too is partly spoken and partly sung. The people all stand. There is no place to sit down. Around the church are prayer stations with icons and candles, where the people stay after the service to say a prayer and light a candle.

The absence of books, even song books, is evident at the churches. The few books that are available are cherished by the members. It is not uncommon to see an elderly lady reading from an old, tattered book of Bible stores to a group of other old people. This happens in the church yard after the service.

Russian Orthodox Churches are usually kept clean and neat. They are beautiful inside and out. They are distinguished by the onion domes, which are usually painted blue. There are also a number of spires. But inside the church the walls are painted with religious paintings and icons. The ceilings also have pictures of apostles and saints. Usually there are pictures of Christ, and a reproduction of the Last Supper in most churches.

Russian young people who come to the churches say they are curious. They have been told that religion is a superstition, and they cannot accept the teachings. But they do exclaim about the beauty of the churches.

Moslem mosques also are located in many cities, particularly in Central Asia and in the Caucasus. They have a round dome, also usually painted blue. Alongside the mosque is a tall minaret, from which a monk calls people to the prayer meetings.

The Moslem faith was widespread in Central Asia and other parts of the Soviet Union. There are quite a number of Soviet citizens who now profess the Moslem faith. There are even some who say that they are Moslems and at the same time members of the Communist Party. The attitude of the Soviet Government is more lax with the non-Russian, Moslem population. This attitude may be related to the close Soviet ties with the Arab world.

There are many Moslem mosques in Tashkent. Many of the Uzbeks live closely to their Moslem faith. The most evident example of this is that they continue to live in mud huts and refuse to move into apartment houses. They claim that their teachings state that they should live close to the ground.

But there are restrictions against the Moslems. The veil is prohibited. The status of women has been changed. Girls attend school and are included into the labor force in the same way as other Soviet women.

Moslem services are also prayer services. There are no places to sit down, except for the prayer rug each member has. The walls are plain. There are no pictures. If there is a picture of a Moslem leader, that picture is covered during the services. People take off their shoes when coming into the mosque also. The Moslems are quite strict about their behavior codes. They want their mosque to keep the sacred atmosphere.

Moslems are also strict in their personal habits. They do not smoke or drink. They emphasize love toward their neighbors and toward strangers. High morality and sexual purity are also emphasized.

Other religions in the Soviet Union include Judaism, Georgian Christians, Armenian Christians, Roman Catholics, Baptists, Seventh Day Adventists, and others.

Judaism is restricted due to the ties with the Jews in Israel. One of the reasons for the greater freedom of the Russian Orthodox Church is its lack of political ties outside of the Soviet Union. The recent activity of the Zionists to encourage Jews to emigrate to Israel has also complicated the relationships between the Soviet Government and Judaism.

There are some synagogues though. One in Tbilisi is very active. Services are held every evening there. The synagogue is very beautiful, particularly on the inside. There are stained glass windows, candles, plaques with hebraic writings. And there are pews for the people to sit during the service. The rabbi has his place on a raised platform in the center of the synagogue, and the men sit in the pews around him. The women sit in the balcony.

There were a large number of Jews in Tbilisi, many of whom have already emigrated to Israel. They fasted during the time of the education payments so that they could raise money for helping certain ones go to Israel. But still the Jews said that they could conduct their services quite freely in Tbilisi. Apparently, there are fewer restrictions in the Georgian Republic than in other places in the Soviet Union.

Stalin allowed greater freedom to the Georgian Republic during the years of his rule. Churches in the Georgian Republic benefit from this freedom, and there is still some carry-over from that.

The Georgian Christian Church is the main benefactor of that extra freedom. It was also the state church of the Georgian people since before the time of the Kingdom of Georgia long before the 1917 Revolution. Actually, the Georgian people received Christianity and had a church before the establishment of the Greek Orthodox Church and of the Roman Catholic Church. Missionaries had come from Jerusalem and taught the Georgians Christianity. This tradition of religious faith has been difficult to counter.

There are lots of Georgian Christian Churches in Tbilisi and in other Georgian cities and villages. Their services are very similar to those of the Russian Orthodox services, but there seems to be a more mystical nature to them. The priest remains behind a screen and his voice could be accepted as the voice of God.

The buildings of the Georgian Christian Church appear to have an upside-down funnel for their spire. The churches are quite plain otherwise both inside and outside. There are also no places for the people to sit down.

The Armenian Christian Church also pre-dates the Orthodox and Catholic Churches. Its center, of course, is in Erevan, but there are also Armenian churches in the Georgian and Azerbaidzhan Republics. They are similar to the Georgian Christian church but there are more pictures of religious scenes on the inside walls of the churches.

The Roman Catholic church is tightly regulated due to its ties with the Vatican. There are few Roman Catholics, except in the Baltic republics. Its services are also limited to the mass. No classes are allowed, and there are no parochial schools.

The protestant churches also do not have any opportunity to grow. Missionary work is prohibited. The Baptist Church in Moscow has a good attendance on Sundays, but the services there are primarily sermons. This Baptist Church has also become a place for foreign diplomats and tourists to attend. In this sense it has become a show place.

There are enough churches throughout the Soviet Union to give evidence to the official statement that there is religious freedom in the Soviet Union. However, there are not enough churches for very many people to attend. Restrictions against teaching and missionary work also limit the growth of churches. The Soviet Government can claim that religion is dying out due to the educational programs in the country. It is said that only the old people are attending church and that the newer generations are rejecting religion. This would indicate that within another 25 years there would be no religion in the Soviet Union. However, it has been more than 55 years since the 1917 Communist Revolution, and there are still many churches. In fact, there are just about as many churches as there were 25 years ago, when the same statements were being made about the dying away of religions. There is now some concern about the vestiges of the past on the part of the Soviet officials. There is also much evidence for the survival of religion in the Soviet Union in spite of the restrictions against it.

Some religious practices have taken different forms and could be maintaining the religious significance or replacing it. Christmas is the main example. New Year's Day has replaced Christmas, but the celebration is almost the same. Starting about the 15th of December there are stands for selling Christmas trees or New Year's trees, whatever a person wishes to call them. Practically every family buys a tree and decorates it in his home. The decorations include lights, tinsel, and other ornaments, just like in other countries. The tree remains in the home generally beyond the New Year's Day and possibly to January 7th. In this way one can celebrate the 25th of December, the 1st of January, or the 7th of January. The 7th is the Christmas day according to the old calendar and is observed by the Russian Orthodox Church.

Not only the trees, but also Grandfather Frost (Santa Claus) is there to give presents to the children. Adults give each other presents too. School is out over the New Year's holidays, and about all for Christmas is there, except for the religious services, which a person could have at church or privately in his own home. At kindergartens there are programs for the children just before the New Year. Grandfather Frost comes and gives the children candy and toys. The parents come and have their children dressed up for the occasion. There are few differences between these programs and similar ones for children in American churches. The main differences other than the lack of religious stories is the presence of fairy stories about animals and legendary characters. Some children wear animal costumes, including the bunny rabbit (reminding one of Easter) and witch costumes (reminding one of Halloween).

Another carry-over from religious practices is the honoring of the dead. This is noted particularly at war memorials. In a rotunda at Volgograd there is an atmosphere similar to that in a religious cathedral. At this rotunda are the names of the war dead listed on the walls all around. In the center of the rotunda is a stone hand holding a gas flame, representing the eternal nature of man (not of the soul, but of the generations of man). But the significant things are the behavior and attitudes of the people who come to honor their dead. These people come many times. As they come into the rotunda, they remove their hats and walk quietly around the rotunda. During this time organ music is playing. One sees tear drops in the eyes of the people. In response to the author's comment that this was a religious experience, a Soviet citizen reacted negatively, but when he changed the words to a "spiritual experience," the Soviet citizen agreed. Each time people come to these war memorials they satisfy a spiritual need.

The moral concepts of religions are available within the pioneer and komsomol teachings. Soviet children are taught to be a friend,

452

comrade, and brother to the other children and to all people. They are taught honesty, respect for persons and property, and moral purity. In place of their devotion to God they are taught patriotism and respect to leaders, particularly to Lenin. In a sense, Lenin is their prophet, and his writings are their scripture.

The concepts of the eternal nature of the soul, the existence of God, and revelation (including the Bible) are rejected by Soviet teachings. The lack of this understanding is the major weakness of Soviet teachings and practices in regard to religious teachings. But there is also a lack of the social benefits of religious worship. Soviet people know other people in their collectives very well, but these people usually are roughly the same age, have the same interests, and are similar in many ways. Without regular attendance in a church the Soviet people do not get well acquainted with a number of people of different ages, different occupations, and different interests. This lack of exposure to a variety of people could tend to restrict a person's perspective on life and to limit the number of friends he has. Such a situation is a reason for the immaturity of the Soviet youth and the narrow attitudes of the adults.

POPULAR DISSENT

Dissent and the control against it appear on the surface mostly in literary and artistic works. The Writers Union, the Union of Composers, and the Union of Artists are the main watchguards against dissent in these areas. Nothing with any significant dissent is permitted to be published in the Soviet Union. Socialist realism is the guard against dissent.

Freedom of speech, of the press, of expression, and of religion and the right to demonstrate do not include the right to dissent against decisions of the Soviet Government and of the Communist Party. In fact, there is very little opportunity for input into the decision-making processes. With the belief that the teachings of Marxism-Leninism are based on objective science, the Soviet citizens consider dissent to be an advocation of nonscientific and false concepts. Such dissent is believed to be anti-social and wrong.

But Soviet citizens do have complaints against the established order. Some say that there is no good music in the Soviet Union. Others complain about the shortage of consumer products and their difficulty in obtaining enough money to buy the things they need. The lack of safety precautions at work and particularly during air flights is another complaint.

Without the opportunity to dissent, many people resort to ways of withdrawal from reality. The two most common ways are heavy drinking and neglect of responsibilities. Drinking has become a real problem. People come drunk to work or don't come to work due to drunkenness. For this reason workers are being restricted against acquiring liquor. Liquor is not sold after 5 p.m. Also movie films propagandize against drinking, and neon signs tell the people to drink more tea and coffee.

But the neglect of responsibilities also reaches family life. Desertion and divorce are very common occurrences. Husbands leave their wives, and in some cases both parents leave their children, who then become welfare cases.

The magazine Krokodil has satire against problems in Soviet society, but other publications have very little of it. Newspaper accounts of problems rarely appear, and when they do appear they are hidden on the back page in a very small article. Even accidents of airplanes, where all the passengers and crew are killed, are treated in this way. The main news in the papers are about economic production and political meetings.

Public criticism is aimed at situations in capitalist countries. Even scientific books start with a criticism of "bourgeois" scientific methods and results before they explain the "objective" methods of Soviet scientists. But there is no criticism of the works of Soviet scientists.

When Americans think of dissent in the Soviet Union, they think of the Soviet Jews. But there are two groups of Soviet citizens, at least, who are worse off than the Jews. The Gypsies have a situation which is probably worse than any other national group.

The Soviet Government has tried to get the Gypsies to conform to Soviet standards. The Gypsy appears willing and agrees to work and send his children to school, but in a few days he hits the road again. When he is brought back to work and to send his children to school, he again agrees, but soon he is gone again. This behavior has been repeated so many times that the Soviet Government has given up on the Gypsies who won't conform. These Gypsies now continue to roam and to live off the land. They are seen at train and bus stations, in public parks, and along the roads. They tell fortunes, beg, and solicit. For stealing they are punished. The lot of Gypsies has become very poor.

Another group of people who have a harder than average life is the Tatars. They have historically been enemies of the Russian people and have been considered as savages, in somewhat the same way that Americans have considered the American Indians. Many Tatars still are farmers and herders, and they are considered to be Cossacks or cowboys, who are looked down upon.

Of course, there are a few Gypsies and some Tatars who have become good Soviet citizens and work in industry. Those who do this are awarded properly and pointed to as examples of equality of races in the Soviet Union. But the lot of Tatars, though not as bad as that of the Gypsies, is not equal to that of other nationalities.

The restrictions on the Jews have to do with religion, Zionism, and other things. Jews have not been allowed to have newspapers in their own language. Early in Soviet history they were assigned a reservation in the Soviet Far East, but few Jews went there, and most of them returned to their former homes. They have not grouped together so they could have an autonomous oblast in the Western part of the Soviet Union, but small groups of Jews live in many places. But many Jews have become well educated and received responsible positions in the Soviet society.

But the problems of all Soviet citizens, whether Gypsy, Tatar, Jew, Ukrainian, or Russian are enough without going into the special problems of particular groups. The organization of all people into collectives on the basis of their schooling or employment is a type of regimentation not known in other societies. The requirement for all people over 16 to have identification booklets (passport), which have a picture, vital statistics, and other information about the person is another restriction. This problem is multiplied by requirements to have other booklets (Komsomol, Party Member, Trade Union, car driver's, car owner's, etc.).

Of course, these restrictions only regulate rather than prohibit movement from city to city or from job to job. Soviet citizens can travel quite freely, and there is no identification check for travelling on local transportation, on busses, or on trains. But the check is made when one buys an airplane ticket, presumably for the security or rather identification of the person in case of a crash.

Every society regulates crime, and the Soviet Union is certainly no exception. Youth colonies are set up to serve as detention camps for young people. These hooligans, as they are called, live and work in these barracaded camps. They do have school programs for them, and life is not too hard for them, but they are confined to the camp. Adult offenders go to Correctional Labor Camps, where conditions are similar to those in Youth Colonies, but their lot is harder. They do manual labor and are detained for a longer period of time, which is based on the seriousness of their offenses. More serious criminals are sent to prisons, and for some crimes people receive capital punishment. But crime is not legitimate dissent in any society.

The average Soviet citizen has little contact with the police. He sees police jeeps going down the main streets with the siren blowing, but he sees little action of the police against his fellow citizens. The most that he sees usually is a drunk being taken to jail. This drunk may be roughed up a little by the militiaman, but this is considered a social problem rather than dissent.

Censorship does effect everyone though. Few citizens could know much about the extent of reading of mail or the tapping of telephones. Foreigners in the Soviet Union know that both exist on their communications. There is a definite censorship of the letters which go to or come from abroad. Letters that don't pass the censor just are not received, and each letter shows signs of being moistened to reseal the letter. International phone calls are monitored too. Noises are not beeps, but there are sounds which reveal the presence of a monitor.

The checks on foreigners leave a question concerning the extent of checks on Soviet citizens. This question, unfortunately, cannot be answered. Mail does travel very slowly in the Soviet Union. It does seem incredible that every letter or even 10% of the letters could be read in transit, but the delay in mail delivery allows time for some checking. The author has no knowledge concerning letters within the Soviet Union which do not reach the addressee.

It is doubtful that all telephone calls are monitored too. But some monitoring is possible.

Soviet citizens do not confide with foreigners over the phone, through the mail, or seldom in buildings. They do this primarily while walking with the foreigner in a park or along a river bank. The reminder that this talk is not to be mentioned to anyone is evidence that there is some danger to the Soviet citizen if his dissent became known. His precaution also indicates that there is on his part a belief that his conversation might be heard other places.

Too close association with a foreigner is also avoided by Soviet citizens. New friendships with foreigners most of the time are quickly terminated. Few Soviet citizens continue to be close friends with them.

Foreign students at a dormitory claimed that their Soviet girl friends were told to leave them alone after the second date. Most of these students had never had more than two dates with the same Soviet girl.

But censorship takes another form too. Certain books disappear from bookstores and from libraries. One such book is the novel by Solzhenitsyn, "One Day in the Life of Ivan Denisovich." It disappeared from the libraries in the late sixties, and copies are not available anywhere.

Most Soviet citizens, with whom the author talked, know nothing about SAMIZDAT, the underground publishing group, or about Andrei Sakharov or other dissenters, who are mentioned in the American press. Either they haven't heard of this dissent or they don't want to talk about it even during discussions on other problems. The author believes that they do not know about these things, because there is no way for them to find out, since these things are not mentioned in the Soviet press.

The main reference to Soviet dissent is to young people who tape music from the Voice of America or other foreign radio broadcasts. They also talk about young people who wear American clothing. A few young men have long hair, but this is a style rather than an indicator of any protest.

The standard belief is that dissent, protesting, and crime are on such a low scale that they are insignificant. Also the mention of police controls against dissent is considered to be American propaganda. But, in spite of these denials, the Soviet citizens do complain against the unavailability of consumer goods, certain books which are no longer available, the lack of safety precautions at work and on airplanes, and the quality of Soviet music.

SOURCES FOR CHAPTER XV - THE SOVIET CITIZEN

Collective farm brigade leader, interview by author, Samarkand,
    August, 1971.
Constitution of the USSR, Moscow, 1971.
Doctors and nurses, Intourist Hospital, Moscow, June, 1962.
Doctors, Kiev City Hospital, Kiev, July, 1964.
Doctors, nurses, and patients, Irkutsk Hospital Compound, July 20,
    1971.
Doctors, Sochi Polyclinic, Sochi, July, 1967.
Gegoriev, N., Soviet Union Today, Moscow, Progress Publishers,
    1971, pp. 168.
Marriage ceremony, Kharkov, July, 1967.
Pravda, Moscow, 1967-1973.
Public Relations Officer, interview by author, Bratsk Power Dam,
    July 22, 1971.
Public Relations Officer, interview by author, Volgograd Tractor
    Plant, Volgograd, August 10, 1971.
St. Louis Post-Dispatch, St. Louis, Missouri, 1967-1973.
Shakhnarzarov, G. Kh. et als., Obshchestvovedeniye, (4th ed.),
    Moscow: Izdatel'stvo Politicheskoi Literatury, 1966, pp. 381.
Shakhnarzarov, G. Kh, et als., Obshchestvovedeniye, (9th ed.),
    Moscow: Izdatel'stvo Politicheskoi Literatury, 1971, 366 pp.
Shakhnarzarov, G. Kh. et als., Obshchestvovedeniye, (10th ed.),
    Moscow: Izdatel'stvo Politicheskoi Literatury, 1972, 368 pp.
Teachers and students, Volgograd Pedagogical Institute, Volgograd,
    September-December, 1972.
Uzbek family, personal interview, Samarkand, August, 1971.

LIVING CONDITIONS

In the large cities many of the Soviet citizens live in apartment houses. This is the goal of the Soviet housing program to make apartments with modern facilities available for all Soviet citizens. But this goal has not been accomplished, partly because of the immensity of the task and partly because of the reluctance of the people. Many people prefer to live in small, wooden homes or even in clay huts (in Central Asia) rather than to live in the apartment houses.

Apartments are usually small, consisting of two or three rooms. Living rooms usually serve also as bedrooms. There is also a kitchen and possibly another bedroom. Shared kitchen facilities and bathrooms are becoming things of the past. Usually a family of three or four people live fairly comfortably and privately in such an apartment.

Apartment houses are usually heated by gas furnaces. Few apartment houses have air conditioning, but it is not needed in most parts of the Soviet Union. Gas is also used for cooking and for operating refrigerators. Kitchens have sinks for doing dishes, cabinets for dishes and utensils, and a table and chairs for having meals. The living room is carpeted, and there are tables, book cases, one or two sofas or cots which serve as chairs and as beds, a wardrobe closet, and probably a television set. Many people now own a television set, and some have pianos. The furniture, appliances, and other household items are personal property, which they buy themselves. The apartment itself is rented for 10 to 30 rubles a month, usually about 10% of the income.

In the cities some apartment houses are attached to others, which form a wall around the city block. The first floor of the buildings on the street side is often used for stores - produce, meat, furniture, clothing, etc. To enter the apartment one walks through an archway between apartment houses and enters the building from the back. Many apartment houses are five or six stories high, and people walk up and down the stairways. Elevators are used only for freight. In the last few years apartment houses are built higher with 13 or even 17 stories. These taller buildings do have elevators for the people.

Within the wall formed by the apartment houses there is a small park or playground for the people who live there. Older peo-

459

ple are seen sitting on the benches reading, and children play on the swings and jungle jim (climbing bars). A kindergarten may also be located on the first or second floor of one of these apartment houses, and the playground is also used by these children. First aid stations and other public services are also available in this or an adjoining apartment house block.

Apartment houses are administered by a housing office, which coordinates with the places of employment, at least for one member of the family. Others in the family may have to ride the busses, streetcars, or subway to work, and housing shortages may make it necessary for all of them to use public transportation. Transportation facilities are quite crowded during rush hours.

Many people live in wooden, single-family dwellings. This is true in the suburbs of Moscow and Leningrad as well as in sections of most other cities. Small towns have few apartment houses, and most of the people live in single-family homes. Some state farms have apartment houses, but people on farms usually have their own home and garden plot. In Siberia wooden homes are much more prevalent than the apartment houses.

Some people who live in the single-family dwellings in Siberia say that they prefer these homes to the apartment houses. They take some pride in their own home, which is often decorated with carvings on the shutters and on the trimmings of the house. Few homes are painted, and those who do paint concern themselves primarily with the shutters. Many shutters in Siberia are painted blue or green, the colors of the sky or water and the forest. One of the reasons why people prefer the individual houses is the opportunity to have a garden and a dog or cat. Apartment houses may have a veranda where the family grows a few plants, but in the gardens at individual houses they can grow most of the vegetables the family needs and some flowers and possibly a fruit tree or two.

Wooden houses are built from boards or from logs. They are usually small, having two, three, or four rooms. Sometimes people add on a bedroom, because families in these homes tend to have more than the customary one or two children. Living conditions in the individual homes are more adaptable to a larger family.

Conveniences, on the other hand, are not as available in these homes. They usually have a wood stove for heating and for cooking. They may have running water, but more often they have to carry the water from an outside faucet, which serves several houses. They do have electricity, as do the apartment houses, but they usually do not have the inside plumbing.

Plumbing facilities are generally of poor quality, even in the apartment houses and in hotels. Leaking pipes are common. Possibly some people prefer having an outhouse than having leaky plumbing facilities in the house.

In the desert areas of Soviet Central Asia many people live in mud or clay homes. The buildings do not resemble the adobe huts of Southwestern United States or Mexico. These Soviet homes appear to be made of wet clay which has been molded into a wall and allowed to dry. This clay makes a wall or fence around the living area. Attached to the fence are two or three separate rooms, also made of clay. In the middle of the fenced-in area is a garden with vegetables and flowers. One of the rooms serves as a living room and kitchen, and the other rooms serve as bedrooms. Some places have a platform of wood in the garden area. This platform may measure about 15 feet square and stand about three feet from the ground. A table with short legs (about 18" high) is placed on the platform, and the people sit on rugs on the platform to eat at the table. The table may be removed in the evening so that the people can sleep on the platform in the open air.

The Central Asian people who live in these mud or clay homes say that they prefer living there. They fear earthquakes and want to stay close to the ground. The lack of other building materials in the desert area is probably a main reason for having such houses. It is also the tradition of the people throughout Central Asia. In the drier areas, such as Samarkand, there is little need to have a water-resistant roof. The roofs there are also made of clay. But in Tashkent people have obtained tin sheets to place over their roofs.

It is primarily the Uzbeks, Tadzhiks, and other people of Central Asia who live in these clay homes. The Russians in this area prefer the wooden houses or the apartment houses. But people living in each type of housing do keep their living areas clean and tidy, as a general rule. They have pride in their homes and do not consider the clay houses or the wooden homes to be less desirable than the apartment houses. They consider the advantages of their own homes to outweigh the advantages of the other types.

There is geographic mobility of peoples, however, in the Soviet Union. The trend is for people to leave the rural areas and the smaller towns and to move to the cities for the benefits of education and occupation. Young people express their desires to move to larger cities, particularly Moscow and Leningrad. There are also people who have been moved to another location for occupational reasons who return to their former homes. People do move to accept better employment, and the new housing provided for them by their place of employment is usually an apartment. The building program of the Soviet Union has emphasized apartment houses, and if people still prefer an individual home, they must build or buy it. This policy causes many people to become accustomed to a new living style in an apartment house.

People who are financially able may build a country house (dacha) on land rented from the government. No one owns the land. It belongs to the government. But a person does have personal possessions, which include all the household items and may include a house. Of course, people do not own housing which they rent to others. It is illegal to do that. But people may share in the ownership of a country house and use it as a vacation home according to a pre-arranged schedule. Some people also move from the apartment house and live the year round in their country home. Retired persons do this. More affluent people also improve their living conditions by moving from an apartment to an individual home in the country or the suburbs. But these homes are still modest. They are usually wooden houses which differ from other such houses in size and paint.

The yards around homes and apartment houses are not lawns in the American sense. The grass is not mowed. It grows as in the forest giving a natural look to the yard. But most of the yard is vegetable or flower gardens. There is usually a fruit tree or two. The yard seems crowded, expecially near the individual homes. The land is used to grow food. Play areas are in the parks and at Pioneer camps. Even near the apartment houses the yards are small parks rather than a family yard.

A Soviet home provides the family with a place to live, eat, and sleep. It is not necessarily the center of the recreational or social life. People do have guests at their homes, but parties have to be held in other places. People do stay home to watch television, play records, play musical instruments and sing, to have people over for dinner, and to play chess. But most social and recreational activities are at public places.

When a person has the opportunity to spend several months in a Soviet city and to see most of the homes in that city, he learns that the housing shortage has not yet been solved and that most families still live in individual houses even in the largest cities. Long distance train travel also reveals to this person that many non-industrial cities, even quite large ones, have only individual houses. In the farming villages there are also no apartment houses. The goal to provide apartment house living for all Soviet citizens is a long way off.

Most of the individual houses are unpainted, and there is no landscaping. There are few sidewalks and paved streets. During dry weather there is a lot of dust, and in rainy season there is a muddy sea.

The summer cottage (dacha) is not a resort home. They are grouped together in an assigned area, and they are very close together. Each house is often no more than 12 feet by 15 feet. Some of these cottages are located in areas far away from trees, streams, or lakes. Still Soviet citizens desire to have a cottage, where they can spend their leisure time.

But no one stays home in the Soviet Union. Life revolves around the large cities in the area. Usually the city which serves as the oblast center is actually the center of economic, social, and political life. This center is connected to the towns, villages, and farm communities by rail or by bus. Local electric commuter trains or local busses convey people to the center and back. In the central region there are also street cars, auto busses, and taxis. All people have access to the large department stores, to the theatres, to the museums, and to all the facilities of the modern cities. And more people are buying cars to ride to the cities or out to the farm communities for things not found in the cities.

Some scarce items may be found in the smaller communities where demand is not as great. Also many city people have relatives in the smaller towns. Smaller towns may also offer advantages such as streams, forests, and a more peaceful life than that found in the cities.

WAGES AND PRICES

Wages and prices in the Soviet Union are determined by governmental policies rather than competition or laws of supply and demand. Monetary policies are a part of the Five Year Plans and are adjusted to conform with the production needs of the whole society. Fluctuations of wages and prices are not caused by labor unions, pressure groups, or industrial enterprises. In addition, changes in the uniformity of wages and prices seldom occur, except for special assignments to places or to work where extra incentives are necessary to attract and to hold workers at these locations. The primary exception is the bonus pay that people receive for living and working in remote places in Siberia, e.g. Bratsk, where a 100% bonus is paid.

The minimum wage is being increased from 60 rubles a month to 75 rubles a month. This wage is paid to unskilled labor in routine jobs. The following chart shows a range of the wage scale for different positions:

60 rubles a month-	minimum wage in Tashkent Cotton Mill
70 rubles a month-	minimum wage in Volgograd Tractor Plant
111 rubles a month-	average wage for workers at the Tashkent Cotton Mill
90-100 rubles a month-	beginning medical doctor
90-100 rubles a month-	beginning engineer
100-120 rubles a month-	beginning teacher (elementary or secondary)
125 or more rubles a month-	experienced engineer
160 or more rubles a month-	experienced teacher (elementary or secondary)
160 rubles a month-	average wage for all workers at Volgograd Tractor Plant
200 rubles a month-	qualified engineer at Volgograd Tractor Plant
250-300 rubles a month-	beginning college professor
305 rubles a month-	section leader of city Party organization at Bratsk
380 rubles a month-	experienced miner at Irkutsk
400 rubles a month-	college professor (after ten years)
500-700 rubles a month-	major college professor
690 rubles a month-	college dean

It is difficult to compare wages in the Soviet Union with those in other countries. On the surface it appears that these wages are low, particularly when one takes the rate of exchange of the Russian ruble with the American dollar. On the exchange the ruble in 1971 was worth $1.11, which means that the range of wages in dollars according to the foregoing chart is $66 to $759 a month, but these figures give a distorted impression.

Rather than having unemployment in the Soviet Union, there is a great shortage of workers. Every enterprise is seeking more employees. Therefore, several members of the family work and contribute to the family income. The husband and wife both work, and the youths out of school also work and bring in income.

The increase in the price of gold in 1973 and the other fluctuations of prices of currencies in the United States and in Europe did not effect the price system of the Soviet Union. The exchange rate for a time in 1973 was $1.27 to one ruble. This meant that the range of wages in the Soviet Union was from $76 to $876, but this did not mean any increase in Soviet wages. It only meant a decrease in the value of the American dollar. This further demonstrates the difficulty in comparing wages in the Soviet Union with those in other countries. The only valid way of comparing wages is to determine the amount of consumer goods those wages can buy in that country in comparison with the amount of consumer goods the wages in the other country can buy. Of course, the standard of living depends also on the amount of goods and services which are provided by the society from public funds.

To understand the real meaning of the income one also has to understand the expenses. Many services and some goods are free or inexpensive in the Soviet Union. A Soviet citizen does not need a high income to satisfy the basic needs of his family. Medical care and education are free. Housing and transportation are inexpensive. These expenses in another society take a large part of the income, but in the Soviet Union they are very low.

The major expenses for Soviet citizens are their costs of food, clothing, furniture, and other houshold items. Recreation is inexpensive and cannot be included as a major expense.

Lower income people usually live in individual houses and have a garden plot. They do not save much in housing costs, but their gardens greatly reduce the cost for food. Their major costs are for clothing, because they get along without much furniture and household items.

Poverty is not considered to be a problem according to many Soviet citizens with whom the author talked. They talk more about needs than about what they would like to have. If they can't afford something, they say they do not need it. A case in point is a car, which is very expensive in the Soviet Union. People say that they don't need a car, because they can walk or use public transportation. Yet many people, even in smaller homes, have their own television set.

Prices in the Soviet Union are quite constant throughout the whole country and from year to year. Rather than having inflation in prices, the trend has been to maintain or to lower the cost of consumer goods. The following chart lists some prices in 1968 and in 1971.[*]

Item	1968 Price	1971 Price
flour	27-41 kopecks per kg. (14¢-22¢ per pound)	24 kopecks per kg. (12¢ per pound)
salt	10 kopecks per kg. (5¢ per pound)	6 kopecks per kg. (3¢ per pound)
sugar	78 kopecks per kg. (39¢ per pound)	78 kopecks per kg. (39¢ per pound)
tea	17 kopecks per 25 gms. (17¢ per ½ pound)	19 kopecks per kg. (19¢ per ½ pound)
onions (dry)	8 kopecks per kg. (4¢ per pound)	12 kopecks per kg. (6¢ per pound)
peaches (fresh)	70 kopecks per kg. (35¢ per pound)	60 kopecks per kg. (30¢ per pound)
pork (fresh)	1.80 rubles per kg. (90¢ per pound)	2 rubles per kg. ($1.00 per pound)
cooking oil (sunflower)	1.55 rubles per kg. (78¢ per pound)	1.55 rubles per kg. (78¢ per pound)
cheese (yellow)	2.50-3.00 rubles per kg. ($1.25-$1.50 per pound)	2.90 rubles per kg. ($1.45 per pound)
men's shoes (dress)	35 rubles per pair ($38.50 per pair)	12-26.80 rubles per pair ($13.20-$29.50 per pair)
man's shirt	7-25 rubles ($7.70-$27.50)	6.50-11.50 rubles ($7.10-$12.65)
man's coat	50-70 rubles ($55-$77)	49.50-119.40 rubles ($54.45-$131.35)
lady's coat (winter)	100-120 rubles ($110-$132)	107.50 rubles ($118.25)

*Prices are calculated at the official rate of $1.11 = 1 ruble

The prices in dollars and cents have been listed in the foregoing chart to provide a means of reference to the reader. However, these prices may cause more problems in understanding than the prices in rubles and kopecks, because the prices or cost of living is relevant only to the income and the other expenses of the family. An example of the income and living expenses of one family in the Soviet Union may give a more accurate picture.

This family has a total income of 400 rubles a month. The father is disabled from the war and is on pension. The mother and one daughter are school teachers. Another daughter is an engineer. The rent for their apartment (including utilities) is 16 rubles a month. Groceries cost them about 150 rubles a month. Since education and medical expenses are free, the additional 234 rubles a month is used for clothes, furniture, public transportation, and entertainment.

Money can be saved at the savings bank and earns 3% interest. Furniture and appliances can be purchased on credit, and loans from the bank also cost 3%. To purchase more expensive consumer items the Soviet citizen saves enough for a down payment (10% or more) and then makes the initial payment and arrangements to pay the balance over a period of time.

Public transportation and entertainment are inexpensive. The following list shows some of these prices:

city bus - 6 kopecks	taxi - 10 kopecks per km.
trolley - 5 kopecks	movie - 25 kopecks (day); 35-50
subway - 5 kopecks	kopecks (evening)
streetcar - 3 kopecks	theatre (drama, ballet, or opera) -
	1-5 rubles, depending on seat and
	on the performance)

Soviet citizens are accustomed to walk long distances both for going places and for recreation. The parks and river banks provide places for recreational walks. Many people live close enough to their place of work to walk every day. These practices help to reduce the costs of transportation and recreation.

Clothing and household items take a large portion of the monthly income. Of course, the costs for these items vary with the needs and ability to pay of the family. However, a listing of some prices will provide an idea of these costs for a family. Also in this list are prices of fresh produce at the farmer's market or bazaar, where the quality of the food may be better and the price higher than in the stores.

Item	Price
sofa bed	60 rubles
piano	370-500 rubles
color TV	550-850 rubles
bed & mattress	51 rubles
sewing machine	74 rubles
wooden table	32-36 rubles
washing machine	71 rubles
book shelves	37-83 rubles
rocking chair	30 rubles
b&w TV	120-432 rubles
motor bike	51-170-350 rubles
car (Fiat)	5600 rubles
car (Volga)	8500 rubles

Clothing

sport coat	26 rubles
man's suit	72-66.60 rubles
trousers	18-26 rubles
sport shirt	11.50 rubles
lady's shoes	27-40 rubles
men's socks	48 kopecks to 3.60 rubles
man's hat	3.40-2.80 rubles
work trousers	10.50 rubles
blouse	10 rubles
skirt	15 rubles

Meat

beef	1.60 rubles per kilogram
pork	1.80-2.00 rubles per kilogram
sausage	2.80-3.00 rubles per kilogram
fresh fish	30-32-50 kopecks per
canned fish	33 kopecks for 250 grams
ground beef	10 kopecks for a patty (about 250 grams)

Item (fresh)	Price (at farmers' market)
cucumbers	40 kopecks per kilogram
potatoes	70 kopecks per kilogram
melons	60 kopecks per kilogram
cabbage	1 ruble per kilogram
ear corn	50 kopecks per kilogram

Item (fresh)	Price (at farmers' market)
grapes	2 rubles per kilogram
pears	1.5 rubles per kilogram
tomatoes	20-40 kopecks per kilogram
red beets	60 kopecks per kilogram
cherries	1 ruble per kilogram
apricots	1 ruble per kilogram
strawberries	2 rubles per kilogram
peaches	60 kopecks per kilogram

Item (canned)	Price (in stores)
carrots	2.70 rubles per kilogram
apple jam	1 ruble per kilogram
tomato juice	63 kopecks per liter
sauerkraut	70 kopecks per kilogram
diced beets	45 kopecks per kilogram
condensed milk	55 kopecks for 400 grams
apples	48 kopecks for 500 grams
borsch	95 kopecks per kilogram
pickles	1.18 rubles for 1950 grams
strawberry jam	85 kopecks for 650 grams
apricot juice	65 kopecks per kilogram

Among other frequently purchased items are books, flowers, ice cream, and soft drinks. These items are sold at small stands on the streets. Books are inexpensive, usually ranging from 35 kopecks to 1 ruble. A few technical books and reference books sell for 3 to 5 rubles. Flowers are sold in bouquets for 30 to 50 kopecks. Ice cream cones, frozen milk bars, and similar products are sold for 13 to 19 kopecks. Soft drinks are purchased at the dispensers for 1 kopecks for mineral water and 3 kopecks for flavored mineral water. Kvas (mildly alcoholic drink, which is very popular) and beer are sold at stands on the street for 3, 5, 10 kopecks, depending on the size of the mug.

There are a few variations in the prices of consumer goods and services, even though most prices are quite constant. A difference of prices in various locations may appear, such as the price of a trolley bus ride in Moscow is 4 kopecks, in Volgograd - 5 kopecks, and in Gorky - 6 kopecks. Special trolley busses that travel a greater distance and have an attached passenger section charge 12 kopecks for a ride in Volgograd. The following items also changed price from 1971 to 1972:

Item	1971 Price	1972 Price
Salt	6 kopecks per kg.	10 kopecks per kg.
Fresh pork	1.80-2.00 rubles per kg.	2.30-2.60 rubles per kg.
Beef	1.60 rubles per kg.	2.00 rubles per kg.
Sunflower oil	1.55 rubles per kg.	1.65 rubles per kg.
Cheese (Yellow)	2.90 rubles per kg.	2.30-2.60 rubles per kg.

However, most prices have remained substantially the same from 1968 to 1972. The problem of a shopper is not to go from store to store to find goods at a lower price. The problem is to find scarce goods, and often it is necessary to stand in a long line to obtain these scarce products.

Yet the wise shopper also learns that different distributors of consumer items do have various qualities of goods and comensurate prices. The second-hand stores (commission stores) do have used furniture and appliances at reduced prices. It has already been mentioned that produce is better and prices higher at the bazaar, but another place is the collective farm store, where food products are sold not by individual farmers but by the collective farm itself. Here the produce is unsorted and may vary from poor to good quality, and the prices may be lower than both at the bazaar and in the store. But the shopper has to watch the collective farm store for bargains. It could save him money.

Conclusions drawn by the author from seeing and talking with many Soviet citizens in various parts of the country are that the people are fairly well satisfied with their standard of living. From work income or from pensions families have enough money to pay their rent, utilities, food costs, clothing costs, and other basic necessities. Free or inexpensive public services satisfy most of their other needs. Such things as cars, televisions, pianos, and stereos are not available to everyone, but the people say they do not need them. Many people have acquired small, black and white television sets, and some people have other luxury items. There are desires, particularly among the younger people, for transistor radios and musical instruments, but these things are not looked on as being necessities. Young people have radios and record players, and guitars and balalaikas are also easily accessible for only 4 to 10 rubles. People do not consider themselves to be poor. They see

At a Collective Farm Market in Rostov.

At a Collective Farm Market in Tashkent.

the availability of more consumer items on the market, and they believe that both the country and the people themselves are becoming more affluent.

According to national policies, no one receives money from investments, rents, business profits, or speculation. There is no stock market. No one can offer property for rent, and no one can employ another person. The only products or services that one can sell are those which he produces himself. All other profit-making activity is considered to be black market operations, which are serious criminal offenses and are punishable by law.

There is a government lottery, which is used to raise revenue. People buy lottery tickets for a chance to win large amounts of money. There are hopes for winning, but none of the people with whom the author talked ever won anything on the lottery or ever knew anyone personally who did.

People become accustomed to living on their work income or pension and do not have dreams of becoming rich. That concept is inconsistent with Communist teachings and with Soviet morality, which condemns profit-seekers.

The essence of this discussion on wages and prices is that Soviet citizens do have a part of their income left over after paying for housing, food, and clothing. This part may be saved for purchasing furniture and household items or for going to the theatre or to the beaches more often. Soviet citizens respond that they live "ne plokho", which means that they are getting along all right.

WORKING CONDITIONS

More than half of the Soviet citizens now live in urban rather than rural areas. An agricultural economy has given way to a highly industrialized one, and the working conditions of the people have changed. Even the work on the collective farms and state farms follows industrial patterns more than that of individual farmers.

The Soviet worker is one member of an organized group, which itself is a small part of a larger enterprise. In turn, the enterprise is supervised by nation-wide or republic ministries according to the comprehensive Five-Year Plans. There is some autonomy for the director of the enterprise who also coordinates with the local Communist Party officials and the local government leaders. Under the director of the enterprise the foreman and their crews carry out the work assigned to them with the encouragement to increase productivity. Each worker has a role which in many ways resembles the role of an assembly worker in other highly industrialized countries.

Most workers have a 40 hour week now. They work seven hours a day for five days and 5 hours on the sixth day. One day a week is the day off. Variations of this schedule are very common. A few people, such as hotel clerks on each floor, work 24 hours or longer a stretch and then have longer periods of time off. Agricultural workers have long hours during the planting and harvesting seasons, but there are times when the work is slack. Miners and others who do heavy work have shorter work weeks. The goal of the 35-hour work week is already in practice for them.

The day shift with Sunday off is the general rule. Work may start at 7, 8, or 9 a.m. The last one to go to work takes the children to grandmother's, to an aunt, to a neighbor, or to the nursery or kindergarten. The first member of the family to return home stops by to bring the children home. The noon meal is provided for the workers and for the children. The family has breakfast and supper together. On the days off the young children stay home with the parents. Their family life is spent together in the evenings and on these days off.

Pay scales follow uniform patterns, as stated in the foregoing section. They do have deductions for trade union fees, but they take home almost all of the monthly pay. Farm workers receive part of their pay in produce, but others receive cash.

Each person who goes to work must have a work booklet. This booklet is in addition to his personal identity passport. The booklet has entries for his description, his place of residence, and his work assignments. This book must be kept up to date and is presented when a person changes work or residence. Entries are also made in the personal passport on these occasions. The work booklet provides evidence of one's capabilities and work status for receiving trade union benefits, e.g. vacation rates, medical care, etc. It is also a type of credentials necessary for seeking new employment. This work book can help the government too in guaranteeing everyone employment and in regulating work discipline. Entries are made for violation of the work rules, e.g. tardiness, drunkenness, lack of diligence, etc.

One of the first things that a foreigner notices in the Soviet Union is the number of women doing various jobs. They work in factories, in construction, in the fields, on landscaping projects, and in management positions. The concept of equality in work, particularly equality of the sexes, is practiced in the Soviet Union. Only in very heavy work or in dangerous positions, such as mining, are women restricted from working. They work along with men in most other tasks.

In factories and at other industrial sites another obvious characteristic of Soviet working conditions is the large number of signs, posters, banners, and placards. Workers are given production figures and percentages and encouraged to meet goals of the Five Year Plans by year, by quarter, and by month. Other advice pertains to safety at work and at home, proper conduct and morality, and dedication to the principles of Communist Construction and Soviet patriotism. A sign at the Cellullose and Carton Plant at Bratsk urged workers to remember that they have a high calling as Soviet workers and should not forget this calling at work and at home.

Incentives are a way of encouraging workers to increase production and to work at projects in remote areas. Bonuses are paid to workers who live and work in Siberia. At Novosibirsk the bonus is a 50% increase in pay for all workers. And at Bratsk that bonus is a 100% increase. Other places and projects may well have similar bonuses. In addition, there are the bonuses paid to workers for increasing and sustaining increased production over a period of time. Some of these bonuses are reflected in the pay, and other benefits come in the form of improved services and facilities for the workers. These benefits may be better nurseries, schools, pioneer camps, vacation benefits, and gardens.

Gardens or small parks are provided for improving the health, both physical and mental, for Soviet workers. Trees and shrubbery are planted, the land is landscaped, flowers are grown, and fountains are built. Such gardens or parks are found at industrial sites as well as near the housing areas. A ratio between the number of people and the amount of greenery in the area is a part of the planned economy.

There is a noticeable difference between cities in the amount of parks, museums, fountains, swimming pools, pioneer palaces, and new public buildings. The priority given to certain cities and to certain enterprises may be a reward for increased production and compliance to specified goals. Bonuses given to the Factory Fund for social benefits are probably used for this purpose.

A sign at the Cellulose Plant in Bratsk. It reads "At work, in the family, among comrades REMEMBER: You are a Soviet worker DON'T STAIN your high calling."

Competition between cities and between enterprises encourages rivalry to outdo the performance and the productivity. It is called "socialist competition," and it is based on the work of a whole plant, a whole enterprise, or even a whole city to increase production and to surpass its competitors. Signs in Moscow and Leningrad show rivalry between them, and figures are given to show how each city is meeting its obligations to the Five Year Plan and is competing with the other city on specific items in this regard.

Honor Boards are displayed near enterprises, city soviets, and in parks to praise outstanding workers. These signs have pictures of the people being honored; and the name, work assignment, and achievement are listed under each picture. Honor Boards are kept current to give recognition to the workers as they deserve this respect for their extraordinary performance.

These types of public incentives and all the political banners, statues, and signs are everywhere in the Soviet Union. One can wonder what the effect is on the Soviet citizen. Their responses to such questions vary, but generally they express acceptance of these manifestations for diligence and loyalty. Some respond that, "If you think there are a lot of banners and signs in the summer, you ought to come to the Soviet Union at the 1st of May or the 7th of November during the celebrations."

Observing Soviet workers provides some understanding of their acceptance of their challenges, but it is difficult to know their actual reactions. The people work much as workers in other countries do. They work a while, then they pause for a rest before continuing on to work. They take breaks from their work. They also do a lot of waiting to coordinate their tasks with the tasks of other workers. They wait for supplies, for parts, for instructions, and for "God knows what." Of course, the Soviet Constitution states that citizens have the right to work and the right to rest. People do become tired, but people also tend to "goof off." It appears that the problems of supervising workers in the Soviet Union is not too different from these problems in capitalist countries. The methods to encourage increased production may be different, but the results do not seem to be too different.

Much of the work in the Soviet Union is mechanized. People have to work along with the pace of the machines. But it appears that the machines are not driving people at too fast a pace. Along the assembly lines in the Tashkent Cotton Mill, in the Volgograd Tractor Plant, and in the Bratsk Cellullose Plant there were few people in comparison to the number of machines. These people were fairly busy, but they had time to complete their tasks easily. Where greater activity was necessary, several people worked together at each station so that the work was not over burdensome.

The common sights in public places in the Soviet Union are the men and women cutting the grass with scythes, women sweeping the streets, women gardening in the parks, and men and women truck and machine drivers which give one the impression of inefficiency. But this picture is not really accurate. The achievements in production and the rapid construction of buildings, power plants, and new cities give another view.

When one considers that there is full employment of both male and female workers and that practically every enterprise is seeking more workers, both skilled and unskilled, he must admit that the total effort is impressive. Added to this are the well-known achievements in industrial expansion and in space exploration. It is apparent that the people recognized on the Honor Boards must be examples of outstanding workers. They and their colleagues who make their achievements possible must be contributing to the rapid growth of the Soviet economy.

The enthusiasm of Soviet citizens in talking about their achievements and their goals is also noteworthy. They are proud of the successes of the country and of their own contributions to these successes. This enthusiasm appears spontaneous, and it must reflect their attitudes toward their work. Rather than complaining about shortcomings, they boast of their achievements and of the announced goals for greater production.

Individual performance and individual advancement is usually portrayed as a part of group or enterprise activity. But the individual also has his personal role and personal drive. He seeks to improve his own lot and takes advantage of situations which help him achieve. He is told that personal achievement comes through group performance, but he also recognizes that advancement comes through individual effort as well.

Mobility of workers from one position to another or from one geographic area to another depends heavily on the present performance and capabilities. A worker who complies with his responsibilities may enroll in evening courses to improve his capabilities. These courses of instruction are free to him, as is all education, but he must match the time released from work with an equivalent amount of his own free time. Usually he has two hours of released time from work and gets paid for full time while he attends evening courses. When he completes the courses, he is qualified for advancement or to change jobs, if the positions are available at that time.

Changing jobs may cause some complications which have to be considered. One problem is the work assignments of other members of the family, particularly if the new job requires a move to a new residence. Another problem is that of obtaining new housing near the place of employment. Housing has to be available. For those persons moving into large cities this problem becomes critical.

Entries are made in the worker's work booklet when he changes jobs and/or changes residence. Advance notice must be given to both the present and the new employing institutions and housing officials. These procedures may become restrictions, if replacements are not readily available. But it is becoming much easier for people to change jobs. The rapid building of apartments has helped that too.

When a person completes full-time instruction in schools, institutes, or universities, he is usually assigned work consistent with his education. These assignments are also consistent with the needs of the society, and often the person is required to move to a less desirable place, possibly a remote area. After working there for two years, the person has completed his obligation and may move to another position and another area, if he is qualified for the vacancy. Bonuses and other means are used to keep workers in these less desirable places, and, of course, there are many people who become accustomed to the new home. Probably there are also people who want to move but for some reason can not do so. One physician in Alma Ata expressed the desire to move back to Moscow, but her husband was assigned to work in Alma Ata. Such assignments are necessary to maintain the needs of the economy and needs of society. Of course, not everyone could live in Moscow either.

Soviet workers do not have collective bargaining. They do have trade or professional unions, but they are not bargaining agents for the workers. Trade unions administer the "fringe benefits" for the workers. They also receive suggestions from workers and from management for improving working conditions at the enterprise level. In addition, they make arrangements for vacations, which are up to 70% pre-paid by the trade union. There are also trade union houses, which serve as offices of the union and as cultural centers for the workers.

Vacations from work are part of the policy of the "right to rest." Workers under 18 years of age have four weeks vacation. People in their twenties usually have two weeks vacation a year, and this vacation period is later increased to three weeks and finally to four weeks. The trade union maintains rest homes and vacation spots for the workers. These areas are usually at a beach, in the mountains, or in a wooded area near a river or lake. The cost to the worker is about one-third of the actual cost, and this includes the transportation to and from the vacation area. Of course, the worker is not obliged to go to the Trade Union sponsored resort. He can take his free time to stay home, to visit relatives, or to go on a vacation to another place with his family and friends. But often the advantages of the Trade Union benefits entice him to go to the sponsored vacation spots.

There are also several holidays, when most of the workers are not required to work. These days are: January 1st, May 1st-3rd, and November 7th and 8th. In addition, women do not work on International Women's Day--March 8th. On these holidays and on other occasions enterprises have special meetings to honor the outstanding workers. These meetings start with a series of congratulations for those presiding at the meeting and also for those workers who are being honored. Bouquets of flowers, telegrams and short speeches are given to honor these people. There is a round of applause for each of the people being honored. These preliminaries are then usually followed by a concert of folk singing and dancing.

But not all work deserves this type of recognition. Much of the work is done sloppily and things are constantly in need of repair or are out of service. Plumbing and electrical equipment are the most common problems of this type. Soviet citizens tend to laugh about it, when they see a sign that reads "nye rabotayet", which means "it doesn't work." But this sign and the one that reads "remont" (repair) are all too common. They are indications of the lack of priority on quality workmanship and on repair work.

Other deficiencies in working conditions are the abuses and the lack of consideration for the consumer as well as the worker. Not only are many public services closed during the day for a clean-up day, inventory, or a lunch break, they are also less than efficient at other times because key people are gone. They may go early and return late for a holiday or their vacation time. But the most common abuse is the "komandirovka" (paid business trip). Many supervisors are on a "komandirovka", which they can obtain quite easily.

Of course, many of these trips are legitimate, but these passes are used for pleasure trips as well. This type of absence from work hampers production and service to consumers.

Another effect of poor quality workmanship is seen in construction of all types. Buildings are shoddy and appear to be old soon after completion. Roads are not built properly so as to provide drainage of rain water, and not only are the roads messy, but they also deteriorate quickly. The response to this problem is that the society is striving to catch up and surpass other industrialized countries. They add that the emphasis now is on "quantity" and that "quality" comes later.

This lack of priority toward quality work effects the appearance and the utilization of the products. It also effects the attitudes of the workers. It has been said that central planning and the lack of individual initiative and responsibility are the causes for poor quality workmanship. But whatever the cause may be, the result is a major deficiency in working conditions and in consumer satisfaction.

Another problem in Soviet working conditions is the rigid adherence to regulations. A book or manual of operations is probably a necessary thing for maintaining work discipline. But Soviet supervisors and workers are very much restricted by the book. Of course, the book does not give all the answers, and in new or different circumstances the supervisor does not know what to do. Possibly the liability is too great for him to risk using his own initiative and improvising, but the result is inaction. He hesitates to do anything until he receives authorization from higher authority, which may take some time, especially if that authority is far away, such as in Moscow.

Parallel with this problem is the tendency for some people to deviate from the book. Any deviation is immediately reported to higher authority, and the responsible person is ordered to stop and desist. He is then reprimanded and possibly punished for that deviation.

Budget problems also effect work plans. There is a direct conflict in the drive for increased and expedited production and the amount of money budgeted for the operation. When the allotted money runs out before the end of the year, there is a curtailment of many projects or possibly the whole work plan. Workers then can not do their work well or may not be able to do it at all. Of course, the director is responsible for following the budget closely and not allowing this to happen. But it is common that toward the end of the year there is insufficient money for unexpected repair work and other operational needs.

PUBLIC SERVICES

Medical Service and hospitalization according to the Soviet Constitution are free for working people. In general, this means that medical care if free for every Soviet citizen. The Government has built first aid stations, poly-clinics, hospitals, sanatoria, and other medical facilities throughout the whole country. There are claims of more hospital beds and doctors per thousand population than in any other industrialized country. Expansion and improvement of medical services and the promotion of the physical well-being of the citizens are major concerns of the Soviet society.

Places of employment are responsible for the good health of the workers. Many measures are taken to promote safety and the prevention of disease. There are educational programs, which include instruction and signs at the enterprise, for keeping people conscious of their own responsibilities. A balance of work and rest is official policy. Rest periods, reduced working hours, and vacations enable people to use time for physical recreation and sports. Conditions at factories and plants are improved by better lighting, cleaner working areas, and pleasant areas for relaxation. Trees and flowers are planted in little park areas at or near the place of employment. The actual responsibility for these employment benefits is taken by the trade or professional unions, where the workers are encouraged to contribute to better conditions for the well-being of everyone. Increased production makes fringe benefit funds available for those purposes, and the trade union members can say how they want the funds used - for better working conditions, for nurseries for their children, for kindergartens, for medical facilities, etc.

Official policies also recognize the role of the trade union in paying a major portion of the vacation expenses to a health resort for the workers. People spend their vacations at these recreational areas near a lake, at a beach, in the mountains, or some place where there are polyclinics, sanatoria, and other health facilities. They swim, sunbathe, and take long walks. Some places may have access to mineral springs, where they drink mineral water and take hot baths. More often people are concerned with getting a good tan.

A strong body and a good tan are marks of good health and a source of pride for Soviet citizens. In addition to their own health-promoting activities at the rest area, they can receive out-patient care at a polyclinic or in-patient care in a hospital or sanatorium for preventive and correctional medical care. Dental work or even major operations are done while a person is on vacation, where he has time and favorable conditions for relaxation and recuperation.

Maternity leaves last for approximately two months before giving birth and approximately two months afterwards. Expectant mothers visit offices for "women's advice" rather than a clinic or hospital, which is for ill people. They are checked periodically for detection of problems and referred to a clinic or hospital only when necessary. These offices of "women's advice" serve a broad range of medical care for women and provide the personal attention that women need not only during pregnancy but also for other female problems. The delivery of babies and the treatment for gynecological problems are performed at the hospitals.

There are several types of clinics. Some are for children. There are also polyclinics, which provide treatment for accidents and minor injuries or illnesses. The clinics and polyclinics are institutions with physicians, assistants, and nurses. They have facilities and equipment for detecting injuries and diseases, but they treat primarily out-patients. Most people have much more contact with a clinic or polyclinic than a hospital for that reason.

Hospitals are usually large buildings or a compound of several buildings for providing in-patient care for ill or injured persons. In large cities the hospitals are in various parts of the city, even in the center area. A hospital may not be recognized and distinguished from other buildings except by a sign or possibly by people visiting patients through a window on the street. The patient opens a window and visits with his friend or relative. In the hospital compounds some patients are allowed to walk around the grounds and sit on the benches, and they sometimes talk to their friends or relatives at the fences of the compounds.

When entering a Soviet hospital one sees quite a different situation. Visitors are not allowed to come in, except on special conditions. A person can not get past the guard without permission, which is usually not given. But those who do get in must wear a white gown over their clothes and put on a white face mask for sanitary reasons. The patients are assigned to beds in large wards or in semi-private rooms. Their beds are low to the floor. The rooms appear clean, but they are not bright and cheerful. The few visitors who are allowed to come into the hospital are ushered around and do not stay long.

Clinics are generally brighter and more cheerful places than hospitals. Both, however, are more utilitarian than aesthetic, as are most public facilities in the Soviet Union until recently.

The medical care at the clinics and at the hospital is good for general practice of medicine. Most of the doctors and nurses are women, but there are also male doctors and orderlies. All hospital personnel wear white clothes or white cloaks over their clothes when they are near the patients. There is unusual emphasis on sanitation.

Surgery and special medical care are performed at hospitals. In some cases there is a deviation from the policy of free medical care when a specialist is needed. But the range and scope of this practice is not widely known.

Psychiatrists and mental hospitals are not as prevalent as one might expect in a highly industrialized country such as the Soviet Union. But there are clinics for people who have sociological and psychological problems. There are also mental hospitals. People who have such problems are counselled at the clinics or offices in order to determine their problems and to suggest remedial treatments. A guiding principle is the teachings of Pavlov concerning "conditioned reflexes," and a person needs to have a new set of "conditions" for correcting the problems. Only within the last few years has much greater attention been given to providing treatment for psychological and sociological ailments. Work and group therapy have been considered to be good methods for remedying these problems. In more serious cases hypnotism is used for helping to detect causes for illness. Electric shock is also used in these serious cases for shocking a person into reality. However, the extent of therapy for mental problems is not known. It appears that many mental patients have primarily custodial care as in many other countries in the world.

Medical research for both physical and mental disorders has a high priority in the Soviet Union. The Academy of Medical Sciences is an extensive organization for the furthering of research in these areas. Much work has been done on the frontiers of medical research, e.g. organ and bone transplants, cures for cancer, and radiation on human genes. This work has both theoretical and practical applications. As in almost all Soviet research medical research is designed to improve the life of man to adapt to his environment in a changing world.

Statistics concerning the expansion and improvement of medical care in the Soviet Union are impressive in comparison with the conditions in the past. The progress has been substantial. Soviet citizens have ready access to medical care. But only medical research has a high national priority. The practice of medical care has a regional or local priority, which is not in comparison with economic production or education. Physicians and surgeons do not command an unusual respect, and their salaries are not high. Low priority is given to the construction of hospital and clinic facilities. Older buildings are used for these purposes. Yet the availability of medical service, the emphasis on preventive medical care, the concern with sanitation, and the dedication of doctors and nurses may compensate for other deficiencies.

In addition to the schools, institutes, medical facilities, and theaters there are many other public services, to which Soviet citizens have to go for their goods and services. Government and Communist Party offices are usually not considered as a part of these public service institutions, because they are more responsible for regulating citizens than serving them. The services that they do render can usually be obtained from the institute where one studies or from the enterprise where one works, because at or near these locations there are local units of the precinct soviet or the Communist Party cell. At these locations the Soviet citizen can have his documents validated and have answers to his inquiries.

One has regular contact with the housing office where he lives, because it is there he pays his rent and utility payments. He also must contact housing offices for obtaining new living space.

Post offices, telephone and telegraph offices, and libraries are available for their respective services. A post office not only receives letters and packages for mailing, but it also provides services for sending packages. A small package may be wrapped for a few kopecks. A larger package must be placed in a wooden box or in a knit bag. One can buy these materials and prepare his own package, or he can pay a few kopecks to have the work done for him. But these services are usually only available at the large post offices. At the telephone office, which usually is together with the main post office, the Soviet citizen may use the public phones for his calls, including long distance or even international calls. He gives his order and then waits for the call to be completed, at which time he is called and told which booth to use. There are also some booths for direct dialing to certain large cities, and in these booths are automatic, coin-operated telephones. The telegraph office is also usually in the same building as the telephone office. One fills out his request and gives it to the girl, who does the rest. She charges a small fee. The postal services, the telephone services, and the telegraph services are all inexpensive. One does not need any documentation to use these services. All he needs is time to wait in lines to receive the service. The only significant regulations are on packages being mailed. Firearms and explosives can not be mailed. Also furs, jewelry, paintings, and other expensive items can not be mailed to foreign countries.

Domestic mail costs 4 kopecks, airmail costs 6 kopecks, and international airmail costs 16 kopecks. Long distant calls vary in cost, but most calls are about 15 kopecks for 3 minutes. International calls from Volgograd to United States costs 7 rubles for 3 minutes.

The most popular store is the department store, where one can buy most consumer items other than food products. Clothing, appliances, cleaning equipment, school supplies, phonographic records, some furniture, hardware, and many other items are available there. The prices are the same as in other stores and are not subject to bargaining. One selects what he wants, tells the clerk, is told the price, pays the cashier, returns to the clerk, gives her the receipt, and picks up his purchase. He usually has to make his way through a crowd and to wait in a line at the cashier's booth to do this.

In the department store there is also a booth where one can buy theater tickets. Another service there is the savings bank. People rarely go to the State Bank. All their financial transactions can be taken care of at the savings bank in the department store. Since there are no checking accounts, the person is primarily interested in depositing or withdrawing savings.

Restaurants cater primarily to people dining out for the evening. It is usually difficult to obtain a table at a restaurant. Most people go to a dining hall (stolovaya) instead. Here the food is not as good, but it is adequate, and the price is more reasonable. But a person usually has to wait in a line and serve himself. But there is a variety of good. Salads, meat dishes, soups, sour milk, juices, bread, and tea are on the regular menu.

There are many book stores, and books are also sold at tables on the street. Books of all kinds are available, but all of them are printed in the Soviet Union. New books are usually first available at the tables on the street. Book stores also receive them soon afterwards. But some books are sold out very quickly, and one has to wait a long time to get a copy. It helps to know the sales girl, who will save a copy for you when it is available.

There are different types of book stores, too. They are political, military, scientific, textbook, or other varieties of bookstores. One has to go to a particular store to obtain a particular book. Hard-to-find books may be at a used book store, where one can look through the books, place an order, or sign up for a book program to receive a set of books. It pays to know the procedures, but even knowing them is not enough. Some people have waited years for a particular book, and this situation is not rare. Some teachers at the Volgograd Pedagogical Institute had waited for years to obtain a Dictionary of the Russian Language, which is somewhat equivalent to Webster's Collegiate Dictionary, but it is for Russian-speaking people. It is logical to expect that each teacher could obtain such a dictionary readily, but that was not the case. Even with all the books published in the Soviet Union there is still a shortage of many books.

A gastronom (grocery store) is the most common food store. It has canned fruit, vegetables, juices, and a variety of other food products. But there are meat stores, fish stores, bakery goods stores, candy stores, and liquor stores. There are also delicatessens, fresh vegetable markets, and other types of food stores. There are also food department stores, which have departments of most of these kinds of stores. A person does not have to go from place to place to try to beat the prices, but he does go from place to place to find what is available. Fresh products often can only be obtained by waiting in a line. The process of buying is the same as at the department store.

Furniture stores, barber shops, dry cleaning pick-up points, jewelry stores, souvenir shops, and many others are in each city. But people in the outlying area have to come to the city to gain access to all these stores. They may have only a small fraction of them in a suburb of a city and even less in a farming community.

Not only is there a problem of the availability of consumer items, there is also a problem of slow service. For instance, the mail moves very slowly from one city to another. But the most common frustration is the waiting for service, often in a long line and even where there is no line. There are many papers that the clerks have to fill out for each transaction, and generally there is no hurry to help a customer.

One may wait while his trousers are patched or his shoes repaired, but some other services take days, weeks or even months. Spare parts are lacking, and it may take two months to get the parts when one repairs his car by himself. But one can use public transportation or even rent a car, if necessary. Car rental is 28 rubles plus three kopecks per kilometer. At that price it would be much better to go by taxi. One can not readily turn in his car and buy a new one. Some people have waited two years to buy a car, and then they have to pay cash for it. With these problems is it apparent why many Soviet citizens say they don't need a car.

Most long distance transportation is by train. People fear airplane accidents, and a train ride is quite comfortable and inexpensive. One can ride a thousand miles for about 20 rubles. In the train there are separate compartments for each four people, and bunks are available for them at night. One can eat in the restaurant car or take his own lunch. Most people bring their own food. But one can also buy a sack lunch with three boiled eggs, bologna, some bread, and mineral water at the railroad stations. This lunch costs a ruble.

The major problem while travelling is obtaining hotel space. Reservations by telephone or telegraph do not always guarantee a room for the traveller. If a person has a komandirovka (travel pass) he can have the reservation made by his enterprise. Official telegrams from enterprises or institutes are more likely to guarantee a room than those sent by an individual. But most Soviet citizens rely on friends or acquaintances to find rooms when they come to a different city. Often they can move in with their friends at home, in a dormitory, or even in a hotel room. Of course, one can also contact the housing office when he arrives at a new location. One must do this usually when he goes to a resort town.

There are lockers in the train station. They are coin operated and a person sets his own combination. These are fairly safe, and one may keep his possessions there for up to three days for only 15 kopecks.

But there are risks while travelling. A wanted poster was noticed in a train station. One person was wanted for moving in hotel rooms with people and then moving out before morning with all the other person's belongings. Other persons were wanted for robbing lockers, and people were advised not to use birthdates or

passport numbers while setting the combination. Hotel rooms
and suitcases also are not very secure. Any key that goes into
the lock can with a little juggling open the lock. It is fortunate
that most Soviet citizens are honest and that there are few problems
of crime, but there is enough danger to warrant a traveller to be
cautious.

A great annoyance for the traveller is the unsanitary condition
of public toilets in the Soviet Union. The conditions may not be
worse than some other European countries, but that does not make
the traveller feel any better. There is always water on the floor.
Usually there is no paper. And often there are only a trough and
a hole in the cement floor. Of course, the hotels have much better
toilet facilities, but there is still usually water on the floor.

Local transportation services are generally good. One may
be inconvenienced by unannounced schedule changes, but the local
trains usually run about once an hour, and the busses at least once
a day. Within the cities the streetcars and autobusses are very
frequent, but still they are very crowded, particularly in rush hours.

SUMMARY

Living conditions in the Soviet Union are "nye plokho" (not
bad) both from the view of the Soviet citizen and from a comparison
with conditions throughout Europe and Asia. Basic needs are satisfied. Everyone works, has a place to live, has enough to eat, buys
enough clothes, and has time for some recreation. The average
citizen, like people everywhere gets up and goes to work each
morning. He works hard, but he does have time to rest and enjoy
himself with his family. In the evening he may go out to a movie
or to the theatre or he may stay home and watch the soccer game on
television. By 11 or 12 p.m. he has gone to bed to rest for another
day.

The advantages that the Soviet citizen enjoys are the guaranteed
employment, inexpensive housing, free or inexpensive public services, and continual opportunities to improve himself. These things
cause a Soviet citizen to believe that he has a good life, which is
getting better all the time.

The disadvantages are generally accepted as necessary in this
phase of social development. They believe that changes will be made
in time as they continue to build Communism.

Of course, they do complain about the long lines they stand
in to buy things, about the crowded trolley busses, the lack of
some consumer items, and the weather, but they believe that their
complaints are no worse than those of people in other countries.
Most of the time the people go along with their routine and enjoy life
for what they have and not worrying about what they don't have.
That is why for them it is easy to laugh at misfortunes, faulty equipment, and inconveniences.

Industrial accidents, airplane crashes, and injury or death in
war are all grieved, but these things are accepted as a part of life
and not blamed on their leaders. They believe that their leaders
are doing all they can to prevent these tragedies.

The real problems of life in the Soviet Union are the things
that most Soviet citizens do not know about, because they can't.
Regimentation, censorship, and propaganda shield and protect them
from knowing about the values of religion, individual initiative, and
free inquiry. Life in the Soviet Union prepares one to conform and
to subject himself to the teachings and leadership of top party officials.

The author had a conversation with a very capable student. He
tried to encourage her to apply herself and to excel in her studies.
When he said that she was a special person who owed it to herself to
become a leader, she was offended and stated that she was just an
ordinary person. She had been taught that the objective of life was to
become a "prostoi" (simple and genuine) person and that putting herself in a special category was selfish and immoral. She wanted to
conform and to follow rather than to excel and lead.

She, like all the other Soviet citizens, can settle back in the
security of guaranteed employment, participation in a collective,
and a life sheltered from "foreign" influences. Her physical needs
will be taken care of, and she can enjoy a measure of happiness,
good health, and success in her work--the three good wishes, which
are shared between friends in letters. But she will never know the
real value of the human soul and her real potential to enjoy life
through her own creative abilities.

SOURCES FOR CHAPTER XVI - LIVING CONDITIONS

Collective farm brigade leader, interview by author, Samarkand,
August, 1971.
Constitution of the USSR, Moscow, 1971.
Doctors and nurses, interview by author, Intourist Hospital,
Moscow, June, 1962.
Doctors, interview by author, Kiev City Hospital, Kiev, July, 1964.
Doctors, nurses, and patients, interviews by author, Irkutsk
Hospital Compound, July 20, 1971.
Doctors and nurses, Sochi Polyclinic, Sochi, July, 1967.
Gregoriev, N., Soviet Union Today, Moscow; Progress Publishers,
1971, 168 pp.
Public relations officer, interview by author, Bratsk Power Dam,
July 22, 1971.
Public relations officer, interview by author, Volgograd Tractor
Plant, Volgograd, August 10, 1971.
Shakhnarzarov, G. Kh., et als, Obshchestvovedeniye (4th ed.),
Moscow: Izdatel'stvo Politicheskoi Literatury, 1966, 381 pp.
Shakhnarzarov, G. Kh., et als, Obshchestvovedeniye, (9th ed.),
Moscow: Izdatel'stvo Politicheskoi Literatury, 1971, 366 pp.
Shakhnarzarov, G. Kh. et als, Obshchestvovedeniye, (10th ed.),
Moscow: Izdatel'stvo Politicheskoi Literatury, 1972, 368 pp.
Teachers and students, interviews by author, Volgograd Pedagogical
Institute, Volgograd, September-December, 1972.
Uzbek family, interview by author, Samarkand, August, 1971.
Wall Street Journal, New York, January 5, 1972.
Work crew, interview by author, Bratsk, July 22, 1971.

8422-0529-2

MSS Information Corporation
655 Madison Avenue, New York, N. Y. 10021

‣ 1751